RUDOLF
HILFERDING

RUDOLF HILFERDING

The Tragedy of a German Social Democrat

William Smaldone

NORTHERN

ILLINOIS

UNIVERSITY

PRESS

DEKALB

1998

© 1998 by Northern Illinois University Press

Published by the Northern Illinois University Press,

DeKalb, Illinois 60115

Manufactured in the United States

using acid-free paper

All Rights Reserved

Design by Julia Fauci

Photographs courtesy of the Friedrich-

Ebert-Stiftung, Bonn.

Library of Congress Cataloging-in-

Publication Data

Smaldone, William.

Rudolf Hilferding : the tragedy of a German Social

Democrat / William Smaldone.

   p.   cm.

Includes bibliographical references and index.

ISBN 0-87580-236-2 (acid-free)

1. Hilferding, Rudolf, 1877–1941.

2. Socialists—Germany—Biography.

3. Sozialdemokratische Partei

Deutschlands—Biography. I. Title.

HX274.7.H55A3 1998

943.085'092—dc21

[B]   97-53284

         CIP

TO MY MOTHER AND FATHER,

THERESA AND GERALD SMALDONE

CONTENTS

LIST OF ILLUSTRATIONS

ACKNOWLEDGMENTS

This work owes its completion to the efforts of a great many people and I deeply appreciate the assistance and support provided by colleagues, friends, and institutions. I would like to thank Professor Jean H. Quataert, my dissertation advisor and teacher, for her indispensable advice, criticism, and encouragement. Thanks are also due to Professors W. Warren Wagar, the late Charles E. Freedemen, Mark E. Blum, Richard Breitman, David W. Morgan, Gerd-Rainer Horn, and Michael Schneider, who read all or large parts of the manuscript critically and made many useful suggestions. I am indebted to Professors Tom Bottomore and Sibylle Quack for directing me to source materials; to Frank Hertz, Susanne Hertz, and Fritz Heine for submitting to interviews; and to Kara Ritzheimer for checking the notes. Working with Mary Lincoln and the staff of the Northern Illinois University Press was a pleasure. Their steady support, professional skills, and good humor were of great assistance.

I wish also to express my gratitude to the many archivists and librarians who helped make my research work an enjoyable and constructive experience. These include the staffs of the State University of New York at Binghamton's Glenn G. Bartle Library, the Friedrich Ebert Stiftung in Bonn, the International Institute for Social History in Amsterdam, the Bundesarchiv branches in Koblenz, Potsdam, and Berlin, the Bayerische Staatsbibliothek in Munich, the Leo Baeck Institute in New York, and the Universitäts- und Stadtbibliothek of the University of Cologne.

The preparation of this book was supported by the generous financial assistance of a number of institutions. These include the Department of History of the State University of New York at Binghamton, the German Academic Exchange Service, the Friedrich Ebert Stiftung, Willamette University, and the J. William Fulbright Foreign Scholarship Board. I would also like to thank Professor Jürgen Heideking and the staff of the Institute of Anglo-American History of the University of Cologne for their hospitality and assistance during my stay there.

Finally, it is impossible for me to fully express my gratitude to Jennifer Jopp, who has supported and guided my work on Hilferding from start to finish. Time and again her substantive and editorial criticisms and her encouragement helped me to move forward. That she could put up not only with the manuscript but also with having to hear about Hilferding and his world for so long is a testimony to her patience and fortitude.

LIST OF ABBREVIATIONS

ADGB   Allgemeiner Deutscher Gewerkschaftsbund (General Federation of German Trade Unions)

AdR   Akten der Reichskanzlei

AdsD   Archiv der sozialen Demokratie (Bonn)

BAP   Bundesarchiv Potsdam

BVP   Bayerische Volkspartei (Bavarian People's Party)

DDP   Deutsche Demokratische Partei (German Democratic Party)

DNVP   Deutschnationale Volkspartei (German National People's Party)

DVP   Deutsche Volkspartei (German People's Party)

ISH   International Institute of Social History (Amsterdam)

KPD   Kommunistische Partei Deutschlands (Communist Party of Germany)

LSI   Labor and Socialist International

NSDAP   Nationalsozialistische Deutsche Arbeiterpartei (National Socialist German Workers' Party; Nazi Party)

RdI   Reichsverband der deutschen Industrie (Association of German Industry)

SA   Sturmabteilung (Nazi paramilitary force)

SAPD   Socialist Workers Party

Sopade   German Social Democracy's executive committee in exile

SPD   Sozialdemokratische Partei Deutschlands (Social Democratic Party of Germany)

SPÖ   Sozialdemokratische Partei Österreichs (Social Democratic Party of Austria)

SS   Schutzstaffel (Nazi paramilitary force)

USPD   Unabhängige Sozialdemokratische Partei Deutschlands (Independent Social Democratic Party of Germany)

RUDOLF
HILFERDING

INTRODUCTION

On Thursday, September 18, 1941, the *New York Times* tersely announced, "Rudolf Hilferding, German Social Democratic Finance Minister in two pre-Nazi cabinets, ha[d] been found hanged in his [prison] cell somewhere in occupied France."[1] Additional information concerning the circumstances of Hilferding's death was unavailable and the report said little else about him. Other events dominated the news. War raged around the globe; the United States watched uneasily as German troops swept across the Soviet Union and Japan continued its aggression in the Far East. To the *Times*, Hilferding's demise, however tragic, was just one more minor event to be dutifully recorded in the paper's inner recesses.

But the announcement of Hilferding's death did not go unnoticed. American and German academics and socialists noted the report and organized a memorial service in Hilferding's honor at the Rand School in New York City. The room in which the service took place was filled to overflowing with political refugees from Germany, Austria, and Russia, as well as representatives from the New School for Social Research, the Social Democratic Federation, the German Labor Delegation, the International Socialist Club, and other organizations. For the participants, Hilferding's passing represented more than just the death of a socialist politician at the hands of the Nazis. Speakers described him as "the great scientific representative of Marxism," as a scholar "who had further developed Marx's teachings," and as an incorruptible politician who placed "logical clarity" ahead of popularity in his political work. In short, Hilferding's mourners regarded him as one of social democracy's most important theoreticians and as a leading political figure in the German Social Democratic party (SPD) and the Socialist International.[2]

They were not exaggerating. For almost four decades Hilferding had been one of Europe's most prominent socialists. As a theorist, his concepts of finance capitalism, organized capitalism, and the total state strongly influenced socialist thought and political praxis both before and after the Second World War. He edited some of social democracy's leading periodicals, was a long-time member of the SPD's executive committee, and played an important role in the party's Reichstag delegation. In 1923, and again in 1928 and 1929, Hilferding served as finance minister in the German government. At the end of the Weimar Republic, as the SPD squared off against its Nazi and Communist opponents, he was a key figure in its leadership. Ultimately, his service to the party and to his country cost him his life.

Before the First World War, Germany was the center of the international socialist movement. The politics of the SPD, the world's largest and best-organized socialist party, had implications for all other socialist parties. Following the collapse of the Second International, the success of the Bolshevik revolution, and the worldwide division of social democracy into socialist and communist factions, the center of the international workers' movement shifted eastward to Moscow, but Germany remained the linchpin of Soviet Russia's survival. Lenin and his supporters regarded a successful proletarian revolution in Germany as essential for the development of socialism in backward Russia and, even after the adoption of Stalin's dictum of "socialism in one country," Germany's economic and political relationship with the USSR was of critical importance. In the interwar era, Germany remained Europe's key political battleground as rival socialist and communist factions fought against each other and against nonsocialist opponents for control of the state.

Thus, as a leader of Europe's "model" Social Democratic Party, Rudolf Hilferding's career unfolded at the matrix of European socialism's intellectual and political life. This work examines his place within this matrix. By focusing on Hilferding's intellectual and political activities as a longtime member of the SPD's oligarchical leadership, it illustrates the interconnections between his development as a theorist, his rise into the party's organizational hierarchy, and from this base, his influence on social democracy's ideology and praxis between 1902 and 1941.

The study of Hilferding's life opens the door to a range of broader issues with which he was connected; for example, the relationship of the bureaucratization of the SPD to the party's growing conservatism, the lack of democracy within the party, and the loss of contact between the leadership and the masses. Whereas most studies of these phenomena begin at the party level, this biography shifts the focus onto an individual party leader.[3] In the German context, the examination of Hilferding's career sheds light on why the SPD was unable to successfully adapt its theory and practice to new and rapidly changing conditions at various key points in its history. As chief editor of *Vorwärts,* the SPD's leading daily paper, Hilferding was an important figure in the party leadership during the crisis of August 1914, when a majority decided to support the government's war effort. As a member of the Provisional Government's Socialisation Commission and chief editor of the Independent Social Democratic Party daily, *Die Freiheit,* he was at the center of events during the revolutionary winter of 1918 and 1919. More important, his government, editorial, and party posts toward the end of the Weimar era made Hilferding simultaneously a key observer and an important actor in the republic's demise. His actions and observations in these and other decisive historical moments provide a unique perspective that helps to explain why the social democratic project failed.

In the broader European context, the examination of Hilferding's career also provides useful insights on a variety of major issues facing the workers' movement as a whole. For all socialists, questions concerning the development of capitalism, the nature of imperialism and social change, the means and ends of socialist transformation, and the organization of a socialist party were—and remain—problems of decisive importance. Hilferding, like many other contemporary thinkers, was deeply engaged with these controversial themes. Based largely on his experience in Austria and Germany, his ideas warrant comparison with other major socialist theorists, many of whom operated in very different environments and drew markedly different conclusions that often challenged his views. For example, in his great work of political economy, *Finance Capital* (1910), Hilferding's argument that the most recent phase of capitalist development prepared the ground not only for socialism but also for imperialist war triggered a heated debate that was joined by Eduard Bernstein, V. I. Lenin, Rosa Luxemburg, and many other socialist thinkers. *Finance Capital* represented a new point of departure for Marxist economic theory and its premises are still of interest to those concerned with contemporary economic problems. Via works such as Lenin's more popular *Imperialism,* it has continued to influence the development of radical political economy in the post–World War II era.

Hilferding's ideas concerning the rise of "organized capitalism" and the transition to socialism also retain much of their relevance in the current period of capitalist development. This phase has witnessed the emergence of enormous international corporations and the expansion of capitalism into areas of the world where centrally planned command economies once operated. Thinking largely with reference to industrialized Europe in the period following World War I, Hilferding's conclusions supporting a gradual evolution into socialism are particularly interesting when viewed in comparison with those of his counterpart Nikolay Ivanovich Bukharin, who worked in the economically backward Soviet Union and adopted a similar outlook.

Hilferding's last major theoretical innovation, developed in exile, was the concept of the total state. Here he attempted to demonstrate the fundamental similarities of the fascist and communist systems, a view that was highly contentious when he presented it, and which remained so after 1945. As he had in his analyses of the capitalist states prior to 1933, Hilferding also drew political lessons from his social and economic appraisal of these regimes. It was here that the democratic socialist dilemma (to use Peter Gay's term) of how to take power and exercise it without betraying the movement's political principles became most apparent, as Hilferding struggled to work out the organizational form and aims of a socialist party forced into illegality by a barbaric state. His dilemma remains one of the central problems faced by democrats and socialists in the contemporary world.

Rudolf Hilferding was not an "independent" or "freestanding" intellectual who could develop his ideas "outside" or "above" the fray of practical political life. From his earliest days in the Social Democratic Party of Austria (SPÖ), he was an intellectual enmeshed in social democratic politics, one for whom the practical application of ideas was a shaping force. A key figure in the development of what historians now refer to as Austro-Marxism, Hilferding occupied a "centrist" position in the socialist political spectrum, where, despite some occasional leftward or rightward shifts, he remained until very late in his life.

As a centrist, Hilferding opposed the revisionist "right wing" of social democracy, which, led by Eduard Bernstein, called on the party to alter its revolutionary Marxist principles and to admit its reformist character. At the same time he also opposed those on the "left wing," such as Rosa Luxemburg, whose radical tactics he regarded as adventurist and ultimately a threat to the long-term interests of the movement. Hilferding developed a position between the reformers and the radicals. He believed that violent revolution was a possible, though not inevitable, means of achieving socialism, but he also was convinced that a parliamentary strategy could achieve the same end and could be justified within the framework of Marxist theory.

At first a student of Karl Kautsky, the center's foremost thinker prior to 1914, Hilferding eventually succeeded Kautsky as German social democracy's leading theorist whose chief task was to ground the politics of the social democratic workers' movement within a Marxist theoretical framework. Like Bernstein and Luxemburg, Hilferding was a democratic socialist; but unlike Bernstein, he was unwilling to break with the basic principles of Marxist ideology that had long been accepted by social democracy. He attempted, rather, to develop a theoretical model tying the party's parliamentary strategy to an analysis of society that retained, if in somewhat altered form, the fundamental categories of Marxism. Such an alternative framework, he thought, could serve as a bridge between the revisionist right and the revolutionary left and thus hold social democracy together.

The centrist project was an ambitious one, and the attempt to carry it out for more than two decades had a profound influence on social democracy's ability to adapt to changing circumstances. After long years of concentration on parliamentary politics, Hilferding and most of the other SPD leaders found themselves unprepared to deal with opponents unwilling to adhere to the norms of parliamentary life. Hilferding knew that the Weimar political system had essentially ceased to function long before Hitler's appointment, but like the majority of his colleagues, he was unable and unwilling to take any initiative that would have risked bloodshed or the possible destruction of the organization to which he had dedicated his life. Fearing civil war and cherishing the hope that the parliamentary system could somehow be salvaged, the SPD leadership decided not to actively resist Hitler's appointment to the chancellorship in 1933. Their failure to act ensured their destruction.

Hilferding's intellectual and political life evolved through three core phases and I have organized this study accordingly. Chapters 1 and 2 trace his career up to 1914. They examine Hilferding's family background, his early intellectual and political development within the Austrian socialist movement, his groundbreaking economic analysis of modern capitalism culminating with the publication of *Finance Capital,* and the ways in which his political outlook, theoretical work, and functions within the Social Democratic party were intertwined.

Chapters 3, 4, and 5 focus on Hilferding's activities between the outbreak of World War I and the collapse of the Weimar Republic. It was during this period that he developed his concept of organized capitalism, which sought to explain socialism's failure in 1914 and the political and economic developments that followed. Hilferding's political outlook and tasks within the socialist movement changed rapidly in these years, largely in response to the volatile conditions in Germany. Traumatized by the war and the division of the SPD, Hilferding participated in the events following the collapse of the monarchy as a member of the left-wing Independent German Social Democratic Party (USPD). At this time, he thought that the revolutionary transformation of German society was possible, and he was active in planning the construction a new socialist republic. The bloody repression of the radical left and Germany's postwar economic and political problems soon convinced him that the revolutionary option was no longer feasible. He then became a strong supporter of the parliamentary road to socialism and worked to bring about reforms within the framework of the capitalist republic.

This project ground to a halt with the Nazi seizure of power, and Hilferding fled Germany just a few weeks after Hitler became chancellor. His departure marked the onset of the third phase of his career (the subject of Chapter 6), in which he fundamentally revised his earlier views on the nature of state power and developed his theory of the total state. During the long years abroad he remained active in exile party politics. Once again he attempted to construct a theoretical and practical program that would hold social democracy's squabbling factions together, and he worked hard to warn the Western democracies of the danger of Nazi imperialism. As the party grew increasingly divided, however, and the European powers adopted a conciliatory policy toward Germany, he found himself politically isolated. In the end, the deterioration of social democracy and the expansion of fascist power led him to distance himself from Marxism and to look anew at the issue of causality in history and the nature of historical change.

Rudolf Hilferding became a convinced socialist as a very young man and he struggled throughout his life for the realization of his ideals. A principled person, he was willing to break with his own party and even with longtime friends when he felt that truth demanded it. If his abhorrence of violence, his ultimate faith in human reason, or simple fear made it difficult for him to advocate bloodshed on the eve of social democracy's destruction, then this is the kind of "weakness" that only very few people can overcome. The tragedy in Hilferding's life lay in his adherence to a political outlook that was incompatible with German reality in 1933.

CHAPTER ONE

THE AUSTRIAN HERITAGE

By discovering the laws of economic and historical development, Marx
created the social theory on which the politics of the workers is based.
Today the international proletariat draws its weapons from the arsenal
of Marxism. —*Rudolf Hilferding (1906)*

R udolf Hilferding grew up in Vienna during the last
two decades of the nineteenth century and it was there that he discovered
Marxism and became a fervent social democrat.[1] His experience as a member
of Vienna's culturally assimilated Jewish middle class, as well as his educational background and an early affiliation with socialist student and political
party organizations, had a profound impact on his intellectual and political
outlook and shaped the course of his entire life. The young Hilferding came
to socialism like so many others subject to rejection and oppression in Austrian society; he joined the workers' movement because he identified with its
goal of universal liberation. As a flexible and critical thinker, as well as a
skilled polemicist, Hilferding quickly came to the attention of leading socialists who kept a sharp eye out for talented intellectuals who could be of service to the party. By the time he left Vienna in 1906, he was on his way to
becoming one of European socialism's leading theorists and had begun a
promising career in the German Social Democratic party organization.

Historical documentation regarding Hilferding's personal life and family
background is scarce, but it is possible to sketch out the basic contours of his

youth and the early development of his ideas.[2] Rudolf was born into the family of Emil and Anna Hilferding on August 11, 1877. His parents were Polish Jews who had migrated to Vienna, yet it is not known if the family was religious.[3] Emil Hilferding was a head cashier for the Allianz insurance company, an old Italian firm. Like many other Jews entering the professions in the latter half of the nineteenth century, he broke with the traditional trading and money-lending occupations of the old Jewish middle class. Although his position as a middle-level professional bureaucrat was a modest one, it appears that the family enjoyed a comfortable standard of living.[4]

According to Rudolf Hilferding's later friend and colleague Alexander Stein, Rudolf and his younger sister, Maria, grew up in the atmosphere of an "enlightened liberal Jewish middle class," whose sons and daughters often displayed a lively interest in scientific and artistic matters as well as strong socialist inclinations. This testimony, when combined with what we know of Emil Hilferding's professional background, indicates that the Hilferding family had adopted many of the dominant cultural mores of Viennese society. Although the Hilferdings may have considered themselves a part of the Jewish community, they appear also to have accepted the language, economic patterns, political views, and cultural baggage of the German-speaking middle class. That the family sent Rudolf to a *Staatsgymnasium* strengthens this assumption. Graduation from this type of high school opened the way for entrance into the university and ultimately a place in the elite professions with their concomitant financial security and social status.[5]

Hilferding's school records indicate that he was an average student with grades ranging from "praiseworthy" in religious studies and physics to "satisfactory" in natural history, philosophy, and languages, to "unsatisfactory" in mathematics. He passed his graduation examination in the summer of 1894 and immediately entered the University of Vienna, where he enrolled in the medical school. His career path was a common one at that time among Jewish students, who were inclined to select intellectual professions, especially in medicine and law.[6]

Although on the surface the young Hilferding appeared to be following a rather ordinary educational and career path, there was another side to him that was more unusual. As a teenager he became interested in socialism, and in 1893, at the age of sixteen, he joined a group of Viennese students who met once a week in the Heiliger Leopold café to discuss socialist literature. In 1895, these students joined forces with another group—made up of young university teachers—to create a larger organization known as the Freie Vereinigung Sozialistischer Studenten und Akademiker (Free Association of Socialist Students and Academics), chaired by Max Adler. The association had no official connections with the SPÖ, but "for three decades [it was] the intellectual and social meeting place of all the socialist students at the University of Vienna." Many of its participants—such as Adler, Hilferding, Karl Renner, Otto Bauer, and Jacques Freundlich—later became prominent

Austro-Marxists and SPÖ members.[7] Although it remains unclear exactly how Hilferding became involved with the association, this organization provided his first exposure to socialist theory and his earliest opportunity to participate actively in the workers' movement.

The intellectual leader of the students was Julius Sesser, a man well versed in socialist literature. Sesser always kept volume 1 of Marx's *Das Kapital* handy for reference during discussions, and he subscribed to *Die Neue Zeit*, the theoretical journal of German social democracy edited by Karl Kautsky. Kautsky's journal circulated among the students and—along with his book, *Marxs ökonomische Lehren*—exerted a powerful influence on them. Sesser's lectures, in combination with Kautsky's works, introduced the students gradually to Marx's own more complicated writings. Hilferding was among Sesser's most promising students. By 1899, he had become the association's president and had published an article on the Austrian factory inspection system in the French journal *Le mouvement socialiste*.[8]

In addition to studying socialist literature, Hilferding and his comrades in the association also participated in social democratic street demonstrations. This activity got them into trouble with the Viennese police. During the May Day protests of 1893, the police arrested Sesser and other association members for singing radical songs and calling for a "red republic." Although the youths were quickly released (one of Sesser's relatives was a highly placed judge), the police continued to harass them. To evade surveillance, the members of the association conducted discussions while walking through the city streets. Hilferding regularly walked long into the night with Renner to discuss Marx's ideas without being disturbed. Police harassment did not deter him or his friends from their involvement in the socialist movement; if anything it encouraged them. According to Renner, the altercation on May Day earned the students the respect of the SPÖ leadership, which then began to pay attention to their group.[9]

What was it that aroused Hilferding's interest in socialism? Why did socialist ideas stimulate a rather average middle-class high school student to diligently study Marxism and actually begin to write about workers' problems? Lack of documentation makes it difficult to answer these questions. It is likely, however, that Hilferding's interest in socialism, at least in part, stemmed from his experience in the gymnasium, where intellectual life was anything but vibrant. As Stefan Zweig has described so vividly in his memoirs, classroom study in the gymnasium was often a stultifying experience designed to promote conformity and obedience to authority, rather than to encourage critical thinking. The oppressiveness of the schools had a twofold effect on the students. Many were "paralyzed" and developed a psychologically damaging sense of personal inferiority. Others, like Zweig himself, were driven to rebel against authority and dogmatism. They searched for and found outlets for self-expression in Vienna's multifaceted cultural scene.[10]

Students hungry for new ideas and new experiences discovered them in

Vienna's cafés, theaters, museums, bookstores, and at the university. They competed with one another in the search for what was new and exciting, and turn-of-the-century Vienna had much to offer. Security may have been the most cherished desire of the city's stolid middle class, but this staid old imperial capital also was home to many of the most innovative elements of modern thought. Psychoanalysis, positivism, Marxism, marginal utility theory, and new forms of literature, painting, architecture, and music, all challenged the norms of the old world and fueled the debates that made Vienna's cultural atmosphere so stimulating. Hilferding and his friends at the Heiliger Leopold were among the rebellious students described by Zweig. In an official world that worshiped conformity, they were attracted to the radical ideas of Austria's growing social democratic movement.

It is also likely that Hilferding's Jewish background influenced his attraction to socialism.[11] Like Otto Bauer and many other Austrian intellectuals of Jewish descent, he found his way to socialism partly because there were few other practical avenues of political expression available to Jews, and partly because the socialist movement offered an ideology of universal emancipation. In a society in which class, religious, racial, and gender boundaries fostered social and political inequality, even the most culturally assimilated Jews faced widespread social and civil discrimination.[12] Ultimately, many Jewish intellectuals found their most comfortable political home in the Social Democratic party.

Earlier, Viennese Jewry had viewed Austrian liberalism as the force for its emancipation and as a vehicle for its participation in Austrian national life, but the rise of the pan-German and Christian social movements and the latter's mayoral victory of 1895 placed the community in a precarious position. The Christian socialists and their pan-German rivals were virulently anti-Semitic and anti–industrial capitalist, and both worked hard to make Judaism and modern capitalism synonymous in the minds of the voters. Except for the Marxist social democrats, who were anathema to virtually all sectors of Vienna's population but the working class, only the liberals had offered the Jews equality as citizens despite their lack of a homeland within the empire. Unlike the other ethnic groups within the national borders, the Jews had no specific area of origin. Now, with the defeat of liberalism, it seemed to many Jews—especially youth from culturally assimilated, middle-class homes—that the solution to their dilemma lay not in assimilation but either in national autonomy within the diaspora or in the foundation of an independent Jewish state—zionism.[13]

Yet, not all Jews who turned their backs on liberalism found Jewish nationalism or zionism attractive alternatives. Some abandoned politics and concentrated on intellectual, business, or artistic pursuits. Others, like Hilferding, turned to socialism, which was just coming into its own at the time when Rudolf entered the gymnasium. Founded in 1889, the Austrian Social Democratic party quickly developed into a significant political force whose ideology provided a radical assimilationist option attractive to many Jewish intellectuals alienated from Judaism.[14]

This ideology achieved concrete political expression in the SPÖ's Hainfeld Program (1889). Written by Victor Adler and Karl Kautsky, the program elaborated the party's goals within a largely Marxist theoretical framework. It declared the SPÖ ready "to liberate the entire people from the chains of economic dependency, to empower them politically and to lift them out of their intellectual degeneration notwithstanding differences of nationality, race or gender." Locating the basic cause of social conflict in the monopolization of the means of production by a few individual owners, the program called for the liberation of the working class through the transformation of the means of production into "the communal property of the whole people." The party's task was to organize this class, to raise its level of class consciousness, and to prepare it intellectually and physically for its struggle. The SPÖ, the program claimed, was an international party that sought to eliminate privilege and exploitation. It called for an end to all restrictions on freedom of association and expression, for universal suffrage, for legislation to improve the proletariat's living standard and to empower the workers economically *(Mitkontrolle der Arbeiterschaft),* for free public education, for separation of church and state, for the creation of a popular militia, and for other democratic reforms.[15]

This, then, was the theoretical and practical program of the movement that attracted the young Hilferding in 1894. It was a worldview that promised universal emancipation and, for Austrian Jews like Hilferding, represented a final step in the process of social integration. Raised in an assimilated family and trained in secular schools, there is no evidence in his voluminous writings or surviving correspondence that Hilferding ever considered his Jewishness to be of importance; he had completely abandoned Judaism and become a socialist well before he left the Gymnasium.[16]

In his essay "The Non-Jewish Jew," Isaac Deutscher describes a type of Jew—among whom he includes Baruch Spinoza, Heinrich Heine, Karl Marx, Rosa Luxemburg, Leon Trotsky, and Sigmund Freud—who, finding Jewry "too narrow, too archaic and too constricting," looked for ideals and fulfillment beyond it. These were Jews who "were born and brought up on the borderlines of various epochs," whose minds "matured where the most diverse cultural influences crossed and fertilized each other." While they "lived on the margins or in the nooks and crannies of their respective nations," they were also "in society and yet not in it, of it and yet not of it." It was this condition, says Deutscher, "that enabled them to rise in thought above their societies, above their nations, above their times and generations, and to strike out mentally into wide new horizons and far into the future."[17]

These thinkers and revolutionaries all had certain philosophical principles in common, despite the many differences in their views. They were all determinists, in that they believed the universe to be ruled by certain laws inherent in it and that these laws govern the process of change. Their thinking was also dialectical, because in their work they closely observed the ways change occurred in all societies, thus making reality dynamic rather than static. All of these thinkers agreed on the relativity of moral standards over time and space; they were convinced that, to be real, knowledge must be active, and finally, they all believed in the ultimate solidarity of man.[18]

Rudolf Hilferding shared the views of these "non-Jewish Jews" and may be counted as one of them. Catholic, monarchical Vienna was a world in which even the most assimilated Jews were never at home. Jews were always outsiders, even when many seemed to reach the pinnacle of professional or social success. At the same time, Vienna was also a cosmopolitan city in a constant state of transformation, in which the mix of cultures and ideologies created a simultaneously rich and conflict-ridden environment. It was within this milieu of contradiction that Hilferding was raised and that he developed his ideas. Like Luxemburg and Trotsky, he thought that Marx's vision was most apt in clarifying the world's condition and providing the intellectual tools to change it. And, like them, he ultimately became convinced that it was necessary to strive for the universal as against the particular, and for the international as against the national, in order to resolve the problems of his time.

Thus, as a teenager, Hilferding had already developed a deep sense of political awareness and become active in the socialist movement. When he enrolled at the University of Vienna in the winter of 1894 he intended to study medicine, but his interests led him to study history, economics, and philosophy also. Like many of his young socialist comrades such as Renner, Bauer, Max Adler, and Gustav Eckstein, Hilferding studied political economy under the supervision of one of Europe's few "professorial Marxists," Carl Grünberg, and attended lectures given by the neopositivist philosopher Ernst Mach.[19] Both men influenced him in important ways.

As Tom Bottomore has pointed out, Grünberg's students acquired from him "a conception of Marxism as a social science, which should be developed in a rigorous and systematic way through historical and sociological investigations." For Grünberg, the materialist conception of history neither was nor aimed to be a philosophical system. Its object was "not abstractions, but the given concrete world in its process of development and change."[20]

Grünberg valued Marx's ideas not as a dogma but as a method of examining the relationship between society's material-economic base and the superstructural spheres of the state, law, and ideology. Because he rejected the notion that Marxism was a rigid set of teachings concerned with the content of history, he was able to question some of Marx's most important postulates such as those dealing with the concentration of capital *(Konzentrationstheorie),* impoverishment, cyclical crisis, and economic collapse *(Zusammenbruchstheorie).*[21] Grünberg's skepticism and his emphasis on Marxism as a scientific method of social analysis strongly influenced the young Hilferding, who, in his own theoretical work, came to regard Marxism as "nothing other than the scientific method for the study of society." Marxism, he insisted, was an "objective, value-free science" in the service of the proletariat.[22]

Grünberg's conception of the historical development of socialism and the role of intellectuals in the socialist movement also had an important impact on his students. For Grünberg, socialism would be established with "logical necessity" once the masses became conscious of the social contradiction between capitalism's "abstract juridical" equality and concrete material inequality. Socialist intellectuals, he thought, would play a key role in developing this consciousness. It was their task to leave the study for the streets, where their words would find a "mighty echo among the propertyless masses. Out of the consciousness of class antagonisms," Grünberg concluded, "blazes up class struggle."[23]

Along with historian Ludo Hartmann, Grünberg founded the Sozialwissenschaftlicher Bildungsverein (Association for Social Science Education), which provided a forum for students and workers to discuss current problems. His stress on the importance of politically educating the masses won the enthusiastic support of his students. Hilferding, Bauer, and many of the other Austro-Marxists went on to help build institutions such as party schools to promote workers' political education, and they viewed their role as intellectuals within the socialist movement as largely an educational one. Hilferding later described Marxists as "the encyclopedists of our time," who, like their eighteenth-century forebears, were charged with the task of carrying out the intellectual revolution that must precede the political and social one.[24] Like Bauer, he worked not to exercise real, day-to-day practical power within social democracy but, rather, to influence socialist politics, both within the party leadership and among the masses. He was active primarily as a theorist and a journalist; thus, as an educator.

Whereas Carl Grünberg provided Hilferding with a view of Marxism as a social science, Ernst Mach reaffirmed the importance of the material world in the process of historical change and the development of ideas. As Mark E. Blum cogently explains, an essential feature of Mach's outlook was his denial that Kant's a priori categories of consciousness existed. To him, absolute laws in thinking, science, or social planning were anathema. Mach's relativism "was based on his view that because material being created and conditioned consciousness, every new historical ordering of environment and society required new measures and values to enable human society to correspond and to cope with what existed."[25]

At a time when many socialists and Marxists were attempting to connect the ethical teachings of Kant to the "scientific socialism" of Marx, Mach's views acted as a materialist counterweight to neo-Kantianism. To Hilferding, Mach's basic perspective in some ways approximated Marx's materialist conception of history, but his later writings show that he was as unwilling to fully accept Mach's "natural-biological" views as he was Kant's a priori categories or Hegel's self-developing idea. Whereas Mach believed that the adaptation of ideas to reality was a biological necessity, Hilferding believed that ideas developed in response to changing material reality and their interaction with one another in the thought process itself. For him "the logical development of theory parallel[ed] the real development of capitalism," but the adaptation of ideas to one another was also the general condition or logical requirement of scientific thinking as such.[26]

Of key importance here is Hilferding's understanding of change. Although he did not think that the development of ideas was solely a biological phenomenon, under the influence of Kautsky, Grünberg, and Mach his view of the Marxist dialectic emphasized the importance of social and economic evolution for the development of a society's cultural and political life. This evolutionary, or gradualist, component of Hilferding's Marxism became increasingly pronounced during the course of his career, especially after the failure of the German revolution of 1918.

One other aspect of Carl Grünberg's teachings had an important influence on Hilferding: his aversion to theoretical dogmatism and his consequent opposition to the formation of separate schools of thought.[27] Grünberg's readiness to integrate and assimilate different aspects of Marxist and non-Marxist thought proved very attractive to Hilferding and his socialist friends. In the context of the revisionist controversy within social democracy at the turn of the century, Grünberg's viewpoint offered them an alternative both to Marxist orthodoxy and to revisionism. In retrospect it is rather ironic, but not surprising, that Grünberg's conceptual openness decisively influenced the principles that joined his students together in what later became known as the Austro-Marxist School.

Following his graduation from the university in 1901, Hilferding began to practice medicine in Vienna, but he did so without enthusiasm. He was more interested in studying political economy and continued to work in this area in his spare time. Soon his interest in economics caused him to consider leaving medicine in order to study political economy full-time. Though at first he lacked confidence in his theoretical abilities, his initial publishing successes and the recognition that followed encouraged him.[28]

During these years Hilferding maintained friendly ties with Karl Renner, Otto Bauer, and Max Adler. The four socialized and traveled together and all were active in social democratic politics. Their common educational experiences, shared political beliefs, and amicable personal relationships provided a strong basis for intellectual cooperation. Although they wrote on a broad variety of subjects, at that time each of these men had a different main interest. Hilferding devoted most of his time to economics, Renner focused on law, Adler on philosophy, and Bauer on the nationality question. Despite these varied interests and important philosophical differences (Adler, for example, was strongly influenced by Kant, whereas Hilferding was not), all of these "Austro-Marxists" shared certain principles beyond their adherence to such key Marxist tenets as dialectical materialism, class conflict, and the alienation of labor.[29] Hilferding and Adler first elaborated these principles in 1904, when they began to publish their own theoretical journal, *Marx-Studien*.

In the foreword to their first volume, Hilferding and Adler described their task as "to further develop the social theory of Marx and Engels, to subject it to criticism, and to place their teachings in the context of modern intellectual life."[30] They wanted to systematically garner what was valuable from Marxism and to link it with the results of contemporary philosophical and scientific work. The editors intended volume 1 to inform the reader not only about "what we want" but also "how we want it," and they regarded its contents "as a kind of program." Thus Hilferding's *Böhm-Bawerks Marx Kritik,* Renner's *Die soziale Funktion der Rechtsinstitute,* and Max Adler's *Kausalität und Teleologie im Streite um die Wissenschaft* were, respectively, works of political economy, law, and philosophy that attempted to achieve the aims described above across disciplinary lines.

Hilferding and Adler eschewed theoretical dogmatism and claimed to be neither orthodox nor revisionist. Citing Marx's own opposition to "the planting of a dogmatic flag," they stressed that the effective power of Marx's thought stemmed not from any particular claim that he had made, but from the spirit in which he had worked. Thus, like their teacher Grünberg, the editors did not see Marxism as a rigid, omnipotent philosophy, but rather as a scientific approach that could be continually developed in light of more recent substantive and methodological advances in philosophy and social science.

This relatively open and flexible theoretical perspective and the view of Marxism as an empirical social science linked Hilferding and his colleagues together as theorists and set them apart from the older generation of orthodox Marxists, whose chief representative was Kautsky. But they were also bound together by practical experience in the SPÖ, experience that taught them that the political unity of the working class was absolutely essential for the success of the socialist movement. The theme of unity recurs often in Hilferding's writings and strongly influenced his work as a party theorist and strategist.

Otto Bauer addressed the importance of unity in an essay on "Austromarxism" that appeared in 1927. Looking back on the history of Austrian socialism, he identified the characteristics that separated Austro-Marxism from other schools of Marxist thought. After discussing the philosophical and methodological perspectives described above, Bauer argued that the trait that made Austro-Marxism especially rare was the continued unity of the Austrian working class at a time when European social democracy had effectively split into separate social democratic and communist movements. The SPÖ, he wrote, was able to avoid a split not only because the workers had the example of Hungary's failed communist dictatorship before their eyes, but also because they understood that for a nation as politically weak and economically dependent as Austria, a dictatorship would have disastrous consequences.[31]

Also important, however, for the party's "immunization" against communism was its intellectual inheritance, particularly the contribution of party founder, Victor Adler. Bauer explained that, during the 1880s, Adler had united the radicals and moderates into one party, and for the next two decades amid difficult nationalist conflicts, he had understood the importance of politically unifying the German, Czech, Polish, Ukrainian, Slovenian, and Italian social democrats. According to Bauer, Adler had handed down to his successors the "will," the "fanaticism," and the "skill" necessary to maintain the unity of the working class. Austro-Marxism, he concluded, was a synthesis of sober *Realpolitik* and revolutionary enthusiasm in "one spirit" *(Geist)*. It had succeeded in uniting the concrete politics of the day with the "revolutionary will to reach the final goal" of socialism.[32] Bauer's essay exaggerates Adler's success in maintaining the unity of the SPÖ's nationalist factions, but it captures the attitude toward party unity shared by Hilferding and his fellow Austro-Marxists.

Although Eduard Bernstein was not the first to suggest that the movement discard its revolutionary rhetoric and concentrate on the struggle for economic and political reforms, it was his theoretical challenge to Marxist orthodoxy in the late 1890s that threatened to tear social democracy apart. Bernstein's "revisionist" writings appeared to systematically undermine revolutionary Marxism's most fundamental principles. In a series of articles culminating in 1899 with the publication of his most important work, *Die Voraussetzung des Sozialismus und die Aufgaben der Sozialdemokratie,* Bernstein questioned the relevance of Hegelianism to socialist theory and, instead, advocated a socialism based on ethical values. He claimed that Marxist expectations regarding the disappearance of the agrarian middle class, worsening economic crises, growing proletarian misery, capitalist concentration, and the disappearance of middle-sized and small producers had not been fulfilled. Most important, he dispensed with the notion that the socialist revolution would follow capitalism's inevitable collapse and substituted for it the ideal of gradualist growth into socialism.[33]

Unlike the young socialist intellectuals of the early 1890s (the *Jungen*), who had criticized German social democracy's reformist practice as a hindrance to the unfolding of capitalism's contradictions and, ultimately, its collapse, Bernstein did not challenge the party's reformist tactics.[34] On the contrary, he demanded that the party dispense with revolutionary illusions, recognize its own reformist character, and cooperate with moderate bourgeois parties in the struggle for progressive change. In so doing he aroused a storm of controversy among social democratic leaders and intellectuals throughout Europe, who had to come to grips with the theory and practice of their own respective parties. The orthodox majority in the German leadership officially condemned revisionism at the Dresden party congress of 1903, but the conflict continued, casting its shadow over social democratic politics for years. The Austro-Marxists played an important role in this debate.

Under Victor Adler's leadership, by 1900 the SPÖ had become a substantial political force. The party claimed a membership of over a hundred thousand in Austria and Bohemia alone and its organization was expanding steadily, establishing links with trade unions, labor organizations, and work-ers' cooperatives throughout the Habsburg domains.[35] Although Kautsky's Marxism clearly shaped the theoretical introduction to the party's Hainfeld Program, the program's reformist components were of decisive importance for the SPÖ's day-to-day practice and actually worked to integrate the party into Austrian political life. Goals such as the achievement of universal suffrage (attained in 1907) and piecemeal economic and social reforms received prior-ity; revolutionary efforts to overthrow the monarchy did not.

During the Bernstein debate, Victor Adler publicly supported the ortho-dox Marxism of Karl Kautsky and criticized revisionist views challenging capi-talism's inevitable collapse and the historical necessity of socialism. But Adler's official condemnation of revisionism stemmed more from his fear of a split in the European socialist movement than from any fundamental dis-agreement with its program. Adler was at heart a reformist politician who be-lieved that the piecemeal improvement of people's lives was "revolutionary" because it raised their social awareness and gave them strength to pursue new goals.[36] In 1901 his reformist inclinations brought him into conflict with Kautskyan orthodoxy. Adler defended changes in the SPÖ's program that wa-tered down its earlier emphasis on workers' growing impoverishment and stressed the party's commitment to the achievement of immediate reforms. These changes led to accusations from inside and outside the SPÖ that its leadership was under Bernstein's influence. In 1904, during the heated de-bate on revisionism at the Second International's Amsterdam congress, the German party leader August Bebel actually accused his friend Adler of being "a revisionist in disguise."[37] Although eventually smoothed over, this episode exemplified the serious personal and political strains caused by the debate over revisionism.

It was within this context that the Austro-Marxists made their entrance onto social democracy's political stage. They rejected being placed in the camp of either revisionism or orthodoxy and hoped to push Marxism in new directions. It was in the process of this development that they trained their guns on Bernstein's theoretical criticisms of Marx and worked to integrate social democracy's reformist practice with the long-term revolutionary aspira-tions of the movement. In so doing they carved out a centrist position that sought to unite socialism's reformist and revolutionary factions. Thus they represented the Austrian wing of the "Marxist center," an international intel-lectual current that developed as Kautskyan orthodoxy disintegrated in the decade preceding the outbreak of World War I.[38]

Hilferding emerged as Austro-Marxism's leading economic thinker. His early essays not only dealt with questions of economic theory but made explicit links between the development of modern capitalism and specific contempo-rary political problems such as protectionism, imperialism, and the use of the mass strike. His engagement in the heated debates surrounding these impor-tant issues quickly thrust him into the center of social democratic politics.

In April 1902, Hilferding sent his first major contribution to *Die Neue Zeit*. His essay was a review of Eugen Böhm-Bawerk's *Karl Marx and the Close of His System* (1896), which criticized Marx's analysis of the commodity and his contention that the source of value is to be found in labor. Böhm-Bawerk was a leading representative of the marginal utility school of economics, which held that value was a subjectively determined category and which attacked all socialist or nonsocialist theoretical systems advocating state intervention in the economy.[39] The popularity of Böhm-Bawerk's text and Bernstein's effort to synthesize marginal utilitarianism with the labor theory of value made it important for Marxists to formulate a response. Hilferding, not yet twenty-five and virtually unknown, boldly took on the challenge. He was very aware that the task of refuting a well-known theorist such as Böhm-Bawerk was no small matter, and he saw his essay as a test of his skills. He asked Kautsky, in an accompanying letter, to evaluate his work and expressed the hope that his contribution to the discussion would be of value.[40]

He need not have worried. The article was sophisticated, penetrating, and long remained the best criticism of subjective value theory from a Marxist standpoint.[41] In explaining his approach to the subject, Hilferding pointed out that since the "psychological school" of political economy attacked the Marxist system as a whole, Marxism had to be defended as a whole.[42] To accomplish this task, he divided his analysis into three sections dealing with broad, overlapping themes: value as an economic category, value and average profit, and the subjective outlook. The essentials of Hilferding's overall argument are located in the last section, which addressed the question of whether the starting point of economics is located on the individual or the societal level.[43]

For Böhm-Bawerk, economics had its starting point in the subjective relationship between the individual and the things that satisfy the individual's needs. In his system, the magnitude of the value of a commodity depends not only on factors of supply and demand but also on the commodity's importance in the eyes of the consumer.[44] Hilferding believed that this incorporation of a psychological or "subjective" dimension to value theory obscures the nature of value itself and makes a clear understanding of capitalist society impossible. Böhm-Bawerk confused the differences between "value" and "price" and ignored the social aspects of production and exchange.[45] Even more important, Hilferding argued, his method of deducing value by observing individual economic relationships did not contain within itself any principle of change. To the psychological school, economic categories were natural and eternal, unhistorical and unsocial, whereas for Marx "economic phenomena are subordinated to objective laws independent of the individual will and controlled by social relationships" (186). Social relationships of production—"wherein commodities play the part of intermediaries"—reproduced themselves in the economic process but were also subject to change and "a new type of intermediation" (186).

Thus, for Hilferding, the labor theory of value was most significant "not as a means for ascertaining prices, but as a means for discovering 'the laws of motion' of capitalist society" (139). The study of these laws was the most important element in any attempt to discern and analyze what he called the "evolutionary tendencies of society" (133). Sociological and historical dimensions assumed the most important place in his analysis of social transformation. He made this clear in a passage that also contains key insights regarding his view of the relationship between social change and human action:

> In his principle of value [Marx] thus grasps the factor by whose quality and quantity, by whose organization and productive energy, social life is causally controlled. The fundamental economic idea is consequently identical with the fundamental idea of the materialist conception of history. Necessarily so, seeing that economic life is but a part of historic life so that conformity to law in economics must be the same as conformity to law in history. To the extent that labor, in its social form, becomes the measure of value, economics is established as a social and historical science. (133)

The defense of the labor theory of value, therefore, was a defense of Marx's sociohistorical method. In Hilferding's view, the prime movers of social change—and, therefore, of social revolution—were economic factors that operated according to certain laws and that conditioned and limited the scope of human action. Unlike Bernstein, Hilferding was certain that these laws, discovered by Marx, were moving society toward socialism. It was Marx's "demonstration of the historical transitoriness of bourgeois relationships of production," he concluded, "[that] signifies the close of political economy as a bourgeois science and its foundation as a *proletarian* science" (196; emphasis in original).

Two problems in Hilferding's analysis of Böhm-Bawerk stand out because they influenced his later work in important ways.[46] The first of these revolves around his equation of "the fundamental economic idea" with the materialist conception of history. This view tends to overemphasize the economic side of Marx's theory of historical change and to minimize other important factors that affect the human condition and the transformation of society.

The second difficulty concerns Hilferding's conception of value, which in some respects differed from that of Marx. Hilferding argued that "a good becomes a commodity solely through entering into a relationship with other goods, a relationship which becomes manifest in the act of exchange and which, quantitatively regarded, appears as the exchange value of the good."[47] Whereas Hilferding emphasized the sphere of circulation in the creation of commodities, Marx held that commodities were goods produced for some sort of market by "private producers more or less separated from one another." Hence Marx's definition focused on the actual relationships of production rather than on the mere act of exchange.[48] As we shall see, Hilferding's view ultimately led him to draw very different conclusions from those of Marx in a variety of areas such as the role of money and the origins of crisis in a capitalist economy.

Hilferding was disappointed when Kautsky decided not to publish his lengthy essay, and he rejected the editor's suggestion that it appear as an independent pamphlet or as three separate articles. A pamphlet would have little impact, and breaking it up he thought would destroy its coherence.[49] Kautsky remained adamant and Hilferding waited almost two years before his essay finally appeared in *Marx-Studien*.

Although Kautsky rejected Hilferding's article on technical grounds, he praised his analysis and asked him to become a regular contributor to *Die Neue Zeit*. His comments overjoyed the young man, whose response reveals his excitement at the prospect:

> It would be an inappropriate claim on your time if I were to fully describe how happy your letter has made me. Just allow me to say that it has helped me make an important decision. Because I was uncertain about how to judge my own work, it was essential to hear the opinion of someone who is, by far, the most competent judge of these matters since Engels's death. My wish to convince myself that I am at least somewhat fit for economic work . . . has been splendidly fulfilled and your letter has encouraged me to continue further along this path.[50]

Hilferding was enthusiastic about continuing his critique of revisionism and thought that this could be most fruitfully done by pursuing new areas of economic inquiry, especially developments in the capitalist economy that had arisen since Marx's death. He explained to Kautsky that these new developments, which could best be observed in New York, would be the focus of his research. In undertaking this study, Hilferding thus began to work out the ideas that eventually formed the nucleus of *Finance Capital*, his magnum opus, published in 1910.[51]

Hilferding's early correspondence with Kautsky is important not only because of what it tells us concerning his hopes and intentions, but also because it marks the beginning of their long personal and political relationship. His flattering remarks may strike later readers as rather obsequious, but they also reflect a real respect for Kautsky that was widespread in socialist circles. As the leading popularizer of Marx's works, the editor of *Die Neue Zeit*, and the chief defender of orthodoxy, Kautsky was the most important Marxist theoretician in the world in the years between the death of Engels and the outbreak of World War I. Hilferding could not have been unaware that establishing good connections with Kautsky would improve his publishing and career chances within the socialist movement. He developed, as well, an intellectual and personal attachment to Kautsky that spanned more than three decades and continued long after Kautsky's influence had waned within the socialist movement.

Soon after he agreed to join *Die Neue Zeit,* Hilferding published an important theoretical article in which he outlined many of the central economic and political theses later developed more fully in *Finance Capital.*[52] The essay was a direct attack on revisionist arguments supporting high protective tariffs and imperialism. At consecutive party congresses between 1898 and 1903, revisionists claimed that German colonialism had little impact on domestic social and economic conditions and asserted that the acquisition of colonial territories was a way to promote the development of the world's productive resources, the extension of civilization, and the expansion of European living space. An overwhelming majority at the congresses rejected these views and condemned "the forcible annexation of foreign lands and the ruthless subjugation and exploitation of the indigenous people," but the issue was so divisive that some revisionist spokesmen were threatened with expulsion from the party.[53] The German debate soon spilled over into Austria and it was in this context that Hilferding's article appeared.

Hilferding analyzed the development of the high protective tariff *(Hochschutzzoll)* that dominated the trade policy of many advanced capitalist states by the end of the nineteenth century. The *Hochschutzzoll,* he asserted, had a completely different function from earlier forms of tariff protection *(der Erziehungszoll),* the primary purpose of which had been to accelerate the establishment of new industries within protected borders. Supporters of the *Erziehungszoll* expected its abolition once these industries became competitive, but this change did not occur. Instead, tariffs were maintained and came to play a completely different role in a capitalist system that was itself undergoing important changes.[54]

Hilferding related these changes to the problem of capital accumulation under modern capitalism. In his view, the development of working-class economic organizations, such as trade unions, made it difficult for capitalists to increase the rate of profit by the extension of workers' hours or the reduction of wages. The capitalists sought new forms of exploitation to raise profits, and they aimed to subjugate "the whole population under the organized power of capital." This "organized power" appeared in the form of cartels or trusts (organizations of capitalists in specific branches of production), which faced the trade unions in the struggle for economic power. Closely related to the establishment of these cartels and trusts was the confrontation over trade policy, which Hilferding described as "nothing more than the struggle between capitalist organizations for state power which should be used to serve their ends." There were, therefore, two simultaneous conflicts: one placing the capitalist against the working class and the other pitting the capitalist organizations against one another. The institution of the high protective tariff resulted from the latter struggle.[55]

The *Hochschutzzoll* enabled the cartels to prevent or limit the import of foreign goods and allowed them to maintain artificially high prices on domestically produced items even when an oversupply should have reduced prices.

In the protected market, the cartels earned exceptionally high profits with which they subsidized the export of commodities at prices that were below cost. Thus, the exploitation of the domestic working class strengthened capital's ability to penetrate and dominate foreign markets. The function of the tariff had changed from one of protection for home industry to one of aggression for expanding national cartels.[56]

The process of concentration in the various branches of industry (cartelization) reduced competition in the domestic market by eliminating smaller, independent firms and increased competition between cartelized industries for foreign markets and natural resources. This development had important implications for the foreign policies of the advanced capitalist states, by which they sought to secure the most favorable terms of trade for their home industries. In the international scramble for raw materials, markets, and colonies, military power became increasingly important, the arms race accelerated, the threat of war grew, and the domestic repression of the working class intensified.[57]

Hilferding saw the repression of the working class as a natural outgrowth of the cartelization of industry and militarization. He pointed out that during periods of prosperity and depression the working class was squeezed to pay for industrial and military expansion. Growing class antagonisms made clear to the proletariat that, in order to put an end to their exploitation, the workers themselves would have to seize political power. For Hilferding, the *Hochschutzzoll* introduced that last phase of capitalist development. It was

> the direct precursor of the socialist society, because it is its complete negation, the conscious socialization of all available economic potential in modern society, but a consolidation not in the interest of the whole, on the contrary, [a consolidation] to raise the degree of exploitation of the whole in a hitherto unheard-of fashion.[58]

Hilferding stressed how the increasing social organization of both capital and the working class shaped the development of class conflict and international relations. His intent was to refute the revisionist claim that cartelization paved the way for the gradual, peaceful evolution of capitalism into socialism. Although Hilferding agreed that cartelization created the economic basis for a future socialist society, he insisted that it also exacerbated class antagonisms. Many of his arguments were similar to those that Kautsky and Luxemburg advanced against revisionism.[59] What set Hilferding apart from them was his emphasis on the increasingly decisive economic and political importance of organized capitalist enterprises (cartels and trusts) in the struggle for economic and political power on an international scale. The *Hochschutzzoll* represented a primary feature of a new and final phase of capitalist development characterized by cartelization, intensifying class conflict, and imperialism.

The notion that the coming of socialism was simply a matter of economic inevitability never appealed to Hilferding. Instead, he believed that the success of a proletarian revolution depended on both society's level of economic development and the pursuit of effective political strategies by an organized working class. These strategies, he thought, required an analysis of the structural changes in the capitalist economy to clarify the tasks of the proletariat in class struggle.[60] The development of a social democratic political program thus depended on establishing a close unity between economic theory and political practice.

Hilferding wrote two important essays on practical political affairs before he left Austria in 1906. Both dealt with the feasibility of using the general strike as a political weapon. In 1902 and 1903, large-scale general strikes occurred in Belgium and Sweden over the franchise issue and in Holland in response to new antistrike legislation. In all three cases the strikes failed, and violent clashes between Belgian and Dutch workers and soldiers presented the socialist leadership with a difficult choice: call off the strikes or risk civil war. None of the socialist leaders was willing to pit unarmed workers against well-organized, disciplined soldiers and they preferred to end the strikes.[61] Despite these setbacks, however, debate concerning the potential of the general strike as a political weapon continued in the socialist press, at party congresses, and at meetings of the International.

In an essay that appeared in October 1903, Hilferding sought to incorporate the general strike into the current parliamentary strategy of German Social Democracy. The SPD had enjoyed a series of spectacular electoral successes and he examined their context by focusing on the historical development of parliamentary institutions as a means for the bourgeoisie to control the state. For him, capitalist development and the rise of the bourgeoisie as a class necessitated the formation of a representative political system. This system ensured that disputes between conflicting elements of the bourgeoisie remained controlled; at the same time it strengthened bourgeois domination over the rest of society.[62]

In Hilferding's view, the bourgeoisie could dominate the parliament only as long as there was no organized, adversarial, class-conscious proletariat. While workers remained disorganized, universal male suffrage represented no threat to bourgeois interests. The bourgeoisie could use the power of the state to pursue its own domestic and international aims, and its interests became closely tied to those of the state and the military. These groups joined forces to maintain their hegemony over the working class.

The development of a workers' party, Hilferding argued, challenged the bourgeoisie's control over the state. Electoral struggle offered workers a peaceful alternative to violent revolution, for a socialist majority in parliament would transform that institution into "an instrument of proletarian dictatorship."[63] It was essential to preserve universal suffrage because it ensured a steady increase in working-class power. Through the parliament, workers could use their growing numerical and economic strength to force the ruling class to make concessions in all spheres of life. These achievements would strengthen workers' resolve and train them in the administration of the state that they would eventually control.

Like Friedrich Engels at the end of his life, Hilferding was convinced it was no longer feasible for workers to fight on the barricades against modern military forces. Instead, he thought they had to use their economic power to defend gains achieved through parliamentary and trade union struggles. He foresaw a strong possibility that the dominant classes, to save themselves, would attempt to restrict universal suffrage and only then should the working class mobilize its economic power in a general strike.

Thus, Hilferding conceived of the general strike as "the regulative idea of social democratic tactics." Workers had to be conscious that only the "will to undertake a general strike" ensured the preservation of the right to vote. But the general strike was not to be used as a regular tactic or an adventurist means of seizing power, it was, rather, a last resort to defend the means for the socialist movement's further development.[64]

Hilferding's argument rested on a historical perspective linking Marx's method of class analysis with his own ideas on political tactics derived from his Austrian experience. Using language emphasizing class struggle, he adopted a tactical position that agreed with the parliamentary strategy backed by the social democratic leadership. Hilferding's thesis conceded the possibility of a violent clash between the proletariat and the bourgeoisie, but it would be a cataclysm initiated by the latter. This argument implicitly removed the initiative in the conflict from the working class and postponed any decisive revolutionary struggle until the distant future. Meanwhile the proletariat, represented by social democracy, could continue along the parliamentary road.[65]

Although cautious, Hilferding's position on the general strike placed him in the radical camp of German and Austrian social democracy in 1903.[66] In that year, at an SPD conference in Bremen, fierce opposition by the trade union and party bureaucracies kept the general strike off the agenda of the forthcoming party congress. In the eyes of its opponents, the political mass strike had no relevance for the German working-class movement and only represented a threat to its hard-earned economic and political gains. In May 1905, the Congress of German Trade Unions proclaimed the general strike to be "indiscussible" despite its acceptance by the International's Amsterdam congress as a means of struggle against "reactionary designs on the rights of the workers."[67]

The Russian revolution of 1905 transformed the context of the general strike debate and again thrust it onto the agenda of the Austrian and German social democratic parties. At the Austrian party congress in October, news of the Russian events inspired delegates to back the mass strike as a means to force political concessions from the government. Victor Adler also supported the idea of a strike, though he regarded it as an instrument to be used for limited political goals and not as a decisive revolutionary weapon. He tempered the enthusiasm of the radicals and won acceptance of the strike as a tool to be used in a highly disciplined manner in the fight for otherwise unachievable goals, such as universal suffrage.[68]

In Germany, the revolutionary events fueled a heated discussion of the political mass strike in the party press and at the Jena congress of 1905. Whereas some intellectuals, such as Rosa Luxemburg, viewed the mass strike as a typical and largely spontaneous element of future proletarian revolutions, others, such as trade union leader Theodor Bömelburg, continued to see it as a threat to the unions' very existence. Social democracy split as the movement's radical intellectuals sought to adapt the tactics of Russian workers to the German situation, while the organizational leadership largely rejected this strategy.[69]

In an essay published just before Jena, Hilferding put forward a compromise position on the general strike that was very similar to that which ultimately attained majority support.[70] The mass strike, he argued, could have a variety of uses in different countries depending on the extent to which class antagonisms had developed between the bourgeoisie and the proletariat. In economically less advanced countries, such as Austria, workers could use the mass strike to win economic and political concessions because the bourgeois parties were disorganized and did not yet regard the proletariat as a threat to their power. In Germany, however, where the level of capitalist development was more advanced and the polarization of classes more acute, the mass strike played a completely different role. A mass strike in Germany would face a united and oppositional bourgeoisie fighting for its existence as a class. Here the mass strike becomes the decisive phase of the class struggle and determines the victory or defeat of the proletariat in the social revolution.[71]

Again Hilferding argued that the German working class had to continue to fight to strengthen and expand the parliamentary system, but now he also suggested that, once a nation achieved a high level of capitalist development (that is, once the material conditions for socialism were at hand), violent conflict with the bourgeoisie became virtually inevitable. When the ruling classes no longer tolerated workers' demands for reform, the struggle for parliamentary concessions would be transformed into a struggle for socialism itself. The mass strike had to be "fought out until the end with a proletarian victory, not a terrible defeat," because "the enemy sees its approaching end and . . . resists with all its might. The mass strike for Germany is only a last decisive means in the struggle between the bourgeoisie and proletariat."[72]

Hilferding's thesis on the mass strike was also a response to hard questions raised by the great French socialist leader Jean Jaurès at the International's Amsterdam congress of 1904. Jaurès differed with Bernstein on many theoretical points but agreed with him that, in certain circumstances, social democracy should form electoral and parliamentary alliances with progressive bourgeois parties in order to achieve reforms. He also supported the entrance of socialist ministers into bourgeois governments that promised substantial social and political improvements. Sharply criticized by the orthodox and more radical Marxists, Jaurès responded by excoriating German social democrats for winning millions of votes but accomplishing virtually nothing in Germany's "pseudo-parliament," the Reichstag. They failed, he argued, because Germany's working class had no revolutionary tradition and because the SPD, despite its ability to recruit members and win votes, was helpless in the face of an authoritarian regime. Jaurès thought it was a serious mistake for German socialists to criticize their French comrades who, though numerically weak by comparison, were struggling for reforms under the more favorable conditions of a republic.[73]

In answering Jaurès, Hilferding adopted a view critical of both the revisionist and the radical positions on the mass strike. He made clear that socialist tactics certainly had to take different national conditions into account, but he insisted that the SPD's lack of parliamentary influence did not result from poor tactics "but was the necessary product of historical development, which must bring about the complete unfolding of the contradiction of bourgeois society before it can be overcome." In his view, then, underlying social relations were the key for understanding the different political conditions in various countries, not the lack of parliamentary development. Hilferding aimed to demonstrate that reformism as a long-term strategy was doomed to failure because the superficiality of its analysis underestimated the fundamental antagonisms of capitalism. As for the radicals, he located their greatest error in their view of the mass strike as only another episode in the class struggle, while he thought it was actually "the moment of decision in the whole war."[74]

Hilferding's analysis of the mass strike in 1905 was more radical than the one he had espoused in 1903, but it remained in keeping with the party leadership's emphasis on parliamentary tactics. By making the bourgeoisie responsible for aggressive action, he appealed to a majority of the SPD's leaders who, like August Bebel, agreed at Jena that the actions of labor's enemies "prescribe our tactic; it is up to them alone whether things will develop peacefully, i.e., naturally, or whether catastrophes will occur."[75] Thus, although Hilferding's "centrist" position ultimately foresaw an apocalyptic clash between the dominant and the working classes, its emphasis on the defensive nature of the mass strike reduced the anxiety of those who feared rash action sponsored by the radicals.

In the face of a possible Europeanwide revolution in 1905, Hilferding's ideas remained consistent with those he outlined regarding the mass strike. He was ecstatic when news of the Russian revolution arrived in Vienna, and his correspondence with Kautsky revealed his youthful exuberance and hopes for the outbreak of a proletarian revolution throughout Europe:

> I can imagine how much the most recent events have moved you. The collapse of Czarism is the beginning of our revolution, of our victory, that is now draw-

ing near. The expectation, which Marx had mistakenly expressed about the movement of history in 1848, will now, we hope, be fulfilled. . . . It is the time of fulfillment, the preliminary work is done. . . . It is a time when one can feel proud and happy to be a Social Democrat.[76]

The realization of these hopes did not, Hilferding thought, require any radical change in the SPÖ's tactics. The goal in Austria remained to win universal suffrage, but the Russian events transformed the meaning of this aim. "Our fight [for universal suffrage]," he wrote, "is only the beginning of a whole series of upheavals and crises that Austria will have to go through until it is transformed or collapses." And the latter eventuality seemed more probable as the revolution in Russia "open[ed] the way for the struggle of nations and the classes inside these nations simultaneously."

The key to the success of the Russian revolution, and eventually the coming European revolution, revolved around the victory of Poland in its fight for independence. A free Poland would become a symbol to all the minority groups struggling for autonomy or independence within Germany and Austria. It would force Germany to intervene in Poland militarily to restore the old order, an action that would unleash a Europeanwide war and precipitate the outbreak of social revolution in Germany. Poland would provide the strongest, most effective impulse to the "permanent revolution."

In essence, Hilferding's view allowed the SPÖ to maintain its current parliamentary strategy though placing it in a new theoretical context. Revolution in Austria was possible, but only after certain external conditions had been met. The party's task was not to prematurely attempt to encourage an upheaval at home. On the contrary, electoral reform remained its chief aim with revolutionary implications in the short term only if national and class conflicts spread throughout Europe. If the revolution in Russia failed, the parliamentary strategy could be continued without interruption.

Hilferding's analyses of the general strike and of the revolution of 1905 illustrate his conception of the passive role of the working-class party in the revolutionary process. Like the Bolshevik leader V. I. Lenin, he believed it was Social Democracy's task to educate the workers about their role in the struggle for socialism, but unlike Lenin, he did not conceive of the party as an elite organization of professional revolutionaries who would lead the revolution.[77] On the contrary, Hilferding was convinced that the class-conscious proletariat would seize state power in response to the intensifying contradictions of capitalism. In the face of crass capitalist exploitation, he wrote, "whoever has not wanted to hear the voice of social democracy must now feel that the conquest of political power is closely bound to his own personal interest."[78]

In Austria, Hilferding thought, social democracy had properly adapted its tactics to local conditions. In a country in which the SPÖ enjoyed "complete freedom of the press, organization, and assembly," it seemed logical to fight for political and economic reforms as a means of building the movement and preparing the workers for the future revolution.[79] His position was similar to Kautsky's, which held that the function of the party was "not to organize the revolution, but to organize for the revolution; not to make the revolution, but to use it." And to organize for the revolution one needed to work in the electoral, legislative, and trade union arenas.[80]

Although the young Hilferding did not think the socialist party should "make" the revolution, he considered himself a revolutionary in the full sense of the term. He wanted to change the world, and although he hoped that violence could be avoided, he accepted its likelihood in the eventual overthrow of capitalism. Once, during the SPD's 1905 campaign for suffrage reform in Prussia, Hilferding expressed this view rather crassly. While talking to a group of leading socialists in the lobby of the Reichstag, news arrived of street battles between demonstrators and police. Upon hearing the report, he rubbed his hands with satisfaction and said, "Everything's going excellently. Now we just need a bad harvest." This comment angered August Bebel, who exploded, "You, you want to be a socialist? You wish for a bad harvest? Don't you think those poor people have it tough enough already?" There is no record of Hilferding's response to Bebel, whom he held in very high regard, but it is likely he was perplexed and embarrassed. He had, after all, merely expressed in concrete terms what he had often abstractly described in his writings, that under capitalism the misery of the masses—whether relative or absolute—will eventually drive them to revolt. Bebel's rebuke implied that he was willing to take up Hilferding's abstract theoretical views for his own political purposes, but he was unwilling to consider their logical consequences.[81]

The altercation with Bebel was a minor one and had no effect on Hilferding's standing with the German party leader. By 1905 his numerous publications placed him in the forefront of social democracy's theoretical discourse and, combined with his social connections, brought him into close contact with its oligarchical leadership. Connections were important, for despite its democratic rhetoric the SPÖ was actually a highly stratified organization controlled by a central committee of between twelve and twenty members. This committee, backed by the party secretariat and parliamentary representatives, usually could impose its will on the party's elected bodies at the local, regional, and national levels. To exercise real influence in the SPÖ, one had to have access to Victor Adler and his closest associates.[82]

Hilferding had such access. He had made the acquaintance of many well-known socialists during his student days. Adler had a keen eye for promising young intellectuals like Hilferding and Bauer and made them into his protégés.[83] Most decisive for Hilferding's career, however, was his cooperation with Kautsky. Not only did his association with *Die Neue Zeit* allow him to publish regularly in socialism's leading journal, but he became an intermediary between Kautsky and Adler and helped smooth over their ideological disputes.[84] In the long run, Hilferding's intellectual talents and personal connections placed him in an excellent position to begin a career in social democratic politics.

In a letter to Victor Adler in October 1904, Kautsky mentioned that he was looking for a possible successor to his post as editor of *Die Neue Zeit*. He said that Hilferding "had made a very good impression on him" and he asked Adler what he thought of the young man.[85] A few months later, he wrote again concerning Hilferding, only this time asking Adler to provide a position for him within the Austrian party apparatus. Kautsky thought that Hilferding was among the most valuable of the contemporary Marxist theoreticians and hoped to convince him to give up medicine and take up political economy full-time. Kautsky worried that Hilferding would reject the "Bohemian" life of a socialist theorist on grounds of economic insecurity. He knew that his friend had recently married Margarethe Hönigsberg, another young physician, whom he had met in the socialist movement. Eight years older than Rudolf, Margarethe was also of Jewish background and had received her degree from the University of Vienna. She wrote frequently for *Die Neue Zeit* and reviewed books dealing with social legislation and medicine. Despite her socialist credentials, Kautsky feared the young couple would be unhappy without a secure social position and asked Adler to provide a post for Hilferding that would enable him to continue his theoretical work.[86]

The correspondence between Adler, Kautsky, and Hilferding provides no clue as to why Hilferding received no position in the Austrian party. He practiced medicine in Vienna for the next two years and often complained about his lack of time for theoretical work.[87] Meanwhile, he and Margarethe moved into new quarters on the Lichtenstein Straße and had their first child, Karl Emil. It seemed that Hilferding, despite his desire to pursue political economy, was settling into the comfortable lifestyle of a Viennese physician. Soon, however, an opportunity arose that he could not refuse.

During 1904 and 1905, Hilferding remained in close contact with Kautsky and visited the Kautsky family at their Friedenau residence in Germany. He enjoyed his visit and expressed his regret at having to return to Vienna. He longed to stay in Berlin, though he feared that, once there, he would involve himself too much with politics at the expense of his theoretical work.[88] Kautsky, meanwhile, used his connections with Bebel to bring Hilferding to Berlin in order to keep him active in the movement.

Kautsky suggested to Bebel, who was looking for new instructors to staff the Berlin Party School, that he consider Hilferding for a position.[89] Bebel recommended Hilferding to the SPD executive committee in July 1906. The committee accepted Hilferding unanimously and offered him a teaching post for six months with a considerable salary amounting to 3,000 marks. In addition, he could earn another 2,000 marks by working at *Die Neue Zeit* and *Vorwärts,* the party's leading daily.[90] Hilferding was expected to teach courses on political economy, sociology, and the materialist conception of history. The executive made it clear that, if he did not want the job, Kautsky would have to fill the position himself, raising the question of who would edit *Die Neue Zeit*. Bebel recommended that Kautsky discuss the matter with Hilferding before the latter made his decision.[91]

Hilferding was of two minds about Bebel's offer. His interest in workers' education had already led him, along with Max Adler and Renner, to found an association called *Die Zukunft* (The Future), which set up Vienna's first workers' school in 1903. He was proud of the school's accomplishments and was certainly pleased at the chance to go to Berlin.[92] Yet there were several obstacles. His lack of German citizenship and his wife's inability to practice medicine legally in Germany were concerns. German regulations against hiring foreigners could prevent them from earning a living. Hilferding also had personal doubts; he did not want to be regarded as an outsider who was too young and inexperienced. He explained to Kautsky that the political tactics used by the Austrian social democrats often differed from those used in Germany. He had certain criticisms of the SPD's methods, such as its use of the *Volksversammlung* (People's Assembly) only as a means of agitation, rather than as a means of *Politik*. It would be better, he thought, to delay his "transfer" to Berlin until he had proven himself and could accomplish something even though he was from outside the German party.[93]

Kautsky was persistent, however, and Hilferding eventually accepted his recommendations to come to Berlin. Hilferding wrote back to him, "The prospect of being able to work by your side and the hope of perhaps being able in some respects to provide [you] relief are too tempting to resist. When I know that my work will enable you to have more free time, then I know that it will be useful."[94] Hilferding accepted the post only on a provisional basis because of the chance that he would be deported and because he was not sure if he would measure up to the job's requirements. Although his correspondence says nothing about whether Margarethe would be able to practice medicine in Germany, it appears that he was no longer concerned about his family's financial situation. His salary was sufficient for them to live comfortably, and he now had his first opportunity to pursue full-time theoretical work.

Although he had already been a socialist for almost half his life, the move to Germany was a decisive step for the twenty-nine-year-old Hilferding. He had now committed himself, however hesitantly, not only to the study of political economy instead of medicine, but also to a career within the Social Democratic party organization. Hilferding had joined the workers' movement as a young man because he was attracted to its emancipatory ideals, and his efforts as a young socialist intellectual had been quickly recognized and rewarded. His ready acceptance as a serious thinker by leading socialists made his move into full-time political and educational work a natural one and cemented his loyalty to the movement. Hilferding was proud to be a Social Democrat; it was this pride, loyalty, and sense of responsibility that motivated his efforts to preserve and strengthen the party when it was racked by dissention, frequent setbacks, and ultimately total defeat.

In 1906, of course, socialism's decisive crises lay in the unknowable future. When he left Vienna, Hilferding's outlook was upbeat; he was convinced that the movement's victory was just a matter of time and the use of proper tactics. Once in Berlin, he intended to continue his studies of modern capitalism and to work to shape social democracy's strategy in light of his conclusions. Hilferding did not have a position of authority in the German party and had no direct input into its decision-making process. His position as a respected theoretician at the Party School and his access to the press, however, would enable him to influence the terms of debate on a wide variety of issues facing the socialist leadership.

It was in Germany that the full weight of Hilferding's Austrian heritage manifested itself. Forged in Vienna's cosmopolitan sociocultural and political milieu, Hilferding's lifelong commitment to the goal of human emancipation and his understanding of the most effective means to achieve this lofty aim always bore the stamp of his youthful experience. Under the different circumstances of his new home and in response to later events, he would, of course, change some of his views, but the ideas and principles that he developed in Austria remained the bedrock of his worldview until the end of his life.

CHAPTER TWO

FINANCE CAPITAL AND THE STRUGGLE FOR UNITY

Industrial profit incorporates commercial profit, is itself capitalized as promoter's profit, and becomes the booty of the trinity which has attained its highest form of capital as finance capital. For industrial capital is God the Father, who sent forth commercial and bank capital as God the Son, and money capital is the Holy Ghost. They are three persons united in one, in finance capital.   —*Rudolf Hilferding*

Once again the road to socialism lies illuminated before our eyes. . . . Our most important task is to take this certainty, which theory gives us, to the masses.   —*Otto Bauer*

The years between his arrival in Berlin in 1906 and the outbreak of World War I were crucial for Hilferding and the workers' movement.[1] During this time, the young theorist established himself as a respected thinker, a leading editor, and a loyal supporter of the leadership that had created the world's largest and best-organized socialist party. Hilferding devoted himself to the task of maintaining social democratic unity in the midst of intense factional infighting. Culminating with the publication of his monumental *Finance Capital,* his effort to build bridges between the party's left and right wings made him a key figure in the SPD's newly emerging majority faction, the Marxist center led by Bebel and Kautsky, which aimed to preserve the revolutionary tenets of the Erfurt Program without altering the party's parliamentary tactics.[2] The division of the SPD after August 1914 marked the failure of the center's project and was a blow from which neither Hilferding nor the workers' movement ever recovered.

Hilferding moved to Berlin just as the SPD began a period of profound expansion that saw the party's membership almost triple from 384,000 in 1906 to over 1 million in 1912. This rapid growth was paralleled by that of the SPD's close ally the General Commission of German Trade Unions, which increased its membership from 1 million in 1904 to 2.5 million in 1914. In addition, the parliamentary arena reflected the socialist movement's growing strength. In 1912 the SPD won 4,250,000 votes (34.8 percent) and was by far the largest party in the Reichstag.[3]

For large numbers of German workers, the SPD represented not only the hope for a better future but also a more acceptable present. The party aided workers with legal problems, helped organize consumer and insurance cooperatives, and offered educational and entertainment opportunities by establishing schools, libraries, and theaters. The SPD functioned as a vehicle for political expression, as a service organization, and as a community providing a sense of solidarity and cooperation. In the context of Germany's ideologically charged and socially fragmented political order, social democracy constructed its own specific milieu, which attracted and retained substantial support among German workers.[4] To its many supporters and opponents alike, social democracy's achievements were impressive, and it appeared that the movement was moving inexorably closer to power.[5]

The young Hilferding shared these sentiments, though he also detected some straws in the wind. Keenly aware of the continued revisionist-radical split in the ranks of the movement's leadership, he worked to develop a theoretical and practical framework that would hold the rival factions together. Although this effort ultimately failed, the experience decisively influenced Hilferding's later career in the socialist movement. Arriving in Berlin as Kautsky's protégé, Hilferding succeeded him during the Weimar Republic as the SPD's chief ideologist. One of the central premises that he adopted from his mentor—and which later shaped his outlook under Weimar—was the idea that the socialist movement must provide the working class with the promise of a radically different social order toward which capitalism was moving and for which the socialist movement was preparing. Unlike Bernstein, the Jungen, or the left-wing faction that later formed around Rosa Luxemburg, Hilferding saw no contradiction between social democracy's parliamentarianism and the theoretical vision contained in its program. He believed that the SPD must use the parliamentary system, even the pseudodemocratic one of Wilhelmian Germany, to build its organization and pursue reforms that, either peacefully or violently, would ultimately lead to the socialist transformation of the social and political order. The establishment of the Weimar Republic only strengthened this conviction.

Hilferding's experiences in prewar Berlin also had important implications for his political career. His theoretical prowess and personal connections with leading socialists allowed him to begin his career at a high level in the party organization and to advance rapidly from there. After his brief sojourn at the Party School, his appointment as foreign policy editor at *Vorwärts,* the party's leading organ, placed him in close proximity to the top leadership. The publication of *Finance Capital* and his contributions to the socialist press, especially to *Die Neue Zeit* and the Austro-Marxist journal *Der Kampf,* enhanced his visibility and influence within the party. By 1914, the thirty-seven-year-old Hilferding was well established in the social democratic hierarchy, though not yet a full member of its highest councils.

The content of Hilferding's theoretical work and his rise in the party hierarchy were closely linked to the SPD's expansion and the evolution of its structure in the prewar era. As Detlef Lehnert points out, the political culture of the social democratic milieu had four main structural components: the trade unions; a "political camp" based on the party's general membership; a "solidarity community" *(Solidargemeinschaft)* of the most committed activists (at most two hundred thousand people), for whom the movement represented a way of life; and a corps of functionaries *(Funktionärskorps)* made up of about ten thousand top-level party workers such as party secretaries, parliamentary deputies, and political officials.[6] It is primarily the latter group that concerns us here. In order to conduct electoral campaigns, communicate with an ever-increasing membership, and provide services, the SPD required a large well-organized bureaucracy. After 1900 the party structure became increasingly centralized with officers from local and *Land* (state) organizations regularly reporting to the national executive committee. Periodically selected by the party congresses, this body initially focused on political tasks but gradually took on more and more administrative functions. Between 1905 and 1912 administrative personnel grew to represent a majority of its membership.

The growth of the bureaucracy enhanced the executive's ability to manage party affairs, but it also created a stratum of workers on all levels that concerned itself more with the health of the SPD's organization than with the realization of its revolutionary aims. Under the leadership of Friedrich Ebert, who was elected to the executive in 1905, this apparatus functioned as an electoral machine that spurned tactics risking voter alienation, state repression, or internal party conflicts. The bureaucracy, as "bearer of an ideology of integration," rejected radical politics and, by 1914, had come to dominate the making of party policy.[7]

This expanding apparatus absorbed the young Hilferding. Intensely loyal to the organization that provided him with a sense of professional and personal identity, he was proud, too, of its achievements. Hilferding cautiously opposed radical extraparliamentary tactics that he felt could threaten the party's organization, yet he was also a man of conviction who did not allow "patriotic" feelings toward the party to undermine what he considered to be fundamental socialist principles. When war came in 1914, he was forced to choose between loyalty to the party leadership's progovernment majority and his commitment to socialist internationalism. He chose the latter. To oppose the war and, ultimately, to break with the party was one of the most difficult decisions of his life.

Before the failure of the German revolution, Hilferding also differed from Ebert and his supporters in one other important regard: he did not believe in the possibility of social democracy's integration into the existing order. On the contrary, he thought that the proletariat could emancipate itself only by conquering political power and transforming the economy. Socialism's victory was only possible, Hilferding was certain, if all segments of the workers' movement, such as the trade unions and the cooperatives, joined forces with the SPD in the political struggle to take control of the state. The paradox of his outlook, like that of the center as a whole, was that, aside from electioneering and organization-building, it left the working class with virtually no active role in the process of self-emancipation. Thus, in practical terms, his view abandoned the field of action to the SPD's conservative elements.[8]

For Hilferding, the SPD was at the heart of the workers' struggle for liberation. When offered the position at the Berlin Party School, he was naturally excited about the prospect of helping to train the next generation of social democracy's leaders.[9] The overtly political nature of the school immediately made it the object of heated controversy. Friction developed between party and union leaders over the school's proposed goals, as the SPD leadership aimed to provide workers with a "simple, serious and needed education" in the interest of political agitation, whereas trade unionists sought to train students in practical union matters and feared placing the education of future union functionaries under party control.[10]

Such fears ultimately led the General Commission of German Trade Unions (ADGB) to found a school of its own in 1905, a separate and very different institution. Marxists such as Hilferding, Luxemburg, Anton Pannekoek, and Franz Mehring staffed the Party School, whereas the Trade Union School, by contrast, employed revisionists such as Carl Legien, Max Schippel, and Bernstein. The institutions' course offerings reflected their different ideological orientations. At the SPD school courses in political economy, the materialist conception of history, and the history of socialism formed an important part of the curriculum. Trade union issues such as health insurance, occupational safety, and trade union history formed the core of the classes offered at the Trade Union School.[11]

The decision to open rival schools disturbed Hilferding. In letters to Kautsky he contrasted the relatively cooperative relations between the SPÖ and the unions in Austria to the often adversarial relations between their German counterparts. He suggested that, as in Austria, one semi-autonomous institution catering to the needs of both the SPD and the unions would have been preferable. Such an institution, he thought, could provide students with a common educational and ideological background, thereby unifying the party and union organizations in which they would later work. Hilferding feared that, instead, the Trade Union School would undercut the SPD, and he regarded the establishment of two different schools as the worst thing to happen to the German workers' movement up to that time. Kautsky eventually persuaded him to accept the teaching post despite his misgivings. Hilferding hoped to help establish the Party School's credibility and anticipated a unification of the two schools.[12]

SPD Party School, ca. 1907. Hilferding is second from the right.
Rosa Luxemburg stands in the middle. Franz Mehring is at the podium.

After his arrival in November 1906, Hilferding taught political economy at the school for one six-month term. Although it is impossible to ascertain exactly who sat in Hilferding's classes, it is known that his students were primarily twenty-five- to thirty-five-year-old workers. Many of the 203 graduates between 1907 and 1914 went on to become editors of social democratic newspapers as well as party secretaries and trade union and cooperative officials. By 1911, thirty-two editors, twenty-four secretaries of various types, and twenty-three trade unionists had attended the school.[13] Thus, the executive had entrusted Hilferding with an influential post. His tenure was brief, but his position certainly enhanced his reputation as a theorist and allowed him to expand his contacts within the party leadership.

Hilferding did not describe his activities at the school in his correspondence, nor are many comments about his teaching abilities available from contemporaries. According to one report, his classroom lectures were disappointing because they were long and boring, but it is difficult to draw conclusions from only one account. His teaching was not a factor in his decision to resign after only one semester; the enforcement of a law prohibiting the hiring of teachers who were not German citizens gave Hilferding the option of resignation or deportation. He choose the former.[14] The SPD replaced him with Rosa Luxemburg, whose recent (and bogus) marriage to a German citizen allowed her to avoid expulsion.

Soon afterward the party appointed Hilferding foreign editor of *Vorwärts*. Assignment to such an important post represented a major step upward within the social democratic hierarchy and illustrated the high degree of trust in Hilferding within the SPD's top leadership. It also assured him of a more than adequate income, especially when combined with his honoraria from *Die Neue Zeit* and *Der Kampf*.[15]

Hilferding was keenly interested in his new job. While still in Austria he had often commented on the quality of the social democratic press in Germany. Except for Franz Mehring's radical *Leipziger Volkszeitung*, he found the press's performance poor in clarifying issues such as the revisionist controversy and the general strike for the workers. He singled out *Vorwärts* as a "miserable failure in all important things" and complained to Kautsky that the socialist press in Germany had completely misunderstood the importance of the Russian revolution and failed to rouse the workers against possible German intervention there.[16]

Personnel problems at *Vorwärts* soon provided Hilferding with an opportunity to shape the paper to his own liking. Soon after Kurt Eisner became chief editor in 1903, serious conflicts arose between the paper's editorial staff and the SPD executive. Eisner's refusal to publish a declaration by Bebel condemning revisionism illustrated the paper's support for the party's right wing, and over the next two years relations between the executive and the editors were extremely confrontational. Disagreements centered on the paper's opposition to the mass strike, its propagation of neo-Kantian idealism, and its view of revolutionary events in Russia. After numerous conferences failed to improve the situation, the controversy was ended only by the resignation of the majority of the paper's editors, including Eisner, and the appointment of a staff more congenial to the executive.[17]

In the wake of this conflict, Bebel suggested that Hilferding become a regular contributor to *Vorwärts*. In October 1905 the party appointed a new editorial staff, headed by Hans Block, and charged it with the task of attracting new supporters to the SPD and educating them on the fundamentals of Marxism. To ensure the realization of these goals, the executive and party press commission stipulated that Rosa Luxemburg should furnish *Vorwärts* with two lead articles per week. Hilferding's appointment was part of a later effort to buttress the Marxist contingent on the paper's staff.[18]

Contributions to *Vorwärts* were generally unsigned, thus making it difficult to identify authorship. It is clear, however, that Hilferding took on a leading role at the paper within a short time. By supporting the Erfurt Program's theoretical principles and the SPD's parliamentary strategy, he provided *Vorwärts* with an editorial "balance" that impressed not only Bebel and the centrist majority in the leadership, but also some reformers, who were chiefly concerned with practical matters. Eventually, Hilferding became chief editor and under his leadership *Vorwärts*'s circulation expanded markedly from 122,000 in 1910 to 161,000 in 1914.[19]

Hilferding's editorial work kept him very busy but it also left him time to participate in social democratic debates on imperialism, militarism, and other issues. Even more important, he continued his economic research and wrote a number of articles on recent developments in Germany and the United States. In 1910 he published his great work, *Finance Capital*, which represented the culmination of these interrelated studies.[20] Hailed by Otto Bauer and Karl Kautsky as a continuation of Marx's *Capital*, the book was a significant theoretical achievement and continues to stimulate debate today.[21] *Finance Capital* established Hilferding as the Second International's leading economic thinker and a major figure in social democracy's emerging centrist faction, which aimed to refute Bernstein's theoretical views while reaffirming the party's practice.

With the exception of Bernstein, reviewers of *Finance Capital* are essentially united in the opinion that Hilferding provided the most thorough early theoretical examination of the processes of concentration and monopolization in industry and banking from a Marxist standpoint.[22] He drew widely from the work of contemporary Marxist theorists such as Bauer and Kautsky and expanded and reformulated many of their ideas.[23] By going beyond the reformist analysis of imperialism worked out by the liberal political economist J. A. Hobson, and by further developing the work of Marxist contemporaries, Hilferding's study of capitalism came to represent the point of departure for all future radical analyses of imperialism and capitalist development. Both V. I. Lenin in his *Imperialism: The Highest Stage of Capitalism* (1917) and Nikolay Bukharin in his *Imperialism and World Economy* (1929) acknowledged the importance of Hilferding's contribution, and other leading theorists such as Luxemburg, Kautsky, and Bernstein all were compelled to deal with his conclusions in their own work.

The strength of Hilferding's analysis lies in the emphasis he placed on the structural transformation of the capitalist economy at the end of the nineteenth century and his recognition of the changes in the power relations of society both nationally and internationally. Unlike Hobson, who saw imperialism as a phenomenon caused by the greed of certain elements of the capitalist class, Hilferding saw the source of modern imperialism in the historical development of capitalism as a whole.[24] Hobson identified symptoms of imperialism such as aggressive nationalism, racism, colonialism, and militarism and he roundly condemned them, but he did not penetrate beneath the surface of the problem, that is, the relations of production and exchange that developed on a world scale as a result of the expansion of capitalism and the development of finance capital. Hilferding's work represents an important contribution to our understanding of how this process unfolds.

In the preface to *Finance Capital,* Hilferding identified "the most characteristic features of 'modern' capitalism," as "those processes of concentration which on the one hand, 'eliminate free competition' through the formation of cartels and trusts, and on the other, bring bank and industrial capital into an ever more intimate relationship. Through this relationship . . . capital assumes the form of finance capital, its supreme and most abstract expression." Without a knowledge of the laws and functioning of finance capital, Hilferding asserted, "no understanding of present day economic tendencies, and hence no understanding of scientific economics or politics" was possible.[25] It was his intention to apply the abstract analytical method of Marx's *Capital* in the study of those laws.

Hilferding divided *Finance Capital* into five parts dealing with money and credit, the mobilization of capital, the restriction of free competition, the phenomena of economic crises, and imperialism. Following Marx, his analysis moved from the particular to the more general aspects of capitalist development, but he also structured the book as a direct reply to Bernstein.[26] Although Bernstein's name appears nowhere in the text, the last four parts of *Finance Capital* parallel those sections of Bernstein's *Voraussetzungen* that analyze the development of contemporary capitalism and reformulate social democracy's tasks. In responding to Bernstein, Hilferding aimed to confirm the basic premises of Marx's economic theory and to defend the SPD's political strategy against reformist and radical critics.

His efforts were not entirely successful. Parts of Hilferding's analysis, especially his theories of money and eco/ nomic crises, break with Marx's own views and are actually more akin to those of Bernstein. In addition, Hilferding occasionally defended arguments that were empirically unsubstantiated and factually incorrect. These difficulties weaken his otherwise powerful argument.

In *Finance Capital* Hilferding analyzed the process by which credit institutions—more specifically, the banks—merged with and gained control over large-scale industry. He began his study with a lengthy discussion of the role of money and credit in the capitalist economy and argued that it was the increasing importance of credit in the process of capitalist development that eventually placed industry in a dependent relationship with the banks.[27] According to Hilferding, "credit first appears as a consequence of the changed function of money as a means of payment. When payment is made some time after the sale has taken place the money due is credited for the intervening period" (82). As capitalism evolved, promissory notes or bills of exchange assumed the function of credit money. These notes, which productive capitalists advanced to one another, Hilferding called "circulation credit" (83). This type of credit functioned as a substitute for money, which facilitated the transfer of commodities without the use of money, thus conserving bullion.

In this system, the credit relationship was one that existed between two or more productive capitalists. If, however, a firm could not raise enough capital by selling its commodities to pay off credit owed to another capitalist, the money had to be obtained from a third party—the banks. The role of banks, therefore, appeared initially to develop out of the need for an institution to regulate and extend credit. More important, however, the availability of circulation credit resulted in the extension of the scale of production far beyond the capacity of the money capital in the hands of the capitalists. The banks became increasingly important as a source of credit when capitalist firms needed to expand to meet the demands of competition with other enterprises (84).

The ability of the banks to concentrate the capital of all classes and to put it at the disposal of the productive capitalists was their most important function in the capitalist economy. "Capitalists," Hilferding pointed out, "thus receive not only their own money capital, which is managed by the banks, but also the idle money of all other classes for use in production" (90). Hilferding called idle money that was converted into active money "investment credit" (92). Unlike commercial credit, which had the function of reducing the costs of circulation, the primary purpose of investment credit was to enable production to expand on the basis of a given supply of money. Industrial capitalists could use the money provided by the banks to expand production by investing either in fixed or circulating capital. It is the investment in fixed capital that is of particular importance to Hilferding's analysis. "So long as the banks merely serve as intermediaries in payment transactions," Hilferding wrote, "their only interest is the condition of an enterprise . . . at a particular time. . . . This changes when the bank begins to provide the industrialist with capital for production" (95). Thereafter, it develops a long-term interest in the prospects of the firm and the condition of the market and "the larger the amount of credit supplied and, above all, the larger the proportion of the loan turned into fixed capital, the stronger, more abiding that interest will be" (95).

How does the bank ensure that its interests are protected? Hilferding dealt with this question in his extension of Marx's and Engels's studies of the joint stock company (or corporation). Building on their conclusions, his analysis stresses the importance of the corporation for the expansion of production, the transformation of private into social capital, the change in the relationship of the capitalist to the means of production, and the cartelization of industry.[28] What was fundamentally new in Hilferding's work was his development of the concept of "promoter's profit" and his emphasis on the power of the banks under finance capital.

In *Capital*, Marx had observed that under capitalism the competitive struggle was fought by the cheapening of commodities. If all other circumstances remained the same, the cheapness of commodities depended on the productivity of labor in the process of production. Competition, Marx asserted, "rages in direct proportion to the number, and in inverse proportion to the magnitudes of the antagonistic capitals. It always ends in the ruin of the many small capitalists whose capitals partly pass into the hands of their conquerors."[29]

Thus, concomitant with the development of the credit mechanism under capitalism, Marx argued that competition led to the increasing centralization of production. Under the pressure of competition, it became more and more difficult for individual capitalists to accumulate enough surplus capital for the investments in production necessary to increase labor productivity. The corporation made possible an enormous expansion of the scale of production, which was impossible for individual capitalists.[30]

Hilferding defined a corporation as an association of capitalists who each contribute a share of capital to the enterprise. The extent of each individual capitalist's influence on the direction of the firm depended on the amount of capital he contributed. Those who owned the most shares (but not necessarily an absolute majority) controlled the corporation, the structure of which entailed an important change in the function of the industrial capitalist and his relationship to his property. The industrial capitalist became liberated from his function as industrial entrepreneur. He was now a money capitalist, a creditor, whose function was to lend his capital and, after a time, to get it back with interest. He had, in general, nothing to do with the use of his loaned capital in production. The shareholder's return (his profit yield per share) on the invested capital depended on the profitability of the enterprise. Unlike an industrial entrepreneur (who tied up his capital in a single enterprise, worked productively only in that enterprise, and whose interests were bound up with it over a long period), the shareholder could recover his profit at any time by selling his shares (or claims to profit) and then seeking out new interest-yielding investments such as those available on the stock exchange. Whereas the industrial capitalist drew a return from his enterprise in the form of industrial profit, the money capitalist's earnings stemmed from the yield on loan capital.[31]

It was in his analysis of the turnover of share capital that Hilferding introduced the category of the "promoter's profit" *(Gründergewinn)*, which clarified the advantages to be gained by capitalists' establishing new corporations. Hilferding observed that the total sum of "share capital" (that is, the aggregate price of capitalized claims to profit) need not coincide with the total money capital, which was originally converted into industrial capital. The discrepancy arose, he asserted, with the founding of a corporation when there was a possibility of selling shares for considerably more than the invested capital if the yield on that capital was higher than the current rate of interest on investments. This action yielded to the seller of the shares an extra profit, which Hilferding named "promoter's profit" and which served as an incentive for the founding of corporations and furthered the concentration and expansion of capital (110–12).[32]

The relative stability of large corporate enterprises even during periods of economic crisis, their secure returns on investment capital, and the promise of promoter's profit attracted large amounts of bank capital for corporate investment. As a consequence, Hilferding argued, banks developed a permanent interest in the profitable operation of firms in which they had invested, and to guarantee their returns they sought to control the use of their loaned capital. Through the purchase of stock, banks could place representatives on a firm's board of directors who could supervise and influence company policy. Moreover, the share system enabled banks to invest in any number of firms simultaneously, to be represented on their boards of directors, and to thereby minimize their risks (120–21).

One of the most important effects of this merger of bank and industrial capital was the placement of control over society's productive forces in the hands of a continually smaller number of decision makers. Hilferding developed this theme not only in his analysis of the effects of competition on the small producer, but also in his examination of the relationship between finance capital and the stock and commodity exchanges. Both of these exchanges, he thought, decreased in importance as bank and industrial capital merged. Whereas during earlier periods of capitalist development both had served in the mobilization of investment capital, with the rise of industrial capitalism the banks began to usurp the functions of these markets. Hilferding argued that even stock market speculation was declining in importance, since the cartelization of industry and the formation of monopolies that can dictate prices meant the "death of speculation" (147–49).

For Hilferding, the role of the banks in the formation of cartels and trusts was decisive. He used the example of bank speculation in the futures trade to emphasize this point. The bank participated in the trade by providing credit against collateral, or it could take advantage of its great capital resources and general overview of the market to enter into speculation on its own account. The bank's aim was to gain control over the market of a specific commodity and to take the place of the merchant in relation to the industrialist. It worked to exclude rival dealers by either buying the commodity directly from the producers or operating on a commission basis and selling it at a lower rate of profit. This activity, as well as the provision of credit and the purchase of shares, brought the bank and industry into close cooperation. The bank established connections with as many enterprises as possible in order to use its influence to cartelize the branch or, in other words, to create a monopolistic combine regulating the commodity's price and securing the industry against the effects of a possible depression (162–63).

In Hilferding's scenario, the banks expanded simultaneously with the growth of industry and gradually became dominant over it due to their control over a greater amount of the total social capital. As the process of cartelization unfolded, the banks also grew and amalgamated. Not only was competition reduced inside cartelized industrial branches, but this tendency also developed in banking. Hilferding suggested that

> with the development of banking and the increasingly dense network of rela-
> tions between the banks and industry there is a growing tendency to eliminate
> competition among the banks themselves and, on the other side, to concentrate
> all capital in the form of money capital and to make it available to the producers
> only through the banks. If this trend were to continue, it would finally result in
> a single bank or a group of banks establishing control over the entire money
> capital. Such a "central bank" would then exercise control over social produc-
> tion as a whole. (180)

Such a "fully developed credit" system, Hilferding argued, was the "antithesis of capitalism" because it represented organization and control over the anarchy of the market. Although it had its "source" in socialism, it was a form of orga-nization adapted to capitalism. It was the socialization of other people's money for use by the few and therefore was a "fraudulent" kind of socialism (180).

Hilferding thought that with the development of finance capital, ulti-mately all independent industries would become dependent on the cartelized industries until they were finally annexed by them (234). The aim of this process of monopoly formation was, of course, to raise profits. For firms inte-grated into the cartel, the abolition of competition could end fluctuations in the rate of profit, smooth out oscillations in the business cycle, and even eliminate certain elements from the process of capitalist reproduction that represented a drain on industrial profit. Here Hilferding specifically referred to the elimination of commercial intermediaries, that is, the merchants, whom he thought would be squeezed out since the cartelized industries could deal directly with one another and thus eliminate the middle man (196). Since the cartel itself presupposed a large bank as creditor for current payments and productive investment in the whole industrial sector, it was in a much stronger position to withstand the impact of a possible depression than any remaining noncartelized industry (223).

The ultimate outcome of this process was the formation of what Hilferd-ing called the "general cartel," a single body that could regulate the whole of capitalist production by determining the volume of output in all branches of industry. Under its control,

> price determination would become a purely nominal matter involving only the
> distribution of the total product between the cartel magnates on the one side
> and all the other members of society on the other. . . . The illusion of the objec-
> tive value of the commodity would disappear along with the anarchy of produc-
> tion, and money itself would cease to exist. . . . This would be a consciously

regulated society, but in an antagonistic form. This antagonism, however, would concern distribution, which itself would be consciously regulated and hence able to dispense with money. (234)

What did these trends mean in terms of the power relations of society as a whole? For Hilferding, finance capital was a power that arose directly from the ownership of the means of production, of natural resources, and of both living and dead labor. Under finance capital, property became concentrated and centralized in the hands of a few capitalist magnates, while the mass of the population possessed no capital. As the "social economy" became more organized, "the problem of property relations" attained its "clearest, most unequivocal and sharpest expression" (235).

Hilferding's conclusions regarding the evolution of the credit system were based on concrete developments of the period, especially in Germany and the United States. From its early nineteenth-century origins the German banking system has been characterized by cyclical crises and a steady process of concentration, and between 1895 and 1924 there was an especially heavy wave of horizontal mergers among privately owned banks, regional *Aktienbanken* (joint-stock banks), and the big investment banks in Berlin. After 1880, German investment banks moved aggressively into the industrial sector providing credit to corporations and buying up shares. To finance very large projects that were beyond the means of both industry and individual banks, and to spread the risk, the banks pooled their resources by forming consortia.

By the end of the nineteenth century, the banks were able to use their capital to gain considerable influence not only over the German coal and steel industries, in which the processes of both horizontal and vertical concentration were well underway, but in the chemical and electrical industries as well. That the interests of the banks and these industries were closely intertwined was reflected in the composition of the industries' supervisory boards; four of Germany's most important banks—the Deutsche Bank, the Bank für Handel und Industrie, the Disconto-Gesellschaft, and the Berliner Handels-Gesellschaft—were strongly represented. Germany's investment banks thus played a key role in the development of the nation's industry. A great deal of power, both economic and political, was concentrated in relatively few hands.[33]

The development of bank power in the United States roughly paralleled that of Germany. In contrast to Germany, however, where the commercial banks initially played a leading role in the establishment and financing of joint stock companies, in the United States, which had a very different history, the private bankers were initially dominant. It was after the process of industrial development was well underway that the commercial banks eventually became ascendant and, for a time, actually held a dominant position in American corporate life.[34]

Whereas Marx had argued that England represented the model of future capitalist development for the continental powers, Hilferding held that in Germany and the United States, "the relation of banks to industry was necessarily, from the outset, quite different from that in England." The difference was rooted in Germany's "backward and belated capitalist development," but nevertheless, the close connection between industrial and bank capital became an important factor in both countries' advance toward a higher form of capitalist organization.[35] Thus, Hilferding believed that Germany and the United States now represented the wave of the future, and in this respect his prediction proved accurate. French, Belgian, and Italian capitalism also experienced the rise of finance capital, though the process unfolded somewhat differently in each nation. English capitalism—once the most advanced—was the last to develop along finance capitalist lines.[36]

While historical development confirmed the general applicability of Hilferding's theoretical model, it also revealed its limits. The power of finance capital rested on industry's need for capital. In Germany, the onset of World War I enabled many industries to amass huge profits and their capital liquidity was strengthened further when the postwar inflation eliminated much of their debt. The big concerns were able to accumulate substantial amounts of capital, which allowed them to finance mergers and new investments without bank assistance. Freed from bank debt and with large amounts of capital on their hands some firms actually sought to take over the banks or found their own.

The stabilization of Germany's currency in 1924 reinvigorated the big investment banks, but the economic disaster of 1929 forced the German state to intervene to prevent the collapse of the banking system. The private investment banks were then merged with public banks. This marked the end of bank dominance over industry and the confluence of industrial, bank, and state power that grew even more pronounced under the National Socialist government.

Between 1850 and 1930 investment banks in the United States played a decisive role in financing the transport and industrial infrastructure, the war industries, and the postwar boom in mergers and acquisitions. But here also the coming of the depression marked the onset of their decline. State intervention reorganizing the banking sector brought about the dissolution of many of the leading investment banks (such as J. P. Morgan), while state-sponsored credit institutions connected with the New Deal, corporate efforts to self-finance investments, and state armaments expenditures further weakened bank power.[37]

Although finance capital would revive after 1945, its temporary eclipse demonstrated its historical specificity. Hilferding's model—stressing the ever-increasing concentration of bank power and suggesting (at least theoretically) the creation of "single central bank" or a "general cartel"—underestimated the importance of countervailing forces within the economy. Hilferding certainly recognized that there were practical obstacles within modern capitalism that hindered the formation of such an all-encompassing bank or cartel. But his conviction that finance capital represented the final stage of capitalist de-velopment prevented him from adequately addressing the tension between his theoretical construct and the realities of the capitalist economy.

Other problems in Hilferding's analysis of the credit system also warrant mention. Not only did he overestimate the banks' ability to eliminate mer-chants from economic life and to reduce stock market speculation, but more important, he exaggerated the dominance of bank over industrial capital. The banks certainly played an important and sometimes decisive role in the process of industrial development, but bank and industrial capital were also interdependent. Accumulated capital under the control of the banks was es-sential for industrial expansion, but production remained the source of bank profit and power. In this sense, bank capital was to a certain extent dependent on industrial capital. In addition, Hilferding's emphasis on the singular role of the banks as providers of industrial capital neglected the development of other financial institutions such as insurance companies, which eventually came to compete with the banks in the search for profitable investment.[38]

Hilferding's analysis of the corporation, in particular his distinction be-tween the concentration of property ownership under finance capital from the concentration of production, was also an important contribution to Marxist political economy.[39] Not only did the system of share capital make possible the mobilization of capital on an ever-increasing scale, but it resulted in the separation of the capitalist from direct control over the means of pro-duction. Whereas Bernstein argued that the development of the joint stock company led to the democratization of property ownership under capitalism, Hilferding convincingly demonstrated the opposite. The share system en-abled an increasingly small number of capitalists to expand their power over broad sectors of the economy. This process of monopolization characterized a new stage of social development clearly different from the period of com-petitive capitalism analyzed by Marx. Whereas Marx and Engels had begun an analysis of the corporation and the credit system, Hilferding extended it by taking into account later developments in the capitalist economy, espe-cially the growing importance of banking in the formation of corporations.

Although Hilferding saw his work primarily as an effort to further develop Marxism, in some areas—such as his theory of capitalist crises—his conclu-sions marked a clear break with Marx's own teachings. Hilferding thought that the process of cartelization had an important effect on the cyclical eco-nomic crises endemic to capitalism. Moving away from Marx's basic proposi-tion that capitalist crises were the result of the fundamental contradiction be-tween the social production of commodities and their private appropriation, he criticized theories that located the origins of crises in the "overproduc-tion" or "underconsumption" of commodities. Such views, he asserted, merely described a general condition of crises but did not explain them or their periodic character. It was not in the sphere of production that crisis originated; on the contrary, they resulted from a "disturbance of circulation" that manifested itself "as a massive unsalability of commodities."[40]

Hilferding argued that disruptions in the specific regulatory mechanism of production—that is, price—prevented prices from giving a proper indication of the needs of production. Such disruptions caused distortions in the proportional relationship between production in the capital and consumer goods branches of the economy and brought on a general crisis.[41] For Hilferding the question then arose: Could the cartels (as Bernstein argued), using their power to eliminate free competition, actually intervene in the economy and reduce the danger of economic crises?

He concluded that they could not. Cartelized industries could certainly withstand the impact of crises more successfully than noncartelized firms, and they could take advantage of their superiority and attempt to undercut their rivals at a time when these could least withstand increased competition. But cartels were unable to prevent crises. Hilferding believed that cartels exacerbated the disturbances in the regulation of prices that lead ultimately to the outbreak of crises. Cartels could end competition within a given branch of production, but they could not alter the competition among capitals for spheres of investment or the effects of accumulation on price structure, which could bring on disproportional relations and crises.

If this were true, then how could the "general cartel" introduce the "conscious regulation" of the whole of capitalist production? Hilferding explained that, although this concept was economically feasible, in the face of social and economic realities such an arrangement actually would be impossible. "It would," he concluded, "inevitably come to grief in the conflict of interests which intensify to an extreme point." The transformation from the anarchic system of capitalist production to one of planned socialist production could not occur gradually. "[It] can only take place suddenly," he declared, "by subordinating the whole of production to conscious control."[42]

Hilferding's emphasis on the sphere of circulation in the cartelization process and in the outbreak of crises must be viewed in the context of his theory of the state in the transition to socialism. Although he did not explicitly develop a theory of the state in *Finance Capital*, his view on the state's role was of key importance to his argument that finance capitalism represented a final stage of presocialist economic development. The underlying centrality of the state in his analysis emerges in the first section of Hilferding's book, in which he developed a theory of money.[43]

According to Marx, in a commodity economy money has the function of the socially accepted general equivalent of all other commodities and it facilitates the exchange of commodities on the market by acting as a general measure of value. Money receives its exchange value in the process of production because, like any other commodity, it represents in abstract form the amount of labor time contained in its production. Marx also made it a point to distinguish between the exchange value of a commodity and its price on the market, which is determined by a number of factors (which we need not deal with here). The essential point is that, for Marx, the exchange value of money originated in production.[44]

Not so for Hilferding, who argued that money was the expression of a social relationship in the form of an object. This object served as a direct expression of value. "In the sequence C-M-C," he explained, "the value of a commodity is always exchanged for the value of another commodity, and money is a transitory form or a mere technical aid, the use of which causes expense which should be avoided as far as possible." In Hilferding's view, money receives its value only in the process of exchange, through its function as a medium of circulation between two commodities. He did not make a distinction between money as a measure of exchange value and money as a measure of price. By emphasizing money simply in terms of its use value (or, more accurately, its technical function in the process of commodity circulation), Hilferding sought to show how money became the object of state policy.[45] In an economy dominated by finance capital (that is, an economy characterized by a certain degree of planning and regulation in which the banks played the dominant role), money policy assumed an important dimension.

Hilferding regarded the social aspect of money—its quality of being the value equivalent of a commodity—as particularly important. He explained:

> This social aspect of money finds its palpable expression in the substance used as money: for example, gold. But it can also be expressed directly through conscious social regulation or, since the state is the conscious organ of commodity producing society, by state regulation. Hence the state can designate any token—for example, a piece of paper appropriately labeled—as a representative money token. (38)

For Hilferding, money became a symbol of society as a whole, a society that could be managed by the state (59). Here we have an example of the state (society's conscious organ) intervening in the financial regulation of the economy. This point deserves special attention in light of Hilferding's stress on the increasing importance of the banks and on the monopolization of whole branches of the economy as a result of the process of cartelization. In his view, what this process amounted to was the socialization of the economy under capitalism in a way that laid the foundation for the establishment of socialism. He declared:

> The socializing function of finance capital facilitates enormously the task of overcoming capitalism. Once finance capital has brought the most important branches of production under its control, it is enough for society, through its conscious executive organ—the state conquered by the working class—to seize finance capital in order to gain immediate control of these branches of production. Since all other branches of production depend upon these, control of large-scale industry already provides the most effective form of social control

even without any further socialization. . . . *Even today, taking control of six large Berlin banks would mean taking possession of the most important spheres of large-scale industry.* . . . In other words, since finance capital has already achieved expropriation to the extent required by socialism, it is possible to dispense with a sudden act of expropriation by the state, and to substitute a gradual process of socialization through the economic benefits which society will confer. (367–68; my emphasis)

Hilferding's comment here on the importance of seizing the banks reveals a key difference between his theoretical perspective and that of Marx. His stress on the sphere of circulation in the process of social transformation stands in opposition to Marx's view, which held that the "credit system will serve as a mighty lever" in the transition to socialism, but "only as one element in the context of other great organic transformations of the means of production themselves." Those who believed otherwise, asserted Marx, were caught up in "illusions about the miraculous power of credit and the banks," which arise out of "complete ignorance of the capitalist mode of production and of the credit system as one of its forms." As one economist has justly pointed out, on the question of the role of the banks in the transition to socialism, Hilferding was closer to St. Simon—who envisioned "a single leading bank that dominated everything"—than to Marx.[46]

Also of key importance here is Hilferding's reference to the workers' conquest of state power. If the working class could only take control of the means of production after it had seized control of the state, how then would this seizure come about? Like Marx, Hilferding thought it was possible, though unlikely, that the working class would come to power by peaceful, parliamentary means, and for this reason he supported social democracy's electoral strategy. In *Finance Capital* he argued that the transition to socialism would most likely take place in the midst of a violent upheaval, the origins of which he located in modern capitalist imperialism.[47]

Imperialism, Hilferding argued, was rooted in the economic policy of finance capital, which had three main objectives: the establishment of the largest possible economic territory, the closing of this territory to foreign competition by a wall of protective tariffs, and the reservation of this area of exploitation for national monopolistic combinations. Building on his earlier research linking protective tariffs and international political and economic rivalry, Hilferding argued that the policy of finance capital would likely lead to war because the expansion of finance capital could not end at national boundaries. With the monopolization of the economy, internal competition decreased, markets became saturated, and profit rates fell. Capitalists were forced to look abroad for new markets, for favorable locations for capital exports, and for sources of raw materials in order to maintain and increase production and the rate of profit. Consequently the state came to assume a central role in the pursuit of these goals in the world economy. According to

Hilferding, the role of the state grew more important in direct proportion to the concentration of power in the hands of a few banking, industrial, and landowning interests.[48]

The protective tariff system, Hilferding argued, created a scramble among the capitalist powers to secure overseas markets and resources among the less developed nations of the world. Worldwide capitalist competition would lead to possible international conflagration and this, in turn, to open conflict between the capitalist and working classes. "Finance capital," he wrote,

> in its maturity, is the highest stage of the concentration of economic and political power in the hands of the capitalist oligarchy, it is the climax of the dictatorship of the magnates of capital. At the same time, it makes the dictatorship of the capitalist interests of the other countries and the internal domination of capital increasingly irreconcilable with the interests of the mass of the people, exploited by finance capital but also summoned into battle against it. In the violent clash of the hostile interests, the dictatorship of the magnates of capital will finally be transformed into the dictatorship of the proletariat. (370)

The proletarian revolution could only be achieved, Hilferding believed, if the workers were organized against their opponents. He found organizations that concentrated their efforts on economic issues (such as the trade unions) incapable of achieving this goal. In his view economic questions were ultimately political ones, thus it was vital "for the working class to secure for itself the strongest possible influence in political bodies and to have representatives who will take up . . . the interests of the workers" (362). The proletariat needed its own political party, which, in conjunction with the trade unions, would represent its interests against those of capital. This party would transform the workers' struggle within bourgeois society into a struggle against bourgeois society.

Hilferding saw countervailing forces within the system of finance capital that, at least in the short run, could work against the outbreak of war. The rise of the workers' movement, he asserted, "has inspired a fear of the domestic political consequences which might follow from a war" (332). In addition, he pointed out that international investors not only competed against one another, but also cooperated in joint ventures that encouraged a certain solidarity of interests. But Hilferding was pessimistic about the prospects for peace. The expansion of capitalism into eastern Europe and Asia, he observed, "has been accompanied by a realignment of power relations which, through its effect upon the great powers, may well bring the existing antagonisms to the point where they erupt in war" (332). War, he was convinced, would unleash "revolutionary storms" (366) that would lead to capitalism's overthrow. Social democracy's task, until then, was to remain the implacable foe of imperialism and militarism, "for only then will the proletariat be the beneficiary of the collapse to which it [the war] must lead, a collapse which will be political and social, not economic; for the idea of a purely economic collapse makes no sense" (366).

The decisive point of Hilferding's thesis was his suggestion, in contradistinction to Bernstein's view, that the economic tendencies of modern capitalist development would likely lead to war, upheaval, and revolution. By tying capitalist expansionism to the outbreak of war and the possibility of violent revolution, Hilferding aimed to strike a blow at reformist expectations of a gradual transition to socialism. He did not argue that Social Democracy needed to alter its political strategy to deal with the future crisis. On the contrary, as he had contended in Austria years before, he thought the party should continue its educational, organizational, and parliamentary work in preparation for the future upheaval. It was this view, which preserved the party's revolutionary theoretical outlook without challenging its reformist practice, that made Hilferding one of the foremost representatives of the Marxist center.

Hilferding was among the first to comment on the rise of the extreme right wing, and he foresaw the development of fascist ideology as a consequence of the development of finance capital. During the transformation from competitive to monopoly capitalism, he argued, the state changed from an advocate of free trade into a defender of the interests of finance capital. This change involved the rise of an aggressively nationalist (and racist) state ideology. The imperialist, Hilferding wrote,

> observes with a cold and steady eye the medley of peoples and sees his own nation standing over all of them. For him this nation is real, it lives in the ever increasing power and greatness of the state, and its enhancement deserves every ounce of his effort. The subordination of individual interests to a higher general interest, which is a prerequisite for every vital social ideology, is thus achieved; and the state alien to its people is bound together with the nation in unity, while the national idea becomes the driving force of politics. Class antagonisms have disappeared and been transcended in the service of the collectivity. The common action of the nation, united by a common goal of national greatness, has taken the place of class struggle, so dangerous and fruitless for the possessing classes. (336)

Thus Hilferding identified several of the fundamental components of what came to be fascist ideology. Nationalism, he claimed, provided a new bond for a strife-ridden bourgeois society and would meet with an increasingly enthusiastic reception as the process of disintegration continued.

Whereas Bernstein and Jaurès opposed colonization that proved "damaging" to the local inhabitants, Hilferding had a less sanguine view of colonial expansion. Both revisionists thought that an enlightened colonial policy would bring the benefits of their "higher" cultures to the colonized peoples, but he harbored no such belief. On the contrary, he argued that "violent methods were the essence of colonial policy, without which it would lose its capitalist rationale" (319). Drawing on examples from the history of European expansion, Hilferding demonstrated that brutal violence in the colonized nations was always needed in order to create the necessary conditions for the valorization of capital, that is, the expropriation of the local population, the introduction of private property, the creation of a population of free wage laborers, and other measures. In the period of finance capital, he argued, the repressive power of the imperial state was of decisive importance because the colonized lands often adopted the national ideals of their oppressors and strove for national independence. Thus it was the state's task to oversee the economic transformation of the colonies and to protect the interests of capital there against internal and external rivals (319–22).[49]

Hilferding's theory of imperialism sparked debate not only with the revisionists but also with Marxist thinkers such as Luxemburg and Kautsky in Germany and Bukharin and Lenin in Russia. In *The Accumulation of Capital* (1913) and her later writings, Luxemburg criticized Marx's and Hilferding's analyses of the reproduction of capital and countered that capitalism could only survive as long as it could expand into noncapitalist territories. Once capitalism absorbed these areas, she thought, expansion ceased and the system entered into a terminal crisis. This view, which focused on the inevitability of capitalism's economic breakdown, contrasted markedly with that of Hilferding, which rejected the idea of such a collapse. It is ironic that in their most important works of economic analyses, it was the radical activist Luxemburg who adopted the more teleological, deterministic, and politically passive interpretation of capitalism's ultimate demise, while Hilferding placed greater stress on the importance of the political realm in the overthrow of the system.[50]

Bukharin and Lenin, on the other hand, accepted the basic premises of Hilferding's work. Their main differences with him centered on their contention that finance capitalism would *inevitably* lead to war and proletarian revolution, and that he had neglected to analyze the "parasitism" of imperialism. The latter criticism, leveled by Lenin, stressed the rise of a small number of "usurer states" such as Great Britain, France, and Holland, which drew vast amounts of wealth out of nations that had become financially dependent on them and were subject to their political and military power. Lenin held that the formation of monopolies and the increasing export of capital in the form of credit tended to hinder technical progress and slowed investment in the industrial states. These tendencies, he thought, did not preclude the rapid growth of capitalism but, rather, increased the sectoral and international unevenness of capitalist development and led to decay even in the nations richest in capital. Such uneven development, Lenin argued, created contradictions that ultimately could only be resolved through the use of force.[51]

Lenin's conclusions were the opposite of those developed by Karl Kautsky, whose views on imperialism were particularly important because he and Hilferding reciprocally influenced one another. Kautsky's early writings on imperialism contained much material from which Hilferding derived his ideas. Kautsky linked colonialism to underconsumption in the home market and industrial capitalism's drive to acquire new markets for goods and capital. He argued that important nonindustrial interests such as the army, the bureaucracy, the aristocracy, and finance capital also had interests in overseas expansion, and at first he was certain that imperialism would inevitably lead to war. Hilferding's theses concerning the power of the banks and the cartelization of industry powerfully influenced Kautsky, but in the years immediately preceding the outbreak of World War I, he became convinced that the development of finance capital could have a nonviolent outcome. He suggested that capitalism might enter into a new phase that he called "ultraimperialism," in which the leading capitalist states would divide up the world peacefully through the creation of some type of international cartel.[52] Following the defeat of the German revolution, Hilferding would incorporate and further develop Kautsky's new thesis into his theory of "organized capitalism."

On the whole, Hilferding's analysis of imperialism was a powerful one. Although it would be inaccurate to claim that the rise of finance capitalism "caused" World War I, economic expansion abroad and perceived conflicts of interest certainly fueled tensions among the leading capitalist states. The completion of the world's division into giant economic areas (for example, colonies and spheres of influence) by the major powers, domestic class conflict, rampant militarism, the arms race, aggressive nationalism, and racism were all factors leading the competing powers into a conflict that had only narrowly been averted on many occasions prior to 1914. Hilferding saw these factors as parts of an interconnected whole, the basic framework of which could best be understood through an analysis of social relations as they developed under the system of finance capital. These relations, which were different than those that existed under the system of competitive capitalism, reflected changes in the structure of the capitalist economy.

Although Hilferding's *Finance Capital* broke with Marx in certain important respects and its value for understanding the current world economy is limited, it was a significant theoretical achievement. By extending Marx's analysis of the corporation and by focusing on the changing relationship of bank and industrial capital, Hilferding's study illuminated decisive aspects of an important phase of economic development that remain influential today. And while *Finance Capital* made Hilferding's reputation as a respected economist, it also reaffirmed his position as a social democratic centrist. His views were welcome to those in the SPD who wanted to refute Bernstein's theoretical premises but also opposed any "radical" shift away from the party's reform-oriented praxis.

Hilferding's editorial work and the publication of *Finance Capital* marked him as one of the SPD's rising stars and eventually brought him into the party's decision-making process at the national level. Rapid growth and the shortage of people with the necessary talents to carry out essential administrative and agitational tasks required the party to employ its skilled personnel in a variety of assignments. Journalists and newspaper editors often held important political posts and Hilferding was no exception in this regard.[53] Beginning in 1912, he represented *Vorwärts* at meetings of the party council *(Parteiausschuß)*, a newly created body of representatives drawn from the *Land* level that was charged with advising the executive committee on political, financial, and other matters.[54] Participation in the council's discussions reflected Hilferding's increased stature within the party. He had become an influential figure in the leadership that shaped socialist politics in the years immediately preceding the war.

What sort of person was this young socialist intellectual? Unfortunately we have few detailed descriptions of Hilferding's personality or lifestyle. Virtually all his contemporaries recognized his intellectual gifts, and Julius Braunthal, a young Austrian socialist who was not uncritical of him, described him as one of social democracy's "brilliant brains."[55] Most accounts agree that he loved to frequent the Café Centrale in Vienna and the Café Josty in Berlin where he would hold forth on various matters, and often at too great a length. As later descriptions confirm, Hilferding enjoyed good food and good company; he was certainly no ascetic. It is also clear that he worked very hard. His editorial tasks at *Vorwärts* and *Die Neue Zeit,* party business, and his own prolific writing wore him down. We know virtually nothing of his relations with his wife and two children at this time, but the family lived in a modest apartment, employed a part-time housekeeper, and took regular vacations. Thus it seems that, like his peers Kautsky and Luxemburg, Hilferding enjoyed the life of a middle-class intellectual.[56]

One of the most detailed commentaries on the prewar Hilferding comes from the pen of the Russian revolutionary Leon Trotsky, whose memoirs, written long after the two men had become bitter enemies, contain some interesting observations. Hilferding and Trotsky met at Kautsky's house in 1907. They then began a correspondence, dealing mainly with political and publishing matters, that lasted about five years. It appears that the two were never close friends but, for a time, respected one another. By 1912, however, Trotsky grew impatient with Hilferding's hesitation to speak out on issues related to internal Russian social democratic politics and on disputes that Trotsky was involved in with socialist leaders in Germany and Russia. He asserted that Hilferding's refusal to write articles for the Russian social democratic press stemmed from his fear of compromising himself, and he attacked Hilferding for not taking the conflicts between the Russian political exiles seriously. Hilferding's attitude and behavior, Trotsky concluded, undermined the basis of their "political friendship," and their correspondence ended soon thereafter.[57]

Trotsky's memoirs, written in 1929, reflect his earlier impatience with Hilferding, but the two men's conflicting views of the Bolshevik revolution certainly exacerbated his hostility when looking back at the past. In 1907, Trotsky remarked, Hilferding was at the peak of his revolutionism, which did not prevent him from hating Rosa Luxemburg and from being contemptuous of Karl Liebknecht. But for Russia, in those days, he was ready, like many another, to accept the most radical conclusions. He praised my articles which the *Neue Zeit* had managed to translate from the Russian periodicals even before I came abroad, and quite unexpectedly for me, he insisted from the very first that we address each other as "thou." Because of this our outward relations took on the semblance of intimacy. But there was no moral or political basis for it.[58]

Trotsky's description here not only reiterates the substance of his earlier view of Hilferding but retrospectively separates him, in his most "revolutionary" phase, from two of the SPD's most radical figures, Luxemburg and Liebknecht. Trotsky did not think Hilferding was of the stuff of revolutionaries. Hilferding, he observed, "regarded the staid and passive German Social Democracy of that time with great contempt, and contrasted it with the activity of the Austrian party. This criticism, however, retained its fireside character. In practice Hilferding remained a literary official in the service of the German party—and nothing more." According to Trotsky, Hilferding was a man who asked "trite" questions and was, like his Viennese friends Bauer, Max Adler, and Renner, representative of a type that "was furthest from that of a revolutionary." Their attitude "expressed itself in everything—in their approach to subjects, in their political remarks and psychological appreciations, in their self-satisfaction."

Trotsky's assertions, though not without foundation, are certainly overdrawn. Hilferding's role in Russian socialist affairs is not clear. In 1907 he suggested to Kautsky that the latter should work to place the menshevik-bolshevik split on the agenda of the International's Stuttgart congress, but nothing came of the idea. Thereafter, it appears that he kept his distance from the issue. He may have wished to avoid compromising himself by taking sides in what Kautsky mistakenly regarded as more a personal than a political conflict. He might also have thought, quite reasonably, that he did not have the knowledge, linguistic skills, or the time to involve himself in the squabbles of the exile community.[59]

More important for us here is Trotsky's characterization of Hilferding as a socialist "literary official" rather than a "revolutionary." Trotsky was right in the sense that, prior to 1914, Hilferding supported a parliamentary social democratic strategy in Germany and Austria and rejected the adoption of more radical tactics that he thought threatened the party's unity and security. On this basis one might argue that Hilferding was not a revolutionary. But to also agree that he was merely a bureaucrat in the party's service would be mistaken. Hilferding certainly worked hard for the SPD, strongly identified with it, and was prepared to promote compromise positions that preserved its unity. He was not, however, willing to abandon what he considered essential socialist principles out of loyalty to the organization. He demonstrated this strength most clearly after 1914, when his opposition to the SPD's support for the war led him to quit the party.

Trotsky's appraisal of Hilferding glosses over the fact that the socialist parties in central and western Europe operated under wholly different conditions from those in Russia. Whereas the Russian socialists were hounded underground and were waiting impatiently for the next antitsarist revolutionary wave, their Austrian and German comrades worked in a relatively tolerant political climate, in which they adopted different forms of organization and tactics. Hilferding's lifestyle, his function as a party intellectual, and his political outlook reflected the influence of this environment. Unlike Trotsky and Lenin, he was not forced to lead the life of a persecuted exile, and from his perspective as a respected editor and economist of a flourishing and legal socialist party, it seemed that conditions in central Europe offered the movement more varied, though still limited, political options. The parliamentary tactic was one of these options, and Hilferding became convinced that, barring any radical change in circumstances, it should be the central element of the party's strategy. In the prewar social democratic debates on tactics, this idea formed the core of his political position.

Hilferding's "centrism" developed as he found himself increasingly at odds with the views of the SPD's right and left wings. In 1907, for example, when reformists claimed that the SPD's strict anticolonialism had undermined its strength in the Reichstag, he sided with the radicals in opposing any concessions to colonialism and militarism. In the pages of *Die Neue Zeit*, Hilferding argued that socialists should defend their principles and reject the demands of the right. Giving up the party's fundamental opposition to the system and searching for allies in parliament would not enlighten nonsocialist workers or strengthen the SPD's organization. On the contrary, by going it alone, social democracy gained advantages. It could demonstrate militarism's and colonialism's intimate links to the interests of the ruling classes; and its demands for military reductions, a peaceful foreign policy, and the creation of a popular militia in place of the professional military would make clear that the SPD sat in parliament as the "single, determined, and ruthless representative of working-people's interests."[60]

Although he sided with the left in the debate on colonialism, in February–March 1910 Hilferding found himself in conflict with his erstwhile allies on the issue of using radical mass action to force the reform of the three-class franchise in Prussia. He did not contest the necessity of mass actions to achieve such changes and was heartened by the extent of workers' demonstrations, but when the latter met with considerable police violence he opposed escalating the confrontation with the state.[61] Sometime later, in a discussion over the use of the mass strike, he dismissed Julius Braunthal's suggestion that the party had missed the chance to take advantage of a revolutionary situation. "It is only Rosa's [Luxemburg's] illusion that you can break up the powerful fabric of Prussian militarism by political strikes," he said. "With an attempt to disrupt the organization of state and society, we would then have given the reaction the pretext for the coup d'état. And we would have been crushed under the formidable weight of the armed forces."[62]

"It is one thing," Hilferding asserted, ". . . to go into the street in a political demonstration as a peaceful citizen, and it is another to stand the tribulations of a revolution. For, don't forget, that political mass strikes must, of necessity, develop into armed insurrection." He agreed that the trade unions would never willingly sanction the calling of a mass strike, but he also contended that ultimately they would be forced to, "because they will not be asked by the infuriated workers" who would "strike without anybody's consent." The German workers, Hilferding insisted, "are the most law-abiding citizens so long as the law stands and so long as they see what they can do under the law. But should the government dare to break the law, the workers will get into a frenzy which knows no bounds."[63]

The exchange with Braunthal illustrates well Hilferding's vision of the proletarian revolution and its relation to the Socialist party. Like Kautsky, he believed that the party would be the inheritor, not the executioner, of capitalist society and that the revolution would be a spontaneous uprising by the workers in response to ruling-class oppression. The SPD's tasks were to prepare the workers for the coming revolution through education and organization, but neither Hilferding nor Kautsky conceived of the party in "revolution-making" terms. Such an outlook set them apart from the revisionists, who demanded that the SPD adopt an openly reformist strategy, and from the party's radical left wing, which hoped to drive the socialist movement forward by linking economic and political struggles and promoting mass strikes.[64] The radicals wanted to channel widespread worker unrest into a struggle not just for specific reforms, but against capitalism itself. Led by such figures as Luxemburg, Liebknecht, Franz Mehring, and Klara Zetkin, they were willing to risk the party organization because, even in defeat, such a strategy would bring about "the ever greater unification of the laboring masses, a unification which prepares the ultimate victory."[65]

From the Magdeburg congress of 1910 until the outbreak of the world war, Hilferding diligently opposed the demands of both the right and the left. Instead, he argued in favor of a "Marxist" political strategy uniting both the reformist and the revolutionary trends in the workers' movement. "In the incessant struggles for reforms," he wrote, "Marxism sees the means to lead the proletarian revolution to victory." The fight for reform teaches the proletariat to build up its own institutions, to know its class enemies, and to recognize the limits of reform under capitalism. It serves the movement's radical aim, because it "awakens the revolutionary idea and kindles the energy for revolution." But it was the masses and not the party, Hilferding insisted, who should take the initiative in using radical means such as the mass strike.[66]

No one on the SPD's radical left, including Luxemburg, denied the close relationship between revolution and the struggle for reform. By playing down the use of the mass strike and by focusing on electoral tactics, Hilferding worked to link the SPD's revolutionary goals with its parliamentary strategy as a means of preserving unity. His formula had the support of a majority in the socialist leadership because it allowed the party to retain the revolutionary tradition that rallied workers to its colors, at the same time representing no threat to the cautious reformism backed by many trade union and SPD leaders.

In the years following Magdeburg, the views of the Marxist center tended to paper over sharp differences between socialist factions. Intense struggles continued over the party's decision to form an electoral alliance with the Progressive party; its policy of voting against the state budget on principle; its attitude toward taxes, imperialism, military spending, and the mass strike.[67] Hilferding's views during these years remained basically in line with his earlier outlook. He stuck to his belief that the class struggle in Germany was intensifying, that parliamentary reforms were unlikely, and that the decisive phase in the struggle for socialism was approaching. At the same time, however, he generally supported the party executive's cautious, clearly reformist program, which by 1912 was obviously tilted toward compromise with the state.[68] Despite a theoretical analysis that was in many ways similar to that of the left, Hilferding continued to regard the radicals' demands as adventurist and a threat to the unity and security of the party.

Hilferding seriously underestimated the depth of the divisions within Social Democracy and the extent to which centrist positions could unite the movement. Although he was convinced that "revisionism was lying on a dead track" and the radicals were mired in "confusion," as an ideology of integration Hilferding's and Kautsky's Marxism did little to resolve the substantive divisions that fractured the SPD, evident in the gravitation of many of the party's best intellectuals into either revisionist or left-wing circles.[69] What prevented the party from splitting was the loyalty of even its sharpest critics and, more important, the lack of an issue serious enough to drive its conflicting factions to the breaking point. This situation changed dramatically in 1914 with the outbreak of World War I. When a majority in the SPD leadership decided to back the monarchy's war effort, the split became merely a question of time.

A variety of factors motivated the party leadership's progovernment policy. Among the most important were fear of a tsarist victory, fear of harsh repression, the perception of popular support for the war, and the hope that, by cooperating with the state, the SPD would gain equality with the other parties. Until the last week of July 1914, the party had criticized Austria's foreign policy and organized large-scale antiwar demonstrations, but by the time Germany declared war on Russia on August 1, 1914, many socialist leaders questioned the viability of their position. For several days it remained unclear what the SPD would actually do. Although the Socialist International had failed to prevent the outbreak of the conflict, no one knew for certain how the individual parties would respond to their respective government's calls for support. In Germany the answer came on August 4 with the Social Democratic Reichstag delegation's unanimous vote granting the monarchy war credits.[70]

The delegation arrived at its decision following a heated debate in which a small minority—led by Hilferding's close friend and party cochairman, Hugo Haase—argued against granting the credits. Defeated by a vote of 78 to 14, the minority agreed to submit to party discipline and to vote with the majority in the Reichstag. Although a facade of unity remained, Haase's prediction that a vote in favor of war credits would be "the greatest misfortune which could possibly befall the party" proved prophetic.[71] As the war dragged on, the conflict between the SPD's progovernment majority and its antiwar minority became increasingly vehement. Eventually the war issue tore the party apart.

Little is known about Hilferding's activities in the summer of 1914, but it is clear that he opposed the war from the beginning. As it had the rest of the SPD leadership, the crisis took him by surprise. At the end of July he was vacationing away from Berlin and the German police used his Austrian citizenship as a pretext to expel him to Austria on the eve of the war. He returned on August 6, but only after Albert Südekum, a leader of the SPD right wing, had appealed successfully to German chancellor Bethmann Hollweg for revocation of the expulsion order.[72]

Although somewhat disoriented by the rush of events, Hilferding arrived in Berlin convinced that the party's vote in favor of granting war credits had been a mistake. He supported Haase against the prowar elements in the leadership and, along with the majority of *Vorwärts's* editors, signed a declaration protesting the actions of the Reichstag delegation, a decisive step that clearly placed him in the ranks of the opposition. The declaration claimed that the Reichstag delegation's decision was unjustified, was a blow to the unity of the International, and made Social Democracy partially responsible for the war and its results. The signers felt compelled to bring their dissenting views to the attention of the party executive, but they refrained from publishing it out of concern that public criticism would endanger the party and its press.[73]

Hilferding's opposition to the SPD's policy was based on his long-held antiwar principles and on his view that the war was imperialist in nature; he did not oppose the majority because he believed that it had broken with any substantial antiwar sentiment among the workers. Although recent scholarship has made clear that working-class opposition to the war was much more widespread than previously thought, there is no evidence that he (or most other dissenters for that matter) perceived the mood of the party's constituency any differently than the majority of the leadership. As Wolfgang Kruse has pointed out, the majority's decision to support the war not only showed the great degree to which the leadership had become estranged from its base but also effectively encouraged the workers to accept the coming of war and undermined the possibility of pursuing a policy more critical of the state. These observations also apply to the opposition, which, though it did not support the war, actually muted its criticism in deference to party discipline and out of fear of repression. It took opposition forces many months to get their bearings and even longer to tap into the popular dissatisfaction that grew as the war went on.[74]

Hilferding's pre-1914 views on the relationship of the socialist movement to war were also held by many others in the prewar SPD. He had always insisted that it was the duty of the International and of the individual socialist parties to do everything possible to avoid international conflict. Militarism and war, Hilferding thought, worked against proletarian interests, and he sharply criticized those in the party who favored supporting German colonial expansion in the hope of winning the cooperation of the bourgeois parties for social and political reforms. By advocating cooperation with imperial governments, he argued, the revisionists undermined the whole concept of working-class internationalism.[75]

The international class struggle, Hilferding believed, had an important national component. The first task of the workers' movement was to "secure the unity and self-determination of the nation and thereby to make the national culture, which up to now has been a privilege of the dominant classes, into the general property of the whole people." To reach this goal the proletariat had to seize control of the state, the bourgeoisie's chief instrument of class domination at home and of expansion abroad. Hilferding thought that each national bourgeoisie developed its own sense of identity (national chauvinism) and strove to dominate the others. Proletarian class consciousness, on the other hand, developed across national borders as workers realized the class basis of their oppression. Although the class struggle in each nation developed under different conditions, any political or economic victory of the proletariat in one country was a victory for the proletariat of other lands. It was the solidarity of working-class interests, Hilferding asserted, that allowed internationalism to develop and overcome national divisions between workers.[76]

The role of the Second International was to bring together the experiences of the workers' movement in each nation. Hilferding believed that the International should formulate general principles for the movement and perform important propaganda functions, but he did not think it should determine the concrete policies of individual parties working under very different conditions. Although pessimistic about the International's ability to solve workers' many problems under capitalism, he did think that by providing a forum it could help the national parties in their fight against imperialism, militarism, and war. In the long run, however, Hilferding thought that a major conflict was probable and that the International itself could do little to stop it. When hostilities broke out in the Balkans in 1912, he considered the outbreak of war between the imperialist powers a strong possibility and called on the SPD to demand peace, the maintenance of German neutrality, and German noninterference in Balkan affairs.[77]

The Balkan war outraged Hilferding, who did not have the oratory skills of the great French fighter for peace Jaurès, but who could also write with skill and passion. He used the pages of *Die Neue Zeit* to pillory the warring states and to condemn the imperial powers for their role in the conflict. He wrote of the slaughter of peasants and workers, of the burning of villages, of the enormous technical progress in the machinery of mass murder, and he sarcastically described how the "civilized" peoples turned away in feigned helplessness. "Such glorious days!" he exclaimed. "This is how the liberal prophecy, that developed capitalism would bring a state of equality, peace and harmony to mankind, has been fulfilled. Instead of the sun of freedom, the eternal torch of war casts its gloomy light over the fields of the dead."[78] Following the model he developed in *Finance Capital*, Hilferding always stressed the context within which the Balkan wars were fought and alliances of the great powers developed. He sharply criticized Germany for using the Balkan conflict to expand the military further against the "slavic threat" and he held Germany responsible for the most recent phase of the arms race, which was transforming even the European republics into servants of militarism.[79]

The rivalry between the Triple Entente and the Triple Alliance reflected British and German competition on a world scale. The purpose of the Triple Alliance, Hilferding argued, was to further the territorial expansion of Germany, Austria-Hungary, and Italy, three states with relatively small colonial holdings. The Entente powers—England, France, and Russia—aimed to prevent this expansion, especially in the Balkans. The alliance system fueled the arms race and the international tensions that repeatedly brought the powers to the brink of war. Hilferding urged the international workers' movement to support neither alliance and to demand the signing of international treaties to settle disputes and to end the arms buildup. In 1913 he still hoped for peace but feared that conflict was much more likely.[80]

Like most other socialists, Hilferding recognized the right of nations to defend themselves (hence his support for a popular militia) but opposed imperialist wars of conquest. What set him apart from the majority of his comrades in the summer of 1914 was that he believed Germany and Austria were conducting an aggressive and not a defensive war, and he was unwilling to place the SPD at the disposal of German imperialism. In the fall of that year he saw that a split in the party was imminent but still hoped that a change in its policy would preserve unity.[81] Like other dissidents, such as Luxemburg and Haase, he shrank at the thought of an open break with the organization, which, as Carl Schorske points out, was "almost life itself to these individuals." During the prewar period's most divisive factional struggles, even the radicals had not broken with the party; and now, in the midst of what they considered an imperialist war, it was still difficult for them to do so.[82] In the end, however, for Hilferding and a minority of party members, there could be no compromise with the majority on this issue. Ultimately, they were forced to leave the party.

As it did for so many others, the coming of the war transformed Rudolf Hilferding's world. For years he had struggled to preserve the unity of the party in whose mission he fervently believed. And now the party's policy, which for forty years had proclaimed a doctrine of international proletarian solidarity, was revealed as hollow. For those who refused to accept this reality, the question was what to do. The search for an answer took time and many of the dissidents came to opposing conclusions.

CHAPTER THREE

THE REVOLUTIONARY

When the locomotive of history comes to a sharp turn, only the stead-
fast cling to the train.   —*V. I. Lenin*

It is socialist and revolutionary to lead the proletarian struggle in
accordance with the respective economic and political conditions.
Loyalty to socialist conviction consists of pursuing tactics not derived
from rigid formulas that serve to maintain illusions, but from the
power relations of the conflicting classes.   —*Rudolf Hilferding (1919)*

T he coming of war transformed Hilferding into an oppo-
nent of his own party; the collapse of the monarchy made him a revolutionary.[1] At the outset, Hilferding hoped the SPD would end its cooperation with
the government and return to its prewar strategy of "principled opposition,"
but instead, the leadership stifled internal dissent and drove the antiwar faction out of the party. When the opposition founded the Independent Social
Democratic Party (USPD) in the spring of 1917, Hilferding joined. Cut off
from his political home and bothered by a sense of his own growing isolation
in the socialist movement, he took this step reluctantly; he saw no other option. He did not hesitate for a moment, however, after mass unrest swept
through Germany in the fall of 1918. Returning to Berlin from service on the

Italian front, Hilferding plunged into revolutionary activity as one of the USPD's most important leaders. As long as he believed conditions existed to make social revolution possible, Hilferding supported a radical agenda. When the revolutionary upsurge ebbed, he called on social democracy to defend the new parliamentary order against counterrevolution and to pursue the struggle for socialism within the framework of a capitalist republic.

In the fall of 1914, the socialist antiwar opposition lacked unity. Composed from all of the SPD's prewar factions, persistent differences among the dissenters hindered their cooperation. Attitudes on key issues shifted as conditions changed, but in general the opposition divided into three groups: the radical left, the center, and the right.[2] Led by such figures as Luxemburg, Liebknecht, Mehring, and Zetkin, the radical left denounced the SPD's August 4 declaration calling for peace "as soon as the objective of security is achieved" and declared that it was impossible for an imperialist war to end without annexations. The radicals considered the fight for peace inextricably bound with the struggle for socialism. They began a campaign based on the International's 1907 resolution calling on workers "to work for the war's speedy termination, and to exploit with all their might the economic and political crisis created by the war to arouse the population and to hasten the overthrow of capitalist rule."[3] On December 2, 1914, Liebknecht became the first to break party discipline in the Reichstag and to vote against the granting of new war credits.

The centrist dissenters, in contrast to their radical counterparts, took far longer to openly denounce the war. Some, like Kautsky, argued at first that socialists had to support the war to the extent that it was a struggle of national self-defense. Although he did not fully accept the government's justifications for the war and was disturbed by the nationalist enthusiasm of many comrades, he moderated his criticism out of concern for party unity. Kautsky expected a short war and hoped that the SPD would survive it intact. Other centrists, like Hilferding and Haase, opposed the war from the outset and wanted to turn the party against it. In the early months of the conflict, however, both men refrained from publicly criticizing the executive because, like Kautsky, they hoped to maintain unity. They found this task increasingly difficult as their opposition to the leadership's policies grew more pronounced.[4]

The centrists began to openly attack the government in the spring of 1915, though they limited their criticisms to domestic issues such as the state of siege and censorship, not its war policy. Only after concluding that the government was conducting an aggressive war did left-centrist dissidents in the Reichstag openly turn against the SPD's support for the state. In June 1915, this group presented the Reichstag delegation and the executive with a petition signed by over one thousand party and trade union functionaries denouncing the imperialist character of the war and calling for an end to the SPD's collaboration with the government. In December 1915, one year after Liebknecht's lone dissenting vote, twenty centrists also voted against war credits. Despite all their hopes of holding the SPD together, the centrists' action was an important step in bringing about its division.[5]

With the exception of a small number of antiwar revisionists, such as Bernstein and Kurt Eisner, radicals and centrists comprised the majority of the opposition to the party leadership, but the two groups found it difficult to work together. The center's refusal in 1915 to condemn the war in principle and its call, when Germany's circumstances were favorable, for a "peace of understanding" met with sharp criticism from the radicals who eschewed any compromises with the regime. Only later, when faced with stepped-up repression from both the party leadership and the state, would the two groups temporarily overcome their differences.[6]

During the fall and winter of 1914 Hilferding's position was close to that of the emerging left-centrist minority in the Reichstag. Under his direction *Vorwärts* attempted to comply with the censor's regulations, but with increasing difficulty. By the end of year the military censors had already suspended the paper twice after its oppositionist editors had ventured beyond the bounds of the permissible. The failure of Hilferding and his colleagues at *Vorwärts* and other important party organs to accede to the government's press restrictions placed the executive in an uncomfortable position. Each time the authorities removed a paper from circulation the party leaders had to request the Reich Office of the Interior to rescind the order in return for promises of good behavior in the future. In addition, the SPD press commission in Berlin and the Berlin party organization as a whole backed the *Vorwärts* editors and made the leadership's position even more difficult. Fearing an adverse reaction within the party, the executive hesitated to discipline the paper.[7]

Hilferding vigorously defended *Vorwärts*. At a meeting of the party council in January 1915, he rebuffed the charge that his "foreignness" made suspect his qualifications as chief editor, and he reiterated his support for the position taken by *Vorwärts*'s editors the previous August. The political and military situation, he argued, was very serious, the fate of the movement was at stake, and now was the moment to prepare the masses for future battles. At issue was not only the collapse of capitalism, but whether the workers had the will and strength to seize power. If either was lacking, then the achievement of socialism would be pushed into the distant future.

Hilferding believed that the party had to end its cooperation with the state. "After the war," he asked, "[how] can we call the masses to action against a regime that we have just supported?" He called for more "active" tactics, such as openly criticizing government policies and refusing to accept appointments to cabinet posts. He also pushed the leadership to reestablish a dialogue in the international workers' movement by making unofficial contacts with the French Socialist Party.[8]

While Hilferding argued for the restoration of an adversarial relationship between the SPD and the state, he pleaded against factional conflict within the party. He insisted that Social Democracy needed unity to carry out its tasks and that the solidarity preserved by Haase on August 4 remained essential. But Hilferding's support for the inner-party civil peace *(Burgfrieden)* was qualified; he wanted unity on the centrist opposition's terms in order to conduct a policy of resistance to the regime. His position is apparent in his assertion that *Vorwärts's* editors could not have behaved differently than they had up to that point, "We may not be allowed to write in the manner we want," he said, "but we cannot write differently." The party would otherwise have to find a new editorial board.[9]

The majority leadership was certainly not sorry to see Hilferding go after the Austro-Hungarian army drafted him in 1915. He probably would have lost his post in any case in October of the following year, when the executive fired the oppositionist editors on *Vorwärts's* staff. By that time, however, he was long absent from Germany serving as a doctor on the Italian front. His correspondence with Kautsky was his pipeline for news on party affairs.

Indeed, Hilferding depended on Kautsky for news, gossip, and reading material. He wrote often; lacking time for lengthy expositions, he sent postcards. He apparently spent little time near the battle front. Initially, the army sent him to Vienna where he served in hospitals for the control of epidemic diseases. Although accompanied by his family and far removed from the war, he was unhappy to be away from Berlin and was concerned that he could be sent to the front at any moment. He also worried about his wife, Margarethe. She had not adjusted well to the return to Vienna or to her own medical work in the hospital. After their arrival she lost weight, became weak, and had to temporarily stop working. A rest in the country improved matters, but Hilferding thought that she was still nervous and needed more time to relax. He, on the other hand, quickly adapted to a new routine that placed him on twenty-four-hour service every three days but also left him time to work in the library. Hilferding also was glad to have his sons, Karl and Peter (born in 1908), close by and commented to Luise Kautsky on their good health and their progress in school. Though he would have preferred Berlin, he hoped he would be able to stay in relatively comfortable Vienna for the duration of the war.[10]

This relatively idyllic situation ended in 1916, when Hilferding began working in a mobile medical unit nearer to the Italian front, though still well behind the lines, at Steinach.[11] The army occasionally sent him to other hospitals where he usually remained for several months. Conditions varied, but it seems that Hilferding did not have a very difficult time during the war. On December 20, 1916, he wrote to Kautsky that his work on typhus and diphtheria was interesting, his relations with his colleagues were good, and he had been placed in charge of the Typhus Department in his *Spital*. He described the food and living conditions as excellent and remarked that he almost preferred where he was to Vienna![12]

Throughout the war Hilferding remained intellectually active and politically engaged. He asked Kautsky to send him theoretical and philosophical works ("the thicker and heavier the book, the better") and published numerous articles dealing with political and economic questions in *Die Neue Zeit* and *Der Kampf*.[13] Kautsky kept him informed of political affairs in Germany, and for the most part Hilferding had access to the German press. In June 1915 he told Kautsky of his great joy after reading *The Demand of the Hour*, a manifesto written by Bernstein, Kautsky, and Haase, which condemned the government's war of conquest and urged the party to call for a peace of understanding instead of annexations. Although the outcome remained unclear, Hilferding expressed his relief that the issue was now in the open and praised Haase for his courage and circumspection in dealing with the SPD leadership. In a letter to Kautsky one month later, he urged that Haase begin to organize the opposition systematically.[14]

As did Lenin's exile in Switzerland, Hilferding's "exile" in the Austrian military gave him the opportunity to ponder the causes of international socialism's collapse in 1914. In October 1915 he published an article entitled "Class Partnership?" which summed up his analysis of the political situation within the SPD and revised the economic theses of *Finance Capital*. The essay is particularly important because it contains Hilferding's first formulation of his concept of organized capitalism, the theoretical construct that underpinned his economic and political analyses for the next two decades.[15]

According to Hilferding, the onset of the imperialist war had brought about the unexpected victory of "opportunism" in the SPD and placed the party under the dictatorship of its right wing. The opportunists had transformed a revolutionary party into a reformist one with the task of adapting the workers' movement to capitalist society. This victory of opportunist ideology, he asserted, endangered the entire workers' movement because it "supported certain tendencies of capitalist development that hinder the realization of socialism."

Hilferding located the success of opportunist ideology in the "social-psychological" effects of capitalist development on the workers. Whereas Marx, observing capitalism in an earlier epoch, had thought that class struggle would enhance workers' revolutionary consciousness, Hilferding claimed that in recent years it had actually had the opposite effect. The more victories the workers achieved in their fight against capital, the more bearable life in capitalist society became. Thus, "the counterrevolutionary impact of the workers' movement had weakened capitalism's revolutionary tendencies" and thereby undercut working-class radicalism.

This process, thought Hilferding, had intensified during the most recent phase of capitalist development. Moving away from his earlier view that cartelization exacerbated economic crises, he adopted a position clearly derived from his concept of the "general cartel." Finance capital, Hilferding now argued, shortened periods of economic crisis, reduced chronic unemployment, and (even more important) tended to transform the anarchy of capitalist production into an "organized capitalist" economic order in which state power played an increasingly decisive role. Instead of socialism being victorious, it was now possible for an organized undemocratic economy to develop, controlled by monopoly capital and the state. The continuation of the war, in which the state's influence over the economy expanded markedly, strengthened the development of organized capitalism.

For Hilferding, the choice was now between organized state capitalism or democratic socialism. To follow the path of the opportunists could only lead to the former. It was the task of the Marxists in the party to struggle against opportunism by instructing the masses concerning their long-term interests. These interests, he thought, would become clearer as the effects of imperialist war grew worse and class struggle intensified. He was sure that the workers would then decide against opportunism and for socialism.

Hilferding's analysis focused primarily on the impact of capitalist development on workers' consciousness, but it clarified neither how the reformists were able to take control of the SPD's apparatus nor the relationship of the party's reform-oriented parliamentary strategy to their success. He shared the view of those socialists who argued that the leadership voted for war because it feared state repression and the loss of popular support. He also agreed that revisionism had prepared the ground for cooperation with the SPD's enemies, and that "the soul of the German people, despite social democracy's massive efforts, remained fundamentally imbued by the cult of violence." But unlike his party comrade Robert Michels, Hilferding did not link the leadership's acceptance of reformist ideology with the growth of the party's organization. On the contrary, he continued to regard the organization's growth as the key to social democracy's success and he saw no connection between the center's support for parliamentary tactics and the strength of reformist influence.[16]

Hilferding's effort to link "opportunism" with recent developments in the capitalist economy was in some ways similar to Lenin's. Both men argued that improvements in the workers' standard of living made substantial sections of the working class receptive to reformism, that the reformist leaders sought an alliance with the ruling elites, and that finance capital and the effects of the war placed socialism on the political agenda. But Lenin also had fundamental differences with Hilferding. He was convinced that capitalism was in its final phase of development and that social democracy should pursue a more aggressively revolutionary policy. Parliamentarianism, Lenin argued, had led to international socialism's collapse in 1914, and it was time to dispense with the "legalism" that had transformed the major social democratic parties into national liberal ones. Revolutionary social democrats now had to reorganize, work illegally, and effectively break with the socialist parties that had backed the war.[17]

These were steps that Hilferding in 1915 was not yet ready to take. He was willing to sharply criticize the nationalists in the party leadership and he hoped to push the SPD into an adversarial relationship with the state, but he was unwilling to advocate a policy that would certainly cause a split. The difficulties inherent in his position became especially clear when he polemicized against right-wing opponents who were willing to break decisively with the party's antiwar opposition. In July 1915, for example, Hilferding published a scathing attack on Wilhelm Kolb, a revisionist leader from Baden, who had recently written a pamphlet extolling the virtues of the party's cooperation with the state. Besides calling on the SPD to work with the bourgeois parties in order to achieve social and political reforms, Kolb argued that the war benefited the German people by strengthening their bonds with the monarchy. He asserted that the "Marxist opposition" was composed of "rootless cosmopolitans" with "criminal views" and demanded their expulsion from the party.[18]

Hilferding responded with a detailed critique of Kolb's basic suppositions. He pointed out that not only were the bourgeois parties unwilling to support social and political reforms that would strengthen the working class but they were also totally uninterested in an alliance with the social democrats. Kolb's program demanded that the workers repudiate their convictions and subordinate their interests to those of the bourgeoisie. Such a policy, Hilferding concluded, was bound to fail and to bring about the disintegration of the party.

Hilferding's arguments, though prescient, lacked effect. Although the center wanted to criticize the right-wing leadership, alter the SPD's strategy, and hold the party together for its struggle with the regime, its practical ability to realize such aims was negligible. The right controlled most of the SPD's apparatus, and many of its supporters were willing to split the party if the opposition's resistance to their policies became serious; thus, the reformists held most of the cards.

Although he feared precipitating a split, Hilferding remained convinced that only sustained criticism could alter the SPD's policy. In this critical situation he rejected the "political quietism" of those who believed the party's new direction was unavoidable and of others who waited for capitalism's inevitable collapse. He held that socialism was not just a question of capitalism's abstract possibilities of expansion but was also a question of the political power of the proletariat. When viewed within the context of capitalism's long-term development, the policy of finance capital—imperialism—was historically necessary and predictable, but Hilferding thought that human action could also change it. To claim otherwise was to accept the status quo, and this he could not do. Despite his wish to maintain unity, he felt compelled to fight his party's wartime policy.[19]

In his struggle against the social democratic accommodationists (Umlerner), Hilferding found himself at odds even with such longtime Austrian friends as Otto Bauer and Karl Renner. Both men enthusiastically supported the war: Bauer was drafted, captured, and then imprisoned in Russia, and Renner wielded his pen in fervent support of the Central Powers.[20] Renner called for the strengthening of economic, political, and cultural ties between Austria-Hungary and Germany. Along with Friedrich Naumann, he viewed the drive for an expanded central European economic and political bloc

(Mitteleuropa) as a necessity in the face of British, French, and Russian competition. Hilferding found Renner's chauvinism repulsive and his economic arguments foolish. He retorted that the elimination of tariffs between Austria and Germany would allow German industry to smother Austrian development and that the establishment of a protectionist central European bloc would drive England, France, and Russia to adopt similar policies. Germany and Austria-Hungary would be economically, politically, and militarily isolated, thereby restoring the international conditions that had led to war in 1914. In Hilferding's view, *Mitteleuropa* was the dream of the German and Austrian ruling classes and, if achieved, it would strengthen antidemocratic forces in both states.[21]

To avoid such a catastrophe, he urged social democracy to demand a postwar policy of international trade and free trade agreements that would prevent the reestablishment of protectionist economic blocs. He did not recognize that behind a policy of "free trade" stand unequal power relations, and he naively asserted that the world's nations could choose either to pursue imperialist policies in their drive to achieve the ever-elusive goal of autarchy, or they could break with power politics and adopt a policy of free trade in an interdependent world economy. Drawing on the ideas of Max Adler, Hilferding proposed a league of nations that would enable peoples to represent their own interests rather than serve the interests of other powers, and he called on the working class to fight against protectionism, imperialism, and the propaganda of those who supported the goal of *Mitteleuropa*.[22]

In the fall of 1915 Hilferding observed that, although it appeared to consolidate power relations in Germany and to justify the right wing's call for accommodation, the war also had the potential to unleash forces that could transform the situation. Less than one year later he was convinced that this transformation was underway. With the war's intensification and expansion, "the historical perspectives [were] increasingly vast." The war altered workers' consciousness as food and fuel shortages and the huge losses at the front fueled the desire for peace, while postwar economic problems certainly would raise questions about capitalism's further existence. In this situation he made very clear that social democracy had to end its cooperation with the bourgeoisie, join in the fight to end the war, and prepare the workers for the struggle for socialism.[23]

He openly admitted the difficulty of achieving these goals. Not only did the state of siege limit the opposition's ability to disseminate information, but the party itself remained under the control of elements determined to continue their cooperation with the regime and to repress internal dissent. Because the opposition refused to cease its criticism of the majority's policy, the possibility of a definitive split loomed larger as the war continued. By the summer of 1916, Hilferding was ready for the break. Declaring centrism superfluous, he called for left unity in the fight for socialism and control of the party and urged its representatives to openly challenge the majority in the

Reichstag. In this "world historical" situation, Hilferding thought, the left had to deal with tactical disputes as they arose, but unity was essential if the movement was to take advantage of any revolutionary situation that might develop.[24]

Thus, by the middle of 1916, Hilferding recognized that the opposition had little chance of altering the course of the SPD, but he hoped that a newly reconstituted left would play an important role in upcoming social and political struggles. Later events would make clear that he underestimated the differences between the center and the left, but his sense that they had much in common was rooted in the reality of wartime politics. As late as January 1916, unity of the opposition had appeared to be an unreachable goal. On New Year's Day, the radicals (now known as Spartacists) organized a conference at which they worked out a program attacking the center's "broad and crooked path of compromise" with national defense. To achieve "the intellectual liberation of the proletariat" they called for a fight against the bourgeois nationalist ideology that dominated the masses. Clarity and ruthless criticism should not be sacrificed for the sake of unity. Within a few months, however, circumstances pushed the Spartacists to soften their stance. Increasing state repression and the party leadership's attempts to stifle internal dissent made cooperation a necessity between the left centrists and the radicals.[25]

As the war dragged on, living conditions worsened, casualties rose, and popular unrest increased. In response, General Ludendorff's military dictatorship moved to root out all opponents of the war. The regime tightened censorship, prohibited meetings, banned individual socialist leaders from speaking in public, and ordered house searches to silence not only the antiwar opposition but also right-wing SPD members who criticized some of the state's domestic policies. It was the left, however, that suffered most, as the government imprisoned leading figures such as Luxemburg, Liebknecht, and Mehring. Haase and other centrist lawyers rushed to take on the radicals' legal cases; at the same time they used the Reichstag to publicize government misdeeds. These actions helped to bring the left and center together.[26]

Meanwhile the party leadership also attempted to silence the opposition. In March 1916 the Reichstag delegation expelled the left centrists after they voted a second time against war credits, and the executive's purge of dissident editors from the SPD's press culminated with its seizure of *Vorwärts* from the Berlin party organization in October. The opposition reacted by setting up a Social Democratic Working Group (*Sozialdemokratische Arbeitsgemeinschaft*, or SAG) in the Reichstag and by informally organizing cooperation among sympathetic groups nationwide. The conflict intensified until January 18, 1917, when the SPD executive used a Berlin conference of centrist and Spartacist leaders as a pretext to expel the opposition.[27] It now remained for the latter to organize a new party. On Easter Sunday, the leading dissidents of the left, center, and right met at Gotha and founded the Independent Social Democratic party (USPD).

From his post on the Italian frontier, Hilferding strained to keep up with events in the party during the winter of 1916–1917. He bombarded Kautsky with requests for information and commented frequently on political events. In January 1917, without explicitly mentioning the expulsion of the opposition, he told Kautsky that he and Haase were constantly in his thoughts, and he expressed particular concern about the fate of *Die Neue Zeit*. As a member of the expelled opposition, Kautsky could hardly hope to remain editor of the party's leading journal and Hilferding was no doubt concerned about his friend's professional future.[28]

Although Kautsky did not lose control over *Die Neue Zeit* until August 1917, Hilferding's last wartime article appeared there in the fall of 1916.[29] Why he ceased publishing remains unknown. It is possible that his medical duties interfered with his studies. In any case, our only firsthand source of information on his views between January 1917 and November 1918 is his correspondence with Kautsky. These letters contain interesting observations on some of the most momentous events of that crucial period.

The fall of the tsar in February 1917 and the Bolshevik overthrow of the provisional government in November transformed the political and military situation in Europe and whetted Hilferding's desire to return to Germany. In a letter written on October 13, just ten days before the Bolsheviks decided to act, Hilferding admonished Kautsky not to be discouraged by his recent loss of *Die Neue Zeit*. Great changes were in the offing and he reminded his friend that he had major services to perform. "The world is renewing itself," he wrote, "though in a different way than we had expected, and your clarity of vision is needed to recognize what is essential and to teach us what is new."[30]

Revolutionary Russia loomed large in Hilferding's mind as a center of change in this process of world renewal. He insisted, however, that Europe's fate would not be decided there; the process that began in Russia could only be successful when completed in the West. Like most USPD leaders, Hilferding anticipated a Europeanwide revolution only after the war had ended, a prospect he considered unlikely until at least the following summer.

Three weeks after the Bolsheviks had seized power, Hilferding told Kautsky that they were largely in agreement about the situation in Russia. His heart, he wrote, was with the Bolsheviks, even though they themselves seemed quite heartless and their intentions were difficult to surmise. Did they want a separate peace? If so, on what terms? Did they think they could actually remain neutral with respect to the Entente? What about Trotsky's claim in 1905 that the dictatorship of the Russian proletariat could only survive if the revolution spread throughout Europe? "The situation is truly incomparable," wrote Hilferding,

> because this combination of revolutionary proletariat and revolutionary peasantry, armed and organized in one army in which the officer corps is in total disarray, has never existed. It has much power on its side. But on the other side

stands not only the whole bourgeoisie, but also the power of all the other states. And that Germany should really make it easy for the Bolsheviks by repudiating its plans in the east thereby helping to stabilize this great revolution in a neighboring country—I'll believe that when I see it.[31]

War, Hilferding thought, would be difficult for them to win given Russia's weakness. Only help from the western European proletariat could save the Bolsheviks, but such assistance seemed unlikely.

In retrospect it is quite remarkable how clearly Hilferding saw the strategic situation facing the Bolsheviks just weeks after their seizure of power. Within months the Germans would force them to accept the humiliating treaty of Brest-Litovsk and, shortly thereafter, the outbreak of a long and bloody civil war coupled with foreign intervention threatened the survival of the revolution. Hilferding's incisive comments make quite clear his early concerns about the nature of the Bolsheviks' aims and about the dilemma in which the revolutionaries found themselves. The events in Russia and Europe over the next three years demonstrate that his concerns were fully justified.

Hilferding's pessimistic view of the revolutionary potential of western European workers in 1917 stands in stark contrast to his earlier assertion that the war would radicalize the German masses. From the evidence at our disposal it is difficult to ascertain what changed his views. The war's long duration, the failure of the USPD to successfully mobilize and coordinate opposition to the regime, and the lack of revolutionary activity among the workers combined to undermine Hilferding's confidence. In early September 1918 he lamented to Kautsky that there were "practically no socialist groups" with whom they could identify, it was difficult for them to express their views effectively, and the slowly changing "historical condition" of the working class hampered the USPD's activities.[32]

These comments illustrate Hilferding's sense of his own political isolation in 1918. With the movement polarized by the war, the political centrism of the prewar years was no longer a tenable position and he felt uneasy about the newly formed and politically divided USPD, whose constituent elements were united primarily by their opposition to the war rather than by any overarching ideological or practical perspective. They also reveal how Hilferding's assessment of the possibilities for popular action had changed since 1916. He was now convinced that the working class was unprepared for revolution anytime soon, and that under such circumstances the USPD would play only a negligible role in shaping the course of events. It was the outcome of the struggles on the battlefield that he believed would be decisive in the future.

Hilferding had not wavered in his conviction that, rather than "make" the revolution, social democracy's task was to prepare the workers intellectually and organizationally for one that they would make themselves, spontaneously, when conditions were right. Earlier, he had accurately recognized that the war was fueling popular unrest, but, as events soon made clear, in the summer of 1918 he underestimated the revolutionary potential of the masses. By the fall, after four years of intense labor, hunger, and millions of casualties, the German workers were demanding peace and the dissolution of the imperial government. The defeat of the German summer offensive in France and Bulgaria's withdrawal from the war convinced the high command that the war was lost. When the soldiers and sailors refused to continue the fight in early November, the monarchy's fate was sealed.

Hilferding rushed back to Berlin during the second week of November. By this time a republic had been proclaimed, the kaiser had fled, and a provisional government, consisting of representatives drawn from the SPD and the USPD, had signed an armistice. Newly established workers' and soldiers' councils acted as focal points of real political power and served as the government's main source of legitimacy. At a moment when Hilferding had least expected it, revolution had come to Germany.

After arriving in the capital, Hilferding immediately threw himself into revolutionary activity. For the next three years, as chief editor of the USPD's central organ, *Die Freiheit*, as ex-officio member of the party's executive committee, and as a member of the government's Socialization Commission, he was a leader in the socialist effort to transform German society. These were years of great hopes and even greater disappointments.

The circumstances of Hilferding's appointment as chief editor are unclear, but Hugo Haase undoubtedly considered him the best choice for the job. Before 1914 the two men had known each other well, and during the war they held similar political views. It is not surprising, then, that the USPD leadership took advantage of Hilferding's editorial experience and appointed him to head the paper.[33] His editorship, as well as his other posts, placed him in a good position to influence debates crucial to the revolution's success. What, for example, would be the role of workers' councils in German society? What did revolutionaries mean when they called for the socialization of industry? What was the relationship between the German and the Russian revolutions? Hilferding's evolving ideas on these and other issues during the immediate postwar years reveal the theoretical and practical difficulties he faced in his dual capacity as party theorist and tactician.

During the weeks immediately following the proclamation of the republic, Hilferding waxed enthusiastic about the arrival of socialism in Germany, despite his recognition that the country faced serious political and economic problems.[34] He argued that (unlike economically backward Russia, with its small urban working class) industrially advanced Germany had a large, class-conscious proletariat and was ready for socialism. In Russia the working-class minority had to use the soviets to assert its hegemony by force; in Germany the transition could be peaceful, democratic, and in accordance with parliamentary norms. He called for the socialization of "ripe" branches of industry, such as mining, but insisted that small-scale and noncartelized industries should be left in private hands. The immediate task of the government, he soberly suggested, was to stabilize the postwar economy by stimulating production to facilitate exports, reduce inflation, and lower domestic prices.

Although he expressed "no doubt" that the working class would confirm its "dictatorship" by electing a socialist majority to the proposed National Assembly, Hilferding knew that the USPD was unprepared to wage a successful electoral campaign that fall. He suggested postponing the elections to facilitate voter registration, the securing of national borders, and the political education of the masses. He warned that the forces of reaction were still strong within the bureaucracy and the military, and that the workers needed to establish control over all politically decisive positions in order to prevent counterrevolution. Without clearly explaining how the workers should proceed, he argued that they should remain vigilant while simultaneously moving forward with the socialization of industry.

Hilferding's views were consistent with those he had developed in Austria and Germany before the war. Now convinced that the working-class majority had conquered state power, he believed it would use its control over parliament to implement radical changes. He rejected workers' councils as permanent political institutions because he feared they would alienate other social groups, anger the Allies, and possibly bring on civil war and foreign intervention. Like his Austrian counterpart Otto Bauer, Hilferding imagined a gradual revolutionary transformation of society with the USPD reuniting the workers' movement and steering Germany toward democratic socialism. The violent suppression of the radical left, the division of the USPD, and the growing strength of the radical right dashed these hopes and convinced him that the revolutionary road to socialism was closed.

The German political situation in November 1918 was confused and volatile. Although the military and bourgeois parties were temporarily discredited, divisions within the workers' movement prevented any formulation of a unified program for fundamental change. The provisional government could not pursue a coherent policy because the various coalition partners had different visions of Germany's future. The SPD leadership wanted to establish a parliamentary republic with broad civil liberties and substantial social welfare benefits; it did not favor more radical change. Ebert, party leader and cochair of the government (Haase was his USPD counterpart), hated revolution "like sin" and aimed to phase out the workers' councils and stifle further revolutionary activity.[35]

The USPD, on the other hand, demanded social as well as political revolution. A majority of the Independents called for a purge of the state bureaucracy and military, the expropriation of industry, and the "dictatorship of the proletariat" during the transition to socialism. This dictatorship, they argued, had been established by the councils and the provisional government. Its task was to oversee the socialization of industry and the democratization of the state. Once completed, the entire population could then participate in elections to the National Assembly.[36] The struggle to realize their respective goals intensified political conflict between the two socialist parties. By the late fall of 1918, as the bourgeoisie and the army began to recover their equilibrium, Germany moved toward civil war.

The USPD itself was divided. The party's extreme right wing, which included Kautsky and Bernstein, argued that the end of the war eliminated the main issue separating the two workers' parties and called for their reunification. The radical left, on the other hand, demanded that the USPD adopt a position diametrically opposed to that of the SPD. Organized primarily into two groups (the "revolutionary shop stewards" and the more radical *Spartakus Bund*), the left feared that calling a national assembly would lead to the creation of a bourgeois republic. Instead it demanded the election of an assembly of workers' and soldiers' councils to erect the future state structure. Most of the USPD leadership—and, at first, the bulk of the party membership—supported various positions between these two extremes.[37] As events unfolded and factional differences in the party intensified, it became more difficult for the leaders to work out a program that would maintain unity.

Like Kautsky, Hilferding hoped for social democracy's eventual reunification, but the SPD's counterrevolutionary policies quickly convinced him that unity was not possible in the near future.[38] At the same time, however, he considered many of the left's demands to be impractical, given Germany's political confusion and economic weakness. Hilferding opposed the USPD's dogmatic adherence to what he considered unrealistic goals and thought that it should adopt a revolutionary program based on the political and economic realities of the moment. He demonstrated his political flexibility in the winter of 1918–1919, as events compelled him to reconsider his earlier rejection of the workers' councils.

By the end of December 1918, the unstable coalition government and the USPD itself were on the verge of falling apart. Throughout the fall, the SPD had blocked all of the Independents' attempts to initiate radical reforms and continued this policy at the Congress of Workers' and Soldiers' Councils that met in Berlin in mid-December. The SPD's large majority easily defeated USPD resolutions calling for the postponement of the elections, the establishment of a council republic, and the concentration of executive and legislative power in the hands of the Central Council, to be elected by the congress. Frustrated by the SPD's strategy, a substantial minority of left-wing Independents called for a party congress to discuss the USPD's continued participation in the government and in the coming elections. Fearing a split, Hilferding, Haase, and the rest of the USPD center and right-wing leaders opposed summoning a congress. On December 15, at a meeting of the Berlin party organization, Hilferding submitted a resolution supporting the USPD's participation in the elections to the assembly. Rosa Luxemburg responded with a proposal calling on the party to withdraw from the government, renounce its participation in the elections, demand a council republic, and immediately summon a congress. Hilferding's resolution won by a vote of 485 to 195.[39]

Although the centrist position had the support of a large majority at the conference, the vote also revealed that the Spartacist proposals could attract many of the party's more radical members. It was their awareness of this possibility that motivated the centrist leadership to oppose convening a congress. Some actually hoped that the Spartacists would leave the party while they were still a small group; at the Berlin conference Haase openly called on them to do so.[40] Two weeks later they followed his advice and on December 30, 1918, founded the Communist Party of Germany (KPD).

Hilferding and Haase hoped that the Spartacists' departure would unify the USPD and enable its leaders to transform the party into an instrument of revolutionary change. They intended to cooperate with the majority socialists and to pressure them to pursue more radical policies. Such a strategy, they thought, would placate the party's left wing and avoid a major split.[41] But the centrists underestimated the depth of the rift in their own party and in the socialist movement as a whole. They did not know that events in the coming months would exacerbate these divisions, and that left-wing sympathy for the Communists would increase, while cooperation between the USPD and the SPD would prove impossible. Contrary to their expectations, the Spartacists' departure ultimately weakened the workers' movement and further undermined hopes for its reunification.

Tensions in the government came to a head on December 29, 1918, as the coalition partners clashed over military policy in the midst of growing civil turmoil. The SPD representatives, fearing the loss of the officer corps's support against the radical left, refused to accept a Congress of Workers' and Soldiers' Councils resolution to replace the old army with a new, democratically organized militia. On December 23, Ebert had precipitated a crisis by calling in troops to quell unrest in Berlin without consulting the USPD. The latter condemned his action and demanded the implementation of military and economic reforms, but the majority socialists refused to budge and the SPD-controlled Central Council supported them. Frustrated, the USPD's representatives—Haase, Dittmann, and Emil Barth—then resigned.[42]

Hilferding supported the USPD leaders' decision. On December 27, 1918, he publicly accused Ebert and his colleagues of attempting to drive the Independents out of the government by presenting them with a fait accompli. The SPD leaders, he charged, had assumed the role of the reactionaries whom they had replaced. They had summoned troops when they felt their authority threatened and they sought the support of the bourgeoisie by using the army to restore order. If the Central Council supported the SPD's actions, the USPD had no choice but to carry on its duties outside the government.[43]

The withdrawal of the Independent ministers was a serious setback for the party. It undermined the center's hope of pushing the SPD toward the left and allowed the SPD control of the state. In early January 1919, with the army's support Ebert's government smashed a popular uprising in Berlin, and both Rosa Luxemburg and Karl Liebknecht were killed. On January 19, the SPD won 37 percent of the total vote in the elections to the National Assembly, while the Independents won less than 8 percent. Their own poor showing and the failure of the socialist parties to win a majority forced the USPD leaders to reexamine their position on the workers' councils. With the socialists reduced to a minority, they sought to promote the workers' councils as permanent institutions that would act as a counterweight to reactionary forces in the assembly.[44]

In early February 1919, Hilferding opened debate on this issue in *Die Freiheit*. In contrast to his earlier position, he now argued that the councils were necessary "to maintain and complete the achievements of the revolution." He called for the annual election of a Supreme Workers' Council that would propose legislation and examine bills before their submission to the National Assembly. Major disputes between the Supreme Council and the National Assembly over legislative proposals would be settled by popular referendum. These functions would establish the councils as permanent organs of workers' power; once anchored in the constitution, they could act to offset the strength of the conservative political parties.[45]

Hilferding believed that a reunified workers' movement was essential to the success of the revolution, but he feared that reunification "from above" would mean capitulating to the goals of the right-wing socialists. Instead, he proposed that workers' councils throughout Germany organize assemblies to elect unification committees composed of representatives from each socialist party. These committees would, in turn, meet to select an executive body that would coordinate the movement toward unity nationwide. As a political basis for unity he put forward an "Action Program" demanding the socialization of industry (especially mining) on national and communal levels and the democratization of factories through the election of councils. Standing on the principles of Erfurt, the unified party would fight for the democratic rights of all and resort to violence only as a defensive measure. Domestically, it would dismantle the old army and bureaucracy, establish a people's militia, and expand the councils system; abroad it would support a democratic peace, the League of Nations, disarmament, national self-determination, and the reestablishment of an international workers' organization. Hilferding hoped that workers would rally around these goals, rectify the political errors of social democracy's leadership, and reunite the parties.[46]

Although designed to reunify the socialist movement as a whole, Hilferding's proposals were barely acceptable to a majority in his own party because they failed to adequately explain how social democracy should achieve its aims. At its congress in March the USPD incorporated most of his suggestions into its new Revolutionary Program, but the dispute over the party's use of parliamentary and extraparliamentary tactics remained divisive. To prevent a split, the leadership drafted a statement declaring that to reach the goal of socialism the party would employ "all political and economic means of struggle, *including parliaments.*"[47] This formula attempted to satisfy both those on the left, who favored the councils, and those on the right, who emphasized working in parliament. The congress adopted the resolution into the new program, but disagreements over its interpretation persisted.

Outside the USPD, Hilferding's proposals for a revived councils system and socialist unity found little resonance. It was too late for such measures. Throughout the winter and spring, government forces had driven the workers' movement into full retreat by bloodily suppressing uprisings around the country. By the summer of 1919, the councils issue was no longer of central importance on the German political scene.

Hilferding's support for the councils as a means of defending the revolution was consistent with the notion of defensive violence developed earlier in his theses on the mass strike. For Hilferding, the councils became a real political alternative only when it appeared that the National Assembly would oppose workers' interests. Despite his hopes that the councils might reinvigorate the revolution, he never really departed from the view that parliament was the appropriate arena for revolutionary change. His occasional deviations from this position arose solely in response to concrete political circumstances.[48]

Few recognized Hilferding's reservations concerning the workers' councils as clearly as Lenin. Two months after the appearance of Hilferding's articles on the councils, the Bolshevik leader responded in *Pravda*. After describing Hilferding as an "ideologically bankrupt leader of the Second International," and the Independents as "petty-bourgeois philistines," he labeled the whole notion of unifying the "dictatorship of the bourgeoisie" (parliament) with the "dictatorship of the proletariat" (the councils) as nothing more than an "ingenius-philistine idea." It represented "a complete abandonment of Marxism as well as socialism [and] ignore[d] the experience of the Russian Mensheviks and the 'Socialist Revolutionaries,' who . . . made the attempt and failed miserably." Such policies, Lenin concluded, made clear that the USPD leaders were "miserable petty-bourgeois, who were dependent on the philistine prejudices of the most backward part of the proletariat."[49]

Lenin correctly sensed that Hilferding and the moderate Independents were hesitant to completely abandon parliamentary politics in favor of the councils. He ruthlessly criticized the effort to blend the two systems because he was determined to undermine any revolutionary political model that differed from the Bolsheviks' model and that might challenge their authority in the newly established Communist International. In 1919, the Bolsheviks expected the "general course" of proletarian revolution to be "the same throughout the world. First the spontaneous formation of soviets, then their spread and development, and then the appearance of the practical problem: soviets or national assembly." It did not matter that social, economic, and political conditions were historically different in Germany; to them the spreading of socialism was the most important task.[50]

The Bolsheviks' strategy necessarily differed from that of the German social democrats for historical reasons. Operating under more oppressive conditions, they had adapted their organizational structure (democratic centralism) and political tactics accordingly. In the revolutionary situation of 1917, the Bolsheviks had few qualms about establishing a minority-led "dictatorship of the proletariat" in a country with a large peasant majority. Like their opponents, Lenin and other Bolshevik leaders willingly used terror to achieve victory in the civil war; they considered their methods necessary to secure the revolution.[51]

Such methods were totally unacceptable to Hilferding and the majority of German socialists. He had received his political education in a party that made electoral work its highest priority, that had operated legally, and that in general tolerated dissenters within its ranks. Its goal was to win a parliamentary majority in order to achieve state power. This was the message that the SPD leaders had pounded into workers' heads for almost forty years prior to 1914. It was also the message that most German workers and their leaders continued to accept after the war. It is not surprising, therefore, that Hilferding, quoting Marx and Engels, announced in November 1918 that "the proletarian revolution is the revolution of the great majority in the interests of the great majority."[52] He was expressing his commitment to a maxim he believed in absolutely throughout his career.

Lenin's critique of Hilferding was harsh, but the logic of his argument is difficult to dispute. In their quest for parliamentary legitimacy, the social democrats effectively relinquished power to their opponents and forfeited their opportunity to implement practical, radical reforms. Hilferding's proposals for the purge of the army and state bureaucracy, the socialization of key industries, and the democratization of the factories would have weakened the institutional strength of the conservative reaction and substantially changed German society. He knew well that such plans were meaningless without political power but, unlike Lenin, he was unwilling to use any means to achieve it.

By late March 1919, a depressed Hilferding saw political mistakes and missed opportunities everywhere. A unified socialist government, he lamented, could have effectively democratized German society, used its moral authority to unify the workers' movement, and won a majority in the National Assembly. Instead, the SPD had turned away from socialism, allied itself with the right (including the military), and allowed the bourgeoisie to retake control of parliament.[53]

Hilferding conceded that the USPD had made mistakes, but the government of Ebert and Philip Scheidemann bore primary responsibility for the revolution's failure. It was the "most fateful misfortune," he bitterly complained, "that such small men were faced with so great an opportunity." Although excellent organizers and propagandists, they were "entirely without vision . . . *petit-bourgeois* who want first of all order."[54] Flattered and corrupted by the compliments of an upper crust angling for favor, "Ebert is delighted, and he thinks that it is his job to reconcile the revolution with the generals and Ruhr industrialists!" (242).

While placing blame for the revolution's failures on the right wing, Hilferding criticized the radical left as well. He spoke admiringly of Rosa Luxemburg's vision and described her as a revolutionary "who knew what she wanted," but he thought that those around her were "romantic revolutionaries" who had "no sense of the realities of power" (243). Conveniently forgetting his own views in December, he asserted that it was the radicals who had forced the USPD to quit the government, thereby precipitating the ensuing futile struggle on the barricades.

Hilferding thought that the proletariat, too, bore some responsibility for the revolution's failures. He believed that a majority of the workers still followed the SPD because their class consciousness was not yet fully developed, and it was this consciousness that ultimately determined the limits of the revolution. Although for decades the working class had accepted social democracy's revolutionary teachings, a long period of peace and steady economic growth had led many to believe "that there was no imminent, pressing need for a revolutionary change of society" (244). Radical ideas were not rooted deeply among workers or even among the intellectuals, "who always have generated the spiritual revolutions" (244). When the sudden collapse of the old regime took them by surprise, "they were content with a political change of society, just because it presented itself" (244).

Hilferding privately conceded that domestic setbacks and the lack of revolutionary activity elsewhere in the West made socialism's victory in Germany unlikely in the near future. The establishment of a "progressive capitalist country" remained possible, but socialism would have to wait "until the next opportunity with which history may provide us" (245). Thus, within six months of the monarchy's fall, Hilferding had lost his confidence in the revolutionary movement's success. He still hoped that the socialization of industry might renew its momentum, but even there he had the feeling that a "blight had killed every revolutionary will" (244).

Hilferding had good reason to be skeptical. As a member of the Socialization Commission, he had worked for months on a project in which the government had no real interest. Established by the socialist coalition in November 1918, the commission's official task was to plan the socialization of those branches of industry considered ready for it. The SPD leadership, however, was actually opposed to such reforms and only agreed to the commission's being formed because socialization had widespread working-class support. Politically impotent, the commission possessed no power to develop its own initiatives and its members were often in conflict. With little financial backing and virtually no support from the Reichsminister of the Economy, Rudolf Wissell (SPD), the commission's prospects for success were poor.[55]

The commission had begun work on December 5, 1918, with Kautsky as chairman. Two weeks later, in a speech to the Congress of Workers' and Soldiers' Councils, Hilferding had outlined a detailed plan for the gradual socialization of German industry.[56] This plan, which made concrete recommendations for radical reform in the midst of an economic crisis, was one of the earliest socialist blueprints for economic change in the postwar period. Hilferding had no illusions about the state of the economy. Opening his speech with Marx's famed phrase "Proletarians! You have nothing to lose but your chains, you have a world to win!" he reminded his audience that, although the revolutionary moment had arrived, the world was not the one they had hoped for or expected. "It is a terrible and tragic fate," he said, "that we have come to power at the moment when the inheritance that we receive is wasted and ruined" (156). The war had devastated the economy. Consumer goods production was low, millions of workers were dead or wounded, raw materials were scarce, and the Allied blockade was causing starvation. The socialization of the means of production, he observed, would never be an easy task, but the economic crisis made it much more difficult. Socialization was possible, but only if the economy revived.

To restart production, Hilferding pointed out, Germany desperately needed to import raw materials, payment for which required an increase in exports of finished products. To ensure uninterrupted and increased production in agriculture and in the export industries, he recommended that these sectors be left in private hands. Which industries should be socialized? Hilferding suggested that the most suitable branches were those "where capitalist concentration . . . has already laid the groundwork for the organized socialist economy" (157). Three specific criteria identified these branches: steady production for a guaranteed mass domestic market; a high level of concentration, in technological and economic terms; and the production of goods that were important to the economy as a whole. The sector that most clearly met these requirements, he asserted, was mining. Once in control of the basic raw materials industries, the government could socialize other branches that depended on their supplies.

What did Hilferding mean by socialization? He rejected outright the idea of simply transferring factories into workers' hands, an action that would result in the formation of competing factory associations without changing the basic character of capitalism. He supported, instead, the creation of an organized economy that would eliminate the chaos of capitalist production relations. Envisioning a long and complex process, Hilferding defined socialization as "the gradual transference of the whole of production over to the control of the community" (157).

In *Finance Capital* Hilferding had argued for the expropriation of the banks as one of the first steps in the transition to socialism, but he now advocated postponing this step. Private bank capital was important for the restoration of Germany's economic stability and he thought it ill-advised to disturb the system in the ongoing crisis. Instead, social control over such raw materials as coal and iron would weaken the independent basis of capitalist industry and banking and open the way to the socialization of other branches of the economy. Hilferding opposed socializing the entire economy and warned against concentrating too much economic power in the hands of the Reich government. He recommended that the production of nonessential items and luxuries remain in private hands, that the central government in Berlin administer mining and transport, and that local and state governments direct most other industries. He said nothing about the socialization of the service industries (158).

Socialization should not proceed, Hilferding contended, through the outright confiscation of all capitalist enterprises. The owners would tenaciously resist and disrupt production. He preferred gradual compensation to expropriated capitalists for the full value of their property and recommended raising the required funds by heavily taxing the remaining capitalists and the wealthy. In this way socialization of the key branches of the economy would not interrupt production or burden the masses (159).

With respect to agriculture Hilferding adopted a different position. Here he thought that the state should seize *Junker*-owned forest and agricultural land without compensation and redistribute the latter to returning war veterans. He opposed the expropriation of peasant property, however, and argued that the government should aid small producers with credit, improved education, machinery, the formation of grain monopolies, and the determination of prices. Hilferding was not, however, suggesting that small-scale production was viable in the long term; he recommended that the state establish model farms to demonstrate the benefits of large-scale production to the peasantry (159).

For Hilferding, socialism was more than just the fight for higher wages, the elimination of poverty, or the raising of the intellectual and cultural levels of the masses. These aims were essential, of course, but also at stake was the ability of humanity "to deal with its great problems, and to replace the brutality, which clings to us all from the period of class domination and the exploitation of man by man, with intellect and ideal[s]" (160). He implored workers and soldiers to look beyond short-term improvements in their own immediate condition and to fill themselves with the spirit of responsibility for the revolution and the welfare of the whole society. To secure the triumph of the revolution, he urged them to be patient during the transition period, to protect their factories against sabotage and bureaucratism, and to struggle for a socialist majority in the National Assembly.

The congress responded positively to Hilferding's speech and unanimously passed a resolution calling for "an immediate start on the socialization of all industries ready for it, in particular the mining industry" (182). The government, however, did nothing. Paralyzed by the crisis that eventually destroyed the socialist coalition, it failed to act on the resolution.

Meanwhile, the Socialization Commission continued its work. On February 15, 1919, it presented majority and minority reports to the cabinet. Hilferding supported the former, which rejected both a return to the free market and the establishment of a state capitalist economy. Instead, it called for socialization as a means of increasing economic efficiency, democratizing the factories, and breaking the power of capital. As a first step, the majority proposed the expropriation (with compensation) of the coal mines and their reorganization into a German coal association under the direction of a hundred-member elected council on which workers, managers, consumers, and the state would have equal representation.[57]

The reforms called for in the majority report were substantial, though limited to mining. Without nationalizing the industry or simply handing it over to the workers, they would have removed it from the control of a powerful and reactionary sector of the German elite and democratized its operations. They also would have demonstrated to the workers that the government was ready to act in their interest as well as that of society as a whole. By democratizing the industry without nationalizing it, the reforms aimed to limit bureaucratization, and by including wage incentives, they rewarded superior organizers, more productive workers, and the most effective salespeople.[58] The Socialization Commission report aroused no interest in the SPD-led coalition government, however. The majority socialists thought it more important to restore the economy first and undertake socialization later, if at all. Their resistance made the commission's recommendations superfluous; the commission ceased its operations in April 1919.

Before the Bolshevik revolution of 1917 and the collapse of the Central Powers one year later, social democrats had said little about the actual construction of socialism. Following the example of Marx and Engels, they hesitated to put forward detailed blueprints of the coming new order and put forward the vague call for the "socialization of the means of production" as the key step toward a classless society.[59] When the old order in Russia and central Europe crumbled, socialist thinkers suddenly found themselves groping to find their way in a new world. Many different "models" for socialization appeared, but the Austro-Marxist and the Bolshevik variants were among the most important. In Germany and Austria, Marxists such as Hilferding and Otto Bauer (who was now Austria's foreign minister and socialization minister) were well positioned to influence economic reform, whereas in Russia the Bolsheviks had absolute power in the areas under their control during the civil war. The two groups developed fundamentally opposed concepts of the transition to socialism.

Hilferding and Bauer were in close communication during the development of their respective socialization plans. Both men equated the "proletarian dictatorship" with workers' control of parliament, and both emphasized the need for the gradual growth into socialism. Bauer's conception of socialization, like Hilferding's, focused initially on heavy industry and mining, rejected outright confiscation, encouraged planning, but did not eliminate the market. The Austro-Marxists agreed that finance capital's higher level of organization and planning had laid the groundwork for socialism, but they worried that precipitous policies could unleash a ruinous civil war that would destroy the economic basis for socialist construction. For this reason, their plans stressed the need to include broad sectors of the population in the economic and political decision-making process. Their suggestions for new institutions such as "economic parliaments" on local and national levels, aimed to win the political support or tolerance of a majority of the population and to avoid violent class conflict. For Hilferding and Bauer, the successful development of socialism was a long-term project that required substantial compromises between social groups.[60]

The Bolsheviks, who intended to hold power at any cost, took the opposite position. By 1919, they were engaged in a brutal civil war in which they quickly placed the production and distribution of virtually all goods under centralized state control. This policy of "war communism" required massive coercion: factories came under military discipline, grain supplies were requisitioned, and resistance ruthlessly crushed. While such measures engendered much popular opposition and intensified civil strife, they also fueled the élan of many who wanted a final break with capitalism. War communism, they thought, would enable them to smash the structures of the old system and begin with the construction of the new.

Nikolay Bukharin, Bolshevism's leading economic theorist at that time, captured the enthusiasm of party activists with his book *The Economics of the Transition Period* (1920).[61] Bukharin's analysis of modern capitalism had much in common with Hilferding's and borrowed heavily from the latter's work. His examination of the transition to socialism, however, moved in a completely different direction. Whereas Hilferding thought civil war would hinder socialist construction, Bukharin held that "it was a pitiful illusion to imagine a transition to socialism without the collapse, without the disturbance of social equilibrium, without bloody fighting."[62] The imperialist war and the overthrow of state monopoly capitalism in Russia, he argued, had necessarily demolished the economic system and its associated political and military structures. The only way for society to recover from this devastation was through the establishment of the dictatorship of the proletariat and the construction of communism. He asserted that in this period of dictatorship, civil war, and economic decline, "new forms of organization arise" that represent the basis of the new system (56–59).

Bukharin believed that the "period of socialist construction will . . . inevitably be a period of planned and organized work," in which the coercive power of the state played a major role (71, 74). "In the transition period," he wrote, "when one productive structure gives way to another, the midwife is revolutionary force." This revolutionary force, "the state of the new class," was essential to destroy the fetters of the old system as well as to build anew. And "the greater this 'extra-economic' power is . . . the less will be 'the costs' of the transition period [and] the shorter will be the period of the transition" (171–72). Bukharin thought that the future communist society would be free of coercion, but until its opponents could be "reeducated," "all forms of proletarian force, from shooting to forced labor" were legitimate (182–83).

The marked contrast between Austro-Marxist and Bolshevik views on the transition to socialism stemmed from their very different conceptions of the proletarian dictatorship and of the dialectical relationship between social development and revolution. After 1918, Hilferding and Bauer worked in states within which traditional parliamentary political structures were reformed but not destroyed. By winning socialist majorities, they aimed to realize their vision of the prewar years, that is, to use parliamentary institutions to carry out the peaceful transformation of the economy. On the other hand, the Bolsheviks—operating under conditions in which the achievement of such a majority was not possible—were willing to completely smash Russia's shaky institutions and, while waiting for the revolution to spread, to hold power by force. Bukharin asserted that there was no historical precedent for a nonviolent social revolution, and he developed a dialectical method that stressed the continual destruction and reconstruction of social equilibrium in the revolutionary process.[63]

Hilferding, on the other hand, adopted an approach that envisioned an organized, peaceful process of social transformation. This stress on evolutionary—rather than revolutionary—change had first appeared in his critique of Böhm-Bawerk, but it became increasingly pronounced after 1914. Whereas in *Finance Capital* Hilferding had written that imperialist war would ultimately unleash "revolutionary storms" that would allow the proletariat to seize power, following the monarchy's collapse he asserted that the dislocations that such storms implied would hinder the transition to socialism. Several factors help to explain the development of his increasingly evolutionary outlook: his prewar conviction that the gradual transition to socialism was possible; his revulsion at the bloodshed caused by the civil war in Russia; and the repeated defeats of revolutionary forces in Germany. As we shall see, with the consolidation of the capitalist republic, Hilferding became convinced that gradual change was the only feasible political option.

By early 1919, Hilferding believed that the stalled revolution had little chance of moving forward, but in the spring of 1920 a new opportunity revived his hopes. In March, a massive general strike defeated an attempt by reactionary officers to seize power (the so-called Kapp Putsch) and led to renewed demands for radical reforms. Under pressure, the government appointed a new Socialization Commission, which included Hilferding among its members. In July 1920, the commission once again submitted two different recommendations. One supported the full socialization of the coal mines following a plan similar to that of the earlier majority report. The other argued for gradual expropriation over a thirty-year period with the capitalists receiving full compensation while continuing to play a leading role in their enterprises.[64]

Hilferding was the leading exponent of the more radical position and tenaciously opposed the efforts of Walther Rathenau to retain the capitalists within the production hierarchy. When Rathenau expressed his doubts that an elected council could efficiently manage the coal mining industry or that council members would even remain interested in their administrative tasks, Hilferding countered by pointing out that the members would be experts who had a direct interest in managing their affairs. He rejected Rathenau's suggestion that workers and capitalists could cooperate as equals in managing industry and argued that numerical "parity" in any administrative body failed to take into account the fundamental inequality between capital and labor. It was not possible, Hilferding was certain, for capitalists and workers to relate on equal terms.[65]

Hilferding contended that Rathenau's scheme for labor and capital to co-operate would only reproduce the hierarchical structures of organized capital-ism and would undermine all attempts to establish democratic-socialist forms of administration. He wanted to expropriate the capitalists and create a new type of economy guided by wholly different principles and economic motiva-tions. This was only possible, he insisted, "when we exclude the capitalists as owners and win hardworking businessmen over as employees, leaders of the socialist economy."[66]

To move decisively away from capitalism, Hilferding argued that socialized industries should only reward those who perform real services in the process of production and distribution. Although he favored compensating nonfunc-tional shareholders for the loss of their expropriated property, he also argued that they should be eliminated from the decision-making process and denied further monetary benefits such as bonuses.[67] As Germany slipped further into economic crisis, Hilferding insisted that the only way out was to break with the profit motive and increase production within the framework of a new, centrally planned system that would meet the needs of all members of society.[68]

It was possible, Hilferding thought, to organize such an economy democ-ratically through workers' councils and economic parliaments, but pushing socialization forward depended on the political mobilization of the workers. In the fall and winter of 1920 his hopes for such a mobilization dissolved as the government resisted economic reforms and the workers' movement con-tinued to splinter. In February 1921, the cabinet of Konstantin Fehrenbach (Catholic Center party) announced its opposition to any socialization pro-gram. It was clear from the beginning that without an absolute socialist ma-jority in the Reichstag the passage of any radical reforms would be very diffi-cult. When the Foreign and Justice Ministries reported that the Allies might confiscate socialized property as a form of war reparations, the outcome was no longer in doubt.[69]

The government's decision clearly repudiated socialization, but by the time of its announcement the issue was no longer a burning one. Events fol-lowing the submission of the commission's report had decisively transformed Germany's political landscape. The USPD, despite the efforts of its leader-ship, was practically destroyed by another split, while a wave of reactionary terror threatened the republic's very existence.

On the surface, the USPD seemed to be the party best equipped to reunite the proletariat in 1920. The Independents published their Revolutionary Program in March 1919, and thereafter membership rose sharply as the SPD-led government suppressed the radical left and alienated many workers. Between January and October 1919, the USPD's membership climbed from 300,000 to 750,000 largely at the SPD's expense. Soon it appeared that the Independents would surpass the SPD in voting strength. In the Reichstag elections of June 1920, they won 18.8 percent of the vote, compared to the majority socialists' 21.6 percent. In the eighteen months since the elections to the National Assembly, the USPD had more than doubled its electoral support. This growth in membership and increased voting strength reflected its ability to take advantage of its position as the major socialist opposition party.[70]

The Independents also built up their organization and press. Hilferding worked hard at *Die Freiheit*, which quickly became Berlin's most widely read daily with a circulation of over two hundred thousand.[71] Hilferding's coworker Alexander Stein was inspired by his chief's untiring leadership and ability to mold the staff into a smoothly functioning, cooperative body. Hilferding was good-humored, innovative, and open-minded, and his subordinates respected him as an organizer, journalist, and party leader.[72] Given his other activities during this time, Hilferding's success at *Die Freiheit* was all the more remarkable. He regularly attended the meetings of the party executive committee, spoke at trade union and party conferences, and was an active member of the Socialization Commissions. That he could take on all these tasks, publish frequently, and direct a major newspaper bespeaks the dedication and energy that he devoted to the socialist cause.

Despite its apparent strength, by the summer of 1920 the USPD actually stood on the verge of collapse. Except for a brief interlude, when its various factions united to support the signing of the Treaty of Versailles, there was continual strife between the party's growing radical left wing and the center and right. Led by Ernst Däumig, Curt Geyer, and Walter Stoecker, the leftists grew increasingly impatient with parliamentary politics and rejected cooperation with the SPD. In the summer and fall of 1919, many worked to reinvigorate the councils movement, but their efforts foundered on disagreements with the SPD and the unions over the councils' future tasks. The radicals hungered for action and hoped that Germany's deepening economic crisis would fuel a new revolutionary upsurge.[73]

With the workers' movement divided, militarily defeated, and disarmed, Hilferding found the prospects for revolutionary action unfavorable and worked to steer the USPD onto a more moderate political course. At the party's Leipzig congress of December 1919, he supported the inclusion of most left-wing goals in a new Action Program but rejected abandoning parliamentary tactics. The latter remained a viable means of struggle, and he insisted that the party should fight to protect the democratic republic because it provided the most favorable conditions for the proletarian conquest of power.[74] Although this position managed to carry the day, the left's vociferous charges that Hilferding (along with other centrists) favored reunification with the SPD, disarming the workers, and dismantling the councils reflected the party's simmering factional antagonisms.[75] Tensions remained especially high on the question of the USPD's relationship to the Comintern, founded in Moscow in March 1919. It was this issue that ultimately split the party.

At the end of the war, any proposal to revive the Second International or found a new international workers' organization faced serious difficulties. The war broke the bonds that had previously enabled the parties to work together, while the Bolshevik victory and the split in German social democracy had changed the face of the international community. Differences of opinion on ideological and tactical matters separated the parties and made their cooperation in a single organization highly unlikely. In early 1919, when the parties of the Second International began an effort to resuscitate that organization, debate began in the USPD over its participation.

Clear divisions quickly emerged. Most Independents regarded the International's behavior in 1914 as a betrayal of socialism and were furious with the recent actions of the SPD. They rejected rejoining the old organization and, like Walter Stoecker, looked forward to the founding of a new "international of action."[76] A minority, including leaders such as Hilferding and Haase, thought that participating at least in the International's early meetings might clear the air and improve interparty relations. They were willing to rejoin if the organization could be revolutionized and could exclude the SPD.[77] Despite these clear differences of opinion, this issue initially did not appear to threaten party unity. In the midst of civil war, most USPD members were preoccupied with domestic problems. The founding of the Communist International, however, changed this situation. Soon many Independents began calling for affiliation with the Comintern, which they considered a truly revolutionary organization.

Lenin had outlined the goals of the Third International as early as 1915. Its task was to organize the workers for a revolutionary "civil war against the bourgeoisie in all countries in order to take over political power and ensure victory for socialism."[78] In 1919, the Bolsheviks established the Comintern to pursue these aims. To join the new organization required unconditional adherence to twenty-one conditions (formally announced in August 1920) that essentially removed all autonomy from the national parties and placed them under the control of the International's Bolshevik-dominated executive committee (ECCI) in Moscow. Following the Comintern's guidelines, all member parties were to transform themselves into Communist parties by rewriting their programs and restructuring their political organizations along democratic-centralist lines. Reformists and centrists, including "notorious opportunists," such as Hilferding, were to be expelled.[79]

Hilferding opposed the USPD's affiliation with the Comintern from its inception because he thought, with good cause, that the party would lose its freedom of action and isolate itself from the bulk of the proletariat, which was opposed to Bolshevism. As an alternative he advocated rebuilding the Second International along more radical lines. The USPD, he asserted, could not participate in an international that included the SPD or that was not prepared to organize for revolutionary action. The majority socialists had served the forces of counterrevolution by allying themselves with the bourgeoisie, disarming the workers, arming the reaction, abandoning class struggle, and using force against socialism. A reorganized international would have to expel such parties and reject reformism.[80]

A radicalized international, Hilferding thought, would have to clarify its goals and tighten its organization. To this end, he proposed a set of political aims and practical measures that attempted to meet the needs of the movement without sacrificing traditional social democratic principles. To abolish class struggle and establish a truly human society, the international must organize the fight to seize political power and socialize the means of production and exchange. It should construct a true society of nations that would include all peoples and maintain world peace. He suggested that the international be organized along social democratic lines but also called for a stronger executive committee empowered to make decisions that were binding on all member parties. Unlike the prewar Second International, the new organization would be able to act. He urged that it adopt both parliamentary and extraparliamentary tactics and stressed the need to combat the influence of bourgeois ideology on the proletariat.[81]

Hilferding was aware of the strong opposition in the party to the USPD's participation in the Lucerne Conference of the Second International, which met in August 1919. In July, he published a series of articles in *Die Freiheit* supporting the party's participation. On July 27, 1919, the USPD leadership decided to send Hilferding and the party's two cochairmen—Haase and Artur Crispien—to the conference in order "to bring the party's revolutionary point of view to bear against the reformist tendencies and counterrevolutionary position of the right-wing socialists."[82]

None of Hilferding's hopes were realized at Lucerne. A majority of the delegates rejected his sharp criticisms of the SPD as well as his proposals for radicalizing the organization. Although the conference went along with a USPD-supported minority resolution condemning the Allied intervention in Russia, the Independents' influence was minimal. To many USPD members, it was now clear that there could be no cooperation with the parties of the Second International, and most expected their leaders to take the next logical step and apply for membership in the Comintern.[83]

Over the course of the next year, however, Hilferding and his allies in the executive did everything in their power to forestall this step. In September, at a meeting of party leaders in Berlin, Hilferding compared joining the Comintern with climbing aboard a sinking ship. It was doubtful, he argued, that revolution could succeed in economically backward Russia where the counterrevolution was gaining strength. Only a socialist victory in the West could concretely aid the Bolsheviks, but this victory seemed unlikely in the near future. Hilferding pointed out that the USPD's affiliation to the Comintern would mean its complete acceptance of the Bolsheviks' program and methods, including terror. These were unsuitable for German conditions and would precipitate a civil war, paralyze the economy, and make the socialization of industry impossible.

Abandoning the Second International, Hilferding insisted, would leave the party isolated and impotent. The USPD could only stay in contact with the masses and push the French and English socialists to the left if it remained within the organization. Thinking along traditional Marxist lines, he argued that the International's future, like that of the revolution as a whole, depended on socialist unity in the West, where the consequences of the war would eventually drive the workers into the revolutionary camp.

Hilferding concluded his remarks by announcing that the USPD's leadership intended to contact all other left-wing groups and, with the help of the French socialists, would attempt to come to an understanding with the Bolsheviks. Time, he said, would work for the Independents. Eventually, it would be possible to create a revolutionary international.[84]

Walter Stoecker spoke for those at the conference who opposed Hilferding's position and rejected his contention that the USPD would have to surrender its independence to the Comintern. Stoecker argued that the Bolsheviks' attacks on the Independents' policies rested on false information and that few programmatic differences actually separated the two parties. He called for a decisive break with the Second International and asserted that, by joining the Comintern, the USPD and other radical parties could build the new international that all socialists wanted. Although no vote was taken, and it is not clear if a majority supported affiliation, Stoecker's view of the Bolsheviks had the sympathy of most delegates.[85]

Following the debate at the Berlin conference there could be no doubt that the USPD's relationship to the Comintern would be a major issue at the upcoming Leipzig party congress. The exchange between Hilferding and Stoecker stimulated a broad discussion on all levels of the party and it soon became obvious that a majority of the membership favored adherence to Moscow. Hilferding continued to firmly reject the Comintern, but he soon gave up his demand to remain in the Second International. Instead he suggested the formation of a new international, one that incorporated the revolutionary parties of the Western industrialized states, in which he thought the fate of socialism would be decided.

On the morning of December 4, 1919, Hilferding opened the Leipzig congress discussion of the Comintern with a speech elaborating his new position.[86] Rejecting any further USPD cooperation with the Second International, he also warned the party against linking its fortunes with those of the Comintern and undertook a detailed critique of Bolshevik policies and the socioeconomic conditions that shaped them. In his view, the political situation in Russia on the eve of the world war had been fundamentally different from that in the West. Russia had been on the verge of a revolution; the bourgeoisie, the peasantry, and the proletariat were poised to overthrow tsarist rule. The structure of Russian society was suited for a "bourgeois-peasant revolution" under proletarian leadership and this, he claimed, was the nature of the revolution that occurred in February 1917 (315).

According to Hilferding, the military and economic disintegration that continued after this bourgeois-peasant revolution made it possible for the Bolshevik party to seize power and to establish a proletarian dictatorship, but political success could not guarantee the victory of socialism in war-ravaged Russia. "In the long run," he explained, "no policy can remove itself from the constraints of the materialist conception of history, or to put it another way, from the determination *[Bestimmung]* of economic relations, and we have learned from Marx that the role of force in economics is limited" (315). Hilferding asserted that the Bolsheviks were aware of the problems they would face if the revolution were confined to Russia. They hoped to spread revolution because they knew that only when Russia was linked to the industrialized West was the transition to socialism possible. The failure of the revolution in the West was a devastating blow to the Bolsheviks' plans. Economically and politically isolated, the only way the regime could overcome its severe domestic crisis was to restore capitalism by loosening state controls on peasant and small producers and by making economic concessions to technical specialists and intellectuals.

The revolutionary government's retreat on the economic front and its resort to terror in the civil war indicated the weakness of the Communist position. It was out of desperation, Hilferding argued, that the Bolsheviks continued to pin their hopes on world revolution, and this same desperation had motivated them to hurriedly form the Comintern. By molding this organization into a reliable instrument of their policy, the Communists intended to use its member parties to carry out decisions made in Moscow's interests. To ensure their control, they would be willing to split workers' parties everywhere and further divide the movement.

Such sentiments were not popular among the Independents, and Hilferding sought to bolster his position by describing Bolshevik behavior toward the USPD. He pointed to Lenin's virulent attacks on virtually every faction within the party, to his withering critique of its Revolutionary Program, and to the Bolsheviks' condemnation of the decision to support the signing of the Versailles treaty. Joining the Comintern, he insisted, meant abandoning the party's principles and surrendering its independence (317–21).

The future of socialism, Hilferding reminded his listeners, would not be decided in the East, where the counterrevolution was on the march, but in the West. Revolution there was not imminent, he conceded, but conditions were gradually radicalizing the proletariat, and the spread of parliamentary democracy gave the socialist parties the most room to maneuver (313–14). Rather than the party's isolating itself by unilaterally joining the Comintern, he proposed founding a new international that would include all parties (even those in the Comintern), that would reject compromise with the bourgeoisie and aim for the establishment of a proletarian dictatorship. Admission to the new international should not depend on the rigid adherence to any particular program. On the contrary, each party should have the freedom to adapt its tactics to local conditions. In closing, he appealed to the delegates to support a conference of like-minded parties that would discuss the rebuilding of the international and establish contacts with the Bolsheviks (321–26).

Hilferding's assessment of conditions in Russia and their impact on the Bolsheviks' policies proved prophetic. By 1921 the failure of the revolution in the West forced the Bolshevik regime to relax its controls over peasant and small producers in order to restart the economy; and his prediction that the Comintern intended to split the workers' movement was also accurate. Hilferding supported close cooperation with the Western socialist parties not only because he believed that the revolution could only succeed in states where modern industry would provide the material basis for a socialist society, but also because he rejected Bolshevik attempts to intervene in German socialist politics. He had always believed that social democratic parties should base their policies on existing conditions in their respective countries, and he was not prepared to allow the USPD to subordinate its interests to those of the Bolsheviks. He consistently supported international cooperation between socialist parties (including the Bolsheviks) but insisted on the preservation of his own party's autonomy.

At Leipzig in December 1919 only a handful of Independents backed Hilferding's position. Much more popular were the views of Stoecker, who supported unconditional affiliation with the Comintern. The factions eventually hammered out a compromise resolution agreeing with the Third International's goal of establishing "socialism on the basis of the councils system by means of the dictatorship of the proletariat" and charged the leadership with negotiating a union of all parties in basic agreement with the USPD's Action Program, including the Third International.[87] This vaguely worded compromise won majority support but did not resolve the issue. The left made this especially clear by pushing through an amendment stipulating that "should the parties of other countries not be inclined to enter the Moscow International with us, the adherence of the USPD is to be undertaken alone."[88] Thus, although a majority of the delegates voted in favor of the compromise, the question of the party's relationship to the Comintern remained open.

Hilferding maintained the views he elaborated at Leipzig throughout 1920, but his critique—of the Bolsheviks' usurpation of soviet power, of their elimination of dissent, and of their use of terror—became increasingly vehement. To those who labeled him a "brakeman of the revolution," he responded that one had to recognize the harsh reality of the Communists' policies. "The brain," he reminded his comrades, "is an organ that inhibits! But that is no reason to deem it counterrevolutionary and shut it down."[89] In August 1920, a schism became unavoidable following the publication of the Comintern's Twenty-One Conditions, which, if accepted, mandated the expulsion of the USPD's center and right wing.

Two months later an extraordinary party congress met in Halle to settle the issue. Gregor Zinoviev, chairman of the Comintern, delivered an impassioned four-hour speech in which he argued that a split in the USPD was necessary to further the world revolution. Hilferding, equally impassioned, provided the minority's reply. Despite his best efforts there was little he could say to sway the views of the delegates, most of whom had been elected on the basis of their position on the Comintern issue.[90] In the end the left won a clear majority with 236 delegates voting in favor of accepting the Twenty-One Conditions and uniting with the small KPD. The other 156 delegates rejected affiliation and remained in the USPD. The party had been devastated. Although it retained about three hundred thousand members and still possessed a sizable press, its total membership fell by more than one-half and it never recovered its voting strength.

We have no record of Hilferding's immediate reaction to the party split; no doubt he expected it and watched its accomplishment with mixed feelings. He doubtless regarded the further division of the workers' movement as a major setback in the fight for socialism, but he may also have felt relieved that the fractious infighting was now over, leaving the USPD free to pursue its goals relatively unhindered by internal strife. Already dubious in 1919 about the revolution's prospects, the defeats of 1920 convinced Hilferding that the socialist revolution in Germany had been halted. Thereafter he worked to re-unify the social democratic left, not in order to push the revolution forward but primarily to protect the parliamentary republic against the growing strength of the reactionary right.

Hilferding explained his priorities after Halle in a speech delivered in late February 1921, at a meeting of the Vienna Union, a new organization established by twenty socialist parties that aimed, ultimately, to reunite the workers' movement.[91] Turning his attention first to the issue of reparations, he asserted that Germany should pay to rebuild destroyed areas in France and Belgium in order to help reconcile the former belligerents and reduce nationalist fervor. Current Allied demands on Germany, he insisted, were unreasonable, impossible to fulfill, and damaging to working-class interests. To pay the enormous sums demanded by the Entente (226 billion gold marks), would require Germany to export as much as possible in order to earn hard currency. Increased exports, however, required the importation of larger quantities of raw materials and food. How, Hilferding asked, could Germany accomplish this feat when foreign markets were shrinking due to the postwar recession and when reparations required all of the nation's import earnings? Exorbitant reparations, he contended, in conjunction with the international recession, would devastate the German economy as inflation and unemployment rose and living standards fell.[92]

A socialist economy with a rational planning system, Hilferding thought, would have facilitated Germany's ability to pay. Under capitalism, international competition made planning much more difficult. He expressed confidence that Germany could meet its obligations by raising production and increasing exports, but only if the Allies refrained from military or economic coercion. He predicted, accurately, that economic sanctions or foreign occupation of the industrial Ruhr or Silesia would fuel mass unemployment, widespread hunger, and political chaos. In such a situation, he asserted, even a socialist seizure of power could do little to improve matters. For this reason, the USPD rejected any policy aimed at inducing such a catastrophe.

Hilferding found the formation of the Vienna Union a necessary response to the bankruptcy of the Second International and the Comintern. Only a class-conscious proletariat could rescue socialism from the failures of the past and make possible the achievement of a just postwar settlement and the reconstruction of economic life. The Vienna Union's task was to push forward the international class struggle against imperialism and to raise the class-consciousness of workers everywhere. Violence, he stressed, offered no solution to the workers' plight except as a response to ruling-class aggression.

As Hilferding's comments make clear, he had not discarded views on the goals and methods of the workers' movement that he had developed before 1914. For him, the enlightenment of the working class, international cooperation, and nonviolent methods of class struggle remained the central elements of social democratic politics. Following Halle, he hoped that the USPD's united front policy would promote the reunification of the workers' movement by drawing all the proletarian parties into a unified struggle for key reforms, such as socialization.[93]

By the summer of 1921, however, right-wing political victories in key *Länder* and increased rightist terror convinced Hilferding that the defense of the republic was the socialist movement's highest priority. The counterrevolution was in full swing. The Versailles treaty and the worsening economic crisis had pushed large sectors of the middle class into the arms of the nationalist right, which held power in Prussia and Bavaria and had consolidated its control over the bureaucracy, the courts, the universities, and the schools. These developments, he believed, created a situation in which proletarian unity was imperative to defend the gains won since November 1918. As a concrete step toward reunification, Hilferding proposed cooperation between the workers' parties on the local level.[94]

This was not the first time that he had urged the USPD to cooperate with its socialist rivals, especially the SPD. Despite his sharp criticisms of the majority socialists, Hilferding had long supported joint efforts in specific situations. In the spring of 1919, for example, fear of nationalist reaction had motivated him to back the SPD-led government's decision to sign the Treaty of

Versailles, and after the Kapp Putsch in 1920, he had been willing to commit the USPD to a coalition with the SPD and the trade unions. In 1921, his hopes that a working union of socialist parties on the local level would lead to unity proved premature. He remained firmly convinced, however, that the differences between the USPD and the SPD became less important as Germany's economic and political crisis worsened. Unity would develop, he insisted, not as a consequence of interparty discussion, but as the result of the workers' struggle to defend their class interests.[95]

A variety of factors hindered cooperation with the majority socialists in 1921. Their adoption in September of the reformist Görlitz Program and their willingness to consider entering a coalition government with the industry-backed German People's Party (DVP) met with a negative reaction among the Independents. Such differences continued to divide the two parties until, as Hilferding had foreseen, the worsening domestic situation in mid-1922 finally brought them together.

Hilferding was elected to the USPD central committee at the party's Leipzig congress in January 1922, but this post did not shield him from the sharp criticism of his colleagues as his views began to diverge from the general outlook of the party leadership. His strong support for unity, his advocacy of indirect taxes as a means of halting spiraling inflation, and his recent doubts about the expediency of the USPD's refusal to consider coalitions with nonsocialist parties, led the executive to accuse him and his colleagues at *Die Freiheit* of violating party principles. Crispien and Georg Ledebour charged Hilferding with attempting to undermine the party's independence by bringing its policies into line with those of the SPD in preparation for reunification. Hilferding did not wish to become the focus of major factional conflict; after defending his tax recommendations on economic grounds and denying any deviation from the party's program, he and most of his staff resigned.[96]

Despite the party leadership's radical posturing during the *Freiheit* affair, within a few months of Hilferding's resignation the political situation in Germany made cooperation between the USPD and the SPD a matter of necessity. On July 2, 1922, following foreign minister Walther Rathenau's assassination by right-wing radicals, the Independents announced their willingness to participate in a coalition government with the SPD and the moderate bourgeois parties in order to protect the republic. Although the bourgeois parties blocked the USPD's entrance into a new coalition, the renewed dialogue between the two socialist parties marked an important step toward unity. In July, their Reichstag delegations began to cooperate and soon afterward negotiating teams worked out a program for reunification. Hilferding was a leading member of the USPD delegation to these negotiations. In September 1922, after each party held its own congress to formally settle the matter, USPD and SPD delegates met in Nuremberg to form a united party.[97]

The Nuremberg congress elected Hilferding to the reunited party's executive committee and he soon became one of its leading spokespersons. In contrast to the hopes he had expressed in November 1918, he now adopted a more sober view of what the socialist movement could achieve, given Germany's political and economic realities. He elaborated his position in a December article in *Die Frankfurter Zeitung*:

> The great goals remain the same, but simple propaganda is no longer satisfactory; it is necessary [for the party] to show the practical way and to place the next step for the carrying out of immediate tasks in the foreground. [The party] must conquer a majority or form alliances in order to carry out the demands [it] made while in the opposition. It must reckon with the call to carry out its program and must, therefore, hold its demands within the limits of the possible. . . . Because the social and political distribution of power is clear cut in a developed democracy, the use of extraparliamentary means is limited.[98]

Hilferding was convinced that the most important result of the collapse of 1918 was the creation of a parliamentary democracy that allowed the parties to represent the people and control the state. He asserted that, in order for democracy to survive and to promote government stability, the parties had to break with the dogmatic interest-group politics of the past and seek to expand their influence among other social groups. He was arguing, in other words, that Social Democracy should strive to become a "people's" rather than solely a "working-class" party.

That social democracy should use parliamentary institutions to promote reforms was a view that Hilferding had long defended, but his outlook in 1922 differed in important ways from that of the prewar years. Before the war, he had never argued so forcefully that Social Democracy had to reach out to nonproletarian groups in order to win a majority, and he had never put such stress on the need for social compromise to make democracy work. On the contrary, he had envisioned the SPD winning a parliamentary majority that—barring civil war brought on by reactionary class forces—would enable the working class to build a new socialist order. The collapse of the workers' movement after 1914 and the civil war that followed the fall of the monarchy fundamentally altered this view. He now believed that it would take time and many compromises to build a unified, class-conscious proletariat and to create a broad, cross-class social consensus that would make socialism possible.

Hilferding thought that the new capitalist republic provided a framework that would allow social democracy to achieve reforms that would lead to socialism. In this sense, this leader of the Marxist center was now standing squarely on the same ground as Bernstein. But willingness to reach out to other groups in order to build social democracy and achieve concrete reforms should not be equated with accepting the revisionists' theoretical or ideological arguments. Hilferding often was ready to alter his theoretical conclusions if he thought empirical evidence demanded it. He remained,

however, fundamentally a man of Erfurt and believed that the historical tra-
jectory elaborated in the old program was correct in its essentials. After reunification, he would work to adapt Erfurt's theoretical principles to the
changes that had occurred in recent years. Along with the revisionists, he saw
reform as the realistic road to fundamental social and political change, but he
was not necessarily willing to follow them theoretically.

Hilferding had come a long way since August 1914, when, as a leading
member of the Marxist center, he broke with the party leadership he had supported for so long. With the collapse of the monarchy, he found himself
forced by circumstances to become a revolutionary activist and he struggled
for the realization of ideas that he hoped would reunite the workers' movement and lay the foundation for democratic socialism in Germany. The defeat
of the socialist revolution and the creation of a capitalist republic led him
back to his roots in the SPD. He had become a faithful supporter of the
Weimar Republic and would remain one until the bitter end.

CHAPTER FOUR

THE REPUBLICAN THEORIST

In Germany we often hear from well-meaning opponents that social democracy has changed, that it is no longer so removed from reality as it was before the war. I believe that our opponents are mistaken. . . . It is not us, it is not socialism, it is not social democracy that has come nearer to reality, but reality that has come nearer to socialism.

—*Rudolf Hilferding (1925)*

Karl Kautsky first envisioned Hilferding as his successor at *Die Neue Zeit* in 1904, but almost two decades passed before Hilferding stepped into his mentor's shoes.[1] Hilferding's appointment, in 1923, to the chief editorship of the SPD's new theoretical journal, *Die Gesellschaft* (Society), marked his accession as the party's "chief ideologist." His direct influence over the SPD leadership, however, surpassed Kautsky's. Unlike his predecessor, Hilferding also served on the party's executive committee and in the Reichstag, where, from 1922 to 1933 he was a powerful influence on the SPD's theoretical and practical policies.

Under Weimar, Hilferding's tasks as a theorist were similar, in many ways, to those of the prewar era when he worked to promote unity in the face of conflict over the SPD's ideological principles and political strategy. Yet now the war, the division of the workers' movement, and the founding of the republic fundamentally altered the context within which he had to operate.

Prior to 1914, social democracy had seen itself as a radical alternative to the imperial status quo; following the monarchy's collapse it became a pillar of the new constitutional order. Many Germans, especially but not solely on the right, associated this new system with defeat, humiliation, and chaos, whereas the radical left, including some social democrats, regarded its creation as either a betrayal of the proletariat or a shabby compromise of its interests. Hilferding strongly believed that for a "politics of the possible" to succeed, the SPD's long-term strategy required participation in government, compromise with rival political parties, and the expansion of its influence among nonproletarian social groups. Such a strategy risked alienating substantial elements of the SPD's constituency, especially that part most concerned with the party's goal of fulfilling the proletariat's historical mission through the establishment of socialism. Here lay the crux of the challenge Hilferding faced: to construct a theoretical framework that would allow the party to pursue a two-track approach in which "every socialist must fight while holding two flags. In one hand, the fight for the present, for the republic of black, red, and gold, but in the other the flag of the future, the red flag of the socialists."[2]

Thus, in his programmatic writings after 1922, Hilferding formulated an

The Party Central Committee, 1926. Hilferding stands in the middle of the second row.
Hermann Müller sits to his left, Otto Wels to his right.

approach that aimed to appeal to the SPD's ideologically committed supporters while compromising with rivals and attracting new social groups, including peasants and white-collar workers, whose interests sometimes clashed
with those of industrial workers. Using organized capitalism as a theoretical
framework, he promoted a parliamentary strategy to enhance the party's influence over the state in order to carry out socialist economic and political reforms. When the SPD pursued this course during Weimar's "golden years" of
relative economic and political stability, it appeared to meet with at least partial success. There is no question that the "social state" expanded substantially and that the SPD began to take on the characteristics of a *Volkspartei*
(people's party).[3] But when Germany's economic and political realities shattered this policy's theoretical and practical premises, neither Hilferding nor
his colleagues in the leadership were able to put forward a viable socialist response to the nation's most pressing problems.[4]

The new SPD executive committee elected at Nuremberg included only
three former Independent leaders: Hilferding, who was elected to the post of
Beisitzer (associate); Wilhelm Dittmann, who became a party secretary; and
Artur Crispien, who was elected cochairman along with Otto Wels and Hermann Müller.[5] Ostensibly representing the reunited party's left wing, none of
these men presented a serious challenge to the reformist consensus advocated
by the twenty-two-member executive. Crispien and Dittmann exerted little
influence, and Hilferding (as we have seen) had come to accept the SPD's
"pragmatic" political course. This outlook made it easy for most majority socialist leaders—such as Wels and Müller—to relegate his earlier criticisms of
their policies to the past. Wels held Hilferding's theoretical talents in high es-
teem, and Müller had long considered him one of the "reasonable" elements
in the USPD. They valued Hilferding's economic expertise and, even more
important, hoped that he could place social democracy's political strategy
within a sound theoretical framework.[6]

In his essays in *Die Gesellschaft,* and in keynote speeches to the party congresses of 1924, 1925, and 1927, Hilferding laid out the basic theoretical
principles and broad strategic aims that justified and guided the SPD's policies until the fall of the republic.[7] "Ten years have passed since the outbreak
of the war," he observed in *Die Gesellschaft*'s inaugural issue, "but the world
has been unable to find its economic, political or intellectual balance."
Whereas Marx had been able to "return to the study" during the "lull" that
followed the failed revolution of 1848, contemporary political conditions
made such detachment impossible. Instead, social scientists had to identify
the key forces and developmental tendencies at work in society and use this
knowledge in ongoing political struggles. The economy, domestic politics,
and the new international order all engaged Hilferding's attention as he as-
sessed developments after 1914.[8]

In Hilferding's view, the economic processes that he had identified before
and during the war were accelerating: the expansion and further concentration

of capital, the formation of cartels and trusts, and the increasing influence of finance capital were bringing the era of capitalist competition to a close. In place of the anarchic system of competitive capitalism, a new system was developing, characterized by economic regulation and planned production. If left undisturbed this process would create a hierarchical social order in which the economy was indeed "organized," but the means of production would remain in capitalist hands (2).

This new system secured capitalists' interests. Improved long-term investment planning by the large corporations, in conjunction with credit regulation by the big banks and the state central bank, were among the means capital could use to reduce the "unsteadiness" of the economy and the impact of crises. A smoothly functioning economy and unemployment insurance would reduce the threat of joblessness, while various forms of social insurance, fewer working hours, and improved wages would make increasingly mechanized, intensive factory work more bearable. As the labor process grew more specialized, Hilferding expected the size of the white-collar workforce *(Angestellte)* to increase. All of these developments, he concluded, would have a stabilizing effect and promote the integration of workers into the economic order.

Despite these conservative tendencies, Hilferding believed that the "antagonistic foundation" of such an economy "compels struggle." The more advanced the organization and the more conscious its regulation, the more the owners' usurpation of economic power and wealth would become unbearable to the masses, who would fight to democratize the system. Thus, "just when [capitalism] has achieved its highest level of organization, it presents the problem of economic democracy" (3).

For Hilferding, the development of economic democracy was part of "a long-term historical process" (3) in which the economy came under constantly expanding democratic controls. In this process, workers acquired the skills and sense of responsibility necessary to participate in the direction of production. Such a psychological change, Hilferding thought, was essential and required not only the "schooling" that one gained in struggle, but also parallel, purposeful educational work *(Erziehungsarbeit)*. In the effort to educate themselves to control production, workers had to overcome the social injustice that denied them access to knowledge, culture, and educational opportunity. By overcoming these as well as economic barriers to equality, they would learn to recognize the differences between political and economic democracy, and that the latter was only possible when everyone had equal opportunity for advancement. Hilferding did not believe that economic democracy would eliminate functional differences in the production process or the naturally differing aptitudes of individuals at work. Its main aim was to ensure each person the same point of departure in the quest for individual achievement.[9]

Hilferding thought that working-class organizations would play an essential role in the achievement of economic reforms. The task of the trade unions and factory councils was to work not only for economic improvements for the workers *(Sozialpolitik)*, but also for the democratization of the production process *(demokratische Produktionspolitik)*. In Hilferding's view, this struggle for democratization transformed the sociopolitical ideology of socialism from a mere abstraction into something more concrete. Socialism was now "the real content of the [proletarian] struggle for influence on the regulated and organized economy."[10]

While the democratization of individual enterprises was important, much more decisive for the transformation of the whole economy was control over the state. "In reality," Hilferding explained,

> organized capitalism means the replacement of the capitalist principle of free competition, by the socialist principle of planned production. This planned, consciously directed economy is subject to a much higher degree of social intervention, which means nothing other than the activity of society's only conscious organization equipped with coercive power . . . the state.[11]

The most important question now facing the working class was how to use the state to democratize the economy and thus aid the transition to socialism. Hilferding fervently believed that the founding of a democratic republic made it possible for the proletariat to use its hard-won political freedoms to win economic freedom as well. The SPD had to pursue a flexible parliamentary strategy that did not rule out forming coalition governments with bourgeois parties in particular circumstances.

In urging social democrats to stand unreservedly behind the republic and to view it as an instrument of socialist transition, Hilferding developed a theory of the state that differed significantly from Marx's. Although he thought Marx had identified a "decisive feature" of the state when he asserted it was both a social and a political institution that functioned as an instrument of the dominant classes, Hilferding felt that Marx's definition was unsatisfactory "because it [was] valid for all state formations since the beginning of class society" (170) and failed to clarify the different characteristics of the state's development. In Hilferding's view, the modern state consisted of a government *(Regierung)*, an administrative apparatus, and a citizenry, but its most "essential element" was its political parties, "because only by means of this medium could the individual express his [political] will" (171). In his model, the "citizenry" spoke through the various parties, and these stood next to the government and apparatus as institutional pillars of the state. Such an analysis, Hilferding asserted, "recognized the basis of Marx's definition, because the struggle between the parties *(Parteikampf)* reflects nothing other than the struggle between the classes. The struggle between the parties, therefore, is an expression of class antagonisms" (171).

Although Hilferding's argument stressed the centrality of class struggle, he broke with Marx by claiming that the parliamentary state, unlike the authoritarian state of the pre-1918 era, was no longer controlled by the capitalist elite. Scornful of those who described the republic as a "bourgeois democracy," he argued that the parliamentary system represented "a completely different technique in the formation of the public will *[Staatswillens]*," and that the latter was composed of nothing other than "the political will of individuals" (172). The state was no longer an organization of the "rulers" *(Herrschenden)* standing in opposition to the Reichstag, "now the rulers had to turn to the citizenry and, in intellectual conflict with [social democracy], allow a majority to confirm their continued domination" (173). Thus, Hilferding saw the democratic state as a neutral institution at the disposal of any political party or group of parties that could win a majority and form a government. Workers had the power to shape state policy in their own interest by actively using parliament. Social Democratic participation in government would open the way for socialism through the achievement of major political and economic reforms.[12]

Hilferding's postwar economic and political analyses did not break decisively with his prewar views. Variations in his conclusions regarding the direction of economic development or the use of political tactics were primarily in emphasis. The theoretical core of "organized capitalism" was already well developed in *Finance Capital,* and Hilferding saw his arguments concerning the growth and increasing concentration of capital confirmed by changes in the economy during and after the war. What was new in Hilferding's analysis stemmed from his acceptance in 1915 of Bernstein's contention that the centralization and concentration of industry and the increased use of planning would ultimately ease the impact of crises. The implications of this shift in his theoretical outlook remained hidden during the war when Hilferding believed that worsening conditions could spark an anticapitalist upheaval. It was only after the social revolution failed, and he had concluded that the revolutionary path to socialism was closed, that his revised "crisis theory" took on more concrete importance. Hilferding became convinced that if the "socialist principle of planned production" could develop under the conditions of the authoritarian *Kaiserreich,* then this process of socialist evolution could be accelerated and completed within the democratic republic.

He did not, however, believe that the evolutionary transition to socialism was inevitable; only continual work in the economic and political spheres would make fundamental change possible. In keeping with this belief, he emphasized the need for the socialist movement to politically educate the masses. Hilferding considered himself a thinker in the tradition of the eighteenth-century philosophes, who had precipitated an intellectual upheaval that opened the way for later political and social revolutions. Shocked by the postwar "rebellion against intellect and science," he urged socialist intellectuals to combat this trend and thereby contribute to the movement's practical efforts. Hilferding once remarked that, "it is the task of socialist intellectuals [and] . . . all socialists . . . to appropriate theoretical insight and thereby become better political counselors." Concretely this meant that activists had to take their views to the masses and educate them concerning the political tasks at hand. Having believed in the efficacy of such political enlightenment since his student days in Vienna, it was only logical that under the parliamentary republic, in which political rivalries supposedly were fought out by intellectual means, he reemphasized the need for education as a prerequisite for radical change.[13]

Hilferding's conclusion that a republican framework channeled class struggle into the electoral arena also reflected his long-held belief that the parliamentary system created the possibility of a peaceful road to socialism. Under the monarchy he had recognized that conservative forces might attempt to block workers' efforts to use or expand their democratic rights, and he had thought that violent revolution would be the likely result. After the consolidation of the capitalist republic, however, his view of the state's neutrality led him to misjudge the nature and function of that institution as well as the strength of the system's opponents. Hilferding was aware, of course, that the republic had dangerous enemies, and he argued repeatedly that republicans had the right and the duty to use all means to defend the state.[14] At the same time, however, he maintained an optimism concerning the stability of the Weimar political system that bore little relation to the antirepublican reality of German society. Hilferding criticized German philosophy for "absolutizing and deifying" the state,[15] but his own theoretical work emulated its "metaphysical" methods and ignored the republic's weakness. By assuming that the parliamentary state was a politically neutral institution, he denied the close connections between Germany's economic and social elites and the state's conservative apparatus. He placed the state outside society, detached from its social roots, and in so doing lost sight of the very social forces that undermined the SPD's reformist project and ultimately destroyed the system.[16]

Whereas Hilferding's views on economic development, political education, and the parliamentary republic were rooted in his prewar thought, his concept of economic democracy developed in light of the events following the German revolution. Before 1918, his writings on the transition to socialism, however vague, had focused primarily on the actions of the revolutionary state in the creation of a socialist economy. The rise of the councils movement had forced him to reconsider his views. Hilferding never supported a "council republic," but during the revolution and afterward he accepted the idea that councils should play an important role in democratizing the production process and socializing the economy. Like Otto Bauer, he was influenced not only by the impact of the councils at home, but also by the growth of a similar "guild socialist" movement in England.[17] The guild socialists aimed to arrive at a compromise between syndicalism and state socialism, both of which they regarded as too one-sided. They agreed with the syndicalist demand for producer control in industry, but they also saw the validity of the state-socialist stress on the needs of the community as a whole. The guild socialists held that one should neglect neither the producer nor the consumer, and their leading exponent, G. D. H. Cole, argued that the historic task of the movement was to "hold the balance between these two schools of thought."[18]

Hilferding developed views on the socialization of production that were much like those of the guild socialists. He stressed that the socialization process had to balance the interests of various groups in order to preserve civil peace, and his suggestions for the reorganization of German industry and the establishment of a "council parliament" were similar to theirs. The guild socialists called for the unification of all (blue- and white-collar) workers in each branch of industry into self-governing guilds. The guilds would, in turn, elect representatives to a national guild parliament that would cooperate with the political parliament and guide British economic life. The parallels between the guild socialists' proposals for Britain and Hilferding's recommendations for Germany are clear and it is not surprising that he enthusiastically welcomed the movement's growth. He was particularly impressed with the guild socialists' view of the trade unions, which they charged with the task of overcoming the barriers between different types of workers and fighting for control over the production process itself. These activities were important, Hilferding thought, because they extended the issue of socialist construction from the formal political arena squarely into the workplace. Now the unions and the party could fundamentally challenge capital "in every sphere."[19]

Although Hilferding regarded the workplace as a key zone of conflict in the fight for socialism, he also kept a clear focus on Social Democracy's fight for state power. Like many other party leaders, he knew that to win power and wield it effectively the SPD would have to expand its political base. In all of his keynote speeches to the party congresses in the mid-1920s, he urged his comrades to fight for the support not only of nonsocialist industrial workers but also of the "intellectual workers" (geistige Arbeiter), the rapidly expanding white-collar workforce (Angestellte), and the peasantry. Hilferding clearly recognized that the white-collar sector was expanding much more rapidly than the industrial labor force. In addition, he found flawed the party's long-held view of the peasantry. Indeed, small-scale peasant production had not succumbed to competition with large-scale farms and it was time to work out a new policy that would meet the needs of small peasants without contradicting working-class interests.[20]

Hilferding's call for the SPD to look beyond the industrial proletariat for support reflected a shift in the leadership's outlook that was expressed in the Görlitz Program of 1921 and continued after the acceptance of the more "orthodox" Heidelberg Program of 1925. By 1930, the party's effort to broaden its appeal had met with modest success. At that time, 60 percent of its membership came from the industrial working class (especially skilled workers), 14 percent from white-collar employees and officials (who comprised about 16 percent of the total workforce), and the remainder from scattered support in other middle-class groups. The party's backing at the polls reflected the changing composition of its membership; 40 percent of its voters after 1930 came from the middle classes. As Peter Lösche and Franz Walter convincingly have argued, toward the end of the Weimar period the SPD certainly was on its way to becoming a Volkspartei, but the republic's short life prevented the completion of this process.[21]

Indeed, the SPD made little headway among Catholics, small businessmen, rural workers, or peasants. The reasons for its difficulties are complex. For example, despite the leadership's insistence on religious toleration, many rank-and-file members sympathized with the "free thinker" movement and were uninterested in reaching out to the religious population. Also, the continued belief among many socialists that socioeconomic development and "enlightenment" would ultimately drive the middle classes into their ranks did little to attract individuals from these groups who resisted the notion that they had interests in common with industrial workers or that they inevitably would be proletarianized. On the other hand, in many cases, when middle-class people did join the party, they often adhered to its radical wing and set up socialist professional organizations (for example, of doctors, government officials, and so on) whose policies and ideas alienated others from the same social station. Finally, social democracy's very success in creating a feeling of solidarity among its members and linking them by means of a vast network of political, economic, and cultural institutions tended to inhibit the party's ability to build bridges to new constituencies. For many socialist workers, the crises of the 1920s and 1930s confirmed the importance of class struggle and the need to stick together within their *Solidargemeinschaft*. This community may have given those most committed to the movement a sense of strength and security, but it also tended to isolate social democracy from potential allies.[22]

Nowhere was the difficulty of reaching out to new constituencies more evident than in the SPD's attempt to win the support of the peasantry. Here we see a clear case in which the leadership's ability to radically change the party's official attitude and policy toward a major social group was only just a start in the process of bridge building. Without the organizational capability to win over the peasants, the social democrats had little chance of establishing ties to a group that, for good historical reasons, was unreceptive to their new message.

Hilferding urged the party to appeal to the peasants because he believed that they would survive as a class. He based his outlook on the mistaken impression that the law of increasing capitalist concentration in industry did not apply in agriculture. In industry, Hilferding argued, the prices of commodities are ultimately determined by the lowest costs of production; in agriculture the situation is reversed. Widespread variations in soil fertility, local farming conditions, the location of markets, and other largely natural factors prevent production from keeping pace with demand and result in a long-term tendency for prices to rise. High prices in turn cause technological innovation and productivity in agriculture to lag behind that of industry; they also allow small peasant proprietors to survive.

Hilferding suggested that the best way to protect the interests of both urban consumers and peasant producers was to reduce agricultural prices by increasing farm productivity. Increased production resulting from improved techniques would maintain peasant incomes and simultaneously stabilize food costs for urban workers. "It was not feasible," he wrote,

> to transfer peasant property into the hands of the state. It was feasible, however, to set up a grain monopoly as a means of making peasant producers independent from wildly fluctuating market prices. At the same time, social [meaning state] influence on price formation would make it possible to influence trends in production.[23]

Despite his disclaimers, Hilferding's analysis marked a significant revision of Marxism and illustrated his misunderstanding of Weimar's agricultural problems. Theoretically, Hilferding's claim that the economic laws of capitalist industry did not apply in agriculture contradicted Marx's most basic arguments concerning capitalism's laws of motion. In practical terms, it was ironic that he postulated a long-term increase in agricultural prices just as a crushing agricultural depression was getting under way. It was true, as Hilferding pointed out, that even in advanced industrial countries various forms of agricultural property continued to exist side by side, including small holdings. But the small peasantry's inexorable decline, however slow, was well underway throughout the modern capitalist states. As useful as some of his concrete suggestions for improvements in the countryside may have been, his economic analysis, drawn up in part to justify a particular political strategy, flew in the face of this reality.[24]

In 1927 the SPD's new agricultural program incorporated many of Hilferding's suggestions for tax and credit inducements, educational opportunities, land redistribution, and government regulation of prices. The peasants, however, largely ignored it.[25] The SPD's organization in the countryside was weak and the party lacked agitators who knew the issues and could effectively speak to rural people. Moreover, the peasants remained implacably opposed to the party's support for free trade, which would expose them to competition from cheap foreign grain. Rather than ally themselves with a party that had long predicted their inevitable demise, the peasants stood together with the *Junker* elite and later with the Nazis to demand protection for a way of life threatened by modernization.[26] Thus, Social Democracy's foray into the countryside failed in the face of conflicting social and economic interests.

The SPD's difficulties in expanding its political base reflect the splintering of Weimar's political culture into ideologically and socially hostile interest groups. Hilferding's own work highlights the extent to which the SPD's commitment to parliamentarianism, however sincere, was fraught with tensions. He encouraged the party to reach out to nonproletarian groups in an effort to build the movement, and in certain situations he advocated compromise and cooperation with rival parties in order to protect the republic. At the same time, however, he never abandoned his understanding of Marx's historical vision and of the unique role of the proletariat within it. For Hilferding, as well as for most other socialist leaders, the party's commitment to the working class remained a powerful one. This continued identification with the interests of the proletariat hindered the SPD's effort to broaden its support. In a republic in which the political culture was extremely fragmented and polarized, during times of crisis the SPD tended to focus mainly on the concerns of its traditional constituency. After the onset of the depression in 1929, this tendency functioned to limit the party's political flexibility and appeal in the face of the republic's most severe challenges.[27]

Hilferding's support for the democratic republic, his emphasis on economic democracy, and his belief that social democracy needed to broaden its social base had much in common with Otto Bauer's view of the situation in Austria. In 1918, with the breakup of the Austro-Hungarian Empire and the collapse of the monarchy, the SPÖ had seemed poised to seize power. The old ruling classes were in disarray and, as Bauer put it, the "workers and soldiers could have established the dictatorship of the proletariat any day."[28] Yet Bauer and the party leadership did not think that a proletarian dictatorship was feasible in Austria. Like their German counterparts, they opposed the council republic favored by the communists and worked to establish a parliamentary regime in which they hoped to exercise power. From late 1918 until 1920, the Social Democrats headed a coalition government, but fear of foreign intervention and internal civil war prevented them from carrying out radical socialist reforms. Ultimately, although the SPÖ remained united, it failed to retain control of the state and left the cabinet after the bourgeois parties won a majority in the parliament. Thereafter the party remained permanently in the opposition and looked forward to a future electoral majority that never came.[29]

Like Hilferding, Bauer considered the parliamentary republic the most favorable political system for the peaceful achievement of socialism. During the 1920s he theorized that, in certain historical situations, the state could not be considered an instrument of the ruling class. Bauer divided Austria's revolution into three phases: during the first year, the proletariat dominated the political system; from 1919 until 1922, a "balance of class forces" characterized the polity; and finally, after 1923, the bourgeoisie established its hegemony over the state. It is the middle phase that is of particular interest here. In this period, Bauer argued, "the republic was not a class state, but the product of a compromise between the classes, the result of an equilibrium of social forces."[30] This condition was not unique to Austria but expressed itself in various ways in different countries: in some states the formation of coalition governments of workers' and bourgeois parties reflected a situation in which neither side could effectively exercise power without at least the tacit support of its opponents; in others, such as Fascist Italy or Soviet Russia, the stalemate between the classes led to the seizure of power by armed parties that subjected all classes to their dictatorship. In Austria, Bauer claimed, the standoff between the bourgeoisie and the proletariat did not express itself in the form of a coalition government, but rather in the confrontation between the parliamentary state and "industrial democracy," which comprised the workers' councils, trade unions, consumer and peasant cooperatives, and organizations of professional employees. The extraparliamentary strength of the latter institutions, combined with the SPÖ's parliamentary influence, limited the power of the bourgeois government and forced it to make substantial social and political concessions to the masses. In the Austrian "people's republic" neither the bourgeoisie nor the proletariat dominated the state.[31]

In contrast to Hilferding, Bauer held that the parliamentary system did not transcend the class character of the state; the state's form depended on a variety of factors that determined the power of different social classes. These included their respective size, the strength of their organizations, their position in the process of production and distribution, and their influence over the military and the press. For Bauer, a parliamentary state could not permanently remain class neutral. Ultimately, it too would fall under the control of the dominant classes.[32] In Austria, the bourgeois parties eventually undermined the "balance of class forces" by establishing firm control over the army and creating reactionary paramilitary organizations. This shift in institutional power, combined with their continued control over the economy, allowed the industrial and financial oligarchy to take the offensive against the workers and to transform the "people's republic" into a bourgeois one. Thus, while Bauer thought that there were historical moments in which no single social class could establish its hegemony over the state, he regarded such a condition as transitory.

Whereas Bauer's theoretical standpoint was somewhat different from Hilferding's, his political conclusions were similar. Bauer believed that, although the consolidation of the bourgeois republic placed Social Democracy on the defensive, the party should do everything in its power to protect the parliamentary order. Even with the bourgeoisie at the helm, socialists could use the system to build up their organizations, fight for reforms and, in the near future, win a parliamentary majority that would usher in the socialist order. Like Hilferding, Bauer thought that to create such a majority the SPÖ had to win over nonsocialist industrial workers while simultaneously expanding its base among white-collar workers and peasants.[33] Both men believed that Social Democracy would gradually grow into power within a republican structure, that working-class unity was essential to this process, and that political adventurism would only hinder the development of socialism. They overestimated their parties' ability to recruit nonproletarian support and underestimated their opponents' strength, and as the fascist and communist movements rose and socialist power declined, they also adopted virtually identical passive defensive strategies that left the initiative in the hands of their enemies. Each man recognized that the republic had dangerous adversaries, and each used militant language in calling on the workers to defend the state with force if necessary, but neither one, either by habit or temperament, was prepared to actually demand such decisive action.[34]

Throughout the 1920s, Hilferding believed that western Europe stood at the threshold of an era of democratic freedom. "Democratic self-government," he argued, "awakened popular interest in social issues, strengthened class-consciousness, and created a state organization that allowed the class struggle to unfold without violent eruptions."[35] In general, he viewed this development as a Europeanwide trend unfolding within different national contexts. International peace was essential for this process to continue, and in his opinion, the prerequisites for it were at hand.

One of the most important results of World War I, Hilferding asserted, was the consolidation of the hegemony of the Anglo-Saxon world. The United States had emerged as the world's strongest economic and military power, while Britain had enlarged its empire and eliminated the German threat. The war had brought both powers into close cooperation, and it was in their mutual interest to continue working together in its aftermath. As the world's leading capitalist nations, both had a common goal: continued economic expansion on a global scale.

Hilferding conceded that, at first glance, peace and cooperation seemed unlikely in the postwar world. Was war not the essence of capitalism? Did the outcome of the imperialist war not simply set the stage for future conflict among the victorious rivals? Would the defeated Central Powers not resort to arms in order to revise the postwar settlement? Was peace possible in the face of Russian instability and unresolved nationality problems in eastern Europe and Asia? Hilferding recognized that these problems threatened peace, but he saw other processes at work, particularly in the economic sphere, that made peaceful relations conceivable even under capitalism. The economy, he suggested, had now reached such a level of technical organizational advancement that capitalist leaders no longer regarded war as an attractive option. To avoid its destructive risks and secure their common interests, cooperation was more economical and effective.[36]

As in the prewar era, capitalist states continued to compete for control over foreign markets and raw materials. War remained an option to resolve conflict, but Hilferding believed it likely only if an imbalance of power developed, and individual or allied states felt strong enough to militarily defeat their rivals. In the 1920s he did not believe such a situation existed; on the contrary, a variety of factors seemed to encourage cooperation, especially between England and the United States. Finance capital in England was far less developed than on the continent, and industry and banking were more concerned with promoting exports and free trade than with protection. At the same time, the British had to deal with the rise of colonial nationalism, and force seemed to be the least useful method of holding their far-flung empire together. Hilferding thought that Britain would seek to appease the nationalists by reorganizing its relationship to the colonies; international peace was a prerequisite for the success of this policy.

The economic condition of the United States also indicated the need for expanded international trade and cooperation. America's growing export industries sought markets worldwide and were especially concerned about the restoration of buying power in war-ravaged Europe, while U.S. banks looked abroad to invest large capital surpluses built up during the war. Hilferding was confident that mutual economic interests, buttressed by close cultural and political affinities, would forge an alliance between the United States and Britain that would promote a policy of "realistic pacifism" *(realistischer Pazifismus)* to maintain international peace. The Washington Conference of 1921 seemed to confirm this view. There the Anglo-Saxon powers signed an agreement with France, Japan, and Italy to limit the size of naval forces and to cooperate on certain colonial matters. Hilferding believed that the "unbridled competition of individual sovereign states" was gradually giving way to a "community of interests." By using their financial and political clout, the Anglo-Saxon nations could peacefully rein in powers such as Japan and France whose interests or policies sometimes clashed with theirs. This policy, the expansion of democracy, and the first steps by the League of Nations toward the limitation of national sovereignty paved the way for a lasting peace even before the victory of socialism.[37]

In *Finance Capital* Hilferding had stressed that imperialism would probably lead to war and revolution, but in the Weimar period he came to accept Kautsky's prewar suggestion that capitalism was entering a new phase of "ultraimperialism" in which "the policy of cartelization" was transferred into international foreign policy. In 1914, Kautsky had pointed out that the dominant capitalist powers eventually could organize themselves into a cartel that would bring an end to the arms race. He thought that social democrats would still have to struggle against such an undemocratic system, but he also postulated that it could maintain peace. Hilferding took up Kautsky's arguments after the war because they were in accord with his own analysis of recent developments. If, on the domestic level, parliamentary means could peacefully transform the organized capitalist order along socialist lines, it was logical that the international extension of this system (the Anglo-Saxon cartel) was also subject to reform. Hilferding rejected the inevitability of either war or peace, but he strongly and rather naively believed that the international situation after 1918 made peace a much more "realistic" option for the world's nations.

Hilferding's theory of organized capitalism is in some ways comparable with the work of Nikolay Bukharin in the same period. By 1921, the destruction of the Russian civil war and the economic failure of "war communism" undermined Bukharin's faith in the possibility of rapidly building communism in Russia and convinced him of the need to restore the economy through a partial restoration of capitalism (the New Economic Policy or NEP). Although he and Hilferding held sharply opposed political views and were operating under fundamentally different economic conditions, it is interesting that they came to similar conclusions about the short-term possibilities for radical economic change in their respective societies. Hilferding believed that even if the revolutionary proletariat could seize power in a violent upheaval, such an action would precipitate civil war, disrupt Germany's advanced industrial economy, and undermine the transition to socialism. As an alternative, he linked socialism's coming with capitalism's gradual "organic development" and social democracy's support for the parliamentary republic. Bukharin also concluded that a gradualist strategy would be more effective but from a completely different political perspective. For him, the socialist transformation could not begin under capitalism but only under the dictatorship of the proletariat. The latter, he insisted, "must destroy the bourgeois state, seize power, and with the help of this lever change economic relations." A lengthy process of development would follow, "in which socialist forms of production and exchange [would] obtain an ever wider dissemination and . . . gradually displace all the remnants of capitalist society."[38]

If one puts aside Bukharin's insistence on the need for a proletarian dictatorship, it becomes clear that he supported an economic strategy quite similar to Hilferding's. Bukharin, too, thought that state power was essential for implementing a long-term "evolutionary" policy of socialist reforms. "For many decades," he wrote in 1923, "we will slowly be growing into socialism: through the growth of our state industry, through cooperation, through the increasing influence of our banking system, through a thousand and one intermediate forms."[39] Thus, although each man certainly had a different political conception of the road to socialism, both adopted a gradualist approach to the problem of socialist economic transition.

Bukharin's analysis of contemporary capitalism also contained many similarities to Hilferding's. Preferring to use the term "state" rather than "organized" capitalism, he also argued that the capitalist economy was overcoming its anarchical nature through "deep internal structural changes," which included continued growth of monopolies, the further centralization and concentration of capital, and the increasingly important role of the state in organizing and regulating economic life. In 1926, Bukharin claimed that the capitalist economies had recovered from the war's destructive effects through organizational innovation and the use of new technology (rationalization). Unlike Hilferding, however, he did not think that these developments stabilized or prolonged capitalism's life in the long term. On the contrary, Bukharin believed that the uneven application of technological advancements in the world economy resulted in disproportional rates of development that would, in turn, fuel international conflict. At the same time, he argued that rationalization might improve labor productivity, but, by increasing structural unemployment, depressing wages, and reducing aggregate demand, it ultimately exacerbated capitalism's crisis of profitability and intensified class struggle in each state.[40]

Bukharin's analysis of the capitalist state was also much different from Hilferding's. He stressed the increasingly complex interconnections between capital and the executive, legislative, and judicial branches of government and asserted that under finance capitalism the state "becomes more than ever before an 'executive committee of the ruling classes.'" Whereas Hilferding thought that the parliamentary state expressed the collective will of individual citizens, Bukharin held that it embodied the interests and collectively expressed will of the ruling classes. For him, parliament was a merely "decorative institution."[41]

Ultimately, Bukharin argued, capitalism's period of relative stabilization would shatter on the shoals of the system's accelerating national and international contradictions. Intensified class struggle and a new round of imperialist wars would be the result. Bukharin thought that socialist evolution within revolutionary Russia was possible because the laws of development were different for socialism than for capitalism. In the case of the latter, however, he believed that crisis and revolution remained intimately bound up with the system and that under finance capital they had become international in scope.[42]

Bukharin's views of "state capitalist" development were echoed by a number of leading communist critics of "organized capitalism." Focusing on Hilferding's argument that the capitalist economy was becoming increasingly stable, they responded by pointing out that, even in an economy in which the trend toward monopoly was strong, capitalist competition could continue as cartels often proved unstable, substitute products were introduced to rival those produced by monopolies, and large firms often broke into monopolized markets in order to diversify their operations. Challenging Hilferding's contention that the democratic state was gradually taking on a larger economic role, they argued that the process was actually reversed; it was the capitalist elite that increasingly exercised its will over the state. Hilferding's critics did not deny capitalism's strong tendency toward large-scale organization and planning, but they took into account the dialectical nature of capitalist development and, unlike Hilferding, recognized the continuing existence of serious contradictions within the system. Whereas the communists' insistence that the coming crisis would open the way for socialist revolution seriously misjudged the situation in Germany, the onset of the depression demonstrated that Hilferding's crisis theory was untenable and made clear that their arguments had been much more realistic.[43]

Although the Bolshevik camp sharply criticized Hilferding's theory of organized capitalism, the theory won widespread support among SPD and trade union leaders until the onset of the economic crisis. Even many left-wing social democrats, such as Max Adler and Siegfried Aufhäuser, accepted the theory's economic premises.[44] We shall examine the left's objections to Hilferding's political conclusions in the next chapter. Crucial here is the question as to why his optimistic economic assumptions met with such broad acceptance. First of all, it is important to recognize that Hilferding developed his theory at a time when much of the left had come to view socialization essentially as an organizational and technical problem. While groups of socialists and communists struggled over various aspects of economic development and political praxis, there was a general fascination with the organizational development of the economy and particularly, "the organizational potential of the state."[45] Many leading nonsocialist thinkers, such as Werner Sombart, shared Hilferding's view of capitalist development, and in 1928 economist Hans Ritschl remarked that "the idea, that we are experiencing modern capitalism's transformation into a late capitalist or early socialist economy, is generally accepted."[46] Thus, different versions of "organized capitalism" strongly influenced the general tenor of economic discourse under Weimar, and many social democrats saw Hilferding's basic concept confirmed by the views of his nonsocialist counterparts.[47]

Second, and more important, most SPD and trade union leaders found Hilferding's theory acceptable because it was well adapted to their reformist strategy. These leaders believed in the goal of socialism; but to achieve it, they thought, required preserving and expanding their organizations. Because Hilferding's theory stressed economic and political gradualism, it represented no threat to the security of the institutions that the movement had worked so hard to build. It enabled social democracy to retain its commitment to the achievement of socialism without having to face the prospect of economic crises or violent revolution. Most SPD and trade union leaders were experienced, practical men who knew that their opponents would fight "socialist" reforms tenaciously, but their conviction that history was on their side also led them to underestimate the extent of the difficulties that lay before them.[48] For leaders who were essentially concerned with organizational and short-term tactical questions, Hilferding's economic theory seemed plausible and his political conclusions made sense. When reality intervened and undermined his strategic assumptions, social democracy found itself poorly prepared to respond.

L. Leontjew once presciently observed that the whole theoretical structure of organized capitalism rose or fell based on the accuracy of its most fundamental premise: that during capitalism's most recent phase of development, the principle of socialist planning had come to replace the principle of capitalist competition.[49] If the premise was correct, then Hilferding's assertion that severe economic crises were a thing of the past would prove itself justified. If it was not, then the latest phase of capitalist development simply laid the groundwork for renewed crisis. The onset of the depression of 1929 made very clear that the latter was the case and revealed that Hilferding had both grossly underestimated the extent of capitalism's contradictions and overestimated its level of organization.

Hilferding misjudged the depth of the German economy's weakness not because he was unfamiliar with its problems but because he absolutized certain tendencies he discerned in capitalism's long-term evolution and regarded contradictory phenomena as aberrations. Beginning with his early economic writings, he had consistently stressed the evolutionary rather than the revolutionary aspects of socialist development and, in 1910, had argued that because finance capital had "already achieved expropriation to the extent required by socialism," it was possible to "dispense with a sudden act of expropriation by the state" and to carry out a "gradual process of socialization."[50] In 1910, however, Hilferding had also clearly recognized that conflicts of interest within capitalism and the continued occurrence of crises would hinder the process of cartelization and the formation of an all-encompassing "general cartel." In that period he analyzed the development of capitalism dialectically and believed that the system's contradictions could only be eliminated through the establishment of socialism. "Planned production and anarchic production," he had argued, "are not quantitative opposites such that by taking on more and more 'planning' conscious organization will emerge out of anarchy. Such a transformation can only take place suddenly by subordinating the whole of production to conscious control. Who exercises this control, and is the owner of production, is a question of power."[51]

Under Weimar Hilferding discarded this argument and the dialectical method. Instead he developed a theory that projected a gradual growth into socialism as capitalist production grew increasingly concentrated, organized, and planned. With economic anarchy and crises no longer a serious hindrance to the creation of wealth, social democracy could work to socialize the economy through progressive parliamentary reforms. Hilferding did not move substantially away from this argument until the collapse of the republic in 1933. His retention of this argument, even in the face of the economic crisis, reflected the strength of his conviction that the evolutionary transition to socialism and the pursuit of a parliamentary strategy were part of an interconnected whole to which there was no acceptable alternative.[52]

Hilferding's theory of organized capitalism presupposed a prosperous economy and stable polity in which the unions and social democracy would be able to fight for change. The economic downturn after 1929 and the political crisis that followed undermined these assumptions. We shall examine Hilferding's and his party's practical difficulties in dealing with these developments below. Here it is sufficient to point out that, in his response to the economic crisis, Hilferding proposed remedies that were generally within the framework of orthodox political economy. Throughout the 1920s he had proposed reforms that he thought were achievable within the capitalist system, and he continued to do so after the onset of the depression. Convinced that capitalism would neither collapse economically nor be overthrown by the proletariat, he articulated what he regarded as a politics of the possible. For him this meant a cautious, in many ways conservative, economic policy that would restore capitalism and secure the republic as a means of keeping the road open for socialist evolution. Under the political conditions of the time, however, such an outlook could scarcely compete with the radical solutions proposed by the SPD's Communist and National Socialist rivals.

In the debates over social democracy's theoretical principles and practical strategy, Hilferding was fond of reminding his comrades that "history is the best Marxist" and that the movement needed to constantly adjust its theory and practice in light of experience and changed conditions.[53] As the events of the late Weimar period made clear, history was a harsh judge of the optimistic conclusions that Hilferding drew from his theory of organized capitalism. The depression, the destruction of the republic, and the resurgence of intense imperialist rivalries, all contradicted the projections of his economic and political analyses. Yet it should not be assumed that the concept of "organized capitalism" is therefore of no value to the contemporary social sciences. On the contrary, as one observer has recently pointed out, Hilferding's optimistic projections were flawed but his conclusions did not *necessarily* flow from his basic and still valid thesis regarding the increasing socialization *(Verge-sellschaftung)* of capitalism.[54] Hilferding derived the core of organized capitalism from his theory of finance capital, and it is unnecessary to repeat our discussion of the ways in which the latter concept helps clarify modern capitalist development.

Organized capitalism assumes its importance as an extension of this theory because it provides useful insights in several key areas. First, it recognizes the growing importance of technical innovations in the economy and their enormous impact on the structure and function of economic and social organizations. With the onset of the "computer age" and the "information revolution," for example, it is now possible for whole branches of the economy to improve their planning and production operations. The anarchy of the capitalist economy has certainly not disappeared, but few would deny that the introduction of computer technology has revolutionized the process of production. Second, organized capitalism emphasizes not only the growing role of the state in the modern economy, but also the increasing importance of non-state organizations (cartels, unions, interest group associations) in shaping political and economic life. Along with the growth of political parties, the expansion of such organizations marks the movement away from the principle of individual competition and toward the principle of collective struggle for the realization of group interests.[55] The developmental tendencies that organized capitalism described have not unfolded everywhere at the same rate or in the same way, yet a number of historians find the concept a useful one for periodizing and analyzing important changes in the capitalist system.[56] Despite its serious shortcomings, then, Hilferding's theory retains explanatory power.

CHAPTER FIVE

THE REPUBLICAN POLITICIAN

We know the way. We know the goal. Our prospects are good.

—*Rudolf Hilferding (1927)*

On February 3, 1932, representatives of the SPD executive, the party's Reichstag delegation, and the Federation of Trade Unions (ADGB) gathered amid worsening economic depression and intensifying political chaos to discuss economic relief measures.[1] With unemployment nearing 6 million and with political violence on the rise, social democracy's leaders were growing desperate. They hoped to come up with a plan to take the wind out of the sails of their Nazi and Communist rivals, both of whom were gaining momentum as the crisis deepened and threatened to destroy the republic.

The proposal they came together to discuss was the brainchild of Vladimir Woytinsky, a Menshevik émigré and head the ADGB's Statistical Bureau; Fritz Tarnow, the chairman of the Woodworkers' Union; and Fritz Baade, a Social Democratic agricultural expert. Professor Gerhard Colm, a like-minded but politically unaffiliated economist from Kiel, explained the innovative WTB plan to the group. In a nutshell, it called for abandoning the conservative deflationary policy of Heinrich Brüning's government, which, the authors believed, was exacerbating the depression. The new plan called on the government to reflate the economy by initiating large-scale public works programs funded by the state through budgetary savings and Reichsbank credits. This Keynesian-like strategy envisioned an investment of 2 billion RM to create 1 million public sector jobs in non-goods-producing industries. Woytinsky and his coauthors predicted that such spending would stimulate demand in the consumer goods industries and thus increase production and employment. The program's limited size and scope would prevent the return of the inflationary conditions of 1923, and (more important) industry could utilize existing surplus capacity to easily meet consumer demand as mass purchasing power increased.[2]

Woytinsky's memoirs provide an interesting glimpse into the SPD's reception of the WTB plan. Responding on the party's behalf, Hilferding attacked it for questioning the labor theory of value and not recognizing that depressions result from capitalist anarchy. "If Colm and Woytinsky think they can mitigate a depression by public works, they are merely showing that they are not Marxists," he commented acidly. The movement's task was "to rise united to the defense of a sound currency and Marxism."[3]

Woytinsky's first thought was that Hilferding was not serious and had merely appealed to clichés lodged in the brains of the SPD deputies, who "listened to him as to an oracle." He countered by pointing out that "the people were at the end of their patience," as workers deserted the SPD for the Communists and the Nazis, and the party must act. The new plan had nothing to do with value theory. The only real question was whether the SPD or its enemies would take the initiative.

Just as Woytinsky felt he was winning support, "a deafening noise came from the head of the table." Wels, the party cochairman, had been sitting "motionless in his armchair [with] his eyes closed and his head sunk on his breast" when suddenly he "pounded the desk with both fists and shouted, 'Shut up! I will not permit . . .'"

"'You will not permit what?' Woytinsky asked.

"'You said "it is not true,"' Wels answered. 'If what Hilferding says is not true he must be a liar! I will not permit . . .'"

At that moment the meeting fell into complete disarray with "a dozen people shouting." Order was eventually restored and the discussion continued, but Woytinsky failed to convince the SPD delegates of the merits of his plan. When the ADGB leader, Theodor Leipart, called for a vote, "all of the representatives of the unions raised their hands in favor of it. All the representatives of the party voted 'nay'."

Woytinsky's description of this confrontation should, of course, be read with caution. He was writing thirty years later, and he and Hilferding had quarreled earlier over value theory when Woytinsky had written for *Die Gesellschaft*. Nevertheless, allowing for some inaccuracy and exaggeration in the details, there is good evidence that Woytinsky's recounting captures the gist of what transpired at the meeting.[4] His exchange with Hilferding reveals much about the latter's role in social democratic politics and his outlook at the end of the Weimar Republic. It illuminates, as well, that many in the SPD's top leadership, especially Wels, held Hilferding in high regard and looked to him for guidance in ideological and economic matters. It also makes clear that he was an ardent supporter of a sound currency and dismissed the idea of reflation as a means of easing the effects of the depression. By discouraging the party and state from pursuing such alternative economic policies, Hilferding helped to limit their ability to respond to the republic's multifaceted crisis.

At first glance it might seem rather surprising that Hilferding, the Marxist theoretician, would adopt such a conservative economic policy in the face of the depression. After all, during the revolution he had been an exponent of radical changes including the socialization of key industries. How, then, did he ultimately wind up advising the conservative Chancellor Brüning and supporting his orthodox economic program? The roots of Hilferding's economic and political views at the end of Weimar Republic may be found in his earlier theoretical work and in his experience as a practical politician and economist after the German revolution. The theory of organized capitalism contained a strong evolutionary component, which, helped along by the SPD's use of parliamentary institutions, envisioned the gradual growth of capitalism into socialism. This vision was the result of Hilferding's study of history, which was informed by his conception of Marxism. Of central importance here is to recognize that to interpret historical development from a Marxist perspective does not necessarily equip an economist with the conceptual tools necessary to repair an ailing capitalist economy. During the German revolution, Hilferding thought that radical measures could quickly transform society, but after it became clear to him that German capitalism would endure, he fell back on the traditional methods of political economy to resolve specific problems.

In many ways Hilferding exemplified the quandary of contemporary left-wing economists in Germany and elsewhere. When considering the complete transformation of capitalism they created various radical plans, but when faced with handling problems within the system, they often resorted to orthodox methods. Hilferding saw it as the practical economist's task to make sure that the capitalist economy functioned well in order to assure its steady movement toward socialism. He believed that this process was advancing under Weimar, and that the republic's early economic crises were rooted in the war and in the peace settlement, not in capitalism itself. In working to resolve these difficulties, he developed no innovative or particularly "Marxist" alternatives.

There is also no doubt that certain economic and political situations shook Hilferding's confidence in the future. The social and political disorder that accompanied the inflation of 1923 was one such traumatic occasion and had an important impact on his later work. His repeated experiences as a participant in the republic's ruthless interest group politics, especially during his two-time tenure as finance minister, formed another. Rather than respond to these situations by striking out in new directions, Hilferding—like the movement he led—tended to rely on older expedients. When these no longer sufficed to deal with the Great Depression and its concomitant political crisis, Hilferding and the SPD faced disaster.

Rudolf Hilferding was one of the republic's most diligent and loyal servants. Working as a parliamentarian, finance minister, and governmental advisor, he courageously took on crushing responsibilities during periods of extreme economic and political crisis. When he thought it necessary, he did not shy away from advocating policies at odds with his own party's position, but such political nerve was offset by a tendency to react cautiously and conservatively to theoretical and practical challenges that required speedy and innovative responses. Hilferding was acutely aware of the severe problems that threatened the Weimar system yet refused to consider anything but the most orthodox economic policies or to break with the SPD's strict adherence to parliamentary norms. Like many other leading social democrats, even in the face of disaster, he deceived himself into believing that the republic would survive.

From the beginning of the republic, respect for Hilferding as a thinker transcended political party lines. Appointments to the Socialization Commission in 1918 and to the Reich Economic Council *(Reichswirtschaftsrat)* from 1920 until 1925 allowed him to make connections with important nonsocialist economic experts and political leaders both at home and abroad.[5] In 1922 the German government invited him to attend an important international conference in Genoa, confirming his considerable stature in official circles. At the conference he served as an economic advisor to the German delegation and also played a key role in the final stage of the negotiation of the Treaty of Rapallo, which reestablished full diplomatic and commercial relations between Germany and the Soviet Union. During these negotiations, Hilferding was in constant communication with such figures as Josef Wirth, chancellor and leader of the Catholic Center Party (Z), and Walther Rathenau, his former opponent on the Socialization Commission, who was now foreign minister and a key figure in the German Democratic Party (DDP). Hilferding functioned as a go-between with the Russians and strove to bring about a Soviet-German agreement. While there is little evidence to support diplomat Harry Kessler's contention that Hilferding was one of the originators of the Rapallo Treaty (Baron Ago von Maltzan, Germany's ministerial director for Eastern affairs, was its chief architect), Kessler's diaries illuminate the important role that Hilferding played in the negotiations.[6] Hilferding's work at the conference reflected his view that the failure of the socialist revolution in Germany required social democracy to work within the institutions of the capitalist republic and to make short-term, pragmatic political compromises that would ensure the movement's long-term success. In accordance with his belief that international economic and political interests in the postwar period created a basis for peace, he regarded the Genoa Conference as an important Allied attempt to bring about negotiated solutions to Europe's most pressing problems.[7]

Germany's leaders initially anticipated using the conference to discuss a revision of the Treaty of Versailles, a measure they considered essential for domestic stability. The French stymied such discussions, however, and thereby drove them into cooperation with the Soviets, whose representatives at Genoa unsuccessfully attempted to reestablish Russia's diplomatic and commercial ties with the Western powers. Before considering official recognition for Russia, the Allies presented the Bolsheviks with a series of demands that required the Soviet state to assume responsibility for the tsar's foreign debt, to compensate all expropriated foreign firms, and to submit to the authority of an Allied-Soviet debt commission that would regulate Russian finances and oversee the return of all expropriated private property to its former owners. Such terms were unacceptable to the Bolsheviks and hindered progress in the negotiations.

For moral as well as political reasons Hilferding also rejected the Allied demands. They effectively blocked German participation in Russia's economic reconstruction and, more important, represented a threat to Russian as well as German independence. The Bolsheviks' acceptance of such terms would relegate the country to the status of a colonial dependency; if the Western powers could assume control over indebted Russia, why not over Germany as well? In Hilferding's view, the Germans had no choice: they must oppose Allied demands and, in order to avoid political and economic isolation, come to an agreement with the Russians. Concern for German interests and not ideological sympathy for the Bolsheviks thus motivated him to urge Wirth and Rathenau to conclude the treaty.[8]

Hilferding's support for an agreement with Russia exemplified his postrevolutionary political flexibility. When Genoa resulted in no fundamental improvement in Germany's situation, he was willing to back a diplomatic and economic alliance with social democracy's Bolshevik opponents. That Hilferding supported the treaty despite substantial opposition to it within social democracy is less important than his view of the treaty as a practical means of securing the republic's economic and political interests. It was this political pragmatism, complemented by his economic expertise, that paved the way for his assumption of a prominent public role in the newly reunited SPD's Executive Committee after 1922.[9]

By this time, Hilferding's economic skills were in demand as Germany's economy steadily deteriorated. War debts, the costs of demobilization, soaring government social expenditures, huge reparations payments, and the printing of excess currency, all undermined the Reich's finances and caused the value of the already weakened German mark to fall precipitously from 493 to 7,589 per U.S. dollar between July and December 1922. Real income levels (especially for the middle class) failed to keep up with the rate of inflation. Other factors aggravated the situation. Agriculture's slow recovery from the war resulted in food shortages, and the complex transition to a peacetime economy caused industrial production to lag. With the return of millions of former soldiers to the labor market, the government passed legislation requiring many factories to employ only part-time workers; under-employment, rather than unemployment, was widespread.[10]

The Genoa Conference failed to ease the German government's financial difficulties, and the Treaty of Rapallo exacerbated its problems by angering the Western powers and frightening Poland. Germany's reparations debt of more than 132 billion gold marks enraged the radical nationalists, and Walther Rathenau's assassination in June reflected the rise of right-wing terror. Backed mainly by the SPD, the USPD, and the Catholic Center party, the Wirth government temporarily forestalled Allied sanctions and the occupation of Germany's most vital industrial region, the Ruhr Valley, by agreeing to fulfill its reparations obligations, but neither Wirth nor his successor, Wilhelm Cuno, was able to put together an effective economic program. In January 1923, after Germany fell behind in its reparations payments, France and Belgium occupied the Ruhr Valley, which unleashed a severe economic and political crisis.[11]

The Cuno government's response was an expensive policy of passive resistance. It encouraged the populace in the occupied zone not to cooperate with the invaders and financed the campaign by paying subsidies to industries, unions, newspapers, political parties, and local governments. Strikes, sabotage, and a wave of unrest swept the Ruhr, bringing production to a halt, while the subsidy system hastened the mark's collapse. Raising funds essentially by means of the printing press, the government exacerbated the hyperinflation that was already well underway, and between January and November 1923 the value of the mark fell from 17,000 to 4.2 trillion per U.S. dollar. Savings and debts disappeared and living standards declined sharply for salaried employees, certain sectors of the proletariat, and people living on fixed incomes. Commodity prices (particularly for food) rose rapidly, causing real income levels to drop even in industries in which wages were tied to the rate of inflation. Unemployment increased sharply in the second half of the year. The wildly increasing rate of inflation threatened to paralyze the whole economy.[12]

While the mark's collapse impoverished many German households, it increased the wealth and power of the nation's financial speculators and some leading industrialists. The latter used the inflation to liquidate their debts, hold down real wages, and weaken the unions. The cartelization of industry accelerated as large firms, especially in heavy industry, took control over smaller, less stable enterprises. For as long as they could benefit from it, few leading capitalists worked to end the inflation. Only when economic chaos loomed did they support a policy of stabilization.[13]

Although not part of the Cuno cabinet, the SPD supported the government's recall of its ambassadors from Paris and Brussels, its decision to cease paying reparations to France and Belgium, and its campaign of passive resistance. Worsening economic conditions and the growth of the radical right, however, forced the party to reconsider its policy. Some right-wing SPD leaders—such as Prussian interior minister Carl Severing, Frankfurt University professor

Hugo Sinzheimer, and *Die Rheinische Zeitung* editor Wilhelm Sollmann—called for Cuno's overthrow and for the SPD's entrance into a "great coalition" with the moderate bourgeois parties. Such a government, they believed, could unite the nation in an all-out effort to overcome the crisis and save the republic. In a letter written to Sollmann on May 30, 1923, Sinzheimer suggested that Hilferding receive a post in the new cabinet.[14]

Sinzheimer's recommendation made sense, for Hilferding was the most prominent socialist in the Reich Economic Council. In October 1922, he had pushed the council's Reparations Committee to discuss immediate domestic measures to stabilize the currency before seeking assistance abroad. Together with Georg Bernhard, editor of the liberal *Vossische Zeitung,* and the Christian trade unionist Friedrich Baltrusch, Hilferding proposed strict foreign exchange controls and the mobilization of state gold reserves to stabilize the mark instead of introducing an entirely new currency, a process that he thought would precipitate an economic slowdown. Despite the backing of the council's economic and finance committees, Chancellor Wirth rejected this policy in favor of one stressing the need to reduce reparations payments and the trade deficit. In the midst of trying to broaden his coalition government with the SPD and DDP to the right, Wirth was not inclined to adopt a policy at odds with the demands of the German People's Party (DVP) for reduced economic regulation (including an end to the eight-hour day).[15]

This 1922 episode is important for several reasons. First, it makes clear that, well before his appointment to the Finance Ministry, Hilferding was in the forefront of the inflation policy debate and was one of those who supported immediate and decisive domestic action to stabilize the currency. Second, his call to convene the Reparations Committee shows that, to solve the nation's crises, he was able and willing to build bridges with prominent leaders from outside the social democratic camp. From the SPD's point of view, his prestige and connections in this important institution made him a logical candidate for a cabinet post dealing with the economy. And last, the government's rejection of his position presaged later events, when his proposals for action would founder repeatedly on the shoals of interest group politics in which parties and politicians jockeyed to defend the interests of their own narrow constituencies.

Despite his initial rebuff, Hilferding did not have to wait long for the chance to remake government policy. By midsummer 1923, despite the call from thirty left-wing SPD deputies to remain in the opposition and work with the KPD "for a decisive struggle against the bourgeoisie," a majority in the Reichstag delegation believed that a great coalition was necessary to save the republic. On August 11, 1923, following a vote of no confidence against Cuno, the socialists called for a new cabinet on the broadest possible basis. Two days later, by a vote of 83 to 39, the SPD delegates decided to enter a coalition headed by Gustav Stresemann, the moderate leader of the DVP, which most clearly represented industrialist interests.[16]

Presented on August 14, 1923, Stresemann's new cabinet included one other representative from the DVP, one independent, two Democrats, three Catholic Centrists, and four Social Democrats. Stresemann named Hilferding, whom he considered a top expert willing to make tough decisions, finance minister.[17] Hilferding was an important participant in the interparty negotiations preceding the new government's formation. His firm support for the coalition, his reputation as a theorist, and the backing of cochairmen Wels and Müller ensured him of the SPD's nomination for the cabinet post.[18] It is important to note, however, that Hilferding had little experience as a practical economist. Although he had served on a number of economic commissions, no administration had accepted any of his recommendations, and he had never overseen the execution of state policy. Now he faced the challenge of ending the inflation and restoring the nation's finances. Success was essential if the republic were to survive. For an inexperienced socialist minister in a cabinet in which the SPD was a minority, this was a daunting challenge.

Hilferding located the origins of the inflation in the deficit spending policies pursued by the Reichsbank during the war and the simultaneous shrinkage of the domestic market. The government had met its wartime needs by borrowing money from the Reichsbank in exchange for promissory notes. Because the bank printed as much currency as the state demanded, the amount of paper money in circulation rose markedly at a time when consumer goods were scarce; the result was a sharp rise in prices. In the postwar period, the government continued to spend without raising taxes to cover ballooning budget deficits. Wages rose but lagged behind the rate of price increases, thus the general level of consumption fell. Germany's inability to export enough commodities to cover the cost of necessary raw material and food imports exacerbated these developments. Germany paid its debts in marks for which there was little demand. The result was a fall in the mark's international value that outpaced its domestic decline. By 1922, Hilferding believed that the inflation had entered a new and final stage in which currency depreciation accelerated primarily because of internal policies that undermined public confidence in the mark. Since the introduction of socialist planning no longer seemed politically feasible, his proposals to the Reich Economic Council aimed not to transform the system but to save it. When he entered the cabinet one year later his goal was much the same—to restore the stability of the currency and, therefore, of the economic order.[19]

On August 9, 1923, Hilferding published an article in *Vorwärts* in which he outlined his plans to stabilize the mark and restore the state's finances. He believed that immediate action was imperative to prevent economic collapse. First and foremost, he argued, the government had to balance its budget by shutting down the Reichsbank presses and raising taxes. Concomitantly, it needed to transform the largely independent Reichsbank into a reliable instrument of its policy. The state could thereby regulate the flow of credit and

The Finance Minister in front of the Reichstag, August 13, 1923.

foreign currency, mobilize the nation's gold reserves, and eventually introduce a new gold-backed mark.[20]

To facilitate the transition to the new currency, Hilferding urged the government to divide the Reichsbank into two departments: a gold-mark department and a paper-mark department. The gold-mark department would have a gold supply worth 300 million RM at its disposal and the power to issue up to 1.2 billion gold marks backed by either gold or "hard" currency (*goldwertige Devisen* or *Handelswechsel*). In addition, the gold-mark department would regulate the issuance of the paper mark, which would remain in circulation with its value fixed to that of the gold mark, while the paper-mark department oversaw the liquidation of excess circulating currency. Hilferding did not believe that paper money necessarily needed gold backing to function successfully as a medium of exchange. In 1923, however, he favored the gold mark as a means of restoring public confidence in the currency.[21]

Hilferding's plans encountered strong resistance both inside and outside the government.[22] The appointment of a socialist finance minister incensed industry representatives in the cabinet and in the bourgeois parties. They resented having to negotiate with an avowed Marxist and former USPD leader, and they fumed over the SPD's demand for heavy taxes on Germany's elites. The ultraconservative German National Peoples Party (DNVP) feared that Hilferding's policies might actually succeed, to the credit of the socialists. The DNVP worked doggedly to undermine his efforts and to achieve an economic solution favorable to the *Junkers* and the industrialists. Karl Helfferich, a seasoned DNVP politician and financial expert, proved Hilferding's most formidable rival.[23]

There were other obstacles as well. Many government officials scorned him for being a "socialist Jew" and took umbrage at his attempt to hold down government salaries. The Reichsbank resisted his reorganization plans, and the Association of German Industry (RdI) and the *Junkers* rejected his proposed tax and currency reforms. He even lacked solid support within the SPD's Reichstag delegation. Many on the left criticized his pragmatism in resolving political questions, while some on the right distrusted him because of his former membership in the USPD.[24]

Hilferding realized that his program required tough and unpopular measures, which his opponents could use to isolate him in the cabinet. On August 15, 1923, he proposed the formation of a multiparty commission to formulate the government's economic plans. With ministers sharing the responsibility for its decisions, Hilferding hoped to protect his own position and encourage cooperation in the cabinet. His suggestion met with little interest, however, exemplifying the opposition that he faced from many of his colleagues in the cabinet. All of them expected him to solve the government's financial problems, but few were willing to accept the political responsibility for the sacrifices that a successful policy would entail. When Hilferding assumed office, the government expected an income of 169 trillion RM for the coming month against expenditures of 405 trillion RM. Of the latter, 240 trillion RM were earmarked for "the Ruhr battle" and thus were untouchable on political grounds. To substantially reduce the budget deficit, then, Hilferding could only fall back on tax increases or draconian cuts in other ministries. Rather than cooperation, such choices fueled conflict among coalition "partners" struggling to protect their own—often conflicting—interests.[25]

Relations between Hilferding and the economic minister Hans von Raumer (DVP) illustrate these conflicts. When, for example, Food Minister Luther (Independent) demanded that the government provide hard currency to import needed foodstuffs, Hilferding agreed, but von Raumer objected. Although he initially called for the seizure of privately held foreign currency and for reductions in luxury imports, von Raumer quickly retreated from these views after considering industrial interests.[26] There were certainly issues on which he and Hilferding could agree. If the socialist finance minister thought that a particular concession from labor, such as a temporary rollback of the eight-hour day, would have broader national benefit, he was willing to go along. Von Raumer, however, focused primarily on industrial concerns. Throughout the fall crisis he tenaciously fought for policies designed to drive wages and employment levels down and called for an end to wage-price indexing, the eight-hour day, taxes on coal, and export controls. Hilferding did not believe that such sweeping concessions to capital would resolve Germany's dilemma. Unlike von Raumer, he did not equate narrow industrial interests with those of the nation.[27]

Once in office, Hilferding quickly realized that the enormity of the budgetary and inflationary crises exceeded his worst expectations. On August 22, 1923, he reported to the Reichsrat that the situation was "very dangerous, practically desperate." Taxes covered only a tiny fraction of the government's costs; workers regarded the currency as worthless; paper money was in short supply forcing businesses to issue trillions of illegal "emergency" marks to pay their employees; and there was a serious shortage of foreign exchange.[28] One week later, Hilferding told Stresemann that it would take time to implement his plans, some of which (especially new taxes on the propertied classes) had met stubborn resistance, but no stabilization program could succeed unless the government immediately ceased funding the enormously expensive Ruhr campaign and put its finances in order. Fearing the domestic political ramifications of such a move, however, Stresemann demurred and urged Hilferding to quickly implement a currency reform in order to strengthen the government's negotiating position with the Allies. Within the month, however, the chancellor would come to admit that his finance minister had been right.[29]

Hilferding's efforts to reform the Reichsbank and to raise capital through forced loans and new taxes also met with little success. The entire cabinet favored replacing Reichsbank President Havenstein and his top deputies but was powerless to remove them. Havenstein had a lifetime appointment, and strongly supported by the bourgeois parties and German officialdom, he and his top officials remained at their posts.[30] And while the Reichsbank leaders defended their prerogatives, so too did Germany's agricultural and industrial elites. On August 18 Karl Helfferich appeared before the cabinet and presented a plan to restore the mark that would simultaneously strengthen the power of Germany's big landlords and industrialists. His proposal was that the government issue a new currency backed by a mortgage on the value of the German rye crop *(Roggenhypothek)*, a move that would have greatly increased the economic power of the *Junkers*. He also demanded lower taxes on industry and argued that the currency reform must be carried out by the professional classes *(Berufsstände)* because "they still have credit and the Reich does not."[31]

On September 6 the RdI presented its own currency reform proposals to the Reich Economic Council. The RdI wanted a gold-backed mark and a new currency bank under state control, suggesting that the bank raise an initial capital of 500 million marks in gold or its equivalent, with a 200-million-mark contribution raised from an industrial consortium and the rest from foreign investors and by public subscription. The new currency would have at least 50 percent gold backing, thus limiting its initial issue to 1 billion marks. The bank was to cut off credit to all levels of state government and locate its basic capital in a neutral country in order to "secure it from possible seizure by foreign or domestic political power holders." As one historian has observed, the RdI's proposal essentially called for government-sanctioned capital flight. Although supposedly state-supervised, the bank's operations would have been subject to decisive influence by the private sector, especially German industry.[32]

Hilferding dismissed Helfferich's scheme because he found the value of rye too unstable to serve as backing for currency and regarded a rye mark as useless for international financial transactions. He also rejected elite attempts to wrest control of the nation's banking system from government hands, insisting that "the primacy of the state had to be preserved" in the making of financial and economic policies.[33] To Hilferding's chagrin, the cabinet, impressed by Helfferich's plan, voted to set up a commission to discuss its implementation.[34] With inflation rapidly accelerating, Hilferding came under intense pressure to present a new and more detailed currency reform plan. During the first week of September, after consulting with representatives of German industry, he worked out a series of new proposals. On September 10, 1923, he outlined his reform package to the cabinet.[35]

The new proposals again reflected Hilferding's willingness to forgo political differences in order to achieve practical results. He still supported a gold-backed currency and a dominant role for the state in the creation of a new bank, but he now adopted some measures proposed by his opponents. He urged the government to set up a quasi-independent *Goldnotenbank* with an initial capital of 180 million marks drawn from the Reichsbank and public subscription. This new bank would have the right to issue 360 million gold marks, which (Hilferding thought) would meet the most pressing needs of the economy. To prevent the new gold mark's devaluation, he now opposed linking it with the old paper mark that would continue to circulate for some time. These measures were similar to those elaborated by the RdI but did not rely on industry for the bank's initial capital or call for its removal to a foreign location. At the same time, the plan also drew on Helfferich's proposals. In response to pressure from Stresemann and others in the cabinet, Hilferding adopted Helfferich's suggestion to mortgage private property *(hypothekarische Belastung des Besitzes)* in order to provide the state with credit and to facilitate the redemption of currency notes.[36]

The cabinet accepted Hilferding's plan and urged its speedy implementation, but several issues provided the RdI, the Reichsbank, von Raumer, and others with enough ammunition to block it. Hilferding's proposal was not as thoroughly worked out as Helfferich's or the RdI's, and there were legitimate fears that it was too deflationary and provided insufficient currency to meet the economy's needs. Von Raumer and Food Minister Luther both pointed out these problems and, although not denying the eventual need for a gold mark, continued to promote Helfferich's plan as a transitional measure. The Reichsbank contended that Hilferding's proposals would take too long to put into effect and that Helfferich's plan, as long as it included no proposals for a rival credit institution, provided a better interim solution. The RdI's leaders, arguing that Hilferding's plan left the bank subject to political influence, dismissed it and quickly moved to undermine the cabinet's new policy. Within a few days they had convinced the leadership of the Catholic Center party's Reichstag delegation to pressure their cabinet representatives into opposing the plan.[37]

On September 13, 1923, the cabinet met once again to discuss the currency reform. Although Hilferding and the other Social Democrats defended their position, the rest of the cabinet now supported Helfferich. Stresemann and von Raumer were anxious to appease the demands of agriculture and industry. They worried about the weakening economy and saw Helfferich's plan as a means to stem the decline. Luther agreed and stressed the need to quickly halt the inflation and increase food supplies. He asserted that a new currency based on the value of rye (later called the *Bodenmark*) would stimulate agricultural production and restore the mark as a means of payment. After considerable discussion, the cabinet accepted Luther's arguments. It resolved to set up a Goldnotenbank as quickly as possible and, in the interim period, to introduce a rye-backed currency.[38]

Hilferding was defeated. Although appointed to chair the committee assigned to prepare the new reform, his position in the cabinet was now extremely weak. Luther had recommended that Stresemann (rather than his finance minister) chair the committee. It was only after the chancellor declined that Hilferding received the post. Despite his marginalization, he considered it his duty not to resign. Hilferding believed that the SPD represented the cornerstone of the republic, and that his resignation could have toppled the already shaky coalition. By staying on, he could work to hold the coalition together and continue to influence financial policy.[39]

Notwithstanding considerable personal friction, Hilferding and Luther worked to put together a new currency reform package. Hilferding's contribution was mostly technical. In order to prevent a resurgence of inflation, Luther accepted his suggestion to reduce the total amount of Reichsbank credit available to the state from 2 to 1.2 billion RM. He also agreed with Hilferding that the new currency bank should eventually be transformed into a Goldnotenbank that would introduce a gold-backed mark to replace the Bodenmark.[40] German industrial and landed elites resisted the tax provisions in Luther and Hilferding's proposal, but even with von Raumer's support, they failed to block its acceptance in the cabinet. On September 29, 1923, three days after the government finally ended the resistance in the Ruhr, Hilferding submitted the currency reform plan as a legislative bill to the Reichsrat and shortly thereafter to the Reichstag. It was never voted on, however, because of the sudden dissolution of Stresemann's cabinet.[41]

During the first week of October, Stresemann announced his intention to request an Enabling Law granting the cabinet extraordinary powers to deal with Germany's worsening economic and political crises. At the same time, the DVP Reichstag delegation, with the support of Labor Minister Brauns and Food Minister Luther, began to press for the elimination of the eight-hour day. Concerned about the growing strength of the extreme right, especially in Bavaria where the government repeatedly defied directives from Berlin, Hilferding and his fellow Social Democratic ministers supported the Enabling Law as "the only way to hold the Reich together." There was strong opposition, however, in the party's Reichstag delegation, which legitimately feared cabinet efforts to reduce workers' legal protections and social benefits. After prolonged discussion with the SPD cabinet ministers, the Reichstag deputies agreed to back an Enabling Law if the government refrained from using it to lengthen the workday.[42]

Once again demonstrating his political flexibility in order to protect the republic, Hilferding supported Vice-Chancellor Schmidt's (SPD) proposal that the cabinet introduce a separate bill that would maintain the eight-hour day, in principle, but allow for exceptions under specified conditions. The cabinet, however, remained divided over this issue. Unwilling to defy his own party by negotiating a compromise, Stresemann resigned on October 3, 1923. President Ebert quickly reappointed him, however, and he attempted to form a new government that included only representatives from the Catholic Center party, the DVP, and the DDP. When both the SPD and the DNVP made it clear they would not tolerate this minority cabinet, Stresemann accepted Schmidt's basic proposal to restore the great coalition.[43]

Hilferding did not return to his post. In the negotiations preceding the cabinet's reorganization, DVP leader Ernst Scholz insisted that Hilferding could not handle the demands of his office and should not be reappointed. Himself disappointed by Hilferding's performance and cognizant of his controversial standing in the SPD's Reichstag delegation, Hermann Müller refrained from defending his party comrade and instead objected to von Raumer's continued presence in the cabinet. The impasse ended with an agreement to drop both men from the government. On October 6, 1923, the politically independent Hans Luther replaced Hilferding as finance minister.[44]

Contemporary appraisals of Hilferding's performance as finance minister were often highly critical. Though widely respected for his theoretical abilities, both friend and foe considered him slow-moving. In response to Stresemann's pleas to spur Hilferding to action, Otto Braun, the SPD's minister-president of Prussia replied,

> If you want me to ask him to write an article today about the currency question, I will. He will do it and it will be a good article. But to [try] to get him to take decisive measures would be a useless undertaking . . . Hilferding would be a valuable scientific advisor for a minister who can make decisions; he is too smart to be a minister himself.[45]

Hans Luther criticized Hilferding's "theoretical manner," which, he wrote, "got on the entire cabinet's nerves," while Gustav Radbruch, Stresemann's Social Democratic justice minister, commented that Hilferding's "theoretical irresolution hindered his own currency policy."[46]

Others looked upon Hilferding's actions more favorably. Heinrich Brüning, a conservative leader of the Catholic Center party and later chancellor, described Hilferding as an "outstanding *Finanzpolitiker*," who "knew what could be done and what had to be done in order to save the nation in the midst of an extreme crisis." Alex Möller, an SPD member in the 1920s and later finance minister in the Federal Republic, concurred. Hilferding, he wrote, "correctly recognized that . . . the currency stabilization could not be carried out before the struggle in the Ruhr had ended." Until then, he "prepared for the currency reform by concentrating first on foreign exchange, tax expenditures, and organizational measures."[47]

The latter view has gained considerable acceptance in recent years. Political conflicts inside and outside the cabinet, not Hilferding's irresolution, were responsible for his "failure" to halt the inflation. Although he could have been more decisive in certain judgments, Hilferding worked under difficult circumstances, under constant attack from all sides. When compared to his successor, he did not perform so poorly after all. Even after the ending of resistance in the Ruhr, it took Luther another six weeks to introduce the new *Rentenmark* and to bring the inflation under control. This time span was roughly equal to Hilferding's period in office and he had done much of the preparatory work.[48]

Hilferding certainly was proud of his party's achievements in the Stresemann cabinet. In a later speech to the Reichstag, he described the SPD's entrance into the government as "an act of rescue that [had] secured the democratic republic" and marked "Social Democracy's greatest accomplishment after the defeat of the Kapp Putsch." As finance minister, he asserted, he had blocked attempts of the industrial and landed elites to take control of the state's money policy, defeated the effort to tie the new currency to the price of the rye crop, limited the amount of the new currency bank's credit, and balanced the budget. The latter measure required ending the Ruhr campaign and was essential to the success of the reform.[49]

Hilferding's claim of victory over Germany's elites was exaggerated, as was his belief that Social Democracy had saved the republic. But he had done much to prepare for the introduction of the new currency, and this reform was essential for the restoration of political stability. Hilferding had not entered the cabinet equipped with an alternative socialist financial program. On the contrary, in spite of what his right-wing opponents claimed, he pursued an eminently orthodox policy designed to meet the needs of industry and agriculture and to shore up a crumbling capitalist economy. Though unwilling to grant the elites a free hand over state financial policy, he was also prepared to concede some of social democracy's most important postwar gains (such as the eight-hour day) in order to hold the cabinet together.

The explanation for Hilferding's orthodox policy and his willingness to make political concessions lies in his view of the relationship of organized capitalism to socialism. Hilferding located the source of the inflation not in organized capitalism itself, which he thought was less prone to crises, but in the economic policies and political antagonisms brought on by war. The crisis, he thought, represented an anomalous situation that could be ended by technical means, but it was essential to act before economic chaos destroyed the republic. This latter possibility was decisive for the socialist movement, for the absence of a democratic political framework would hinder the evolutionary transformation of the organized capitalist economy into a socialist one. Thus, unlike many left-wing socialists and the Communists, Hilferding did not see the crisis as an opportunity to push forward the socialist revolution, but rather as a danger to the parliamentary system. The aim of his financial policy was to salvage that system by restoring the capitalist economy and setting it back on its evolutionary course.

It is important to note that Hilferding's practical experience during the inflation crisis strongly influenced his increasingly orthodox economic policy ideas. During the inflation's initial postwar acceleration, Hilferding had called for socialist reforms to end the crisis, but after 1920 he abandoned such radical dreams and worked to salvage the existing system while protecting workers' interests. To this end, in his speeches to the Reich Economic Council in 1922, Hilferding stressed the need to stabilize rather then replace the currency because he feared that the latter alternative would bring on a depression. At that time he thought the state could use its gold reserves to provide needed foreign exchange and thus gain breathing space to implement strict exchange controls and budgetary reforms. He did not advocate using gold as backing for a new currency.

One year later, however, with the situation out of control, Hilferding saw a new, gold-backed mark as the nation's only way out. Indeed, the reform he advocated in September 1923 called for such a radical contraction of the money supply that, fearing a sharp economic downturn, conservatives in the cabinet objected. Thus, the socialist finance minister adopted anything but a "Marxist" or even "Keynesian" policy to end the inflation. On the contrary, he resorted to orthodox tools of political economy that, ironically, implied exactly the kind of contraction that he had initially hoped to avoid.[50]

During his tenure in office, Hilferding especially focused on reducing the state's enormous budget deficit, which, in that particular conjuncture, played an important role in accelerating the inflation. The effort to balance the budget left him permanently preoccupied with the issue, and he came to equate deficit spending with unsound financial practices that weakened the currency. Although the post-1929 depression unfolded amid very different historical circumstances, the experience of 1923 entrenched Hilferding's economic thinking along exceedingly orthodox lines, a development that had profound implications for social democratic policy during Germany's greatest crisis.

Following his dismissal from Stresemann's cabinet, Hilferding pressed the SPD's Reichstag delegation to continue backing the great coalition in order to hinder a rightist putsch.[51] On October 7, 1923, in a speech to the Berlin party organization's general assembly, he described the grave political situation. In the Rhineland and the Ruhr, separatists appeared to be on the verge of seceding from the Reich, while in Bavaria a nationalist minister-president, Gustav von Kahr, aimed to eliminate workers' political influence. Kahr's coming to power, Hilferding argued, was a signal for well-prepared right-wing forces around the country to move against the Reich government; he saw the Kustrin military garrison's foiled plan to march on Berlin and seize power in late September 1923 as only one example. Only the SPD's control of the Prussian and Reich Interior Ministries, he claimed, had enabled the government to suppress the putsch attempt. If the party had not been in the cabinet, the republic would have fallen.[52]

For that reason, Hilferding asserted, the party must stay in the cabinet. He now doubted the republic's survival. The army's loyalty was questionable, and the fascists had plenty of weapons and good leadership. The proletariat could do little to oppose them. The workers were politically divided and unarmed, the party press was in decline, and the Communists had split the unions. In every Western country social democracy was on the defensive and stood on the precipice of defeat. With the workers turning in increasing numbers to fascism, Hilferding saw no way out of social democracy's dilemma. "Every day the counterrevolution moves forward," he lamented. "If the workers continue to mistrust [their leaders], then nothing can save the situation."[53]

These remarks reveal much about Hilferding's attitude toward the masses and, more generally, about the widening gap between Social Democracy's leaders and the party rank and file. Hilferding recognized that the SPD was on the verge of disaster, and he knew that its failure to adequately address workers' immediate concerns was driving many into the ranks of the extreme right and left. He reacted, however, not by listening to the masses, whom his party claimed to represent, but by criticizing their lack of trust. Hilferding did not suggest any radical alternatives to meet workers' needs and restore their confidence. Such policies risked further polarizing the political situation. To defend the republic and avoid civil war, Hilferding and most other SPD leaders saw collaboration with the moderate bourgeois parties as the only responsible policy.

Hilferding's concern for the republic's survival was well founded, yet the republic managed to hang on. In early November, the SPD quit Stresemann's cabinet after he ordered the forcible removal of Saxony's Social Democratic and Communist coalition government but did nothing against the right-wing regime in Bavaria. Despite the SPD's departure, the minority cabinet held firm. On November 9, 1923, the Bavarian police put down Adolf Hitler's Beer Hall Putsch, a week later the government introduced the new currency, and there was progress in negotiations over reparations. At the end of the month, Catholic Center leader Wilhelm Marx organized a new cabinet.

The SPD remained in the opposition but tolerated Marx's government. Although Marx intended to ask for another Enabling Law and to weaken laws protecting the eight-hour day, a majority in the party leadership, including Hilferding, feared that overthrowing him could destabilize the new currency, undermine the reparations negotiations, and bring about Social Democracy's exclusion from the government in Prussia. As it had most party leaders, the experience of the great coalition had sobered Hilferding, and after the Reichstag delegation voted in favor of the Enabling Law, he concluded that it was time for the SPD to return to the opposition. From there the party could criticize the government, avoid accusations of collaboration with the bourgeoisie, and rebuild its political base.[54]

The May elections of 1924 strengthened this conviction. Along with the moderate bourgeois parties, the reunited SPD suffered a stunning defeat and received only 6 million votes (20.5 percent), a postwar low, and 100 seats in the Reichstag. The Communists, on the other hand, with 3,700,000 votes (12.6 percent) markedly increased their strength, as did the parties of the radical right: the DVP, the DNVP, and the fascists. Hilferding believed that to recover from this setback the SPD needed to win back the workers' confidence. The party previously had entered into coalitions only because most of the others wanted to avoid the hard foreign policy decisions required after the war. It had assumed this responsibility knowing that many workers would not understand the necessity of this policy to open the way for socialism. The negotiation of the Dawes Plan regulating reparations payments and the stabilization of the currency eased the crisis and allowed the SPD to move away from its coalition strategy and focus more clearly on proletarian concerns. To grow and expand its base, the party had to defend the eight-hour day, collective bargaining, free trade, progressive taxation, acceptance of the Dawes Plan, and Germany's entrance into the League of Nations. "What we want," Hilferding asserted, "is not a coalition strategy, but a socialist majority in the Reichstag."[55]

The inclination to withdraw from coalition politics was a logical reaction to the difficult circumstances in which the movement found itself. Since the party had participated in seven of the republic's first nine governments, many workers linked its policy with the privations of those years. Coming on the heels of the sharp economic downturn that followed the currency reform, the May electoral debacle reflected public dissatisfaction not only with the SPD but with all the parties of the Weimar coalition. By moving into the opposition, the party was able to use the controversies surrounding the Dawes Plan and its implications for German sovereignty to recoup its strength. To win back lost voters and cultivate its core working-class constituency, the SPD could selectively support or criticize the foreign or domestic policies of minority cabinets that were dependent on its tolerance to survive.[56]

This strategy bore fruit in the elections of December 1924. Campaigning under the slogan "The Enemy Stands on the Right!" the party won 7,880,000 votes (26 percent) and gained 31 additional seats in the Reichstag. At the same time, however, certain limitations were apparent. Although the SPD gained largely at the expense of the KPD, which won only 9 percent of the vote, it fared poorly among salaried employees, rural workers, and small businessmen. Substantial numbers from these groups had backed the party immediately after the revolution, but many abandoned it during the subsequent crises and attached themselves to the nationalist right.[57] Hilferding and many other Social Democrats clearly understood the importance of making gains among these constituencies if the SPD was to win a majority. They were to find, however, that it was difficult to accomplish this goal while also promoting industrial workers' interests.

Following the December 1924 elections, Hilferding and most other SPD leaders opposed entering into another coalition government until the party could do so from a position of strength. In a letter to Kautsky he observed that the voting results signaled a turning point for Social Democracy, but full recovery was a long way off. In 1912, the SPD had won 35 percent of the vote compared to 26 percent in 1924. To bring the party's strength up to its old level required the elimination of the KPD.[58]

One year later, Hilferding still believed that both sustained political work and economic prosperity were necessary before the SPD could enter a new coalition that would enjoy a strong prospect of success. He also remained suspicious of some of the SPD's potential partners, such as the DVP, which he felt had played an especially obstructionist role in Stresemann's cabinet.

This attitude strongly influenced his opposition to DDP leader Erich Koch-Weser's attempt to construct another great coalition in December 1925. Although Koch-Weser extracted substantial concessions from the DVP concerning SPD demands for increased unemployment benefits and reduced taxes on low-income groups, Hilferding remained unimpressed. He still considered the DVP unreliable and, more important, wanted economic conditions to improve before joining a new government. A new period of prosperity would strengthen the party and improve the chances of forming a workable coalition.[59]

Hilferding thought it more important for the party to remain in the opposition than to join a shaky coalition with untrustworthy partners. He was, of course, by no means opposed to the coalition strategy in principle and steadfastly defended it against its critics on the left. But he insisted that the SPD only enter into coalitions either under especially favorable conditions or to defend the republic in a severe crisis. In the meantime, he advocated backing minority bourgeois governments that excluded the extreme right.[60]

Dismissal from the Finance Ministry did not diminish Hilferding's status among the SPD's top leaders; on the contrary, his star continued to rise. After appointing him chief editor of *Die Gesellschaft,* the executive named him chair of the party's program commission (following Kautsky's return to Vienna) and placed him on the SPD's national list of Reichstag candidates, a position that virtually assured his yearly reelection without his having to personally campaign. According to party secretary Fritz Heine, Hilferding was "the most respected Marxist theoretician in the executive and was the most brilliant theorist the party ever had."[61] It was this respect, rather than any particular political post, that gave Hilferding his authority. As a Beisitzer in the executive his functions were mainly advisory. He voted in that body's decisions but had no practical power in the day-to-day management of party affairs. But Wels (who directed the SPD's organization) and Müller (who held together the Reichstag delegation) depended on Hilferding's intellectual talent and political judgment. Wels, in particular, remained impressed with Hilferding's theoretical abilities, and it was largely due to Wels's efforts that the executive placed Hilferding on its Reichstag list.[62] In the eyes of the party's leaders, Hilferding was one of the few prominent social democrats that were capable of giving theoretical expression to the majority's practical program. As long as his views did not threaten their parliamentary strategy, they were willing to entrust him with the formulation of the party's ideological tenets and long-range goals.

As a leader of the SPD's program commission, Hilferding faced the difficult challenge of developing a document that would overcome important divisions in the party after reunification. The Görlitz Program of 1921 represented an important milestone in the SPD's gradual transformation from a workers' into a people's party. Although it continued to recognize socialism as the party's goal and retained the language of class struggle, it also strongly reflected the dominance of revisionist thinking within the leadership and marked a clear break with the theoretical principles of the old Erfurt Program. Whereas the latter argued that urban and rural small producers would be eliminated by the development of large-scale capitalist production, Görlitz implicitly rejected that supposition. Instead, it asserted that small producers, wage workers, and salaried employees had common interests. By extending its influence among these groups, the party leaders aimed to broaden the SPD's political base in order to win a parliamentary majority. At Görlitz they set the party's course in this direction without encountering much internal opposition.[63]

Reunification altered this situation. Of the USPD's total membership of 290,000 in the fall of 1922, over 206,000 joined the SPD, which already had a membership of over 1 million. These new members were highly critical of the party leadership's willingness to collaborate with the bourgeois parties and held fast to traditional socialist principles stressing class struggle and a political strategy of fundamental opposition. Within a short time, a coherent and growing left-wing opposition emerged led by Paul Levi, cofounder and former chairman of the KPD; Kurt Rosenfeld, former Prussian minister of justice; and trade unionists Robert Dissmann and Toni Sender. In 1927, the left had the support of a quarter of the delegates to the party congress at Kiel, and in 1929 it comprised approximately half of the SPD's membership. Largely excluded from the majority-controlled media, it published its own journals, such as the Berlin-based *Sozialistische Politik und Wirtschaft* and the semimonthly *Klassenkampf*.[64]

Along with the majority of social democracy's leaders, Hilferding vehemently opposed the left's blanket rejection of the coalition tactic and grew increasingly impatient with its critique of the parliamentary system. He clearly sympathized, however, with those who longed for a return to the ideological traditions of the Erfurt Program. Although it avoided the agrarian question and, like Görlitz, abandoned old notions of workers' growing impoverishment, the new program accepted by the Heidelberg congress of 1925 held fast to most of Erfurt's economic analysis and to its call for the transformation of capitalist private property into social property.[65] Clearly drawing on Hilferding's theoretical perspective, the program declared that the drive to monopoly, "leads to . . . the organization of the economy into cartels and trusts. This process unites industrial capital, commercial capital, and bank capital into finance capital" (7).

Hilferding's view of historical economic trends, thus, remained rooted in the analytical categories that had shaped his prewar work; he continued to reject the central tenets of revisionist economic theory. At the same time, however, by exhorting workers to struggle against finance capital within the framework of the republic, Heidelberg also illustrated his firm adherence to a reformist strategy. "The working class," the program asserted, "cannot lead the economic struggle or fully develop its economic organization without political rights. The preservation and strengthening of the democratic republic is an absolute necessity in the workers' struggle for liberation" (8).

The Heidelberg Program proclaimed the solidarity of interests among wage earners, salaried employees, and intellectuals and called for a series of broad practical reforms, including a unitary state with a strong central government and the thorough democratization of the state administration, the justice and educational systems, and the military. Progressive tax reform was also on the agenda, as was social legislation to improve workers' living standards and to strengthen the trade unions. Unlike its predecessors, and closely reflecting Hilferding's views, the new program farsightedly asserted that international economic development made imperative the formation of a "United States of Europe." In essence, Heidelberg represented a compromise between those in the party loyal to the ideological traditions of Erfurt, and others who sought to expand the SPD's base among nonproletarian voters. As he had done throughout his career, Hilferding worked to bridge differences between the party's conflicting groups.

Hilferding's effort to unify the party ideologically had much in common with that of Otto Bauer in Austria. In the SPÖ's Linz Program of 1926, Bauer also stressed the need to rally diverse segments of the working class for a unified struggle against capital and he, too, emphasized the democratic republic as the most favorable political framework for the achievement of socialism. Bauer differed most from Hilferding in his belief that the republic represented a class state under the control of the bourgeoisie. There were moments, he thought, when no single class could dominate the state and "cooperation between hostile classes" was possible, but only temporarily. Due to capitalism's inherent contradictions such cooperation had to collapse, making coalitions only "a transitory phase in the class struggle for state power, not the goal of the struggle itself."[66]

Thus, for Bauer, the usefulness of socialist participation in coalition governments was questionable. He consistently favored a policy of opposition through which the SPÖ would win power by achieving an electoral majority. Even in emergency situations he opposed the party's entrance into coalitions in order to avoid the political damage that might result. Bauer's view was less flexible than Hilferding's. Hilferding's attitude toward the republic was generally more optimistic than Bauer's, and he believed that social democracy could win broader support for itself and for the democratic state by participating in reform-oriented republican governments.[67]

The general economic analysis of the Heidelberg Program met with little criticism, but the SPD's left wing challenged its political conclusions and criticized its reformist emphasis. When Paul Levi suggested that Hilferding's view of economic and political evolution had little to do with the reality of the movement's recent experience or the demands it would face in the future, the latter retorted that Levi and his supporters had a much different conception of revolution than his own. Revolution, Hilferding argued, was bound up with capitalist development and its inherent class antagonisms, not with revolutionary phrases, and he defended the party's use of a coalition strategy as a means of moving the class struggle into the government itself. Levi was wrong, he claimed, to suggest that the SPD would be satisfied with a "bourgeois republic," but he insisted that the political democracy offered by the republic was essential for the achievement of economic democracy and socialism. For Hilferding, extraparliamentary tactics remained primarily defensive measures against threats to the republic.[68]

Despite the left's dissatisfaction with the party's strategy, internal conflict remained relatively subdued from 1925 to 1928, during which time the SPD remained in opposition. During these years, Hilferding promoted and edited *Die Gesellschaft*, which, like its predecessor *Die Neue Zeit*, aired the views of many of Germany's leading liberal and leftist thinkers on a variety of issues. Among the many contributors to this high quality publication were Hilferding, Kautsky, liberal historian Friedrich Meinecke, trade unionist Fritz Naphtali, sociologist Ferdinand Tönnies, historian Arthur Rosenberg, philosophers Hannah Arendt and Herbert Marcuse, and Menshevik leader Alexander Schifrin.[69]

With a readership of about forty-four hundred, *Die Gesellschaft* circulated mainly among social democratic political leaders and intellectuals. Hilferding encouraged articles on virtually all topics related to problems of the democratic republic and socialism. The latter included studies of the SPD's programmatic and practical efforts to broaden its membership base and mobilize new sources of support, and many of these essays questioned notions long accepted by the movement. Hilferding did not, however, open *Die Gesellschaft*'s pages to those who impugned ideas he considered unchallengeable. Woytinsky, for example, left the journal after Hilferding blocked one of his articles for being "contrary to the spirit of Marxism," because of its criticism of the concept of surplus value.[70] Over twenty-five years after he answered the criticisms of Böhm-Bawerk, Hilferding was unwilling to publish material challenging economic, ideological, or political views that he equated with fundamental social democratic principles. A tough political infighter, he denied the SPD's left-wing access to *Die Gesellschaft* and ignored its vehement objections to this exclusion. Although he was willing to review "scientific" works by leftist opponents and strongly supported communist David Riasanov's work on the *Marx-Engels Gesamtausgabe*, he did not hesitate to use *Die Gesellschaft* to publish anti-Bolshevik polemics.[71]

Hilferding's role at *Die Gesellschaft* in many ways paralleled that of his mentor, Karl Kautsky. Like Kautsky, he saw it as his duty to articulate and defend the party's Marxist outlook, a task he carried out against perceived challenges from the right as well as from the left. Kautsky once remarked to Bernstein that he agreed with many of Bernstein's criticisms of Marxism, but "Should the materialist conception of history and the view of the proletariat as the driving force of the coming revolution ever be overcome [*überwunden*], then I would be finished and my life would no longer have meaning."[72] Hilferding's attitude was similar. He, too, was deeply attached to the materialist conception of history and the role of the proletariat within it. Under Weimar, it was Hilferding who articulated this theoretical outlook, which remained of central importance to the movement's identity as well as to his own. On many specific points of social democratic theory and practice he could be flexible; but challenges to his fundamental worldview met with resistance. He held fast to this outlook until the events of 1933 shattered his confidence beyond repair.

In addition to his editing duties, Hilferding also took on important responsibilities in the Reichstag. As the SPD's chief economic spokesman, he supported free trade, bilateral trade agreements, tax and budgetary reforms, and social welfare legislation. Between 1924 and 1933, he delivered dozens of speeches on these issues and, in the course of often heated debates, made many enemies on the right and on the left. Nazi leader Gregor Strasser referred to him as an "East-Galician-born negroid Jew"; other antisemitic nationalists labeled him "Jewish louse" and "alien" even though he had become a citizen in 1918.[73] Karl Korsch, a KPD Reichstag deputy and leading intellectual, attacked Hilferding's and Kautsky's reformism and labeled them "social democratic agents of capitalism's war," who had "disgracefully abandoned the true theory of Karl Marx and of the First International."[74] On the other hand, Hilferding also earned the respect of some leaders in the moderate bourgeois parties. He befriended the right-wing Catholic leader Heinrich Brüning and DDP leader Oscar Meyer and worked together with them during the republic's later years.

Hilferding survived the traumas of war and revolution but his marriage did not. Although virtually nothing is known of the circumstances of his relationship with Margarethe, it is possible that his penchant for high living and his hectic public life strained their marriage to breaking point.[75] In any case, she did not return to Berlin with him in 1918, and they officially divorced in 1923. Shortly thereafter, Hilferding married Rose Lanyi, a Czech-born physician and translator, who remained with him until the end of his life. We know little about their day-to-day relationship, but it is clear that they lived well. As one of the top leaders of social democracy, Hilferding was constantly in the company of Germany's leading cultural, political, and intellectual figures. Alone or with Rose he often appeared at or hosted affairs attended by government officials, key party leaders, writers, and artists. Harry Kessler described one breakfast that the Hilferdings attended in a way that tells us much about the political atmosphere in Germany at that time:

> Breakfast at the Nostitzes' included the Hilferdings, Georg Bernhard, Ernst Toller, Annette Kolb, [and] Professor Haas. Pretty formless conversation. I said . . . that in Paris one moves from salon to salon, whereas in Berlin I always feel as though I am going from one public meeting to another. In fact, this breakfast was just like a public meeting with everyone haranguing everyone else and claiming to be right without elegance or wit. Not a single well-turned phrase, not one well-aimed shaft, just loud-mouthed opinions.[76]

Rudolf and Rose Hilferding, 1928.

If Hilferding had financial difficulties before his divorce, they ended with his election to the Reichstag in 1924. As a deputy he earned the considerable salary of 9,000 RM per year.[77] This sum, when added to his income from *Die Gesellschaft,* enabled the Hilferdings to live comfortably in Steglitz, a solidly middle-class district in Berlin. It would be an exaggeration to describe Hilferding's lifestyle as extravagant by the standards of Germany's economic elites, but he certainly enjoyed dining in first-class restaurants and prided himself as an expert in fine foods and cigars. His tastes, however, were less refined than he thought. One acquaintance of the family later recalled how Hilferding's friends would sometimes switch his expensive cigars with cheaper ones and laugh as he smoked them and extolled the virtues of his "very fine" cigars.[78] As a young man, the dark-haired and mustachioed Hilferding had been of medium build. By the mid-1920s, the bespectacled intellectual was balding and had grown quite corpulent. Lord d'Abernon's comment that Hilferding "looks too prosperous to be a fighter" was fitting.[79]

Hilferding had little contact with rank-and-file party members or working people. He often wrote for or spoke to working-class audiences, but this activity was largely one of political education rather than interaction. It was among intellectual and political elites that he was willing to engage in dialogue. In 1919, for example, he became involved with efforts to set up a private "revolutionary" political club "where one could speak among open-minded people" without concern about party affiliation. Joined by publisher Paul Cassirer, diplomat Harry Kessler, poet Theodor Däubler, USPD leaders Hugo Simon and Rudolf Breitscheid, and others from communist and moderate republican circles, he attended irregular club meetings dealing with a variety of pressing issues.[80] He was also considered, along with such figures as physicist Albert Einstein, *Die Vossische Zeitung* editor Georg Bernhard, and historian Hans Delbrück, for membership in a proposed organization modeled after the English Fabian Society, in which leading intellectuals would meet with the aim of clarifying recent political, economic, and ethical developments.[81] A socialist theorist enmeshed in republican politics, Hilferding was well connected with Germany's political and intellectual elite.

As a prominent socialist intellectual and politician, Hilferding often circulated among Germany's most important republican thinkers and politicians. This focus was, however, also symptomatic of the growing gulf between the SPD's top leadership and its rank and file. Like Bauer, Lenin, and most other contemporary socialist thinkers, Hilferding essentially agreed with Kautsky's view that workers developed an anticapitalist instinct in the process of class struggle, but the development of a revolutionary socialist consciousness required the intervention of socialist theorists and the organized workers' movement.[82] Although he did not deny Kautsky's assertion that socialist thinkers could also learn from the workers, his belief in the party's role as educator decisively influenced his attitude. It was the party's job to teach the masses and to pursue policies thought to represent their interests. It was the workers' task to learn what was in their interest and to join the SPD in the struggle for their emancipation. Hilferding's outlook assumes particular importance when viewed in connection with the SPD leadership's autonomy vis-à-vis its constituency. He entered the executive at a time when it had reached the zenith of its control over the party organization. Most Social Democrats did not challenge the top leaders' authority, even if their policies appeared flawed, but when opposition did arise the executive's decisive influence over the selection of congress delegates and over the socialist press made it virtually impossible to replace executive members.[83] Thus, Hilferding did not have to worry unduly about losing his post if he supported unpopular views or failed policies. His relatively protected position—combined with his view of the socialist theorist as teacher—over time tended to produce an attitude of intellectual arrogance that made it difficult for him to accept criticism, especially from the left.

Among Hilferding's closest social democratic associates after 1918 was Rudolf Breitscheid. Breitscheid was also a leader of the USPD's moderate wing. He participated with Hilferding in the "revolutionary" club and, after reunification, became a member of the SPD executive wherein he focused on foreign policy issues. He and Hilferding had similar political views and often appeared together at private functions.[84] Although their personalities sometimes clashed and (especially after 1933) they occasionally differed politically, the two men remained loyal friends over the years and were virtually inseparable in the months preceding their capture by the Gestapo in 1941. Contemporary reports indicate that Hilferding also worked amicably in the executive with Wels and Müller. He regularly discussed the contents of his major speeches with Wels, who once playfully, but respectfully, joked that "if you poked Hilferding in the stomach, something brainy would come out."[85] For his part, Müller insisted on naming Hilferding to his cabinet in 1928 and stuck with him during the ensuing crises. When Müller died in 1931, Hilferding praised the chairman's accomplishments as a statesman and party leader. In a letter to Kautsky he wrote, "Hermann Müller's death was a great loss. I was able to work well with him, and through him I could almost always carry out my policy"; he and Müller had agreed on most issues.[86]

Karl Kautsky's return to Vienna in 1924 greatly saddened Hilferding, for by that time they had developed a deep personal attachment. To Hilferding, Kautsky was more than a teacher or party comrade, he had become a father figure as well. In their correspondence he often reminded Kautsky that he missed him. One letter, written in November 1924, tells us much about the nature of their relationship and provides a rare glimpse of Hilferding's private side. It is worth quoting at length:

> [It was] you [who] intervened decisively in my life and brought me to Berlin. You and Luise took me in like a son and your house became like home to me. You were always the benevolent friend, and I always felt secure and protected in

this friendship. You only disappointed me once, when you left Berlin. I felt your absence immediately, but it weighed upon me more the longer you were away. It's strange, I'll never feel completely at home here and today even less so than when Bebel and you represented the party. I have no real friends here, scarcely anyone with whom I can argue about serious problems and—remarkable but true—I can't get over the disappointment of 1914 as easily as you. I couldn't hold you here and believed I had no right to do that. I think that Vienna must be more comfortable for you than Berlin because that's where the children are and it's warmer and more human there. . . . [This] had to be said, so that you know how strong my feelings are, how thankful I've always been to you and how happy I was to have the good fortune to work with you intellectually. Perhaps between 1914 and 1918 we had some tactical differences, but in all important points we were in agreement.[87]

This letter reveals that, by the middle of the 1920s, Hilferding had become uneasy about his place within the SPD leadership. He clearly was uncomfortable with the generation of party leaders that had replaced that of Bebel and Kautsky. The latter group had drawn Hilferding into the leadership, and he was loyal both to its members and to their ideas. The events following the disaster of 1914 had shattered many of that generation's expectations, and Hilferding's remarks indicate that in 1924 he still had not recovered from the blow. The changes in the SPD's leadership left him feeling isolated and alone; Kautsky's departure from Berlin represented one more break with his pre-1914 world, when social and political battle lines seemed clear and the movement appeared to be united and moving inexorably toward the goal of socialism. Hilferding now recognized that the SPD was in a state of transition, but he still wished to hang on to pieces of the past. Thus his friendship with Kautsky, forged during that earlier time, was so important to him. After Kautsky's return to Vienna, Hilferding was determined to preserve their ties and remained a devoted friend until the older man's death in 1938.

Politics dominated Hilferding's life and colored virtually all of his personal relations so it is natural that contemporary appraisals of his talents and character generally depend on the commentator's political perspective. Most social democrats would probably have agreed with Alexander Stein's description of Hilferding as one of the movement's "most significant theorists" and "able" leaders, and many nonsocialist moderates, impressed with his rejection of radical political and economic strategies, were equally complimentary. Heinrich Brüning, for example, considered him a "realist," who had broken with "pure Marxism" and thus become "the only one who could provide a new theoretical basis for the social democratic parties." The DDP leader, Oscar Meyer, described him as an "outstanding personality . . . [a] man of the most noble desires, thorough education [tiefe Bildung], and never failing goodwill."[88]

Some social democrats, however, saw things differently, however. Otto

Braun, the longtime minister-president of Prussia, came to despise Hilferding when the latter, as *Vorwärts*'s editor in October 1914, refused to accept an article by him because of their opposing points of view on the war. Braun never forgave Hilferding and referred to him in his diary as a "Slovenian racketeer *[slowenische Oberschieber]*." In 1923, Braun criticized him scathingly for his indecisiveness as finance minister and, five years later, actually blocked his comrade's appointment to a professorship at the Berlin College of Trade. Without stretching the example too far, Braun's attitude provides further insight into Hilferding's standing in the party leadership. Like many others who criticized Hilferding, Braun respected his abilities as a thinker but thought little of his practical talents. He also regarded him as an outsider, and his slur against Hilferding echoes earlier comments in the Parteiausschuß by those who wondered if his "foreignness" compromised his loyalty as *Vorwärts*'s editor during the war. Given such sentiments among at least some of his colleagues, it is not hard to understand Hilferding's remarks to Kautsky in which he described his sense of isolation in Berlin. The Jewish outsider from Vienna never felt fully accepted even in the movement that promised him a home and to which he had dedicated his life.[89]

Other socialists also criticized Hilferding's character, though for different reasons. Paul Hertz, an SPD financial expert and later coeditor with Hilferding of *Die Zeitschrift für Sozialismus,* established close political ties with him in the mid-1930s. After they had a political falling out, Hertz commented acerbically that "engagement and loyalty to his friends were not among Hilferding's strengths." Carl von Ossietzky, a leading left-wing republican journalist, harbored similar views. In 1924 he published an article entitled "Rudolf Hilferding: The Man without a Shadow," in which he skewered Hilferding's abilities and personality. Hilferding, he wrote, may in fact have been social democracy's top intellectual, but among aging party leaders who had long ceased to think about anything other than the "politics of the possible" this was not saying much. With his "schooled brain" and his "eye for the possible" he fitted in well with this group.[90]

Ossietzky characterized Hilferding as a man of reflection rather than initiative. Against his better knowledge, he had hesitated to fight the radicals in the USPD in 1919. By the time he moved decisively against them, they had seized control of the party. If Hilferding had fought the opposition in 1919 and 1920 (when it was strong) as vehemently as he fought it now in the SPD (when it was weak), "perhaps social democracy would have been spared some of its trials of the last few years."[91]

According to Ossietzky, Hilferding's work usually merely stated what was already obvious to all and entailed no risk of challenge. He had managed to become social democracy's oracle because of his ability to make it appear that he had arrived at his opinions "scientifically." He was cold, schoolmasterly, arrogant, and had much knowledge but little wisdom. "There is an icy barrier around him," Ossietzky wrote, a zone in which there is no emotion. His speech is that of a man who occupies himself only with the great questions and does not worry about details. He remains always the learned Marxist, believes in systems, and is mathematically exact. But he is without the essentials of a leader. He is without flash and does not have a sense for the irrational behind things . . . . No heart, no fist. A head. But the head of a party that no longer makes any momentous claims, moves at a leisurely pace and, like a parvenu, uses intellectuality as a facade.[92]

In Ossietzky's view, Hilferding was simply not equipped to lead social democracy to victory. When *Vorwärts* had backed the SPD's counterrevolutionary postwar policy, he had missed the chance to build *Die Freiheit* into "an intellectually representative organ of German socialism." As finance minister, he had surrounded himself with reactionaries and done nothing. Hilferding had constantly failed at the critical moment.[93]

Ossietzky's judgments are not groundless, but they are grossly exaggerated and in consequence represent an unfair appraisal of Hilferding's character. Hilferding certainly had an arrogant streak, made serious political mistakes, and may occasionally have been slow to react in certain critical situations, but he was not the heartless pseudointellectual Ossietzky portrays. During the revolution and the inflation crisis he acted resolutely and courageously to defend what he believed were socialist principles and to protect the republic. Ossietzky ignores the context that hindered Hilferding's actions during the USPD's internal crisis and during his tenure as minister. Where Ossietzky was most prescient, however, was in recognizing that social democracy's leadership under Weimar had lost much of its vigor; its staid parliamentary tactics and close association with the status quo did little to inspire a frustrated younger generation or to win over social groups who blamed the republic for their problems.

Hilferding and the majority of social democracy's leaders thought otherwise. To them, the SPD's tactics were on the right track. Remaining in the opposition allowed the party to recover some of its electoral strength in the December ballot of 1924, and as the economy improved, its organization began to recover as well. Indeed, the mid-1920s witnessed a historical highwater mark for the growth of the movement's cultural organizations. Attracting hundreds of thousands of workers, social democratic associations of all types—ranging from singing and sports clubs to trade union, "free thinker," professional, and prorepublican paramilitary organizations (the *Reichsbanner*)—flourished and represented a point of pride for Hilferding and other SPD leaders. It was here that social democracy's core supporters created a finely interwoven *Solidargemeinschaft* that, for many, represented the nucleus of the future socialist society. As Peter Lösche and Franz Walter point out, the expansion of the party's organizations into virtually every sphere of cultural life conformed with the model of gradual socialist transformation put forward by Hilferding. It was no accident that his theory of organized capitalism and economic democracy were popularized precisely during the years of the cultural organizations' greatest prosperity.[94]

There was also substantial progress in the area of social policy. During the mid-1920s the Reichstag enacted a series of reforms that were quite favorable to workers. These included the implementation of binding arbitration by the Labor Ministry, the restoration of the eight-hour day in large firms, the Labor Courts Law of 1926, and in 1927 the Employment Facilitation and Unemployment Insurance Act, which established insurance paid for by the contributions of employees, employers, and the state. The government expanded health, disability, and social insurance programs, improved occupational safety standards, and increased investment in public housing. These were concrete gains and their achievement demonstrated how the establishment of political democracy had shifted the social balance of power since 1914. With capital now forced to recognize unions and with social democracy able to influence state policy, Germany's economic elites—however resistant—could no longer avoid making substantial concessions either in the workplace or in the sphere of redistributive taxation.[95]

In addition to these improvements, many SPD leaders also thought that the alignment of Germany's political parties had shifted in their favor. Industrialist Paul Silverberg's address to the RdI in September 1926 convinced Hilferding and others that the DVP was moving away from the extreme right and could become a viable partner in a coalition government. In Hilferding's view, Silverberg's approval of the government's foreign policy, his recognition of the republic, and his call for the SPD to enter the cabinet reflected the growing strength of the export-oriented "finished product industries" within German capitalism. Unlike the declining "raw material and heavy industries," in which capital still fought to hold down wages and operated according to the *Herr im Haus* principle, the finished product industries were expanding rapidly and were willing to pay high wages to keep production going. The growing importance of these industries in the German economy was symbolized by the RdI's support for the Dawes Plan, the Locarno Treaty, and Germany's entrance into the League of Nations. Thus, a significant portion of industry was now ready to break its ties to the reactionary DNVP and to end its opposition to the republic. The movement of industry toward the center, Hilferding thought, created the possibility for a broad coalition of republican parties that could pursue the practical goals elaborated in the SPD's own program.[96]

Hilferding developed this argument further at the Kiel party congress of 1927. There he reelaborated his theories of organized capitalism and economic democracy, reviewed the SPD's policy through the mid-1920s, and called on the party to consider joining a new coalition. He justified this tactical shift by arguing that the transition from organized capitalism to socialism required the conscious political activity of the working class. The capitalist republic provided the political framework to make this transformation possible, but only if the workers gained influence over the state. The party, he asserted, had to convince the workers that money, trade, tax, labor, and insurance policies were political policies, and that progressive change depended upon the growth of their political power: "We must hammer it into the head of each worker that the weekly wage is a political wage, that it depends . . . on the strength of the parliamentary representation of the working class." Participation in the government, he insisted, would enable the SPD to fight for reforms that prepared the way for socialism.[97]

Hilferding also saw working in coalition governments as a strategy to prevent the nationalist right, especially the DNVP, from coming to power. Remaining too long in the opposition effectively meant abandoning the government to socialism's enemies and would make reform of the army, government, and economy impossible. It was essential, Hilferding thought, to mobilize the workers in the fight for democracy, for if the proletariat failed to develop a democratic political consciousness, the republic could fall victim to the attacks of the reactionary right. Joining an effective reform coalition would increase workers' awareness of their power within the democratic republic and strengthen their resolve to protect it.[98]

As he had in the past, at Kiel Hilferding stressed the SPD's need to broaden its base of support. In addition to proposing a new agricultural program designed to attract small farmers, he urged the party to unite "the whole working class" under its banner by drawing workers' support away from the Christian trade unions, the KPD, the Center, and the DNVP. Hilferding believed that Germany's social structure made a "proletarian" majority in the Reichstag possible, but he did not adequately address the different ways wage laborers and salaried employees perceived themselves and thus left unclear what steps were necessary to win nonindustrial workers' support.[99]

The left opposition at Kiel responded sharply to Hilferding's conclusions. Led by Toni Sender and Siegfried Aufhäuser the left argued that, under organized capitalism, capitalist domination of the state was stronger than ever. To enter a coalition with capital's representatives would only confuse the very workers whom the party was trying to recruit. Although the opposition did not dismiss the political freedom gained under the republic, it warned against harboring "democratic illusions" about the system and about the antisocialist parties' respect for its rules. Entering a coalition, they argued, required too great an accommodation with the party's enemies. Instead the party should remain outside the government and develop a program designed to win over nonsocialist workers. Hilferding brushed aside these objections by reemphasizing his central arguments. He knew that the bulk of the party leadership backed him. When the left proposed a resolution calling on the SPD to remain in the opposition, it received only 83 votes with 255 opposed.[100]

The Kiel congress marked the high-water mark of Hilferding's influence within the socialist movement. Along with a majority in the party leadership, many German trade unionists agreed with his basic views. In 1928 the Hamburg Congress of Free German Trade Unions (ADGB) adopted the concept

of economic democracy into its official program. As presented by union
leader Fritz Naphtali, economic democracy did not entail the rapid socialization of the economy but aimed to restrict the autocratic management of industry and to increase trade union influence on the economy. These were
moderate measures intended to adapt the unions' strategy to the development of organized capitalism. Like their SPD counterparts, most union leaders believed that the democratization of the economy was essential to the
gradual evolution of socialism. Their immediate goal was not the sudden
overthrow of the system but the achievement of reforms.[101]

The arguments Hilferding put forward at Kiel rested on a fundamental
misreading of German reality. It was true that some business sectors—such as
the prosperous chemical, electrical, and finishing industries—supported Silverberg's advocacy of cooperation between capital and labor, but a majority
of big capitalists, especially in heavy industry, were furious at their relative loss
of economic and political power under the republic and rejected his proposals. Indeed, the country was about to experience a renewed wave of open
warfare between labor and capital as the latter chafed under the system of collective bargaining and state arbitration of industrial disputes. The lockout of
250,000 Ruhr steelworkers in 1928 was only the opening salvo in this struggle. Although the effort failed to undermine the arbitration system, it marked
the growing radicalization of industry's critique of the Weimar system.[102]

Serious problems also made it difficult for the SPD to achieve the majority
it craved. Hilferding and other leaders certainly recognized the need to
broaden the party's appeal but, aside from drafting a few programmatic documents, actually made only halting efforts to do so. The failure to develop a
clear strategy for reaching out to groups that were underrepresented in its
ranks (such as youth, peasants, the self-employed, and white-collar workers)
was partly due to the continued attachment of many in the leadership, including Hilferding, to the idea of the SPD as a party of industrial workers.
Otto Wels's proclamation at Kiel that "The fight is for the political soul of
the German working class" reflected this sentiment and drew no criticism
even though the party was about to unveil its new agrarian program![103] And
while the leaders vacillated, many activists focused primarily on strengthening
their own institutions and promoting the solidarity of industrial workers,
their traditional constituents.

In a society riven by class and other social conflicts, it was difficult for the
social democrats to build bridges between their own and other, often antagonistic, social milieus. The SPD's slowness in building cross-class support was
not of major importance to the functioning of the Weimar system during its
years of relative economic and political stability. After the onset of the republic's fatal crises, however, this factor had major implications as the party's support base narrowed and, simultaneously, the other parties of the Weimar
coalition either collapsed or moved to the right.[104]

Hilferding urged the Weimar SPD to pursue a "politics of the possible," but as Richard Bessel notes, "successful democratic politics must be based upon a clear recognition of what in fact is possible."[105] Following Kiel, the party's policy rested on anything but such a clear recognition. On the contrary, it was based on an unrealistic assessment of the economy and of what could be accomplished within a coalition government. The optimistic scenario of Hilferding's theory of organized capitalism was predicated on continued economic expansion without serious cyclical downturns. It did not recognize Germany's persistent unemployment and shaky state finances as symptoms of fundamental economic weakness that would make it very difficult to preserve, much less extend, the social state.[106] At a time when the country stood on the brink of economic disaster, the SPD proclaimed the expansion of the government's *Sozialpolitik* as a major campaign theme for the May 1928 elections.[107] As was the case in most other political circles, the rapid deterioration of the German economy surprised and unnerved the ill-prepared social democrats.

The SPD emerged from the May 1928 elections as Germany's largest party with almost 30 percent of the vote and 153 seats in the Reichstag. It was twice as strong as the DNVP and three times as strong as the KPD, and the executive decided to enter and lead a new great coalition. After a month of difficult negotiations with the bourgeois parties, Hermann Müller assumed the chancellorship of a government that included three other Social Democrats, two representatives from the DDP, two from the DVP, and one each from the Center and the Bavarian People's Party (BVP). With Müller's backing, Hilferding once again took over the Finance Ministry.

As in 1923, Hilferding's second term began under inauspicious circumstances. Despite the relative prosperity of the postinflation years, well over 1 million workers remained unemployed and government income did not suffice to meet the increased costs of its expanded bureaucracy, social programs, and economic subsidies (especially in agriculture). The state had covered its debts by using surpluses accumulated immediately after the currency stabilization, but by 1928 these were exhausted. Forced to borrow in order to cover repeated budget deficits, between March and December 1928 the government increased the national debt from 792 to 1,337 million RM. The financial situation for the following year threatened to deteriorate even more. According to the stipulations of the Dawes Plan, in 1929 Germany had to resume making full reparations payments to the Allies.[108] Hilferding believed that in this crisis it was important for a Social Democrat to head the Finance Ministry in order to prevent a resurgence of inflation and to protect workers' interests. Confident of his ability to deal with the situation, he shrugged off Heinrich Brüning's suggestion that he avoid placing himself in the same vulnerable position he had occupied in 1923. In retrospect, it is hard to imagine that two years later Hilferding did not wish he had followed Brüning's advice.[109]

The Social Democrats entered the government without clearly defined goals. Although they certainly hoped to carry out reforms favorable to workers, conflicts of interest within the cabinet prevented it from uniting behind a specific program. On a variety of issues, including the building of pocket battleships, tax policy, and unemployment insurance, the right-wing parties forced the SPD to make one concession after another to maintain the coalition. In the face of fierce resistance from the right, it proved impossible for the socialists to carry out any major reforms. From the Müller cabinet's inception in June 1928 until its fall in March 1930, the SPD was barely able to defend the workers' interests, much less promote them.

Hilferding took over the Finance Ministry determined to implement an orthodox budgetary policy that would bring order to the state's chaotic finances. In a speech to the Reichstag delivered in March 1928, he had called for reduced military expenditures and had specifically criticized the navy's plans to build the first of the four pocket battleships permitted by the Treaty of Versailles. While opposing reductions in social spending, he favored granting the finance minister the right to block new expenditures that were not balanced by increased revenues. He stressed the importance of attracting more foreign investment in industry. If used properly, he thought, foreign capital could reduce Germany's growing unemployment. He also advocated the formation of a unitary state in order to reform Berlin's tax relationship with the *Länder* and thereby reduce administrative costs.[110]

His plans immediately encountered resistance. The first major struggle occurred when the bourgeois parties in the cabinet demanded the construction of the pocket battleship. The vast majority of social democrats opposed this project, and the party had campaigned vigorously against it by stressing the need for social rather than military spending. It seemed inconceivable to most SPD members that their leaders would suddenly alter this policy.[111] Yet the socialist ministers faced a serious dilemma. During the summer the DVP and the Reichswehr pressured them to begin the project. Fearing that resistance to the right's demands would destroy the coalition, on August 10, 1928, Müller and his socialist colleagues in the cabinet agreed to support the battleship's construction. The decision unleashed a storm of disapproval within their own party.[112]

Outrage swept through all levels and all factions of the SPD. Most of its newspapers and many politicians and officials joined the chorus of rank-and-file members who condemned the ministers in meetings held around the country. The Reichstag deputies were incensed and, together with Party Council and the Prussian Landtag delegation, upbraided and reprimanded the socialist ministers at a meeting held in Berlin on August 18, 1928. During the proceedings the ministers found it difficult to defend themselves against the mistrust engendered by their policy. According to Landtag delegate Toni Jensen, Hilferding was "completely passive" even as his friend Breitscheid "demagogically" attacked him and his colleagues. The acrimony that characterized the meeting reflected a very real struggle between the Reichstag delegation and the SPD's cabinet representatives over the making and execution of policy. In this case, the delegation fully asserted its authority, but the conflict continued. Caught between the squabbling in the cabinet and the interference of the deputies, Hilferding found the situation "unbearable" and complained that the delegation was floundering in "complete confusion . . . without leadership or direction." He had no solution. No longer members of the delegation, neither he nor Müller could control it or restore its members' trust.[113]

On November 14, 1928, the SPD Reichstag deputies unanimously voted to reject the battleship and the next day ordered the socialist ministers to vote with the delegation against their own policy in the Reichstag. When the DVP and Center then informed Müller that they might abandon the coalition if he voted against his cabinet's policy, the government seemed doomed.[114] Müller responded by making clear to the DVP and Center party ministers that if Reichstag defeated the SPD's motion, the cabinet could rest assured of the socialist ministers' support. On November 16, the SPD's attempt to block the battleship project failed by a vote of 225 to 203. SPD ministers Hilferding, Müller, Severing, and Wissell all followed the instructions of their Reichstag delegation and voted against their own policy, but the bourgeois parties remained in the coalition. The cabinet had survived, but only because the socialists had abandoned their principles and granted the militarists an important victory.

This fight was but a prelude to the interparty conflicts that arose as the coalition's so-called partners struggled to deal with Germany's deteriorating economy. By February 1929, unemployment had reached 3 million, and the Reich Unemployment Insurance Agency (Reichsanstalt)—funded by a 3 percent tax on wages and salaries and a 3 percent employers payroll tax—was financially overburdened. The year before, the government had helped to finance its operations with loans totaling over 250 million RM, but no relief was in sight. By early 1929, the state budget deficit already had reached 738 million RM and, to make matters worse, reparations obligations were expected to rise more than 20 percent over the previous year, to 1.5 billion RM.[115]

In his early theoretical work, Hilferding had recognized that a coordinated credit and investment policy by the banks and the state could ease the impact of capitalist crises. His experience in 1923, however, had greatly magnified his fear of inflation and now caused him to shy away from such ideas. In his March 1929 speech presenting his new budget to the Reichstag, Hilferding argued that Germany's most pressing economic problem was a shortage of investment capital to stimulate production and provide jobs. High taxes and excessive government spending discouraged saving and hindered capital formation, while new loans to cover the budget deficit only increased the state's debt and rekindled the danger of inflation. The only solution, he asserted, was to cut income taxes and balance the budget by reducing spending on all levels and raising indirect taxes.[116]

Hilferding called for "socially bearable" government spending cuts wherever possible and proposed a freeze on the central government's payments to the *Länder*. But even if the Reichstag approved his plans, Hilferding knew the deficit would fall to only 379 million RM. To bridge the gap, he called for new indirect taxes, most notably on beer and brandy, as well as modest increases in inheritance and property taxes. In order to stimulate capital accumulation, he recommended a 5 percent income tax cut for those earning between 8,000 and 25,000 RM yearly. In addition, he hoped that a new round of negotiations in Paris between Germany and the Allies would result in substantially reduced reparations payments. Such a reduction would ease the budget crisis, free more capital for investment, and allow the government to further reduce income taxes.[117]

Hilferding's plan encountered strong resistance from the DVP, which opposed any new taxes and demanded reduced government spending, a further reduction of Reich payments to the states, and the taxation of public enterprises to balance the budget. When the DVP threatened to leave the cabinet, the SPD compromised once again. In March and April, committees of experts from the Reichstag delegation of each coalition party worked out a new plan, which they completed on April 9, 1929. This plan, which had the DVP's support, eliminated most of Hilferding's suggested tax increases and called for deeper budget cuts.[118]

The new proposal dissatisfied Hilferding; the cuts were too deep and were so economically unfeasible that they would have to be restored by the end of the year. He thought that the experts had overestimated the government's future income, allotted insufficient reserves to make up for unexpected revenue shortfalls, and relied too heavily on the successful reduction of reparations payments. Nevertheless, Hilferding supported the new plan in order to secure the cabinet's unity. "A stable government," he concluded, "was indispensable if we are to achieve our most important political goal, the success of the Paris negotiations."[119]

In late June 1929, the Reichstag approved a new budget that looked little like Hilferding's original plan. The SPD and the BVP had eliminated the beer tax; the income tax reduction was postponed; and the right wing blocked the inheritance tax and reduced the new property tax by half. To cover the deficit, the experts cut spending by an additional 180 million RM and conveniently revised upward their estimates of government income for 1929. Hilferding's politically expedient decision to accept this program ensured the failure of his economic policy later on. By agreeing to the extreme cuts demanded by the conservatives, the government helped slow an economy that was desperately in need of stimulation. The number of government contracts to industry fell, and there was less money available for public works projects, housing, and transport. The reductions exacerbated unemployment, which in turn fueled rising unemployment insurance costs.[120]

Hilferding's efforts to deal with the latter problem bogged down amid the conflicting interests of the coalition parties. To shore up the Reichsanstalt's finances, he proposed its reorganization, an increase in workers' and employers' contributions to the insurance system, and the formation of a reserve fund of 150 million RM for loans to the Reichsanstalt in an emergency.[121] Rudolf Wissell, SPD labor minister, opposed these suggestions because he regarded some of them as contrary to social democratic principles. Accepting the organizational reform and a 1 percent increase in worker and employer contributions, he also demanded increased unemployment benefits and the system's expansion to include previously ineligible categories of workers (seasonal laborers, for example). Wissell wanted to protect and improve workers' living standards and advocated increased property taxes to pay for extended benefits. But Hilferding, backed by Müller, resisted proposals that he thought would weaken the government's finances.[122]

While the SPD ministers argued among themselves over the future of the Reichsanstalt, Germany's industrialists began an offensive to roll back the wage and benefit gains made by the workers just a few years earlier. The DVP and the industrialist organizations aimed to minimize government expenditures and to resist SPD attempts to raise or extend insurance benefits. They wanted to "adapt" Germany's social insurance system to the needs of the economy and demanded a "free market" as "the decisive prerequisite for a return to prosperity and the final liberation of the German people." With these goals in mind, the DVP and its allies worked to undermine government-sanctioned binding arbitration in labor disputes and to weaken the unemployment insurance program.[123]

Although Hilferding's economic proposals did not go as far as those of the right-wing parties, his policies were not fundamentally different. Deficit spending, he believed, had to stop, even if it meant limiting benefits to widows, orphans, and lightly wounded war veterans.[124] Such views were bound to meet with tenacious resistance within the SPD. In his dispute with Wissell, the latter had the support of top party leaders including Wels, Braun, and Friedrich Stampfer, the bulk of the Reichstag delegation, and the whole of the party's left wing. *Vorwärts* accused Hilferding of being willing to dismantle the insurance system while lowering the taxes of the rich. The trade unions made it clear that the SPD should risk the dissolution of the cabinet before it surrendered its principles on social issues.[125]

In early October 1929, just as the cabinet neared collapse, the coalition parties finally reached a compromise. The SPD, the DDP, and the Center agreed to a 0.5 percent increase in worker and employer contributions to the insurance fund and also agreed to grant benefits to unemployed seasonal laborers until March 31, 1931. Stresemann begged his party comrades not to destroy the coalition over this issue, and the DVP reluctantly agreed not to vote against the proposal in the Reichstag. The bill became law on October 12, 1929.

For Hilferding, this compromise was a defeat. The new plan failed to make the insurance system financially solvent, and in 1930 the Reichsanstalt required government loans amounting to 624 million RM.[126] For the SPD,

however, the bill's passage was a victory, because it ensured, at least temporarily, that the government would not abandon its social responsibilities.
Hilferding was trapped between his socialist principles and the practical measures he thought necessary to resolve the financial crisis. Social democracy, he
believed, represented "the collective interests of the proletariat," yet as finance minister he found himself advocating policies that strengthened the
economic power of capital at the workers' expense.[127] By arguing that such
tough remedies were economically necessary, he placed himself at odds with
the vast majority of the SPD's rank and file and even with many of his supporters within the leadership. As the state's financial crisis worsened in the fall
of 1929, few social democrats were willing to defend Hilferding's position in
the cabinet.

In June 1929, Germany and the Allies agreed to a new plan that resched
uled Germany's reparations payments, provided for withdrawal of all Allied
troops from the Rhineland, and ended Allied controls over the Reichsbank.
The Young Plan granted Germany fifty-nine years to pay its obligations in
yearly installments that were half a billion RM lower than those required under the Dawes Plan. Months of further negotiations were necessary, however,
to work out the details. In addition, the German government's support for
the plan polarized public opinion to such an extent that it took the Reichstag
until March 1930 to ratify it. These delays prevented Hilferding from immediately using the newly available funds to shore up state finances. As revenues
plummeted, he had to cover expenses by resorting to short-term, high-interest
loans that increased the Reich's total debt. At his request, in October 1929
the Allies granted Germany credits amounting to the yearly difference in reparations payments between the Dawes and Young Plans. At the same time, he
successfully negotiated a loan of 125 million U.S. dollars from the Swedish
match producer Ivar Krueger. The agreement required Germany to repay the
loan over fifty years at 6 percent interest and to establish a match monopoly in
which Krueger played a role. This was to go into effect in tandem with the
Young Plan.[128]

Hilferding's support for the Young Plan and his resort to foreign credits
raised the ire of the nationalist right and angered the president of the Reichsbank, Hjalmar Schacht. Schacht had participated in the Paris negotiations and
had even signed the Young Plan, but shortly afterward he had distanced himself from this action. Shifting sharply rightward politically and determined to
establish the Reichsbank's control over the government's money policy,
Schacht became one of Hilferding's most virulent critics.[129] Hilferding and
his state secretary, Johannes Popitz, found him difficult as early as the Young
Plan negotiations, when Schacht refused to cooperate in discussions of the
budget crisis. Their relations deteriorated rapidly thereafter. During the summer and fall of 1929, the Finance Ministry secured important loans and
sought new creditors in negotiations carried out largely separate from the
Reichsbank's own similar activities. Irritated by the Finance Ministry's inde-

pendent actions, in December Schacht blocked an important loan that Hilferding was negotiating with Dillon Read, an American bank consortium. On December 4, 1929, Schacht demanded that the government resort to Article 48 of the constitution (which allowed the chancellor to rule by decree in an emergency) in order to bring the state finances in order. Hilferding labeled this proposal a "policy of disaster" that would "arouse a storm that even a dictatorship could not withstand." Had the parties not blocked his planned tax increases, he argued, the 1928 budget would have been balanced. With Müller's backing, he rejected Schacht's suggestions to cut costs by delaying the payment of government salaries and halting the central government's support for the states. Balancing the budget, he asserted, had to be done in an orderly fashion and without taking drastic action against the masses. The Young Plan would make this possible; in the meantime the state could meet its expenses by further borrowing.[130]

Angered by the cabinet's refusal to accept his demands, on December 6, 1929, Schacht publicly denounced the Young Plan and attacked the Reich's financial policies. The latter, he claimed, were in complete disarray, and even if the Young Plan went into effect the reduction in reparations payments would do little to improve the state's finances.[131] Schacht's assault embarrassed Hilferding and the cabinet. It cast a shadow over Hilferding's financial program for 1930, which he presented on December 9, 1929. Like his earlier proposals, this one called for a mixture of new indirect taxes, administrative reforms, and income tax reductions designed to stimulate capital accumulation and balance the budget. It, too, immediately sparked controversy within the cabinet and the Reichstag as each party defended its own interests. On December 16, 1929, just after the coalition had survived a vote of no confidence and had negotiated a compromise budget, Schacht intervened again by charging that the latter was unsatisfactory because it failed to begin repaying the national debt. He demanded that the government raise 220 million RM in new taxes and cut expenditures by another 280 million RM in order to repay 500 million RM of the debt in 1930. If the cabinet rejected his proposals, he threatened to block desperately needed foreign loans.[132]

Schacht's actions brought the government to its knees and forced Hilferding out of the cabinet. The DVP's Reichstag delegation began calling for his resignation on December 14, 1929, and six days later DVP ministers Curtius and Moldenhauer informed Müller that, unless Hilferding stepped aside immediately, they would leave the cabinet.[133] With his finance reform "derailed through outside intervention" and the coalition on the verge of collapse, Hilferding asked Müller to relieve him of his duties.[134]

The chancellor hesitated to grant his request. He knew that, despite the SPD's general dissatisfaction with Hilferding's policies, a majority in the Reichstag delegation opposed his dismissal because it would weaken the party's position in the cabinet. He also worried about the repercussions of Hilferding's absence from the negotiations to finalize the Young Plan. On

December 21, 1929, he discussed the situation with the cabinet and it became clear that to save the coalition Hilferding would have to go. Reluctantly, Müller accepted his resignation.[135]

The reaction of most social democrats to Hilferding's resignation was similar to that of 1923; in general his reputation as a theorist remained undiminished, but most thought him a failure as a practical politician. Some of Hilferding's socialist critics, such as Wilhelm Keil and Friedrich Stampfer, blamed many of the government's economic troubles on Schacht, the DVP, or even on Hilferding's assistant, Popitz. But virtually all observers, including the relatively supportive SPD Press Service, criticized Hilferding's inability to make and carry out tough decisions against his opponents in the cabinet.[136] These criticisms are only partially justified. Hilferding did make tough decisions, and his budget proposals made clear that he would oppose his own party when he thought it necessary. He was not, however, able to overcome intense opposition from both sides of the political spectrum. Rather than risk the government's dissolution, he was ready to compromise with the coalition's conservative parties, but in vain. Ultimately, the conservatives used him as a scapegoat for the financial disaster and drove him from the cabinet even though his policies differed little from theirs, while the SPD grew impatient when his proposals worked to the disadvantage of its constituency. Hilferding argued that his program defended the long-term interests of the proletariat, but this position attracted little sympathy from party leaders concerned with worsening economic and political conditions.

Rudolf Wissell's remark that Hilferding had "carried out the policy of the DVP" was accurate.[137] Hilferding joined the cabinet in 1928 intending to restore and improve, not to radically alter, the capitalist state's operations. As in 1923, his task was to reset the course of the capitalist economy. Once he perceived that conditions were worse than anticipated, he advocated drastic and unpopular steps to keep the capitalist ship afloat. This outlook explains why Hilferding entered the cabinet without an alternative socialist financial program to deal with the crisis. With the onset of the depression, he resorted to inadequate methods of supply side economics to restore the state's finances and create investment capital. In essence these were policies demanded by the German right, and they strengthened the SPD's nationalist and communist enemies. Without an economic program of its own, the SPD had little to offer to increasingly desperate workers, many of whom were now considering political alternatives to the party's left and right.

The SPD's left wing recognized this danger early. Its leaders, among them Kurt Rosenfeld and Max Seydewitz, insisted that the party withdraw from a coalition in which it had to make such concessions. They called on the SPD to make demands that would clarify its position to the masses and win increased support against the growing Fascist threat. In answer to Hilferding's financial proposals, the party organization in Saxony published a program calling for increased inheritance taxes, reduced indirect taxes, lower tariffs, and 20 percent salary reductions for the most highly paid government officials. It also demanded cuts in pension payments to those receiving over 12,000 RM per year and a 500 million RM reduction in the military budget. These proposals contrasted starkly with Hilferding's because they decreased the share of national income going to the rich while improving the workers' position. Both he and the leftist leaders knew that the SPD's coalition partners would reject them. Unlike Hilferding, however, the leftists were willing to destroy the coalition in order to promote a program that would strengthen the party in its traditional constituency. They saw little value in remaining in a cabinet that weakened its ability to attract workers' support.[138]

The measures demanded by the left might have benefited workers to some degree but would not have been enough to pull the German economy out of its tailspin. In addition, it should be noted that although there was disagreement on how to divide the economic burden, the left's program—like Hilferding's—called for increased taxation and reduced government spending to balance the budget. On that goal there was agreement, and until the summer of 1931 no one in the social democratic camp or among its adversaries put forward an economic plan that was not deflationary. Labor and capital may have been at war over wages, unemployment insurance, workplace control, collective bargaining rights, and the system of state arbitration of contract disputes, but union and party leaders basically agreed with their capitalist opponents that a deflationary fiscal policy was the way out of the crisis. This fact, when viewed together with his perspective on the evolution of organized capitalism, helps to further explain Hilferding's reliance on orthodox methods to deal with the crumbling economy. As Knut Borchardt points out, virtually no one among contemporary economists understood how to react to the deepening economic crisis because all the previous postwar downturns had been relatively brief affairs that had quickly righted themselves. Time was required for economic policy makers such as Woytinsky or State Secretary Schäfer—operating in very complex social and political contexts—to develop proposals for the types of reflationary countermeasures later considered standard by economists operating after 1945. It was these types of proposals that Hilferding rejected because of his fear of inflation and his understanding of the workings of capitalism.[139]

Like his left-wing comrades, Hilferding viewed the growth of the extremist parties with dismay, but he dismissed their arguments for withdrawing from the cabinet. He remained convinced that the SPD could do more for the workers and the republic from inside the government than from without, and he insisted that the party remain in the coalition. In March 1930, when the SPD finally left the cabinet after renewed conflict with the DVP over unemployment insurance contributions, Hilferding opposed the move. From the outside, he argued, it would be impossible for the party to build up a reliable republican administrative apparatus, and it would be more difficult to protect government social programs from right-wing attacks.[140]

Hilferding believed that leaving the government risked the republic. Heinrich Brüning's conservative minority cabinet had little support in the Reichstag, and his intention to govern by means of Article 48 threatened the parliament's power. The inability of the Reichstag to form a majority government, Hilferding argued, resulted in the expansion of the Reich president's functions (since he had to sign all emergency decrees) and made it easier for anti-democratic forces to undermine parliamentary rule. It was not a violent putsch from without that endangered parliament but, rather, the threat from within the body itself.[141]

Events soon substantiated Hilferding's fears. In April 1930, Brüning survived an SPD-inspired vote of no confidence, but he failed to win parliamentary backing for an economic program calling for lower unemployment benefits and wages, higher income taxes, no reduction in military spending, and new appropriations for a second pocket battleship. Ignoring SPD efforts to compromise, he attempted to carry out his program first by winning the support of the DNVP and then by resorting to Article 48. When the DNVP rebuffed his overtures and the Reichstag blocked his initial decrees, Brüning decided to break the deadlock by dissolving parliament and holding new elections on September 14, 1930.

The plan backfired. Largely by drawing supporters away from the moderate bourgeois parties and mobilizing new voters, the Nazi party achieved its first major electoral victory and gained 18 percent of the vote and 107 seats in the Reichstag. The KPD also did well with 14 percent and 77 seats. Although Brüning's Catholic Center party had increased its number of delegates from 77 to 89, and the SPD remained the strongest single party with 143 seats (down 10 from 1928), the anti-Republican DNVP, NSDAP, and KPD now controlled 225 of the Reichstag's 577 seats; Brüning's support was weaker than ever.[142]

The extent of the Nazi breakthrough surprised the SPD and sharply reduced its tactical options. Although most party leaders agreed that their first duty was to protect the republic, they disputed the best means. Some, such as Otto Braun, advocated entering into another coalition government. This suggestion found little resonance, however, since many in the party feared internal squabbling and further erosion of electoral support that governing in the crisis could entail. Even if the socialists had seriously considered joining the government, however, the idea was moot since Brüning, ultimately intending to restore the monarchy, had promised President Hindenburg to exclude the socialists from his cabinet. Other Social Democrats such as Siegfried Aufhäuser and Toni Sender argued for a policy of opposition. They believed that the best way to protect the republic was to end collaboration with the bourgeois parties.

A majority of the party leadership did not view opposition as a viable option. If the SPD worked against the minority coalition, it risked either the government inviting the Nazis to share power or another election that could strengthen the extremists. The cautious executive decided that to defend the republic the party had to back the "lesser evil" and "tolerate" Brüning's cabinet. This decision, which the leadership believed was the only really responsible one, set the direction of party policy for the next two years, during which it resolutely supported Brüning and tolerated policies that were anathema to most SPD leaders as well as to the rank and file.[143]

Hilferding was a leading advocate of toleration and saw no other way to prevent the nationalists and the fascists from coming to power and destroying the republic. Elaborating his views in a postelection article in *Die Gesellschaft,* he asserted that the causes of the radical right's mass appeal were clear. The war, inflation, and the depression had ruined millions of small urban producers, traders, and peasants, drastically reduced their living standards, and driven them into the ranks of the proletariat. These embittered people often blamed the republic for their plight. Desirous of quick solutions, disillusioned with democracy, and uninterested in the socialist movement's methodical struggle to change the system, they sought another revolution to save themselves—a third Reich. The discontented masses were abandoning the traditional parties, including the antirepublican ones, and turning to "the new saviors standing at the door," the Nazi party and the Communists.[144]

Hilferding believed that the Nazis represented the most immediate threat to the republic. Accurately describing the NSDAP as a "catchall" party with support from virtually all social groups including the military, the aristocracy, the old middle class *(Mittelstand),* the peasantry, officialdom, and even the working class, he acknowledged its great success in using antirepublicanism to unite disparate elements into a powerful political movement. Hilferding feared that as national socialism grew, it would be increasingly tempting for a right-wing cabinet to invite its leaders into the government. Such a move would be disastrous because the Nazis would use the state's resources to expand their power. They would penetrate the government's administrative apparatus, the Reichswehr, and the police. "Once such a government is formed," he predicted, "it would be very difficult to remove." Together with their reactionary partners, the Nazis would destroy the republic.[145]

Given his later response to Hitler's appointment to the chancellorship, it is amazing with what clarity Hilferding recognized the fascist danger and anticipated the tactics the Nazis would employ. He had no new ideas, however, to ward off this threat. Hilferding hoped that the SPD eventually would rejoin a government with the "rational republican" parties of the Weimar coalition, but he realized that such a move was impossible at the moment. By supporting Brüning, the SPD served the republic as a protective wall until political and economic circumstances improved.[146]

In the weeks following the September 1930 elections, Hilferding joined other members of the executive in a campaign to convince a recalcitrant party to get behind the toleration policy. On October 4, 1930, facing a hostile Berlin audience, he criticized those who favored allowing the Nazis to enter the cabinet in order to "expose" the reactionary nature of the right. Once in power, he did not expect the Nazis to give it up, and he argued forcefully that extraparliamentary efforts to dislodge them, such as a general strike, had little chance of success when so many workers were unemployed or under the sway of the unreliable KPD. His listeners were not convinced and passed a resolution calling for opposition to Brüning's cabinet and, if necessary, extra-parliamentary action to defend the republic.[147]

A few days later, in Breslau, Hilferding addressed another resistant crowd. This time he stressed that not only would opposition to Brüning bring the Nazis to power, but it would also undermine the SPD-led Prussian govern-ment and reduce Germany's ability to attract much needed foreign loans. Toleration, Hilferding asserted, would give the party breathing space to pre-pare itself to fight later on. Although many speakers at this meeting opposed propping up the minority government, this time there was no resolution for or against toleration.[148]

Hilferding's reasons for supporting toleration remained basically the same until the fall of the republic. For him, parliament was the central arena of struggle and he, like the entire executive, had little enthusiasm for action in the streets. Not only did the latter risk violence, which he deplored, but he also believed that the party could not win such a struggle. Social democracy not only had failed to win majority support under Weimar but, after 1930, found itself in constant retreat. It could still count on its core membership but Hilferding was certain that, with the unions weakened by the crisis, the movement's possibilities for extraparliamentary struggle were sharply cur-tailed. Thus, he placed his hopes in the party's ability to restore the integrity of the Reichstag, the key institution of republican democracy.

Despite considerable antitoleration sentiment among the rank and file, by mid-October 1930 the executive not only had won over a large majority of the Reichstag delegation to its policy but had also convinced most of the op-position leaders to get on board, if not out of conviction then by virtue of their sense of discipline. Together with their union allies, the socialists adopted a defensive policy to block the radical right's entrance into the government, but they also hoped to convince Brüning to rein in his attack on social services and to adopt policies that would raise wages and create employment.[149]

Hilferding was a key contact with Brüning. For years the two men had worked together in the Reichstag as financial experts in their respective dele-gations and as representatives to international trade conferences in London (1926) and Rio de Janeiro (1927). Over time they became friends, and Brün-ing viewed Hilferding as a skilled expert and a person who, in working with rival parties, put cooperation and responsibility above political partisanship. During Brüning's chancellorship, Hilferding advised him on financial policy and, along with other top SPD leaders such as Wels or Müller, sometimes met with him on legislative and other matters.[150]

Indeed, it was Hilferding who invited Brüning to meet with him and

Müller one week after the elections in order to discuss the composition of his future cabinet. The talks were vague and noncommittal but, at another meeting one week later, the socialists made it clear they would tolerate the cabinet despite his rejection of their moderate demands for the abolition of the poll tax, the restoration of cuts in sickness and unemployment insurance, and the submission of July's emergency decrees to the Reichstag for passage as individual laws. Thinking that Brüning would make some concessions to stabilize his government, the SPD leaders had overestimated their leverage and were unprepared to change course.[151]

Hilferding and Brüning agreed that it was important for Germany to pursue a deflationary economic policy but for very different reasons. Hilferding was convinced that, unless the government pursued such a course, the capitalist economy would not be able to right itself and resume its progressive expansion. Brüning, however, also subordinated domestic economic policy to his foreign policy, which, first and foremost, aimed to remove the burden of reparations. He was willing to use the economic crisis, even at the cost of delaying a recovery, to prove to the Allies that Germany could not pay. Although the socialists did not know it, he was also determined, once the reparations issue was resolved, to radically alter the constitution, bring back the Hohenzollerns, and form a right-wing cabinet. The man upon whom Hilferding and his colleagues were counting to protect the republic had no intention of doing so.[152]

As the economic situation worsened (unemployment reached 6 million by 1932) and political violence increased, Hilferding increasingly feared civil war. Convinced that the working class was too weak to seize power by force, he grew impatient with comrades who called for more radical tactics. Throughout 1931 dissatisfaction with toleration grew as Brüning muzzled the Reichstag and, in June, issued draconian emergency decrees cutting wages, unemployment benefits, and social services. In March and April 1931, Hilferding, Wels, Breitscheid, and Hertz met with Brüning to try to find out the exact nature of the impending cuts and to protest against his intention to prorogue the Reichstag until November. Hilferding made clear that the SPD would not support social spending cuts or new protectionist trade measures, but Brüning made no commitments. When it became certain that he intended to issue his emergency decrees without parliamentary interference, Hilferding pathetically requested the chancellor to inform the SPD of the decrees' content before the party congress scheduled for the end of May. Otherwise, he feared, party members might think the leadership was feigning ignorance before their expected announcement in June.[153]

Hilferding's foreboding concerning the upcoming Leipzig congress was well founded. In acrimonious debates the leadership fought to convince the party to provide the Reichstag delegation (where it had majority support) with complete freedom to respond to the June 1931 decrees. Numerous dissenters from virtually all factions expressed their frustration with toleration.

While moderate leftists like Sender and Aufhäuser demanded that the SPD at least consider a change of policy, right-wing leader Wilhelm Dittmann, reversing his usual role, called for a shift away from concern with parliament and toward extraparliamentary action. Finally, a small minority on the far left demanded a return to outright opposition. Although the executive soundly defeated these challenges and carried the day, internal fissures were obviously widening.[154]

The announcement of the June 1931 decrees led to a groundswell of opposition to toleration and support for the left within the party and the ADGB. The leaders of both organizations issued public protests and intensified their criticism of the cabinet, but they never seriously considered altering the policy.[155] In *Die Gesellschaft*, Hilferding sharply attacked Brüning's refusal to amend the decrees, to summon the Reichstag, and to negotiate with the parliamentary budget committee. At the same time, however, he noted that the Reichstag had ceased to function as a democratic forum and that, if convened, the cabinet would probably fall and open the way to dictatorship. The party, then, had no choice. It had to continue to tolerate "the lesser evil." Ironically, Hilferding hoped that Brüning might succeed in eliminating the reparations payments. Such a victory, he thought, would strengthen his hand against the radical right.[156]

Divisions within the SPD intensified in the fall of 1931, when the executive expelled leftist leaders Rosenfeld and Sedywitz for their continuing agitation against its policy. When several other left-wing leaders and large numbers of youth followed them into the newly founded Socialist Workers Party (SAPD), Hilferding became depressed. He was not sorry to see Rosenfeld and the other leaders go. On the contrary, he thought they were quite "miserable" and he had long ago lost the desire to argue with such "difficult" people. He wished, however, that the party had handled the confrontation differently and was very concerned about the growing anger and disorientation of the social democratic youth.[157]

Although only a few thousand members left to join the SAPD, the split marked a low point for social democracy's morale, and Hilferding shared the sense of helplessness that permeated the movement in the face of Germany's multiple crises. He remarked to Kautsky that worst of all "is that we can't say anything concrete to the people about how and by what means we would end the crisis." Capitalism had been shaken "far beyond our expectations," but no socialist solution was at hand. As the Communists and the Nazis gained support, the political crisis deepened "because the struggle to preserve democracy alone does not satisfy the psychological needs of the masses."[158]

Hilferding did propose a number of actions to deal with the economic crisis. To end the credit shortage and promote international cooperation he urged the relatively stable French and U.S. banks to place their gold reserves back into circulation. He insisted that the powers abandon protectionism and support free trade in order to revive commerce and growth. Domestically, he called for state regulation of banking and production, but his suggestions were vague. In essence, Hilferding continued to back the same supply side policies that he had supported during his tenure as minister. Fearful of renewed inflation, he succeeded in convincing Wels and other SPD leaders to oppose trade union plans for large-scale public works projects financed through deficit spending.[159]

By the fall of 1931, the latter option was certainly receiving closer scrutiny across the political spectrum. While Woytinsky and Tarnow worked out their reflationary strategy for the ADGB, several government officials—such as the finance minister Hermann Dietrich, his state secretary, Hans Schäffer, Ernst Wangemann of the Statistical Office, and Wilhelm Lautenberg of the Economics Ministry—developed similar strategies of their own. Germany's deplorable condition was such that even big business was turning against the chancellor's policy. Brüning himself thought it was time for a change, but he wanted to wait until after the reparations issue was resolved.[160]

It is an irony and a tragedy that, by arguing against reflating the economy, Hilferding helped delay the implementation of alternative policies that might possibly have altered the political situation in Germany. Every day that passed without action to stem the deepening crisis cost the cabinet and the republic legitimacy they could ill afford to lose. Brüning, backed by conservative circles as well as by social democracy, had decided to continue the deflationary policy carried out under Müller. Given his political outlook and the state of economic thinking at the time, a policy of deflation was logical. It was not inevitable, however, and there were alternatives, which Brüning chose not to consider for political reasons. Hilferding argued against them because he did not believe that capitalist crises could be ended by means of public works or credit creation. On this issue he was more conservative than many on the right.

It is arguable, of course, that by the end of 1931 the depression had reached its final stages and that no policy change could have been executed in time to save the republic.[161] But it is also true that by waiting for the depression to bottom out, Hilferding and those who supported his position gambled in a situation that they knew was extremely dangerous. Hilferding did not know what to do as the apogee of the crisis approached; he could only recommend holding on.

Such a strategy gave German voters little to hope for, whereas the Nazis did not hesitate to make sweeping promises. On May 10, 1932, Nazi leader Gregor Strasser presented the Reichstag with an ambitious job-creation scheme financed by the state through deficit spending. His speech circulated widely and appealed to people anxious for the government to take action. Hilferding rose in parliament the following day to answer Strasser, and his speech brilliantly revealed the differences between Strasser's intellectually bankrupt "socialism" and the ideals of Marxism. It did not, however, present a convincing alternative to Strasser's proposals for the immediate amelioration of the crisis. As various groups moved forward with plans to reflate the economy, Hilferding steadfastly opposed them, and the SPD provided only tepid support for the trade union proposals that spring.[162]

Hilferding often said that if the existence of the republic were threatened, the proletariat had the right and the duty to use any means at its disposal, including the most extreme forms of violence, to come to its defense. He also believed that the successful defense of democracy depended on the will of the masses to act.[163] As Donna Harsch argues, by 1931 the will to act was strong among the socialist rank and file, and social democracy appeared to be preparing seriously for decisive action in the streets. In December 1931 the party, the trade unions, and the Reichsbanner formed the Iron Front, an extraparliamentary alliance of prorepublican forces against fascism and reaction. The impetus for the formation of the alliance came from below. As the political situation deteriorated, many social democrats pressed their leaders to form a common front and go on the offensive. Party activists such as Sergei Chakhotin also pressed for new propaganda and mass mobilization techniques stressing simple, positive, powerful messages to inspire a more radical élan. The SPD leadership realized that it could not abandon the streets to its enemies, and that it had to somehow rejuvenate the spirit and enthusiasm of its followers. For these reasons it agreed to go forward with the alliance.[164]

The response was overwhelming. Tens of thousands of social democrats took part in actions around the country, holding meetings and demonstrations in factories and neighborhoods, and often challenging the nazis on their own ground. The Reichsbanner stepped up its paramilitary training and street-fighting activities and, in some areas, began stockpiling arms. After long hesitation, the party leadership accepted the use of provocative new symbols and messages in SPD propaganda. These activities and a radicalized proletarian-oriented rhetoric raised rank-and-file morale amid what Breitscheid and Wels described as "civil war conditions."[165]

Yet, the social democratic leaders were unwilling to fight this civil war. On the whole they considered the Iron Front an electoral instrument in the fight to protect the republic. Holding fast to the constitution, they sought more effective means of mobilizing their supporters but also feared provoking their enemies into open warfare. In the end, neither the growing strength and violence of the NSDAP and the KPD nor the paralysis of the Reichstag, nor the illegal dissolution of the SPD-led Prussian government, was enough to move Hilferding and his colleagues to alter their stance. Their understandable reluctance to shed blood and their (probably correct) conviction that they could not win in such a confrontation undercut their will to use extraparliamentary means to save democracy.[166]

The destruction of Otto Braun's cabinet in Prussia most clearly revealed the social democrats' unwillingness to resist aggression. In May 1932, Brüning's cabinet fell when President Hindenburg, under the influence of reactionary advisors, lost faith in his chancellor's conservative loyalties and replaced him with Franz von Papen, also of the Center party. The SPD leaders despised Papen and regarded his cabinet as a front for the military and the Nazis; and Papen, whom one historian has described as "the worst selection since Caligula appointed his horse as consul," did nothing to discourage these suspicions.[167] On June 4, 1932, he dissolved the Reichstag and called for new elections in July. Ten days later, he imposed 1.5 billion RM in new taxes on the general populace while simultaneously attacking the social welfare and unemployment insurance system. On June 16, he lifted the government's ban on the Nazi SA and SS paramilitary units and thereby unleashed a wave of violence. In street battles in July alone, Nazi terror was responsible for over thirteen hundred casualties including ninety-nine deaths.

Hoping to ensure the NSDAP's backing for his cabinet, Papen next moved against the socialist-led coalition in Prussia. On July 20, 1932, following a bloody, Nazi-provoked street fight in Altona, he accused the Prussian coalition of failing to maintain order; he deposed the cabinet and appointed a Reich commissioner to oversee Prussian affairs. Papen quickly purged the administration of any potentially hostile officials and took control of Germany's largest police force.[168]

Fearing that the Reichsbanner was too outgunned and undertrained to face the Reichswehr, the nationalist Stahlhelm, and the Nazi SA, the top social democratic leaders, including Hilferding, decided not to resist Papen's action with violence. The workers' movement was divided; it was unclear if a general strike would receive enough support to be effective; no one was sure exactly where the Prussian police would stand; and the leaders dreaded the possibility of a bloodbath. Instead of resorting to armed resistance or a general strike, they attempted to attain redress through the court system, ultimately a futile gesture. Whether this decision to refrain from armed resistance was justified has been the subject of much debate. What is clear, however, is that despite their rhetoric concerning the defense of the republic, social democracy's leaders were not prepared to summon their troops into action if the outcome was in doubt.[169]

In the July and November elections of 1932, the SPD's fortunes continued to decline as its electoral support fell to 20 percent and 120 seats in the Reichstag. Although Nazi strength, after peaking in the summer, also declined in November, the NSDAP remained the largest party in the parliament with 196 seats. The big winners in the fall were the Communists, who won almost 6 million votes and 100 seats.[170] The Reichstag was yet more polarized and Papen had little support. On December 3, 1932, Hindenburg replaced him with General Kurt von Schleicher, who was no more able to put together a parliamentary majority than his predecessors. He resigned on January 28, 1933. Two days later, Hindenburg appointed Adolf Hitler chancellor.

During the critical latter half of 1932, the SPD drifted. Isolated in the Reichstag, the party had little influence on political events. In August, Hilferding had called on the party to tolerate Papen's cabinet in order to forestall Hitler's entrance into the government, but the decision was essentially out of social democracy's hands.[171] Following the November 1932 elections he urged the leadership to fight Papen "with no holds barred" in parliament because it had no other options. Talk about using extraparliamentary means of coming to power was dangerous, because "the party did not possess any."[172] On December 1, 1932, he wrote to Kautsky of his hope for "at least a chance of a slight relaxation" if Schleicher came to power, but he was very worried. Not only were the Nazis still strong, but the Communists seemed to be gathering momentum and were poised to catch up to the SPD in size. "It is not a pretty picture," he soberly observed, and "adventurist blunders would only make the situation worse."[173]

In the January 1933 issue of *Die Gesellschaft*, Hilferding argued that there were three possible solutions to the crisis.[174] The first was the appointment of Hitler as chancellor. This event had not occurred because Hitler was unwilling to lead a coalition government unless he had total control. Absolute power was necessary because without it he would have to sacrifice certain goals cherished by the Nazis' often conflicting constituencies. Splits among these antagonistic elements would lead to the movement's disintegration and Hilferding believed that full power was now beyond Hitler's grasp. After the NSDAP's electoral setback in November, Hitler was in a less favorable position to demand sole control over the state.

The second choice was the maintenance of Papen's reactionary government. This regime, Hilferding argued, had intended to undermine the constitution and restore the monarchy, but in doing so it would have radicalized broad sections of the population until rebellion threatened the state. The leaders of the state bureaucracy had wanted to avoid such a crisis, and they had convinced Hindenburg to dispose of Papen and to appoint Schleicher. But Schleicher's appointment did not represent a return to parliamentary government. It was a presidential regime that was not responsible to the Reichstag, and its lack of popular support doomed it to failure. It was the SPD's task, Hilferding asserted, to oppose Schleicher and to struggle for a return to parliamentary rule. This alternative was only possible, however, if the party also defeated the Communists and reunited the proletariat. A united front with the KPD was not feasible, for in such an alliance, the Communist leadership would work to subjugate the masses to its will and to destroy social democracy. It would undertake adventurist actions that could allow the fascists to unite with the state against the left and thus ensure the victory of counterrevolution. In the struggle for democracy, Hilferding believed, it was just as important for the SPD to fight against communism as it was to fight the presidential regime.

Thus, for Hilferding, as for most other SPD leaders, the rift with the Communists had become unbridgeable. Under Weimar both parties had ceaselessly attacked one another, and in 1925 the Communists had adopted the line that the SPD endangered democracy even more than the fascist parties. KPD chief Ernst Thälmann claimed that Hermann Müller's government was "an especially dangerous form of fascist development, the form of social fascism. . . . Social fascism consists in paving the way for fascist dictatorship under the cloak of so-called 'pure democracy'."[175] Such arguments made any rapprochement impossible between the two workers' parties. In a letter to Kautsky written in 1931, Hilferding remarked that intellectually and morally the Communists and the Nazis were not much different from one another; two years later he had not changed his mind.[176]

Hilferding concluded his January 1933 article by claiming that the SPD's policy of toleration had prevented the growing Nazi party from entering the government. Now that it was in decline, the possibility of a fascist seizure of power was reduced. But the future remained uncertain. Although the SPD and the Center party had held the fascists at bay, economic developments ultimately would determine the course of political events.

By January 30, 1933, Hilferding knew that he had misjudged the political situation and that Hitler's appointment loomed. To discuss their options, the SPD and trade union leaders gathered in the Reichstag. Hilferding counseled caution and insisted that any preemptive action by the SPD to prevent Hitler from coming to power would only lead to armed conflict with the SA and the Reichswehr. Instead, he urged the party to decide whether it would tolerate a cabinet of professional bureaucrats *(Beamtenkabinett)*. After considerable discussion, the leaders issued a statement that the party and trade unions were ready to "support unconditionally any government that sets itself the goal of ending the anarchy in the country and restoring legal, constitutional conditions." The SPD leaders learned of Hitler's appointment soon afterward, but they did not stir themselves to action. They rejected calls for a general strike and could only agree to issue an appeal to the masses to support the dissolution of the Reichstag and new elections.[177]

Over the course of the next seven weeks, social democracy's leaders remained paralyzed as the Nazis methodically consolidated their power. Through a combination of terror and manipulation of the law, they eliminated the communist opposition and severely restricted the social democratic press and the party's preparations for the upcoming elections on March 5, 1933. Despite all that he had written concerning the Nazis' methods and goals, Hilferding rejected the demands of the more radical party leaders for mass action. Instead he opted for a parliamentary "fight for freedom" in which the SPD would call for rent reductions and the expropriation of heavy industry, the banks, and large landowners as a means of winning over the KPD's supporters. More radical actions, he asserted, would only lead to civil war.[178] One party comrade has vividly described Hilferding's reaction to his proposal for a general strike in February:

> [He] was sitting in a comfortable easy chair with warm felt slippers on his feet and remarked with a benign smile that I was a young firebrand and that political skill consists of waiting for the right moment. After all, he said, Hindenburg is

still the President, the government is a coalition government, and while Hitlers come and go, the ADGB is an organization that should not risk its entire existence for a fleeting political purpose.[179]

For Hilferding, the right moment never came. Within weeks Hitler was able to assume dictatorial powers. In June 1933, the SPD was banned.

In virtually all of his writings prior to Hitler's appointment, Hilferding had recognized the danger that fascism posed to the republic and he had argued long before 1933 that the antirepublican parties had succeeded in undermining the function of the Reichstag. These sober analyses and his repeated exhortations to defend the democratic order with all means if necessary lead one to ask why, with thousands of armed Reichsbanner men waiting for their signal, did Hilferding not urge his colleagues to support violent resistance? The answer lies partly in the concrete obstacles recognized by the party leaders but more significantly in the experience, basic principles, and hopes that most of them shared.[180]

Like Otto Bauer in Austria, Hilferding had spent his political career engaged in a struggle to realize the goals of socialism by peaceful means. Each placed great faith in the parliamentary order as a guarantor of future progress, and both were proud and protective of the organizations they led. They had always held that workers should use violence only as a defensive measure, and they were convinced that, as in 1918, when revolutions occurred they were the result of spontaneous mass action. After many years of leadership in which they had grown accustomed to the norms of the Rechtsstaat and the parliamentary order, neither Hilferding nor Bauer was able to adjust to the strategic challenge of fascism. Most important, both were humane men who, when finally forced to act, could not bring themselves to urge the spilling of blood. The main difference between Germany in 1933 and Austria one year later was that, in Germany, the party membership followed the instructions of its leaders and did not violently resist fascism, whereas in Austria a part of the membership broke with its leadership and fought in spite of its leaders' intentions.[181]

Hilferding fled Germany at the end of March 1933. He escaped with the aid of Heinrich Brüning, who had received word from Nazi sources that a part of the SPD leadership would be arrested after the Reichstag passed an enabling law on March 23 granting Hitler full power. Brüning immediately informed Hilferding and urged him to leave Germany at once, along with Wels and Breitscheid. Shortly after the law's passage, Hilferding left Berlin and headed north to the border where SPD Reichstag delegate Otto Eggerstadt helped him slip into Denmark. According to Brüning, Hilferding had just barely avoided arrest. On the day after his departure, Nazi storm troopers ransacked his apartment. He never returned to Germany.[182]

CHAPTER SIX

THE SWORD OF DAMOCLES

Indeed, I have never been afraid of the truth and I believe that "non-conformism," . . . the rebellion against traditional views, dogmas, and simplistic conceptions, belongs to the essence of my thought. Perhaps the only advantage that the emigration has is complete independence and freedom from the considerations that active politicians have to take into account, but this does not exclude the possibility that one will fear taking the wrong road after considering the consequences of moving significantly away from one's earlier views.

—*Rudolf Hilferding (1937)*

From Denmark Hilferding went to Saarbrücken and then to Paris, where he met with other German political refugees and contemplated the future. Like many of his companions he was in shock. The political movement to which he had devoted his whole being lay in ruins, and the republic in which he had placed such great hopes was dead. At the end of May 1933, in conversations with other exiles in Paris, the horrified Hilferding described the gruesome tortures employed by the Nazis against their opponents. He knew what awaited him if he returned to Germany; it was doubtless with a profound sense of despair that he contemplated life in exile. In June he moved on to Zurich, where he lived until 1938.[1]

He remained politically active. For the rest of his life, Hilferding worked to make sense of social democracy's defeat and to rebuild the outlawed and fractured party. Although the world economic crisis and the Nazi seizure of power had discredited many of his theoretical and political views, a majority in the SPD's exiled executive (the Sopade) remained willing to seek his advice and to employ his talents. The executive's core did not change after the disaster of 1933, and few of its members could claim to have understood its coming better than Hilferding. Leaders such as Wels, Hans Vogel, and Sigmund Crummenerl still regarded him as a leading theorist, a skilled journalist, and an internationally respected figure whose loyalty was beyond question. With their support, Hilferding took on an important role in the Sopade's effort to reformulate and propagate its message to the German people and to reconstruct a unified movement. Thus, his fate remained bound to that of the party; when the Nazi tidal wave engulfed Europe and destroyed social democracy as an organized force, he was among the thousands of social democrats who perished along with it.

Once in exile, Hilferding began to rethink the theoretical and practical ideas that he and the bulk of the party leadership had accepted under Weimar. The Nazi triumph illustrated the bankruptcy of the SPD's rigid adherence to parliamentary tactics; it forced the party leaders to reconsider their political strategy and its theoretical underpinnings. During this rethinking process, Hilferding fundamentally revised his views on the nature of state power and developed a theory of the totalitarian or "total" state. At the same time, he worked to reorient Social Democracy's practical strategy in light of the completely transformed political situation, a particularly daunting task. After all, how could a party steeped in democratic tradition effectively challenge a barbaric state without sacrificing its own principles? This is a problem that democratic and democratic socialist revolutionaries have long faced and continue to struggle with in the contemporary world. Hilferding and his colleagues failed to resolve it adequately, and this failure, with their movement under relentless attack, undermined its strength.

In early April 1933, Hilferding wrote to Kautsky outlining his thoughts on the evolving situation. He knew then that Nazi rule would not soon end, a circumstance that doomed the SPD as a legal party. Germany, he thought, was in a transition phase as the Nazis consolidated their power. When the SPD's legal existence no longer served their purposes, they would ban it. This action would clarify the political situation and require the SPD to reevaluate its tasks, a process in which Hilferding hoped to play an active role. The psychological depression that had followed his flight from the Nazis had begun to abate, and Rose's safe arrival had greatly relieved him.[2]

Not surprisingly, Hilferding also had the past on his mind, and in this letter he reviewed the events of the last two decades. Unlike Kautsky, he now seriously doubted the future of democracy. They both had been right, he claimed, to see bolshevism as the "greatest danger," and its seizure of power as "counterrevolutionary." Recent events, however, had been so shattering that he could not yet draw any clear conclusions about the historical significance of the SPD's defeat. He could only say that its consequences would be far-reaching and would affect some of Social Democracy's fundamental views. In this regard he was referring not to Marxist theory, but to the SPD's political conduct.[3]

Hilferding did not criticize the SPD's political actions during the republic's waning days. On the contrary, he insisted that its policy had been "inevitable and correct." Other tactics would have brought about similar results. He also asserted, however, that the SPD had "underestimated [unterschätzt] the working-class's will to preserve democracy and to place politics and freedom over material [well-being] under all circumstances." This comment is particularly interesting because it contradicts the view he had expressed throughout the Weimar years concerning workers' political consciousness. As late as October 1932 he had told Kautsky that the political situation was becoming increasingly critical "because the struggle to preserve democracy alone does not satisfy the psychological needs of the masses."[4] Now, following the Nazi seizure of power, he seemed to concede that the party had indeed erred by not taking advantage of proletarian support in its fight against fascism, and he seemed to imply the existence of a rift between the workers and the leadership, a division that he and most other SPD leaders had previously always been unwilling to recognize.[5]

It is possible that the shock of the Nazi victory led Hilferding to believe that perhaps the leadership had, after all, lost contact with the masses and therefore failed to take full advantage of their support in the fight for the republic. If this was the case, however, he soon changed his mind. In September 1933, he reiterated to Kautsky that SPD policy in the republic's last years "could not have been much different," it was between 1914 and the aftermath of the Kapp putsch that "the worst errors were made." It did no good to rehash the leaders' mistakes. More important was to recognize that, however "understandable given the historical situation," the working class itself had failed. "If one wants to overcome the German workers' lack of a will to freedom and their repeated capitulation to nationalism," he wrote, then this failure "cannot be left uncriticized."[6]

Thus, it was the workers themselves—rather than their political leaders—who were primarily responsible for social democracy's defeats. Despite over fifty years of social democratic tutelage, Germany's workers had not developed a deeply ingrained, democratic political consciousness, and it was their "lack of a will to freedom" that undermined their resistance to Nazism. For Hilferding, in the last analysis, the actions of social democracy's leaders, even those who backed the counterrevolution in 1918, were not decisive either in the postwar upheaval or in the debacle of 1933. As he had argued throughout his career, it was the SPD's task to enlighten, organize, and lead the workers in the struggle for reforms; in a revolutionary situation, however, it was the workers who were responsible for taking action, not the party leaders. This attitude raises several important questions: When does leadership end and spontaneous action begin? How should workers, long accustomed to the party's guidance, suddenly decide to "act" on their own and to what ends? Before 1933, Hilferding had not dealt systematically with these problems and had generally argued that workers would undertake revolutionary action in response to ruling-class violations of their rights. Fascism's triumph forced him to examine these questions more closely.

As early as April 1933, Hilferding recognized that opposition to Hitler would be extremely difficult. The Nazis, he believed, would seize control not only over the state bureaucracy, but over the trade unions, the schools, and most industrial, trade, and agricultural organizations as well. A diplomatic success would further strengthen their position. He worried about the future of Western democracy itself and feared that Allied inclinations to compromise with the Nazi regime could prevent a realistic assessment of the changed political situation, especially in the sphere of foreign policy.[7]

Hilferding's appraisal of the Nazis' intentions was on the mark. By late spring, the NSDAP had smashed the unions and subjugated most of Germany's social, economic, and political institutions. Although the SPD remained legal, the Nazis arrested hundreds of party leaders, drove many more into exile, and banned the socialist press. On April 27, 1933, the executive called a conference in Berlin that aimed "to rejuvenate" the party's weakened organization and "make it more active." The conference elected a new executive designed to placate each of the SPD's conflicting factions without challenging the old guard's predominance. Chaired by Wels and Vogel, the twenty-member body now included nine "new" personalities: Paul Hertz, Erich Rinner, and Otto Ollenhauer represented the "youth"; Karl Böchel, Georg Dietrich, Franz Küntsler, and Siegfried Aufhäuser represented the "left"; Paul Löbe and Wilhelm Sollmann represented the "right."[8] For the first time since 1922, Hilferding was not reelected; unable to reside safely in the country, he could not participate in the executive's regular deliberations.

On May 4, 1933, two days after the Nazis arrested the top trade union leadership and seized the unions' property, the SPD executive sent six of its members abroad as a precaution. Although Berlin remained the executive's official headquarters, the majority instructed Wels, Vogel, Crummenerl (the party treasurer), Stampfer, Hertz, and Ollenhauer to establish a party center outside the country. This action was timely. On May 10, 1933, the Nazis seized SPD's funds and property. Although the party remained legal, the leadership could do little to stem the disintegration of its organization.

Over the course of the next several weeks, conflict arose between the executive members outside the country, who wanted to build a revolutionary underground movement, and those in Berlin, who—under Nazi pressure—were ready to support Hitler's foreign policy in order to demonstrate the party's loyalty to the state and remain legal. When the Reichstag delegation endorsed a speech by Hitler calling for international "justice" and "equality" for Germany, it precipitated a split with the Wels group. On May 29, 1933, the "representation abroad" condemned this action and asserted that saving the old party organization was no longer as important as saving the soul of social democracy. A new organization, built along lines suited to the radically altered situation, would bring the party's message to the German people. With these goals in mind, Wels and his colleagues set up their headquarters in Prague and began publishing a weekly newspaper, *Neuer Vorwärts*.[9]

Hilferding was appalled at the actions of the Berlin party leaders, who continued to claim that they constituted the SPD's legitimate leadership until the Nazis banned the party altogether on June 22, 1933. On June 11, he wrote to the Sopade that the events in Berlin were "painful" but not of decisive importance because a Social Democratic Party loyal to Hitler would not win much support. He was uncomfortable with the "moral impression" provided by the Berlin leaders' policies but also thought they helped make the Sopade's actions more understandable to the public. The exiled executive had acted not only out of political necessity but also to save the party's honor.[10] A few days later, Hilferding told Paul Hertz that attempts to placate the Nazis through good behavior were useless. The Nazis tolerated no opposition, and the Berlin leaders' strategy only damaged the SPD by confusing the masses and driving them toward the Communists.[11]

The latter prospect particularly alarmed Hilferding. Even in exile the communists continued to denounce the socialist leaders as social fascists. They worked to destroy the SPD by initiating a united front from below that encouraged demoralized and disorganized Social Democrats to join the KPD as individuals. If successful, this plan would have robbed the SPD of whatever rank-and-file support remained.[12] Hilferding urged the Sopade to act decisively to derail the KPD's strategy. He encouraged it to reestablish the party's press in order to make its views clear to the masses. A party weekly, he suggested, should be an organ of "struggle and information," while key theoretical and political issues such as socialist construction, foreign policy, and trade union policy should be discussed in a separate journal. Of central importance was the question of democracy. By focusing on its centrality to the socialist project, social democracy would clearly differentiate itself from communism.[13]

Hilferding's priorities in the spring of 1933 were clear. He rejected all compromise with the KPD and its sympathizers and anticipated the publication of a manifesto proclaiming social democracy's principles and goals in the struggle against fascism. The manifesto, he advised the executive, should not dwell on the party's past sins, but should stress that the epoch of its reformist strategy had ended, while at the same it remained committed to democracy.[14]

Hilferding's exhortations did not fall upon deaf ears. The Sopade intended to concentrate its resources on the party press in order to combat Nazi propaganda and to organize resistance. It had located the party's headquarters in Prague to use the Sudeten-German Social Democratic party's printing facilities in Karlsbad and to take advantage of Czechoslovakia's close proximity to Germany. Using an intricate network of border secretaries, the executive could communicate with underground activists. At great risk, these dedicated social democrats smuggled people, information, and printed matter across the heavily forested frontier. Starting in 1933, the Sopade regularly transported thousands of copies of *Die Sozialistische Aktion,* its miniaturized version of *Neuer Vorwärts,* over the border for distribution by party operatives. In 1934, using information gathered by the underground, the executive began publishing regular reports describing the situation in Germany. Edited by Erich Rinner, these *Deutschlandberichte* provided the SPD leadership with the bulk of its information on the situation in the homeland between 1934 and 1940.[15]

The Sopade had plenty of journalists to staff its new publications. Among the thousands of German refugees living in Prague were dozens of penniless socialist journalists and party functionaries. Within a few months, the executive created a paid staff of about twenty full-time employees in Prague and between fifty and one hundred others scattered throughout Europe. The party also had many part-time paid and volunteer employees, and there was no shortage of contributors to its press.[16] Hilferding served the SPD both as an official and as a journalist. Along with Wels, from 1933 until 1939, he

Hilferding and Wels (with cane) at a meeting of the Socialist International, London, 1938.

represented the Sopade on the executive committee of the Labor and Socialist International (LSI), the successor organization to the Vienna Union and
the Comintern's chief rival. Since the Sopade was in dire need of the LSI's
political and financial support, his position was an important one.

Beginning in June 1933, Hilferding became a regular contributor to *Neuer
Vorwärts,* which Friedrich Stampfer edited. Writing under the pseudonym
Richard Kern, for the next seven years he published over 250 articles on a wide
variety of subjects. More important, however, in July 1933 the executive appointed him chief editor of the party's new theoretical journal, *Die Zeitschrift
für Sozialismus (ZfS),* which appeared for the first time in October 1933. The
selection of Hilferding for this position did not go unopposed. Executive
member Wilhelm Sollmann—himself editor of *Die Deutsche Freiheit* in the
French-occupied Saarland—argued that, because the public associated Hilferding's name with the failed policies of the past, it made no sense to appoint him
to such a high-profile post. If Hilferding became editor, Sollmann thought, it
would be difficult to convince the masses that the SPD had assumed a new
course. Instead, he recommended making him a contributing editor, a position
that would allow him to use his "enormous knowledge and his dialectic" to
strongly influence the journal, without occupying the top spot.[17]

A majority in the Sopade ignored Sollmann's suggestions and also turned
a deaf ear to Karl Böchel's claims that, under Hilferding, the journal would
avoid discussion of past mistakes and lack a clear political line. Hilferding's
relationship with Wels certainly cooled during the exile years, and he sometimes opposed the chairman and his allies on important issues, but the
Sopade's majority still admired his intellectual abilities and knew they could
count on his loyalty in a situation in which they had few friends. It was this
combination of their respect for his theoretical and journalistic talents and his
accord with their political outlook that secured him this influential post in the
party's press.[18]

What was the SPD's message in the summer of 1933? In the June 18 issue
of *Neuer Vorwärts,* the executive published a manifesto entitled "Break the
Chains," in which it promised "to fight against the reactionary dictatorship of
monopoly capitalism and its Nazi cohorts and for the establishment of
working-class rule in Germany." By using radical language appealing primarily to the workers, the Sopade hoped to control the SPD's left wing, to combat Communist efforts to win over the party's rank and file, and to distance
itself from the remnant of the Berlin leadership. The Prague exiles knew that
they had to make their total opposition to the Nazis absolutely clear to retain
their following in Germany.[19]

A few weeks later, they published a more detailed program. Entitled "Revolution against Hitler," it declared the party's abandonment of reformism and
its adoption of "revolutionary" means to combat the Third Reich. The new
program reflected the SPD's efforts to counter Nazi propaganda's portraying
socialists as unpatriotic conspirators. It announced the party's opposition to

foreign military intervention in Germany and called on the German people to liberate themselves from fascism. Revolution, the program asserted, could only come about "through the evolution of oppositional forces inside the country." The party's first important task was "to assist, sponsor, and direct this process" by telling Germans the truth. Through popular enlightenment, the Sopade hoped to create a revolutionary core of "Socialist schooled workers" who would fuse with other disenchanted social groups in the fight for liberty.[20]

The SPD's second major task was to collect and organize forces that, "at the critical moment in the life of the regime, can effect its overthrow." Arguing that freedom and socialism were inseparable, the Sopade claimed that only social democracy could lead the coming revolution, but it also now stressed that Hitler's regime "must be overthrown through the mobilization of the widest coalition of all strata of society." A class alliance in the struggle for popular liberation was the goal, not the dictatorship of the proletariat. The SPD eschewed bolshevik methods and aims and emphasized that the movement would never substitute a bolshevik penitentiary for a fascist one. In essence, the Sopade now called for an uprising "in the spirit of the liberal-democratic revolutionaries of 1848."[21]

The sharp contrast between the messages contained in "Break the Chains" and "Revolution against Hitler" reflected important divisions among social democrats over the movement's strategy and goals. The conservative majority in the Sopade faced repeated challenges to its authority, especially from forces on the left, which aimed to change the SPD's leadership, structure, tactics, and aims. One such group, known as New Beginning, demanded the total reorganization of the party along democratic centralist lines. Completely breaking with social democratic tradition, it called for the formation of an underground party of elite revolutionary fighters to organize and lead a rebellion against fascism in Germany. This struggle would be long-term, was not inevitable, and required training and mobilizing new cadre to lead the masses once Nazi economic mismanagement had fueled social polarization and created a revolutionary situation. New Beginning's supporters criticized the dogmatic, Comintern-controlled KPD and rejected cooperation with it, but they also spurned the "economic determinists" in the social democratic "old left," including the Sopade.[22]

Other dissidents included the Revolutionary Socialists, led by Karl Böchel and Siegfried Aufhäuser, both trade unionists and new members of the executive. They demanded that the SPD break completely with reformism and reestablish its ties with the revolutionary tradition that led from "Marx and Engels via Wilhelm Liebknecht and August Bebel to Luxemburg and the Hilferding of *Finance Capital*." The SPD, they argued, had to replace its old leadership, discard its outworn ideology, reorganize its structure, and fill its ranks with revolutionary cadre guided by a new apparatus and new policies based on revolutionary Marxism.[23]

The radical demands put forward by New Beginning and the Revolutionary Socialists were unacceptable to the Sopade's conservative majority, which considered itself the SPD's legitimate leadership. Hilferding agreed and remained a firm supporter of the majority until the Sopade's virtual dissolution in 1940. He did not, however, always find himself in accord with the majority on theoretical and practical questions, and his early recommendations concerning the party's organization and tactics placed him closer to the left than to the right. Ultimately, Hilferding once again found himself in the role of mediator as he attempted to work out ideological and practical political compromises among the party's conflicting factions. Such efforts exposed him to sharp criticism from all sides and led to his increasing isolation within the party. Over the years, as it became clear that compromise was not possible and that the SPD was helplessly adrift, Hilferding's bitterness and despair deepened and strongly influenced the direction of his theoretical work.

As editor of the *ZfS*, Hilferding's task was to preside over the ongoing and vituperative debates on the SPD's future theoretical principles and strategy. During the summer of 1933, he was in constant communication with Paul Hertz, his coeditor in Prague, and with the Sopade itself. Hilferding thought that short articles written in a popular, unscientific style would make the journal accessible to a wider readership. He thought that the publication of long, complicated essays on political economy, law, and philosophy would limit available space for broad discussion of issues. Hilferding hoped to publish the journal every other week so that its articles remained current, and he recommended a length of about thirty-two pages per issue. It was clear that financial constraints represented a serious obstacle to the realization of these plans, and he was probably not surprised when he learned that the *ZfS* could appear only monthly.[24]

In June 1933, Hilferding wrote to the Sopade outlining the major themes to be discussed in the new journal and sketched out his own views on the economic and political situation. Some of his arguments were new and controversial and broke fundamentally with the ideas he had propounded under Weimar. In May 1933, he had written to Kautsky that the party's theoretical premises essentially had been correct; by the summer, however, he had begun to change his mind.[25]

Hilferding argued that "the latest phase of capitalist development created new problems not only for Germany, but also for the rest of the world." What had happened in Germany, he thought, was only an extreme example of similar occurrences elsewhere. The specific German situation resulted from a variety of historical circumstances: the lack of experience with political democracy, the strength of nationalism after the defeat of 1918, the impact of the Treaty of Versailles, the inflation of 1923, and the widespread hatred of the working class. German developments were not, however, all that different from those in other lands. "The world economic crisis," Hilferding asserted, "had created analogous, if not exactly the same conditions in many different countries" (1).

In Germany, the "change" (that is, the new political situation) had shaken the position of the big bourgeoisie. Whereas earlier the banks and heavy industry had controlled the economy, they now found their power threatened by the petty bourgeoisie (*gewerbliche Mittelstand*) and the peasantry. The political and economic influence of the latter groups had grown with the establishment of democracy after the war, and with the onset of the crisis, they used their strength to advantage. To Hilferding, this development was also true for the United States. "In [the] farming regions . . . the peasant rebellion resembles that of Holstein," he wrote. "The influence of bank capital is in complete retreat, [while] the struggle against interest slavery through inflation, the expansion of credit and . . . public works programs is becoming the substance of politics. Sociologically Roosevelt is, with strong qualifications of course, not so far from Hitler" (1–2).

Hilferding stressed that the state now exerted increased influence in the economic sphere even to the point of violating the rights of private property owners. State intervention was especially marked in agriculture, where governments set up monopolies to market grain and fix prices. Ideas about capitalist planning were widespread. "In short," Hilferding wrote, "the rebellion against the crisis leads to a progressive intellectual, political, and economic revolutionization from which social democracy must draw its conclusions" (2). Unlike the communists and many others, he did not think that fascism, in any form, was a necessary stage of capitalism. It was a particular kind of political response shaped by specific social factors.

The Nazi seizure of power clearly had forced Hilferding to reevaluate his earlier theoretical arguments stressing the evolutionary road to socialism. It was not the proletariat but the radicalized petty bourgeoisie that was using the state to transform organized capitalism to suit its own ends. In Germany, for historical reasons, the rebellion against big capital had assumed a fascist form, but Hilferding believed that the general aims of the rebels everywhere were the same: the defense of the old middle classes by means of state intervention. In the face of these developments it was imperative for social democrats to reaffirm their support for democracy and their opposition to communism. For if they capitulated to the communists, he insisted, the struggle to restore democracy in Germany and elsewhere would be lost. When he turned to the discussion of social democratic tactics, he continued to emphasize this theme.

Hilferding supported "all means" to overthrow fascism, but he worried that "revolutionary work" would naturally develop into an "extremely radical ideology." He feared that, if democracy were pushed into the background, it would blur the differences between social democracy and "pure bolshevism." In his view, democracy was a "prerequisite" for a socialism that does not just improve productivity and living standards but also "raises the level of culture, which cannot exist without intellectual freedom" (3). It was, then, essential for workers to realize that a bolshevik dictatorship, like a fascist one, would not be a temporary condition. "Dictatorship," he wrote, "despite other intentions at the time of its founding, creates the precondition for its [own] continuation" (3). Only decisive political action could successfully overthrow the fascist regime, but Hilferding stressed that the fostering of a democratic consciousness among workers was extremely important for the future.

Hilferding viewed the *ZfS* as a forum for the discussion of virtually all issues pertinent to building the movement, but he also thought it should work to influence the Sopade's allies. This was especially true in the area of foreign policy. The SPD had to recognize that in the current situation the term "imperialism" was a communist shibboleth that served to confuse rather than clarify matters. The "war question" was a question of the warlike attitude of broad sectors of the population, not a question of imperialism. In the current situation, the SPD needed to convince the LSI to drop its demands for German equality and disarmament, and it had to resist calls for foreign intervention in Germany. Hilferding clearly recognized that if Nazi Germany achieved equality with its neighbors, the threat of war would certainly escalate; he hoped that through a popular revolution the German people would themselves oust the Nazis and avoid war.

Taken as a whole, the views Hilferding elaborated to the Sopade formed the nucleus of his analysis of the European situation throughout the 1930s. As he had during the republic, he fervently opposed bolshevism and stressed democracy as the core element of any future socialist system. He drew no distinction between "bourgeois" or "working-class" democracy and rejected the notion of a workers' dictatorship following the overthrow of Nazism. Yet some of his basic ideas had changed. The economic crisis and the Nazi triumph forced him to rethink his view of organized capitalism and to promote violence as a means of transforming the system. Despite his antibolshevism and loyalty to the Wels group, Hilferding was moving leftward. By the end of the year, he would write the most radical program in the history of German social democracy.

During the summer and fall of 1933, Hilferding worked regularly and settled into a new routine. Zurich's central location enabled him to travel easily to Paris, Brussels, and Prague in order to represent the party at conferences or to attend important Sopade meetings. He wrote weekly for *Neuer Vorwärts* and prepared to publish the first issue of the *ZfS* in October. He and Rose lived modestly in the Touring Hotel Garni, where rooms cost between five and seven Swiss francs per day. It is doubtful they had escaped from Germany with many belongings or much money, and Hilferding's income from his party work was necessarily low. The couple earned enough to survive, however, and he traveled constantly on SPD business.

Hilferding's articles in *Neuer Vorwärts* sharply criticized Nazi socioeconomic and political policies and stressed that they would lead either to economic disaster or war. The Nazi state, he argued, was bankrupt and could only forestall disaster by extorting money from the workers and falsifying its books. To pay for agricultural subsidies and for public works programs, the

German government was depressing workers' wage levels and reducing the standard of living. Such a policy, however, could not be pressed too far, and the regime would have to borrow even more money to remain solvent. Hilferding predicted that Finance Minister Schacht's financial machinations could not solve the budget crisis and would probably antagonize Germany's foreign creditors. The government would resort to the printing press to cover its debts and thus increase the danger of renewed inflation.[26]

For Hilferding, the introduction of the "Führer principle" into the factories and the destruction of the unions symbolized the enslavement of Germany's workers by monopoly capital and the state. Capital could now organize the economy as it wished, so long as the Nazi state approved. Capitalists and Nazis had formed an alliance; monopoly capital dominated workers and consumers, while the National Socialists held unlimited political power. Hilferding rejected the Nazi boast that they had ended class struggle in Germany and restored the "corporate state" (Ständestaat) of the Middle Ages. Such a claim he considered merely "camouflage for the most modern [method] of ruinous exploitation."[27]

Hilferding insisted that class struggle was not over. In July 1933, when Interior Minister Frick announced there would be no "second revolution," Hilferding astutely pointed out that this comment signaled the abandonment of the "socialist" portions of the Nazis' program. They were betraying the interests of those who had carried them to power—the petty bourgeoisie, national socialist workers, and the peasantry—and were acting to strengthen capitalism. "The promises to big capital," he wrote, "are being completely fulfilled and the promises to the middle class are being kept in so far as they are compatible with the interests of capital." For the "cheated, exploited, and oppressed masses," however, Nazi policies brought only disappointment. In the end, Hilferding thought, this disappointment would strengthen popular resistance to Hitler's regime.[28]

Hilferding's writings in the summer of 1933 reveal that he was not sure of the relationship between big capital and the state under fascism. On the one hand, he told the Sopade that bank and industrial capital were retreating in the face of an anticapitalist petty bourgeois and peasant rebellion. On the other, he wrote in Neuer Vorwärts that Germany's capitalists were under the Nazi state's full protection. By the fall, however, he had clarified his position in the inaugural issue of ZfS.

The German working class, Hilferding wrote, had made great economic and political gains after 1918, but it was neither strong enough nor intellectually prepared to transform capitalism. Other groups such as big capital, the Junkers, the Mittelstand, and the peasantry, despite conflicting interests, feared and resisted workers' efforts to expand their political and economic influence and strongly supported reactionary nationalism. The depression enabled the NSDAP to unite the main antirepublican groups under its banner, to defeat the divided working class, and to seize power. The new Nazi "total state" aimed to expand its control into every sphere of society.[29] It obliterated all other political institutions and extended its authority over all economic, social, and cultural institutions. The state intended to depoliticize the populace and eliminate any opportunity for the people to participate in local or national decision making. The Nazis wanted to "atomize" individual citizens, force them into state-controlled organizations, and transform them into state slaves.[30]

Hilferding argued that, unlike earlier counterrevolutionary states, which were controlled by relatively small minorities, the National Socialist dictatorship commanded broad support. Decisive elements of the bourgeoisie united with the Mittelstand and peasantry to back the Nazis, and many intellectuals and professionals joined them as well. These groups even supported or tolerated bestial Nazi atrocities against their political opponents and the Jews. With both the Protestant and the Catholic churches remaining loyal to the state, and nationalist fervor spreading among Germans in the border regions, Hilferding thought that the German people had disgraced themselves in the eyes of the world; they could win back their honor and respect only by overthrowing the Nazi regime (4–6).

Hilferding was convinced that the Nazi regime's deficit spending would ultimately devastate the economy and reduce its popular support. To prevent the erosion of their political base, he predicted that the Nazis would turn to "the insane ideas of the Pan-Germans" (8) and feverishly pursue rearmament, militarize social and economic life, and promote international hostility. He regarded such popularly supported radical nationalism, combined with Nazi efforts to achieve economic autarchy, as extremely dangerous. Only Germany's military weakness had thus far prevented it from taking aggressive action, and this was why the Nazis were adamantly demanding "equality" from the other European states. Once they had achieved this goal, he believed, they would use their power to extort concessions from other countries and thus increase the probability of war.

National socialism, Hilferding concluded, was "the deadly enemy of the German people and of humanity" (9), but it had not altered capitalism in any fundamental way. The class conflicts inherent to capitalist society remained. As Nazi policies led the nation to economic ruin, fascism itself "would become the victim of those class antagonisms and class struggles" (9). The Nazis had used class antagonisms to seize power, but in the long run could not master them. Already in 1933 Hilferding thought that the Nazis' procapitalist and pro-*Junker* policies had reduced their support, and he expected this process to continue as the economic crisis deepened and its foreign policy failed. Here was cause for hope that widespread unrest would drive the Nazis from power before they plunged Europe into the abyss.

But Hilferding also emphasized that material want and political disillusionment alone would not bring down the National Socialist state. The overthrow of the "total state" could be achieved only through a "total revolution" backed by mass movements. This revolution required a great deal of mental, technical, and organizational preparation; above all, it would need leadership. The SPD had two main tasks in the current situation: first, to organize illegal operations in Germany and build cadre to carry on the struggle; and second, to prepare itself intellectually to lead the fight and to exercise power after the revolution (10).

The *ZfS* had a key role to play in the SPD's process of intellectual clarification. It provided a forum in which socialists could freely debate principles and tactics and analyze their mistakes. Ruthless criticism was necessary if the journal was to be a truly revolutionary organ, but the point was not to find scapegoats for the SPD's failures. What was most important, wrote Hilferding, was to strive to understand events by using a "truly Marxist method." Marxism, he declared, "does not ask: what should be? On the contrary, it asks: what will develop?" From its "perception *[Erkenntnis]* of social existence" (10), Marx's method could derive the desires and goals—the social consciousness—of classes. Social democrats could use this analytical tool to examine the underlying causes of their recent defeat and the important questions facing the party in the future. To demonstrate the party leadership's tolerance of dissent, Hilferding was willing to open the pages of the *ZfS* to all social democratic points of view but insisted that there could be no room for "patent slogans" or "dogmatism" in the journal (11).[31]

By the fall of 1933, Hilferding clearly had changed some of his most fundamental views regarding social democratic theory and practice. In the theoretical sphere he had essentially abandoned his view of the state as a neutral institution or, as he had argued in *Finance Capital,* as an instrument of the ruling class.[32] Now he saw the German state as an independent power in its own right with ultimate authority over all spheres of life. Although he still believed that the regime's economic failure would undermine its popular base, Hilferding's future work increasingly stressed the state's relative independence from the economy.

Of equal importance to this theoretical shift was the practical role he now assigned to Social Democracy in the coming revolution. By calling on the SPD to recruit members "who can take over the active leadership of the mass movement" (10), for the first time in his career Hilferding called on the party itself to push the revolutionary process forward. His new view of the state led him to conclude that it was necessary for the SPD to fundamentally transform its organization and strategy in the struggle for power.

Hilferding further elaborated his new position when the Sopade requested him to revise the party program during the winter of 1933–1934. Factional conflict within the leadership made the formulation of the program extremely difficult and the executive hoped that Hilferding could provide a compromise draft. He sent the draft to Prague in early January 1934, where, after heated discussion, it won the approval of the Sopade's right-wing majority. On January 28, 1934, it appeared in *Neuer Vorwärts* under the title "The Struggle and Aim of Revolutionary Socialism."[33] Despite its acceptance by the execu-

THE SWORD OF DAMOCLES 187

tive's reformist wing, this "Prague Manifesto" was undoubtedly the most radical programmatic statement ever put forward by the SPD. Arguing that "in the fight against National Socialism there was no place for reformism or legality," the manifesto called for the "conquest of state power, its consolidation, and the realization of socialism." The old party apparatus could not carry out these tasks in the changed political situation. It was, therefore, necessary to transform the SPD from a reformist into a revolutionary organization.

In 1918, the manifesto explained, Social Democracy had come to power as a result of the monarchy's collapse rather than from an organized, revolutionary struggle by the working class. When the SPD assumed power, it committed "a grievous historical error" by not purging the state bureaucracy and the military apparatus. The new situation in Germany made a repetition of 1918 impossible. After destroying the Nazi state, a strong revolutionary regime would hold power. This government, sustained by "the revolutionary mass party of the working class," would consolidate the revolution's control over the state, crush the roots of opposition, and transform the administrative apparatus into an instrument of mass rule.

Social Democracy opposed fascism's overthrow through foreign military intervention and aimed to prevent a war that would threaten the unity and independence of the German nation. The manifesto urged the European powers to grant no military concessions to Hitler's Germany. It advocated, instead, a "total moral, intellectual, political, and social revolution," in which the workers formed an alliance with all other social forces fighting the Nazi regime. Since they were all enemies of the dictatorship, Social Democrats, Communists, and members of other leftist splinter groups were actually "equal socialist revolutionaries." Working-class unity, the manifesto declared, "becomes a necessity" imposed by history itself.

Hilferding closed the manifesto by emphasizing the SPD's defiance of Nazi power and harking back to the party's traditional ideological principles and beliefs. Not only was capitalist development "creating its own gravediggers," but Social Democracy led the fight for what it called "the great and immortal ideas of humanity":

> We are the bearers of the great historical development since the overcoming of bondage in the Middle Ages. We carry on the immortal tradition of the Renaissance and of the humanism of the English and French Revolutions. We do not want to live without freedom and we will conquer it, freedom without class domination, until the complete eradication of all exploitation and all domination of man by man!

As this passage makes clear, Hilferding's willingness to adjust the SPD's organization and tactics to changed conditions did not mean that he was also willing to break with the party's traditional goals. For him, the manifesto aimed to clarify the reasons for the party's new course, but it was not the place for a detailed analysis of fascism, economic questions, past SPD policies, or the characteristics of a future postrevolutionary regime.[34]

Hilferding's decision not to examine some of these issues in greater detail left the manifesto filled with ambiguities. It demanded the SPD's reorganization into a revolutionary elite, but it contained no details on the party's future structure. It called for a violent anti-Nazi revolution and the establishment of a strong revolutionary regime but shied away from concrete discussion of the new government's form or the measures it should employ to consolidate its power. On one hand, Hilferding emphasized the "sustaining" role of the working class in the revolutionary government; on the other, he stressed the need for proletarian unity with the petty bourgeoisie and the peasantry. The call for a total revolution made no mention of the transformation of the economy.

Many of the manifesto's ambiguities resulted, in part, from Hilferding's attempt to placate the Sopade's various factions.[35] To satisfy the left, he demanded the party's reorganization, encouraged socialist and communist unity, and pointed to the need for a strong revolutionary government following the overthrow of the Nazi regime. To win the support of the right, he avoided any reference to the left's call for the replacement of the Sopade and called on the SPD to forge a multiclass alliance against fascism. Hilferding's concessions to the right made his draft acceptable to a majority in the executive, but it did not satisfy the left. In the end, the manifesto did nothing to unite social democracy's disparate groups.

The equivocations contained in the manifesto and in Hilferding's later programmatic writings also reflect his difficulty in dealing with certain crucial questions facing social democracy. Nowhere is this better illustrated than in the discussion of the party's reorganization. Throughout his career, Hilferding had condemned Bolshevik methods and rejected the Leninist conception of a revolutionary "vanguard" party. With the SPD driven underground, however, he called for its transformation from a mass party into an elite formation of professional revolutionaries. This elite would be organized into decentralized conspiratorial cells, unified through ties to a central party leadership outside Germany, the Sopade. It was the exiled leadership's responsibility to work out effective forms of struggle and to provide all possible support to the underground.

In the coming anti-Nazi upheaval, Hilferding argued in an essay published in early 1934, the movement would have to smash the total state by using revolutionary tribunals against fascist criminals and by purging the bureaucracy, the courts, and the military. To secure its power, a new government would have to expropriate—without compensation—the banks, heavy industry, and the *Junkers*. These measures would constitute the regime's "minimum program," and Hilferding asserted that no elections would be necessary to legitimate its actions. The revolutionary government's very existence would demonstrate its mass support.[36]

Thus, basing his views on a radically altered political situation, Hilferding found himself advocating organizational and tactical policies that were, in essence, Leninist in conception. He was extremely ambivalent about taking this step. At heart, he rejected Bolshevik conceptions of the "dictatorship of the proletariat" (148) and the vanguard party. In all his writings, both before and during his exile, he stressed the indivisible links between socialism and democracy, fearing that in Germany, as in Russia, a revolutionary dictatorship might turn against the workers themselves. He failed, however, to work out a specifically "social democratic" organizational alternative that could function under the conditions of fascist repression. Instead, he warned against the dangers of a dictatorship that would contradict the communist manifesto's goals of "free association" and the transcendence of the old antagonism between state and society. He remained trapped between his rejection of Leninism and his commitment to traditional social democratic organizational forms and methods of decision making (151–52).

While Hilferding in the early years of his exile devoted much attention to organizational questions, he also began to rethink his view of Marxist theory. Although he had never accepted the widely held notion that socialism was inevitable, prior to 1933 he did not question Marx's conclusions that capitalist development prepared the ground for socialism and that the class-conscious proletariat would be the agent of its own liberation. The Nazi victory and the SPD's subsequent inability to influence events led him to reconsider these beliefs. Gradually, he moved away from class analysis as a means of understanding the dynamic of future development and stressed the role of subjective factors in the historical process. In his early 1934 article, Hilferding observed that many Marxists overemphasized economics and class relations in their analyses of social and political change. This tendency led to the neglect of other important influences—such as the role of ideas in history—on the formation of class consciousness. "The Marxist conception of history," he wrote, "makes the historical conditions under which ideas are realized into the object of research" (146). It does not reduce the value of ideas but shows how they arise within certain historical relations and "take on a value of their own for which people are ready to live or die" (146). To dismiss ideas and the struggle for their realization was a "deformation of Marxism" (147).

Many German Marxists, Hilferding charged, had "relativized" the struggle for ideas throughout the SPD's history. Under the German Empire, the party had adopted a radical program that was politically unrealizable given the power relations at that time. The struggle for humanity remained abstract, while trade union and parliamentary efforts to improve living standards and introduce social reforms were more concrete. In spite of its "radical revolutionary" ideology, the SPD came to expect economic development to strengthen the proletariat, change power relations, and make the conquest of state power possible. The political impact of this deterministic outlook was profound. It reduced Social Democrats' readiness to fight for political goals that were not immediately tied to "the final goal of socialism" (147).

Ultimately, the theoretical and practical stress on economic change hindered the party's ability to fully understand contemporary conditions and to compete effectively in the political arena.

Hilferding's critique of Marxist "economic determinism" was, in many ways, a valid attempt at self-criticism. Although he had always recognized the importance of both, he had also tended to compartmentalize "ideas" and "economic relations." Throughout his career, he had stressed that capitalist development strengthened the position of the working class in relation to other social classes. Social Democracy's task, he had argued, was to organize this growing majority to win control of the parliament. At the same time, he emphasized the necessity of educating workers on the centrality of democracy to socialism and understood that noneconomic factors—such as religion and nationalism—played an important role in the shaping of people's political attitudes. It was not until after the disaster of 1933, however, that Hilferding seriously began to reconsider the relationship of class and noneconomic factors in the context of unfolding political struggle. He became convinced of the need for Marxists to view ideas as more than mere reflections of the social relations from which they arose, but also as important historical factors themselves. In essence, he was introducing Marx's concept of the dialectic into his theoretical framework.

Both Marx and Engels had emphasized the dialectical relationship between society's "economic base" and its "legal and political superstructure"; Engels himself had pointed out that, in certain historical periods, "the warring classes balance each other so nearly that the state power, as ostensible mediator, acquires, for the moment, a certain degree of independence from both."[37] Neither Hilferding's critique of economic determinism nor his initial description of the autonomous and dominant role of the state in totalitarian societies marked a methodological break with Marxism, and in fact, his early post-1933 theoretical work may be seen as a return to, rather than a departure from, Marx's method. Hilferding did not move decisively away from Marxism until his analysis divorced the "subjective" actions of the totalitarian leadership from the broader sociopolitical context. His dissatisfaction with Marxist analytical methods became increasingly pronounced during the latter half of the 1930s and must be seen in light of his personal sense of despair and frustration in the face of the apparent omnipotence of the fascist and communist regimes.

Hilferding's writings in the fall and spring of 1933 and 1934 represent his last major efforts to explicate the Sopade's strategy and goals. During the course of the next seven years, he wrote regularly but focused primarily on more specific economic and political issues. In particular, he urged the Western powers not to appease Germany. He rightly identified the latter's aggressive intentions and called on the democracies to rearm and organize new defensive alliances. Hilferding sharply criticized strong pacifist elements in the British Labour Party that were demanding disarmament; he thought it imperative for England and France to stand united. Convinced that the British and French socialists and the LSI all underestimated the German military threat, he hoped to alter their view. His efforts were in vain.[38]

Between 1934 and 1941, Hilferding watched helplessly as the social democratic movement disintegrated and the Nazi juggernaut rolled over Europe. The executive made no effort to transform the party along the lines suggested in the Prague Manifesto, and the disputes between communists, New Beginning, and the left and right wings of the Sopade remained unresolved. As the exiles bickered, the Nazis systematically crushed resistance groups inside Germany. The Gestapo rounded up thousands of social democratic activists, and many of them were tortured and killed. Nazi agents penetrated the party organization, broke up SPD smuggling operations, and assassinated or kidnapped a number of SPD leaders living in exile.[39]

As the Sopade's strength inside Germany declined, so did its position in Prague. Financially drained, its publishing house operated at a loss; it was difficult to pay party employees; and the circulation of *Neuer Vorwärts* stagnated around five thousand. The financial situation was so precarious that during the winter of 1935–1936, the party even considered selling the Marx-Engels archive to the Bolsheviks. The executive sent Hilferding to Paris to discuss the transaction with the Soviet emissary, Bukharin. Negotiations dragged on for several weeks. The Soviets were willing to pay 5–10 million Swiss gold francs for the documents and to provide the SPD with photocopies of them all, but only if the Social Democrats promised not to use the money for anticommunist purposes. Hilferding was unsure about the sale. Although he recognized that the funds would be of enormous assistance to the party, he was unsure if the soviets would actually adhere to the agreement. Eventually, Wels scrapped the deal with the Russians and sold the archive to the Institute for Social History in Amsterdam.[40]

The SPD's financial crisis limited its activities and matters worsened when it encountered increasing pressure to leave Czechoslovakia. As Nazi military and political power grew, the Czech regime found it difficult to resist German demands to ban *Neuer Vorwärts* and to outlaw the Sopade. By the winter of 1937–1938, it was apparent that the executive would have to leave Prague. With the permission of the French Popular Front government, it transferred the party's seat to Paris the following spring.

Hilferding's fortunes mirrored those of the party. His work at the *ZfS* was both time-consuming and frustrating. Financial problems plagued the journal, there were constant publishing delays, and the editors had difficulty finding high-quality contributors. With Hilferding in Zurich, it fell to Paul Hertz, his coeditor in Prague, to represent the *Zeitschrift*'s interests in the executive. Both Hilferding and Hertz had political enemies there, and as the party's financial problems multiplied, sentiment grew to stop the *ZfS*'s publication. Despite Hertz's repeated pleas to come to Prague and help fight for the journal, Hilferding demurred. Tired of political infighting and convinced that he could accomplish little, he was unwilling to involve himself in the Sopade's factional squabbles. In 1936, the leadership shut his journal down.[41]

Hilferding had serious disagreements with both left and right wings of the Sopade. He opposed attempts by Böchel, Aufhäuser, and Hertz to bring the SPD into cooperation with the KPD and other leftist splinter groups. In 1936, for example, when Communist leader Walter Ulbricht approached him with the suggestion that the KPD and the SPD together might publish a resolution in support of peace and begin discussion of cooperation against the Nazis, Hilferding reacted with caution. He found a Social Democratic declaration of a nonaggression pact with the KPD acceptable and thought it appropriate for both sides to publish separate statements clarifying the similarities in their foreign policies, but he would go no further.[42] Convinced that the Communists ultimately aimed to destroy Social Democracy and erect a dictatorship, he opposed any serious consideration of joint actions. In early 1935, he made his position clear to Hertz:

> Ever since bolshevism produced a socialism that is based on force, repression, and terror, the only correct question for me has been: freedom or slavery? Socialism . . . can mean both, and the real tragedy is that freedom and socialism are no longer identical . . . I cannot, therefore, compromise on the question of dictatorship. . . . Dictatorship is not transitional or educational, but makes the dictators increasingly despotic, and that is the case in Russia as well as in Italy or Germany. For this reason, I reject any cooperation with the Communists, as long as they are for dictatorship and terror. I cannot understand how one can protest together with murderers and terrorists (and today more than ever that is what Stalin's worshipers are) against murderers and terrorists.[43]

Hilferding did not think the leadership of the other leftist groups any more capable of unifying social democracy than the Sopade. Prague at least "offered security against the Communists" and all the other groups to which he was opposed, such as the Trotskyists, the Socialist Workers' party, and Böchel's group. He saw no other alternative.[44]

Hilferding's opposition to the Communists also placed him at odds with Otto Bauer, whose works in exile adopted a naively optimistic view of Bolshevik Russia. Like Hilferding and Kautsky, in the years immediately after 1917, Bauer thought that Russia had entered its bourgeois democratic phase of development, and he dismissed the possibility of building socialism in a backward agricultural country. Believing that the revolutionary dictatorship would ultimately disappoint and turn against the masses, he had stressed that revolutionary social democrats needed to constantly emphasize what separated them from their Bolshevik and reformist rivals. During the 1920s, however, Bauer developed a more supportive attitude toward the Soviet Union and argued that its "despotic socialism" represented an attempt to transform a society in which the prerequisites for democracy were poor. Although he rejected such a model for western Europe, he believed it was possible for a society first to develop socialist features (economic planning, for example) and later to develop democracy. After the collapse of the Austrian Republic in 1934, Bauer's view of the USSR became even more positive. Arguing that the recent growth of its economy had laid the basis for socialism, he asserted that the latter's realization now depended on Russia's democratization. Bauer did not regard democratization as a foregone conclusion, and he recognized the possibility that the Soviet governmental and technical apparatus could hold power indefinitely. But to protect the revolution's gains and to make democratization possible, he argued that all socialists were bound to defend Soviet Russia in case of war.[45]

By the mid-1930s, Hilferding, too, accepted the possibility of a "socialism" without democracy, but he had long been highly critical of Bauer's views on the Soviet Union. Under Weimar he had publicly said little about Russian development, but his letters to Kautsky show clearly that he had a more realistic view of soviet prospects and the nature of the regime than Bauer. In 1926, for example, he pointed out that when the Bolsheviks began to replace used-up fixed capital in their industries, they would face a severe crisis. To finance recapitalization, they could either look to the West for credits (and thereby revise their overall foreign policy) or return to a policy of "pure communism" and terrorism against the peasants. The latter policy, Hilferding thought, would result in a catastrophe, and he hoped that the Soviets would choose the less drastic option. This policy, while it would also exacerbate class antagonisms, held more promise of a political transformation.[46] When, instead, Stalin initiated his "revolution from above," it confirmed all of Hilferding's worst fears. He compared it to the impoverishment that resulted from the mercantilist policies of early capitalism and saw little chance for democratic change.[47]

Thus, Hilferding opposed Bolshevism and Nazism in equal measure and rejected Bauer's and any other position advocating tolerance or support of the Soviet regime. "I feel separated from Otto Bauer, my best friend," he wrote sadly to Hertz. But he angrily denounced calls for a united front with the Communists or claims that, in the international class war, it would be progressive if the fascist states defeated the English and French bourgeoisie. The left socialists, Hilferding exclaimed, "are even more idiotic than the Communists!" Rather than a united front, he asserted, the SPD's goal should be "the liquidation of the Communist parties in West and Central Europe."[48]

Hilferding's harsh criticism of the left was matched by his sharp attacks on the party's right. In 1936, for example, he blasted Stampfer, the editor of *Neuer Vorwärts,* for his optimistic views on the domestic and international situation. Stampfer was deceiving himself, Hilferding thought, when he suggested that the German military would overthrow Nazism or that Hitler's foreign policy "had nothing." Actually, the opposite was true. Hitler had "the strongest military in the world"; he had moved decisively into the

Rhineland and he was forging a strong alliance with Italy. Austria, trapped between Germany and Italy, would soon be annexed by the former; Poland had to choose between an alliance with the fascist camp or one with the Soviets. Not only did Stampfer completely misunderstand the international situation, he also misunderstood the nature of the Nazi system itself and focused too much of his attention on Hitler as an individual, and not enough on his function within the National Socialist system. "The German state," Hilferding lectured his comrade, "had its own laws . . . which were carried out not by Hitler, but by a collectivity of leading men who control the Foreign Ministry and the General Staff." Because the guiding principle of their policy was "the primitive logic of violence," these men saw war not as a catastrophe but as a boon. They expected to win, "and today, there is much evidence that they will win."[49]

The only thing that he and Stampfer agreed upon, Hilferding concluded, was that *Neuer Vorwärts* had little influence on public opinion. This circumstance did not disturb him, however, because his main intention was not propagandistic, but rather, to simply tell the truth. He reminded his colleague that he could not alter the fact that truth was bitter and destroyed illusions. The latter was particularly important, because the fight against fascism would only succeed when one ceased to deny reality.[50]

Hilferding's sharp but honest criticisms of the left and the right mark his increasing isolation within the socialist movement. In May 1935, he told Hertz that he was "not in complete agreement with any group" and that his own conception was not yet clear. He felt that the whole workers' movement was in crisis and wished to distance himself from factional struggles "until objective facts and objective development" made it possible for him "to work out a new thematic formulation [and] a concrete political foundation."[51]

Hilferding's effort to remain aloof from factional disputes, his pessimistic appraisal of the movement's situation, and his blunt criticisms of the party leadership did not win him many friends in the executive. His relations with Wels grew strained after 1933, and even Hertz—with whom Hilferding had worked and corresponded honestly for many years—eventually turned against him. In 1938, Hertz campaigned hard against Hilferding's formal election to the executive. "Hilferding's pessimism in regard to any mass movement or any illegal movement is so great," argued Hertz, "that no one could expect any support from him." In the end, the executive decided against his admission. Since Hilferding's post in the LSI already gave him the right to participate in the Sopade's discussions, the leadership decided there was no need to make him a formal member.[52]

The strains of exile took their toll on Hilferding. Not only did he and Rose have few financial resources, but they also had to worry about their status in Switzerland. It was always possible that the Swiss, under Nazi pressure, would force them to leave. The Hilferdings knew that the Nazis had not forgotten them, and they lived in constant fear of the Gestapo. In June 1935, the German government stripped Rudolf Hilferding of his citizenship, while the newspapers labeled him a traitor and blamed him for the inflation of 1923 and the financial crisis of 1928 and 1929. In 1938, his picture was displayed in a Berlin exhibition entitled "The Eternal Jew."[53]

Prolonged insecurity and the woeful state of social democracy sometimes drove Hilferding to despair and undermined his ability to work and keep up with his correspondence. In July 1935, Rose described one of his depressions in a letter to Hertz:

> Today I am writing to you behind Rudi's back so that you will not have to wait in vain for [his] reply. I returned to Zurich at the beginning of July and was absolutely shocked by the condition in which I found him. I have never seen him so depressed, so lifeless, and without hope. He drags himself around, can't work, eats practically nothing, sleeps for hours on end, and is irritable and unapproachable—in short it is heartrending. He stayed like this for ten days, during which [time] I was often ready to leave, but I said to myself that I had to bring him out of this numbness and persevere. Above all the article for the *Zeitschrift* was pressing; each day he tore up what he had just written.[54]

Eventually, Hilferding returned to work, but this passage reveals how difficult it was for him to deal with the repercussions of social democracy's defeat and the tensions of life in exile. Feeling himself isolated from each of the party's factions, he saw little hope for the future.

Early in 1938, the Hilferdings followed the Sopade to Paris. The decision to move was a logical one. The LSI had transferred its headquarters to Brussels in 1935, and there was no longer any need for Hilferding to travel to Prague. Hilferding's correspondence with Hertz indicates that he and Rose were also having difficulty renewing their visas. When France's socialist premier, Leon Blum, allowed the Sopade to establish its headquarters in Paris, it must have greatly relieved the Hilferdings. Hilferding knew Blum fairly well and probably encountered little difficulty in acquiring visas for himself and Rose. When they arrived in Paris, they rented a cheap furnished room in the student quarter.[55]

Over the course of the next two years, Hilferding advised the Sopade and wrote for *Neuer Vorwärts*. Despite his unhappiness with the situation in the party, it appears that he never seriously considered any other course. He could have dropped out of politics and sought safe haven overseas. Like many other famous German intellectual or political exiles, he could have secured a university teaching position in England or the United States. Such a move, however, remained out of the question. His dedication to the workers' movement, which he had demonstrated throughout his career, took precedence. For Hilferding, the withdrawal from politics would have meant the acceptance of social democracy's total defeat and the negation of everything he had ever worked for. He could not take this step.[56]

The coming of war in 1939 did not surprise Hilferding. He had long foreseen Nazi aggression; he had published numerous articles analyzing the expansion of Germany's war economy and attacking Allied appeasement. It was only a matter of time, Hilferding warned, before rearmament either destroyed the economy or resulted in a "total war" for the goal of "living space."[57] This analysis of Nazi policies took shape in the context of a broader discussion among socialist intellectuals concerning the "totalitarian" nature of the communist and fascist regimes. While editor of *Die Gesellschaft,* Hilferding had established close ties with many Menshevik exiles (most notably Alexander Schifrin, Boris Nikolaevskii, and Iurii Denicke), who were well informed about conditions in the Soviet Union and were constantly evaluating developments there. In exile, he remained on good terms with the Mensheviks, and many of them contributed regularly to the *ZfS.* Unable to read Russian and without intimate knowledge of Russian conditions, Hilferding refrained from direct participation in their debates prior to 1933. He played a more active role, however, following Hitler's seizure of power.[58]

By 1936, Hilferding's theory of the total state had assumed a much clearer form than in the early exile years and it formed the centerpiece of his analysis of international developments. In his view, the causes of the next war would be different from those of World War I, which had its origins in the international competition spawned by the development of finance capital. The next war would result from the unlimited growth of state power in the "totalitarian" countries. State power, he thought, had increased enormously during World War I, as governments subordinated society to their war-fighting needs. People recognized the state's ability to organize and direct the economy and accepted this notion even after the war's end. The state was no longer the instrument of society's dominant economic class, it had become independent of society, a power unto itself.[59]

According to Hilferding, governmental authority achieved its highest degree of control over society in the "totalitarian state," in which the state apparatus took possession of society and restructured society as it saw fit. Social strata could be leveled, reorganized, or left alone: the state "nationalized" (*verstaatlicht*) society. The totalitarian state surpassed all others in the extent of its means of control. The military, the police, the courts, and the bureaucracy were dependent on and subordinated to the state, and together formed an "interested mass base" at its disposal. The state also increased its role over the "autonomous" economy, which now had to subordinate its interests to the regime's own political goals. It dominated or destroyed all social organizations and won supporters by attracting people into the hierarchical party or state apparatus and granting them social and material privileges.

Hilferding argued that although the influence of classes had not been extinguished, class interests now were subordinated to those of the state. The dictators attracted mass support by promoting nationalist solutions to serious domestic economic and political problems. After the establishment of the totalitarian regime, the chief goal of the state apparatus was to consolidate and expand its power. The state used every means at its disposal to create a war economy and build a powerful military. With superior military power, the regime staved off domestic economic ruin by seizing and plundering neighboring territories.

For Hilferding, World War I had brought an end to the "classical policy of imperialism," or what he also called the "policy of finance capital." In the postwar period, the totalitarian dictatorships pursued policies that had very different motives. Germany and Italy "did not need areas in which to invest surplus capital." On the contrary, they needed to annex already developed areas "in order to alleviate the food and raw material shortages created by their own insane power policy." In essence, Hilferding argued, the dictatorships were carrying out a "new type of original accumulation." To save their own economies, they had to seize needed resources by force. In the long term, however, such a strategy could not solve any of the basic problems inherent in their war economies. The regimes would have to constantly renew their aggression and expand their territories in order to ease "the consequences of the economic policies that drove the dictators into war."

This analysis of the totalitarian states that Hilferding put forward in 1936 makes clear that he was gradually moving away from Marxism. In 1934 he had urged Marxist thinkers to strike a better balance between objective and subjective factors in their analysis of events, but within two years he had begun to place decisive emphasis on the subjective will above all else. By asserting that the state apparatus stood apart from society and essentially operated under its own laws, and by arguing that class interests were of secondary importance to those of the "state," he adopted a position that had little in common with Marx's views. Although he recognized that the totalitarian regimes had broad popular support and that economic factors remained important for the making of state policy, Hilferding also abstracted the totalitarian power holders from society itself and placed state power at the center of his analysis of political and social development.

In April 1940, Hilferding published an article in the Menshevik journal *Sotsialistischeskii Vestnik* in which he deepened his critique of Marxism by analyzing the nature of the soviet system. Entitled "State Capitalism or Totalitarian State Economy," the article aimed to debunk R. L. Worrall's argument that the USSR was a capitalist rather than a proletarian state. Worrall asserted that although the Bolsheviks had abolished private property in the means of production, capital accumulation continued under the aegis of the Soviet government. Economic control rested in the hands of the Stalinist bureaucracy, the functions of which were similar to those of its capitalist counterpart. In essence, therefore, the Soviet Union was a state capitalist—rather than a socialist—society.[60]

Hilferding agreed that Bolshevism had not transformed Russia into a proletarian state, but he firmly rejected Worrall's other conclusions. "A capitalist economy," he asserted, is governed by the laws of the market (analyzed by Marx), and the autonomy of these laws constitutes the decisive symptom of the capitalist system of production. A state economy, however, eliminates precisely the autonomy of economic laws. It represents not a market but a consumers' economy. It is no longer price, but rather a state planning commission that determines what is produced and how. (334)

In a planned economy, Hilferding observed, the accumulation of capital ceased, but the accumulation of the means of production and products continued. He believed that Worrall's analysis failed to distinguish between the process of accumulation, which occurred in virtually all economic systems, and the accumulation of capital (value), which is specific to a market economy. Since the capitalist appropriation of surplus value ended with the suppression of the market economy and the introduction of planning, so too did the accumulation of value. Accumulation, however, continued under a planned economy as the state guided the production and distribution of all types of goods (use values).

Hilferding rejected Worrall's and Trotsky's notion that the bureaucracy "ruled" in the Soviet Union or anywhere else. The bureaucracy was composed of varied elements including all sorts of government officials ranging from minor postal and railway employees up to generals and even Stalin himself. "How," he asked, "could this variegated lot possibly achieve a unified rule?" His answer was that it could not. The bureaucracy had no power of its own and was merely "an instrument in the hands of the real rulers" (336). Its hierarchical organization was subordinated to a "commanding power." Hilferding declared:

It is Stalin who gives the orders to the Russian bureaucracy. Lenin and Trotsky[,] with a select group of followers who were never able to come to independent decisions as a party but always remained an instrument in the hands of the leaders (the same was true later with the fascist and national socialist parties)[,] seized power at a time when the old state apparatus was collapsing. They changed the state apparatus to suit their needs as rulers, eliminated democracy and establishing their own dictatorship, which, in their ideology, but by no means in practice, was identified with the "dictatorship of the proletariat." Thus they created the first totalitarian state—even before the name was invented. Stalin carried on with the job, removing all his rivals through the instrument of the state apparatus and establishing an unlimited personal dictatorship. (336–37)

Hilferding emphasized that, despite different points of departure, the economy in all the totalitarian states had lost the primacy it once held under bourgeois society. Economic groups were still very influential, but the state—led by a small ruling clique—now dominated the economy. In his view, "this was why the subjective factor, the 'unforeseeable,' 'irrational,' character of political development, has gained such importance in politics" (337). Hilferding did not expect his views to win much support among other Marxists. In anticipation of their criticism he observed:

> The faithful believe only in heaven and hell as determining forces; the Marxist sectarian only in capitalism and socialism, in classes—bourgeoisie and proletariat. The Marxist sectarian cannot grasp the idea that present-day state power, having achieved its independence, is unfolding according to its own laws, subjecting social forces and compelling them to serve its ends for a short or long period of time. (338)

The Soviet Union, Hilferding concluded, was neither capitalist nor socialist. It represented a new type of system that he called a "totalitarian state economy," toward which Germany and Italy rapidly were moving. A Marxist analysis of this system was still possible, he thought, but only if Marxist theorists altered their "rather simplified and schematic conception of the correlation between the economy and the state, and the economy and politics, which developed in a completely different period" (339).

Hilferding's views on the totalitarian state economy had both theoretical and political implications. By postulating the creation of a new type of economic system, he challenged the traditional notion among social democrats that capitalism would inevitably lead to socialism. Hilferding's stress on the irrational subjective factor as the key element in the political domination of social and economic life implicitly refuted his own long-held belief that knowledge of the laws and functioning of the economy was essential for the development of "scientific politics." It was thus no longer necessary for the SPD to base its political strategy on an explicitly Marxist theoretical analysis of social and economic development. Following World War II, this outlook won many adherents within the social democratic movement. Its widespread, though not total, acceptance allowed the party to eventually break with its traditional Marxist ideology and to adopt a socialist worldview based on ideas drawn from Christian ethics, humanism, and classical philosophy. The SPD was then able to develop specific policies that appealed to a broader electoral constituency.[61]

Many aspects of Hilferding's theory of totalitarianism later became central to the Menshevik interpretation of the USSR and also won broad acceptance in Western academic and foreign policy circles.[62] The theory gained credibility despite its important methodological weaknesses. It divorced the Nazi and Soviet leadership from the sociopolitical context of their respective societies and ignored the complex interrelationship between the political sphere, in which economic interests are implemented, and society's economic foundation. Given the impact of Hitler's brutal seizure and consolidation of power in Germany and Stalin's equally bloody "revolution from above," it is not surprising that Hilferding essentially took his earlier view stressing the "primacy of the economy" and turned it on its head. His outlook, however, was shortsighted. In the long run even the omnipotent Soviet state was unable to overcome the economic problems that its place in the world economy and domestic mismanagement caused. The weakness of the communist economic system was a central factor in the Soviet state's rapid dissolution after Gorbachev assumed power in 1985.

Hilferding also exaggerated the similarities between Nazi and Soviet societies. Nazi Germany, despite its rhetoric, did not destroy capitalism. The Nazis used the system pragmatically in order to achieve their political goals. There was no radical restructuring of society, and Germany's capitalists largely cooperated with the NSDAP in return for lucrative profits and the preservation of their social privileges. It is true that the German state intervened in the economy when it encountered occasional resistance or when it was deemed necessary to meet particular military or political ends, but Nazi actions did little to alter the system as a whole. For the Nazis to transcend the limits of capitalism would have required much more radical economic policies than those they pursued.[63]

The Soviet Union, on the other hand, swept away the basic structures of the capitalist economy, and the functioning of its system depended on a wholly different constellation of social forces than existed in Germany. In the USSR, the Bolsheviks destroyed the capitalists as a class and basically eliminated the market. The state developed a plan for the production and distribution of goods. Thus, the Soviet and Nazi economic systems differed markedly from one another and Hilferding's attempt to develop a fascist-communist totalitarian model simply does not hold up.

Hilferding certainly expected his comments on the Soviet state to stimulate further theoretical discussion, but for him the time for such debate was over. Within weeks of his article's appearance, Nazi armies overran northern France. Paris fell on June 14, 1940, and Hilferding fled to the west and south among hundreds of German exiles. He left Paris in the company of his friend Rudolf Breitscheid, Breitscheid's wife, Tony, and Erika Biermann, the daughter of Hermann Müller and now Rudolf Breitscheid's secretary. For reasons that remain unclear, Rose Hilferding stayed behind and was unable to leave Paris for eight months. She never saw her husband again.

Hilferding and his friends went first toward the Atlantic coast where they hoped to find a ship that would transport them to safety. They traveled toward Agen, south of Bordeaux, but the approach of German troops forced them southward in the direction of Toulouse. Along the way, they encountered Leon Blum, who agreed to help them reach the port of Marseilles. There they hoped to receive immigration visas from the U.S. consulate. Their situation was desperate. On June 22, 1940, the French government capitulated and agreed to allow the Nazis to occupy the northern half of the country. The south remained under French administration, headquartered in Vichy, but this gave the refugees little encouragement. They were well aware that the French, as part of the surrender terms, had agreed to hand over all German nationals demanded by the Nazis.[64]

Hilferding, the Breitscheids, and Biermann were among hundreds of other German exiles who arrived in Marseilles in early July. The situation there was very fluid. It took time for the Nazis to establish their control over local French security forces, and for a while the refugees could move about in the open. Even though Hilferding and his companions had no residence permits, the French authorities allowed them to reside unmolested in the Normandie Hotel.

At first it seemed that their prospects for escape were good. In reaction to the Nazi conquest of France, President Roosevelt eased U.S. immigration restrictions on certain categories of European refugees. When Hilferding and Breitscheid applied for emergency entrance visas, the American consulate complied and they received their papers at the beginning of August 1940. Under normal conditions they could have left immediately for the United States, but conditions were not normal. To ensure the capture of German refugees, the Nazis forced the French to require everyone wishing to leave the country to apply for an exit visa. German officials stationed in Vichy could review all such applications. When the French authorities rejected both Hilferding's and Breitscheid's visa requests, their only recourse was to leave by illegal means. Their situation was precarious and grew increasingly dangerous the longer they remained in Marseilles.[65]

In early August, a representative of the New York–based Emergency Rescue Committee (ERC), Varian Fry, arrived in Marseilles. Carrying a list of numerous German exiles, Fry's task was to facilitate the escape of as many prominent refugees as possible. Fry made every effort to help Hilferding and Breitscheid get out of France. There were two possible escape routes: either by ship to Oran or Casablanca or by land across Franco's Spain to Portugal. The latter route would be especially dangerous for them; as staunch opponents of Franco's regime, they would certainly be delivered to the Nazis if discovered en route. After discussing the situation with other refugee leaders, Fry decided to prepare for their escape by ship. When presented with the plan, they hesitated. Hilferding was inclined to try the Spanish route, and Breitscheid had little faith in either choice. For several days they vacillated.[66]

The two friends made no attempt to conceal themselves while they debated what to do. Every day they sat for hours in the same café on the Boulevard d'Athènes. Their behavior angered other refugees, who feared that by exposing themselves to arrest, they threatened the security of the entire German émigré community. When Fry and others brought this sentiment to their attention, Hilferding and Breitscheid refused to consider going underground. Breitscheid even declared that Fry's suggestions were "complete madness." Hitler, he said, "will never dare to demand our extradition." Such statements, however, were purely rhetorical. Hilferding and Breitscheid knew they were in danger. Soon after their conversation with Fry, both men began to carry poison in their vest pockets.[67]

Eventually, they decided to escape by sea. In early September 1940, after encountering a number of difficulties, Hilferding secured a place on a ship to North Africa. Breitscheid arranged to follow him two days later. On the day of Hilferding's scheduled departure (September 13), however, the French authorities arrested both men. Without explanation, the police ordered them to leave Marseilles and to go immediately to Arles, where they were to take up residence in the Hotel du Forum. The police escorted them to the railway station and confiscated their French papers before putting them on the train. Upon their arrival, they were placed under house arrest.[68]

In Arles, Hilferding and Breitscheid continued their efforts to secure exit visas. They still had their U.S. entrance visas and hoped somehow to arrange to leave France. Hilferding wrote to Pierre Laval, vice-premier of the Vichy regime, and to friends in the United States such as Heinrich Brüning, in an attempt to secure their help. Laval sent no reply, but Brüning did his best to convince U.S. officials to intervene with the French on Hilferding's behalf. Evidence indicates that Brüning also sent Hilferding money through the Unitarian Friends Service Committee, which, like the ERC, was working to save prominent refugees from the Gestapo.[69]

The efforts of Hilferding's friends took many months to bear fruit and the fall of 1940 passed without incident. For Hilferding, the long waiting period was unbearable; by October he was very depressed. He had heard nothing from Rose since his departure from Paris and felt isolated and alone in Arles. He had very little money and no winter clothing. Worst of all was the constant fear of extradition. "The Damoclesian sword of extradition still hangs over me," he wrote to his friends Oscar and Margarethe Meyer. He blamed himself for not having understood in time the gravity of the situation, and he now realized how grim the outlook was for the future. "For some time, I had come to terms with life," he wrote, "but, . . . now it has again become more difficult to think about the end. [This is] probably a consequence of the long period of uncertainty."[70]

Hilferding's mental and physical condition declined as winter approached and he still had no word of Rose. He wrote to the Meyers:

> I am leading a life of total loneliness. Because of my friend's [Breitscheid, W.S.] difficult character, the isolation is terrible. I was sick recently, a terrible sciatica after a cold. I was in great pain [and] could not go out, but neither could I lie in bed because of the lack of cleanliness. Along with that came terrible sleeplessness, which was a consequence of the pain. For a while I was practically psychotic from confinement. . . . It is very cold, the hotel has no heat, and there are frequent storms. All this would be nothing if there were just some hope of improvement, and if it was not so sad about Rose. I still have not heard anything and my recent hope indirectly to hear something has gone unfulfilled. The separation from Rose was also a mishap in another respect. I am convinced that if we had stayed together, her superior knowledge of the language would have helped me.[71]

Although officially under house arrest, Hilferding was not strictly confined to his hotel quarters and was allowed to move about Arles. To distract himself, he spent much of his time in the local library. There he began to write what he described as an "epilogue" or "criticism of Marxism."[72] The critique opens with a discussion of the relationship of violence to economics and then turns to the development of the state, the subjective factor as an element of historical causation, and the usefulness of Marxism as a tool of social analysis. In essence, it summarizes and further elaborates the theoretical views that Hilferding had developed after 1933.[73]

One of the central theses of Hilferding's essay was that force was the decisive factor in history. It was not the economy that determined the content, aim, and result of violence; on the contrary, "it was the Germanic and Mohammedan conquest that brought about the agrarianization of Europe, the end of trade, the decline of cities, feudalism, and serfdom" (295). It was these types of violent upheavals that precipitated decisive historical transformations, rather than economic causes. Hilferding had long believed that Marxism was an "objective, value-free science," that could identify capitalism's "laws of motion" and thereby make "scientific politics" possible. Now, in "Das historische Problem," he argued that "violence is blind and its results are not predictable. This means that the knowledge of historical laws encounters limits, and that we cannot not speak of 'necessity' in Marx's sense, but only of 'chance' in the sense of Max Weber."[74]

These statements indicate that Hilferding was now willing to dispense with Marxism as a method of historical analysis, but his subsequent comments seem to contradict this view. Although he believed that, at certain points in history, violence could usher in a new phase of historical development, he also thought that the causes of such struggles, such as the increasing tensions that resulted from capitalist development, could be discerned and analyzed. One could examine the sociological conditions that made warfare possible and determine its content and scope. "Economic relations," Hilferding insisted, "require their realization in politics." He did not, however, clarify how this assertion could be made to agree with his claim that "blind force" itself was the decisive factor in history (296).

As he had in many of his post-1933 writings, Hilferding now emphasized the importance of state power as an independent force. "The political problem of the postwar epoch," he wrote, "consists of the change in the relationship of state power to society brought about by the subordination of the economy to the coercive power of the state" (296). The formation of the all-powerful state altered the previously dominant historical and social laws of development. Since the state could intervene in every sphere of social life, the policy makers in its apparatus held immense power. This new situation had important implications for Marxism, because it raised the question of what determined the leadership's subjective will. In place of the "objective context," it now appeared to Hilferding that "a purely psychological problem" had developed (298).

In Hilferding's view, Marx had put forward a "sociological conception of history" (300), which focused its analysis primarily on the sphere of production relations. While he thought that production relations were certainly of great importance in shaping people's consciousness, Hilferding did not believe that by analyzing them one could fully explain the reasons why legal, religious, and moral attitudes change. Historians, he said, had two tasks. On one hand, they had to analyze production relations in order to discern the interests of social groups. On the other, they had to study the psychological effects of these interests on the behavior of these groups and to take all other possible psychological influences into consideration. For Hilferding, history was essentially the study of "causality" and "the determinants of the will" (312). The degree to which psychological analysis succeeded in showing how various interests and motivations were linked to the historical behavior of specific social groups was decisive for determining the scientific merit of any historical representation.

Hilferding was convinced that Marx's concept of class needed further development and revision. Marx's definition, he thought, was correct in terms of its economics, but it inadequately considered the other factors that influence the formation of class consciousness. Broad economic definitions of class could not explain group behavior. It did not, for example, effectively explain the alliance between Germany's small peasants and the *Junkers*, two groups with very different and often conflicting interests. Nor was it completely successful in analyzing the relationship between poorly paid unskilled workers and highly skilled workers and technicians. These workers all received wages, but they also formed very different social groups. In Hilferding's view, Marxist theorists had to recognize the complexity of modern society's structure. It would be better to examine "social groups" rather than "classes" in order to achieve a more accurate understanding of the "socially effective interests" that influence them (318–19).

Hilferding's essay was an erudite work that indicated the author's broad knowledge of economics, history, and philosophy and exemplified his willingness to rethink many of the ideas that had long guided his actions. As a critique of Marxism, however, it suffered from his own serious misunderstanding of Marx's work. Throughout his career, Hilferding and most other social democratic thinkers had generally undervalued the dialectical principles central to Marx's and Engels's conception of the historical process. They neglected the political side of Marx's analysis and tended to focus primarily on his study of the economic development that would ultimately bring about an increase in proletarian political power. Instead of seeing a dialectical relationship between what Marx referred to as society's "economic foundation" and the "legal and political superstructure" that arose from it, Hilferding tended to neglect the political or "subjective" dimension of Marx's thought.[75]

Following Hitler's seizure of power, Hilferding ascribed to Marx the determinist elements of his own theoretical work. In response to his earlier emphasis on the economy, he stressed the importance of human subjectivity and the autonomous, all-powerful state in the unfolding of events and ultimately came to see blind force as the decisive factor in history. In general, Hilferding's theoretical effort lacked clarity and coherence. On one hand, he argued that violence, the state, and ideas were in themselves independent causal factors in history. On the other, he remained attached to a strongly evolutionary and materialist outlook and insisted that when studying human history, the problem "is [to determine] how the natural and the fundamental . . . relations of production affect people's consciousness and behavior."[76] Hilferding did not link these seemingly contradictory elements into any kind of dialectical relationship, and it is unclear how he would have resolved this dilemma had he finished the work.

Unfortunately, circumstances intervened to prevent Hilferding from completing his critique of Marxism. Around January 20, 1941, he received a telegram from Brüning in the United States announcing that the French had agreed to grant his exit visa. Breitscheid went immediately to the deputy chief of police in Arles and asked if he and Hilferding could safely present formal visa requests to the French authorities and if these requests would also be subject to review by the Germans. The deputy chief replied that he would have to inquire in Vichy. Two days later, he informed Hilferding and Breitscheid that there "was not the slightest danger" and urged them to apply immediately for visas.[77]

A few hours later, the deputy chief appeared at the Hotel Forum and explained to Hilferding and Breitscheid that it was no longer necessary for them to send their applications to Vichy. The authorities there had already agreed to grant the visas, and they could receive them in Marseilles. The chief of the Marseilles "pass department" then came to Arles personally and arranged for their travel papers. On January 27, 1941, Hilferding and Breitscheid took the train to Marseilles. Along with Tony Breitscheid and Erika Biermann, they immediately went to the police station and received their exit visas. The police forbade them to cross the Spanish border and recommended that they make immediate arrangements to go by ship to Martinique.

The next ship was scheduled to depart on February 4. There were no more private cabins available, but one could still get a bunk in a larger sleeping cabin. Hilferding decided to sail on that ship; the others elected to wait for the next ship on February 18. After months of crushing anxiety and fear, it appeared that Hilferding would be able to leave France after all. On January 31, however, disaster struck. The deputy police chief in Arles (where they still lived) told Hilferding and Breitscheid that the Vichy government had without explanation revoked their exit visas. He repeatedly assured them, however, that they had nothing to fear and were under his personal protection. With his word of honor, he promised that if the Germans entered the unoccupied zone, he would guarantee their security.

About a week later, Hilferding and Breitscheid found themselves under police surveillance. When they inquired why, the police told them there had been a misunderstanding and the surveillance ceased. Once again the authorities assured Tony Breitscheid and Biermann that they had nothing to fear.

At 11:30 A.M. on February 8, 1941, a Saturday, two policemen and a "special police commissar" came to the Hotel Forum and ordered Hilferding and Breitscheid to accompany them to the local police station. Upon their arrival, they learned that the Nazis had discovered their location and were on their way to Arles to arrest them. The police, however, assured Hilferding and Breitscheid that they were still under their protection. They told them that, after hiding for a few days, they would receive Spanish visas and would be able to escape. After the commissar explained that they would be taken to police headquarters in Vichy, Breitscheid became suspicious and accused the French of plotting to extradite them. The official replied, "You have a very low opinion of France, Herr Breitscheid," and vehemently denied his accusations. After calming the two men's fears, the police took them back to their hotel to pack. They told them to bring few clothes but as much money as possible. The latter, they said, would be much more useful in the days to come. When Tony Breitscheid insisted on accompanying her husband, the French at first resisted but eventually gave in.

Hilferding, the Breitscheids, and their police escort left in the middle of the night for Vichy. They arrived at 11 A.M. Sunday morning and the two men were taken to the national police headquarters. Tony Breitscheid remained free, but the French prevented her from seeing either her husband or his friend. The police took away Hilferding's and Breitscheid's belongings, searched them, and placed them in separate rooms under heavy guard. Later that day, they announced that the two socialist leaders would be handed over to the Nazis, who had repeatedly requested their extradition since December 17. Both men were surprised but took the news courageously. The French explained to them that Fritz Thyssen, a leading German industrialist and one-time Hitler supporter, had already been extradited and was being held with his wife in Germany. They told Hilferding and Breitscheid to expect a similar fate.

At around 7 P.M. Sunday evening, the police finally allowed Tony Breitscheid to visit her husband. After he explained the situation, she immediately ran to the U.S. Embassy, but there was no one there. She wrote a note describing what had happened and asked the doorman to deliver it to the ambassador as soon as possible. At 5 A.M. the next day, Tony returned to police headquarters and paced up and down the street for two hours before she could get in. She was able to talk to both men for about an hour before returning to the embassy, which was still closed. She left another message requesting the ambassador to intervene on the prisoners' behalf and then set out for the French Interior Ministry. On her way, she realized that there was no public transportation until 9:30 A.M., so she returned to the embassy. There she learned that the ambassador could do nothing to help her companions. The ambassador's secretary explained that the Nazi government's request was fully justified under the terms of the German-French armistice, and the Vichy regime had no choice but to comply. Upon leaving the embassy, Tony hurried to the Interior Ministry but was turned away at the door. At 10:45 A.M., she returned to police headquarters, where she was allowed to speak to Breitscheid for a few minutes before he and Hilferding were driven off in separate cars.

The French drove the two friends to the Nazi Security Service office, where SS *Hauptsturmführer* and Criminal Commissar Hugo Geissler greeted them scornfully with the words, "Now, you social democratic toads!"[78] The Nazis then loaded them once again into separate cars and took them to Paris where they were imprisoned in the Gestapo dungeon of Le Santé on the night of February 10, 1941. They were locked in separate cells.

By the time he arrived in Paris, Hilferding had lost all hope. The movement he had worked for all his life was in ruins, he was cut off from his friends, and he had heard nothing from Rose for almost eight months. In Nazi hands, he could look forward only to imprisonment, torture, and probable death. He and Breitscheid had long feared that this situation would arise and had begun to carry poison as a last possible means of escape. Sometime during the trip to Paris, Hilferding decided to act. In his cell he managed to take an overdose of veronal sleeping pills that he had successfully concealed on his person. By the next morning, he was senseless. Breitscheid heard a guard tell his chief that he "could not get Hilferding up," and the head of the prison medical staff, Dr. Schumann, later reported that an empty bottle of veronal had been found in his cell. Although the Gestapo transferred Hilferding to the prison infirmary, nothing was done to revive him. Within two days he was dead.[79]

AFTERWORD

Over fifty years have passed since Rudolf Hilferding's death and during that time he has virtually disappeared from public consciousness. His activities and ideas have been examined by many scholars, but aside from the relatively few people who take a serious interest in German or economic history or who may have been alive when he was active, it is difficult to find people in Germany today who recognize Hilferding's name or can tell you anything about him. In contrast to the public honors bestowed upon so many other social democratic political figures in German history, no street or plaza, to my knowledge, bears his name and no statue or plaque reminds us of the price he paid for his convictions.[1]

There are several explanations for this situation. The first of these concerns the period in which he was most influential. Hilferding attained the height of his public renown not during the pre-1914 "glory years" associated with the SPD's founding and growth, nor during the post-1945 period in which the party once again became a major force. Rather than being connected with these relatively successful phases of the SPD's history, his political reputation is most closely tied to that of the failed Weimar Republic. In the post-1933 studies of this era, Western historians have devoted much more attention to the leading Nazi personalities—the winners in the struggle for power—than to the defeated social democrats. Whereas biographical studies of the latter are scarce, academic and popular works on the Nazi leaders abound. The Nazis attract the lion's share of historical interest because their political victory and the enormity of their crimes tend to overshadow all else.

The political concerns of the Socialist and Communist parties after World War II also tended to discourage interest in Hilferding and the Weimar Social

Democratic leadership. At the end of the 1950s, the SPD jettisoned its adherence to class struggle and its critique of private property. By moving away from Marxism and adopting a socialist vision based on other philosophical currents, the party expanded its nonproletarian base of support and increased its political strength. The latter goals were certainly ones that Hilferding had also envisioned, but he had been a Marxist theoretician, and (the flexibility of his Marxism notwithstanding) for the postwar SPD such a weltanschauung was of little use. With his theoretical views no longer relevant to the party's new outlook, Hilferding became a figure of primarily historical interest for German social democrats.

In communist-controlled East Germany, Hilferding's reputation met with a somewhat different fate. There the Socialist Unity Party continued to hold his early theoretical work in high regard and it moved quickly to publish a new edition of *Finance Capital*. But the East German historians' view of Hilferding was marked by a slavish adherence to Lenin's theoretical and political criticisms of him and no biography appeared. Much more concerned with elevating the role of their own leadership in the struggle against fascism, East German historians produced few biographical works focusing on the Weimar SPD.

Hilferding has faded from the historical memory of the postwar generation, but the legacy of his political and intellectual career remains important. Having spent his entire life enmeshed in social democratic politics, the story of Hilferding's career is, in many ways, also that of German social democracy in the first half of the twentieth century. Hilferding wanted to change the world; and for over four decades as a leading socialist thinker and politician he worked to synthesize thought and action. That he ultimately failed to achieve his aims in no way reduces the relevance of his experience or the significance of his ideas for those in the current generation concerned about problems of empowerment and leadership as well as economic development.

When speaking of Hilferding the politician, the gap between what he thought of himself and what he was mirrored the party's own misperception of its image. Like most of his colleagues in the party leadership, Hilferding was a sincere believer in democracy and toleration for opposing views, yet he became a member of a party oligarchy that was virtually irremovable and that grew increasingly intolerant over the years of challenges to its authority. Hilferding thought it was the SPD's task to educate the masses politically and to prepare them to take and exercise power on their own, yet in practice he often supported policies that discouraged spontaneous mass action or deviations from the course charted by the party leadership. Although he worked hard to effect the democratization of German political and economic life, he was uncertain if the masses were actually prepared to lead or to rule, and it was this uncertainty that produced a fundamental tension in his thought concerning the relationship of the party leadership to the rank and file and the masses. His experience in this regard exemplifies a problem that modern socialist parties continue to face not only in states where parliamentary politics are the accepted norm, but also in places where the workers' movement has had to face repressive governments.

With the collapse of the communist states in eastern Europe and the establishment of parliamentary governments and a capitalist economic order there, Hilferding's view of the state also provides interesting lessons for the current generation. Although he recognized that the Weimar republic was threatened by a variety of problems, Hilferding exaggerated the ability of the parliamentary order to withstand social dislocation brought on by economic crises, a miscalculation also made by many contemporary parliamentary regimes, especially in eastern Europe. In the euphoria that followed the collapse of "communism," many new governments have attempted to leap into "free-market" capitalism, and the result has been severe social and economic dislocation accompanied by political crises. Hilferding may have misjudged the strength of Weimar Germany's political institutions, but in laying out his thoughts on the transition to socialism, he also stressed that success depends on the establishment of the broadest possible social consensus as a means of preventing destructive civil conflict. In the contemporary movement away from central planning and toward a capitalist market, his argument is no less valid.

Although the end of the Cold War has been hailed by many as the triumph of capitalism and even "the end of history," most of the economic and social problems of Hilferding's time have in no way been resolved, and many have grown worse. Under "real existing capitalism" even the most advanced capitalist welfare states find themselves beset by serious structural crises that fuel unemployment, impoverishment, and social polarization. Conditions in most of the "underdeveloped" world are much worse, and the gulf between the wealthy North and the poor South is growing. In this context, Hilferding's economic writings still provide much food for thought not only on the origins of these developments, but also on the possibilities for democratic change.

Finance capital lost its dominant economic position in the decades following World War I and the onset of the Great Depression, but there is considerable evidence that its power has at least partially revived in the contemporary capitalist economy. A few examples suffice to illustrate the general point; the case of the United States is particularly compelling. As early as 1967 (thus, well before the "merger mania" of the 1980s), six major New York banks alone held at least 5 percent of the outstanding stock in 965 companies.[2] Since many analysts consider a 5 percent holding sufficient to control a firm (and almost all, including those in government, view that amount as at least influential), this one example clearly illustrates finance capital's continued clout. As one Reagan-era study of American business observed, "at the pinnacle of the American financial and industrial structure are the money-market banking institutions, located mainly in New York." Through their control over the flow of capital and an elaborate interlocking personnel network, these banks "are the only institutions capable of coordinating the broadest spectrum of American business."[3]

Since the late 1970s, investment banks have played a key role in the corporate takeover process that has decisively shaped the American and international economic order. By providing advice and credit and by purchasing stocks, firms such as Salomon Brothers, Goldman Sachs, and Morgan Stanley have benefited from and encouraged a wave of mergers and acquisitions that continues to concentrate economic and political power in the hands of a few giant corporations. The results of Morgan Stanley's 1988 business year reveal the enormous scale of this process. In that year Morgan Stanley took part in 190 merger and acquisition transactions worth 156 billion dollars or a sum amounting to three-fourths of the state budget of West Germany! Bank profits from these operations totaled almost 10 billion dollars.[4]

America's investment banks have wielded great power in recent years, and so have its commercial banks. In one study of the banking system, William Greider demonstrates that not only is the United States' central bank, the Federal Reserve, subject to practically no effective governmental oversight or control but its "preferred interest group" is composed of the six thousand commercial banks in the Federal Reserve System. Greider argues convincingly that, through its control over this and other institutions, the creditor class—composed of bondholders, commercial bankers, the four hundred thousand Wall Street professionals and their customers the investors—has been able to shape government economic policy in its own interest. By radically cutting tax reductions on corporations and the rich, slashing funding for government services to the poor, pouring public investment into the military-industrial complex, crushing the trade unions, and deregulating financial and industrial activity, Reagan and his successor administrations greatly increased the wealth not only of capital as a whole, but of the financial sector in particular.[5]

In Germany, too, although the structure of the banking system is somewhat different than in the United States, finance capital wields great power. Three of the country's largest corporate credit institutions—the Deutsche Bank, the Dresdner Bank, and the Commerzbank—participate in the operations of hundreds of the most important domestic and foreign financial and industrial firms and thus play a decisive role in Germany's economy. The Deutsche Bank, for example, is one of the ten largest banks in the world. It is a major shareholder in virtually every economic sector from insurance and real estate to heavy industry, and in 1993 it serviced over 220,000 firms with credit totaling 160 billion DM. Along with Germany's other major banks, the Deutsche Bank uses its control over vast capital resources to shape state economic and political policy at home and abroad.[6]

Finance capital, Hilferding once pointed out, "detests the anarchy of competition and aims at organization—though, of course, only in order to resume competition at a still higher level."[7] Recent developments in the world economy confirm this view. The emergence of giant transnational corporations since 1945 reflects the globalization of the world market in which capital knows no national loyalty. Many of these corporations, among them transnational banks, have come to rival the national state in their ability to shape the world economic and political order.

In the international arena, corporate banks play a key role as providers of credit to private business and government. One study, carried out by the UN Commission on Transnational Corporations, illustrates their decisive importance in extracting wealth from the developing countries. According to the UN, corporate banks based in the Western industrialized countries transferred 132 billion dollars in interest payments out of Latin America alone between 1980 and 1986. Thirty of these transnational banks dominate the lending field in which the total debt of the developing countries rose to over 1 trillion dollars by the late 1980s.[8] These banks, through their control over scarce capital resources, often have decisive influence over the domestic and foreign policies of the debtor states.

While the private banks have moved decisively into the world market, the establishment of large, state-supported, international credit institutions such as the World Bank and the International Monetary Fund has also encouraged the internationalization of capital. These institutions use their financial power "to promote the interests of private, international capital in its expansion to every corner of the underdeveloped world."[9] Like the private corporate banks, their control over capital resources allows them not only to promote "development" projects, but to directly and indirectly shape the economic—and ultimately the political—policies of their clients.

The shift of corporate interests from the national to the international level again illustrates the historical limitations of Hilferding's model of finance capital. Hilferding examined capitalism at a time when "protection" was the order of the day, but today transnational corporations demand a state policy of "free trade" that weakens the power of local governments, trade unions, or any public institutions that may "intervene" in economic life.[10] They want a policy that eases the movement of industrial and money capital throughout the world in order to find the most favorable conditions for investment. Recent revisions of the General Agreement on Tariffs and Trade, the establishment of a free trade zone in the European Community, and the signing of the North American Free Trade Agreement reflect transnational capital's success in shaping government policy.[11]

Hilferding hoped that the socialist movement would be able to create a society in which the liberal political freedoms won in the wake of the French Revolution would be complemented by the achievement of economic democracy for the mass of the population. For him, democratizing the economy meant not only empowering workers in the production process but also including the majority of the people in economic decision making. Although his proposals for transforming the economy foundered on socialism's political weakness, the ideas he espoused retain their currency today. If the socialist movement in the post–Cold War era is to move forward, it will not be able to dismiss questions of ownership and empowerment faced by Hilferding and his generation. Their experience and ideas represent an important element of socialist history that cannot be ignored in the modern era.

NOTES

INTRODUCTION

1. *New York Times,* September 18, 1941.

2. An unpublished description of the ceremony may be found in the Paul Hertz Nachlaß, Film XL 54 A–J, in the Archiv der sozialen Demokratie (AdsD), Bonn (hereafter cited as Nachlaß Hertz).

3. Among the most important general studies of the SPD are Wolfgang Abendroth, *Aufstieg und Krise der deutschen Sozialdemokratie* (Frankfurt am Main, 1964); Carl E. Schorske, *German Social Democracy, 1905–1917* (Cambridge, Mass., 1955); Richard Hunt, *German Social Democracy, 1918–1933* (New Haven, 1964); Georg Fülberth and Jürgen Harrer, *Die deutsche Sozialdemokratie, 1890–1933* (Darmstadt, 1974); W. L. Guttsman, *The German Social Democratic Party, 1875–1933* (London, 1981); Richard Breitman, *German Socialism and Weimar Democracy* (Chapel Hill, 1981); Heinrich August Winkler, *Von der Revolution zur Stabilisierung, Arbeiter und Arbeiterbewegung in der Weimarer Republik, 1918–1924,* 3 vols. (Bonn, 1985), *Der Schein der Normalität . . . 1924–1930* (Bonn, 1985), and *Der Weg in die Katastrophe . . . 1930–1933* (Bonn, 1987); and Donna Harsch, *German Social Democracy and the Rise of Nazism* (Chapel Hill, 1993).

CHAPTER 1. THE AUSTRIAN HERITAGE

1. Epigraph is from Rudolf Hilferding, review of Anton Mengers "Volkspolitik," *Die Neue Zeit* 25.1 (1906–1907): 480. Unless otherwise noted, all translations are mine.

2. Although most of Hilferding's writings and speeches are available in published and nonpublished form, few documents related to his personal life or party work survive, and what remains is scattered in various European and North American archives. It appears that most of his private papers were lost or destroyed during the Nazi period as were many SPD and government records pertaining to his activities.

3. Emil Hilferding (1852–1905) was from Brody, and Anna Liss (1854–1909) was from Lemberg. See Wilfried Gottschalch, "Hilferding, Rudolf," in *Neue deutsche Biographie* (Berlin, 1972), 9:137. Hilferding's birth was registered in the Israelitische Kultusgemeinde, Wien 1, Schottenring 25. See Minoru Kurata, "Rudolf Hilferding, Wiener Zeit: Eine Biographie (1)," *Economic Review* 26.2 (October 1975): 18.

4. Kurata, "Hilferding (I)," 18–19; Arthur J. May, *The Hapsburg Monarchy, 1867–1914* (Cambridge, Mass., 1951), 177–78. My comments on the circumstances of Emil Hilferding's employment are drawn from information provided by Dr.

Joseph Kolb of the Allianz Versicherungs-Aktiengesellschaft based in Munich. Dr. Kolb described the job of the "Hauptkassier" very succinctly: "Hauptkassierer war die Art von Vertrauenstellung, die man durch Fleiß, Ehrlichkeit und saubere Handschrift erlangte—also eine bescheidene Position" (The head cashier was the kind of position of trust that one reached through hard work, honesty, and neat handwriting—therefore a modest position).

5. Alexander Stein, *Rudolf Hilferding und die deutsche Arbeiterbewegung, Gedenkblätter* (Hamburg, 1946), 5. On Jewish cultural assimilation in Vienna see Marsha Rosenblitt, *The Jews of Vienna, 1867–1914* (Albany, 1983), 3; Steven Beller, *Vienna and the Jews, 1867–1938* (Cambridge, 1989), esp. chap. 4.

6. Minoru Kurata, "Rudolf Hilferding, Wiener Zeit: Eine Biographie (2)," *Economic Review* 29.2 (1978): 26–27.

7. Karl Renner, *An der Wende zweier Zeiten* (Vienna, 1946), 245, 250 (279); Tom Bottomore and Patrick Goode, eds., *Austro-Marxism*, texts translated by Tom Bottomore and Patrick Goode, with an introduction by Tom Bottomore (Oxford, 1978), 9; Kurata, "Hilferding (I)," 23.

8. See Hilferding, "L'Inspection du travail en Autriche," translated by Camille Polack in *Le mouvement socialiste* 13, July 15, 1899, pp. 101–11. For background on the Socialist Student League see Kurata, "Hilferding (II)," 25–26; Renner, *An der Wende zweier Zeiten*, 246–47. Renner thought that more was learned from Sesser's lectures at the Heiliger Leopold café than would have been from the most hard-working of school teachers.

9. Renner, *An der Wende zweier Zeiten*, 250–51.

10. Stefan Zweig, *Die Welt von Gestern* (Stockholm, 1944), 50–55. Arthur Schnitzler's *Jugend in Wien* (Vienna, 1968), chaps. 1–3, confirms many of Zweig's observations.

11. I am indebted to professor Tom Bottomore who made available to me a copy of a manuscript by the late Morris Watnick, which deals with Rudolf Hilferding's background and with Jewish assimilation in Vienna. The material contains many useful insights regarding the socioeconomic context of Hilferding's early life.

12. Compare Rosenblitt, *The Jews of Vienna*, 47–49; May, *The Hapsburg Monarchy*, 175–81; and John W. Boyer, *Culture and Political Crisis in Vienna: Christian Socialism in Power, 1897–1918* (Chicago, 1995), 26, 29–31.

13. Carl E. Schorske, *Fin-de-Siècle Vienna: Politics and Culture* (New York, 1979), 115–18, 130; Rosenblitt, *The Jews of Vienna*, 161.

14. Robert Wistrich, *Socialism and the Jews: The Dilemmas of Assimilation in Germany and Austria-Hungary* (London and Toronto, 1982), 209.

15. "Beschlüsse des Parteitages der sozialdemokratischen Arbeiterpartei Österreichs am Parteitag zu Hainfeld (30.–31. Dezember 1888 und 1. Januar 1889), ergänzt am Parteitag zu Wien (Pfingsten, 1892)," in *Austromarxismus: Texte zu "Ideologie und Klassenkampf" von Otto Bauer, Max Adler, Karl Renner, Sigmund Kunfi, Béla Fogarasi und Julius Lengyel*, ed. Hans-Jörg Sandkühler and Rafael de la Vega (Vienna, 1970), 370–71.

16. Three substantial collections of Hilferding's correspondence survive. The most extensive of these are his letters to Karl Kautsky, followed by those to Paul Hertz and Leon Trotsky. Even when writing to good friends such as Kautsky, Hilferding mainly dealt with party affairs and theoretical matters. He rarely wrote regarding personal matters and said virtually nothing about his family history.

17. Isaac Deutscher, "The Non-Jewish Jew," in *The Non-Jewish Jew and Other Essays* (Oxford, 1968), 26–27.

18. Ibid., 35–36.

19. On Grünberg see Günther Nenning, "Biographie Carl Grünbergs," in *Indexband zum Archiv für die Geschichte des Sozialismus und der Arbeiterbewegung* (Graz, 1973), 126–28; Bottomore and Goode, *Austro-Marxism*, 9–10.

20. Bottomore and Goode, *Austro-Marxism*, 10.

21. Nenning, *Indexband*, 73–75.

22. Rudolf Hilferding, book review of G. Maier, "Soziale Bewegungen und Theorien bis zur modernen Arbeiterbewegung," in *Die Neue Zeit* 25.2 (1906–1907): 299–300; and *Finance Capital: A Study of the Latest Phase of Capitalist Development,* ed. Tom Bottomore, trans. Morris Watnick and Sam Gordon (London, 1981), 24.

23. Nenning, *Indexband*, 59–63, 65 (65).

24. See Julius Braunthal, *In Search of the Millenium* (London, 1945), 243.

25. Marc Blum, *The Austro-Marxists, 1890–1918: A Psychobiographical Study* (Lexington, 1985), 20. On Mach see also K. D. Heller, *Ernst Mach: Wegbereiter der modernen Physik* (Vienna, 1964).

26. Rudolf Hilferding, "Aus der Vorgeschichte der Marxschen Ökonomie," *Die Neue Zeit* 29.2 (1910–1911): 620–23 (623).

27. Nenning, *Indexband*, 123–24.

28. Stein, *Rudolf Hilferding*, 5; and Hilferding's letters to Karl Kautsky, April 23 and May 21, 1902, KDXII, 580, 581 resp., International Institute for Social History, Amsterdam (hereafter cited as ISH).

29. The nature of Austro-Marxism remains the subject of considerable debate. See Blum, *The Austro-Marxists,* 19–21; Bottomore and Goode, *Austro-Marxism,* 2–3; Raimund Loew, "The Politics of Austro-Marxism," *New Left Review* 118 (November–December 1979): 15–17; Ernst Glaser, *Im Umfeld des Austromarxismus: Ein Beitrag zur Geistesgeschichte des österreichischen Sozialismus* (Vienna, 1981), 22–29.

30. Rudolph Hilferding and Max Adler, preface to *Marx-Studien: Blätter zur Theorie und Politik des wissenschaftlichen Sozialismus, erster Band* (Vienna, 1904), ii–viii.

31. Otto Bauer, "Austromarxismus," in *Austromarxismus,* ed. Sandkühler and de la Vega, 49–51.

32. Ibid., 51.

33. Helga Grebing, *Der Revisionismus: Von Bernstein bis zum "Prager Frühling"* (Munich, 1977), 16–45; Peter Gay, *The Dilemma of Democratic Socialism* (New York, 1952), 61.

34. On the Jungen see Stanley Pierson, *Marxist Intellectuals and the Working-Class Mentality in Germany, 1887–1912* (Cambridge, Mass., 1993), 19–26.

35. Vincent Knapp, *Austrian Social Democracy, 1889–1914* (Washington, 1980), 40–41.

36. Ibid., 113–15, 61.

37. Ibid., 124.

38. Norbert Leser, *Zwischen Reformismus und Bolschewismus: Der Austromarxismus als Theorie und Praxis* (Vienna, 1968), 177–78; Grebing, *Der Revisionismus,* 60.

39. On Böhm-Bawerk's thought see Henry Spiegel, *The Growth of Economic Thought* (Durham, 1983), 537–43; and Paul Sweezy's introduction to *Karl Marx and the Close of His System,* by Eugen Böhm-Bawerk, and *Böhm-Bawerk's Criticism of Marx,* by Rudolf Hilferding (New York, 1949), v–xxx.

40. Hilferding to Kautsky, April 23, 1902, KDXII, 580 (ISH).

41. See Paul Sweezy, *The Theory of Capitalist Development* (New York, 1942), 26.

42. Hilferding, *Böhm-Bawerk's Criticism of Marx,* 122.

43. Sweezy points this out in his introduction to ibid., xx–xxi.

44. See Joseph A. Schumpeter, *Ten Great Economists* (New York, 1951), 169.

45. Hilferding, *Böhm-Bawerk's Criticism of Marx,* 138–39. Quotations in the following two paragraphs are from this work, and pages will be cited parenthetically in the text.

46. Minoru Kurata, "Die Entstehung von Hilferdings *Finanzkapital,*" *Review of the Liberal Arts* 62 (1981): 72–73.

47. Hilferding, *Böhm-Bawerk's Criticism of Marx,* 128.

48. Ronald Meek, *Studies in the Labor Theory of Value* (New York, 1956), 152.

49. Hilferding to Kautsky, May 21, 1902, KDXII, 581 (ISH). Kautsky's side of the correspondence has not survived. The details provided in this letter, however, make the substance of the discussion clear.

50. Ibid.

51. Ibid; and Kurata, "Entstehung," 68–69.

52. Hilferding, "Der Funktionswechsel des Schutzzolles: Tendenz der modernen Handelspolitik," *Die Neue Zeit* 21.2 (1902–1903): 274–81. This was not Hilferding's first publication in *Die Neue Zeit.* Only a few months before, he had published an article entitled, "Zur Geschichte der Werttheorie," 21.2 (1902–1903): 213–17, where he had again criticized subjective methods of economic analysis and pointed out problems in Wilhelm Liebknecht's view of value theory.

53. Eduard Bernstein, *Die Voraussetzungen des Sozialismus und die Aufgaben der Sozialdemokratie* (Berlin, 1921; reprint, Bonn, 1971), 210; Julius Braunthal, *History of the International,* vol. 1, *1864–1914* (New York, 1967), 307–9 (308).

54. Hilferding, "Der Funktionswechsel," 275–76.

55. Ibid., 275.

56. Ibid., 277. See also Hilferding's study of the Austrian sugar industry in "Das Zuckerkontingent," *Die Deutsche Worte* 23 (1903): 278.

57. Hilferding, "Der Funktionswechsel," 278–80.

58. Ibid., 281–82.

59. For a good summation of Kautsky's response to Bernstein's views see Gary P. Steenson, *Karl Kautsky, 1854–1938: Marxism in the Classical Years* (Pittsburgh, 1978), 126–29. For Rosa Luxemburg's position see "Sozialreform oder Revolution," in *Ausgewählte politischen Schriften in drei Bänden,* vol. 1 (Frankfurt am Main, 1971).

60. Hilferding to Kautsky, May 21, 1902, KDXII, 581 (ISH).

61. Braunthal, *History of the International,* 1:292–95.

62. Hilferding, "Zur Frage des Generalstreiks," *Die Neue Zeit* 22.1 (1903–1904), 136–41.

63. Ibid., 140.

64. Ibid., 141. For Engels's view on socialist tactics see his "Einleitung" [zu

"Die Klassenkämpfe in Frankreich 1848–1850" von Karl Marx (Ausgabe 1895)] in Karl Marx and Friedrich Engels, *Werke* (East Berlin, 1964), 7:511–27.

65. Hilferding made this exceptionally clear in a letter to Kautsky: "it is a question of the possibility of maintaining our previous tactic, especially when our successes place it in question. And I believe that the only effective protection of the right to vote lies in the power of the workers as producers, which, when used, appears in the form of the general strike." See Hilferding to Kautsky, August 31, 1903, KDXII, 582 (ISH).

66. In the case of the general strike, members of social democracy's various factions often crossed political lines to support or to oppose the concept. Bernstein provides a good example of this tendency: on this issue, his support for the general strike as a means to defend or acquire universal suffrage placed him in the same camp as Hilferding. See Schorske, *German Social Democracy*, 34.

67. Ibid., 34–35, and Braunthal, *History of the International*, 1:(299).

68. Knapp, *Austrian Social Democracy*, 135–37; Hilferding to Kautsky, October 27, 1905, KDXII, 596 (ISH).

69. Schorske, *German Social Democracy*, 36–42.

70. Braunthal, *History of the International*, 1:300.

71. Hilferding, "Parlamentarismus und Massenstreik," *Die Neue Zeit* 23.2 (1904–1905): 815–16.

72. Ibid., 809, 815 (815).

73. Harvey Goldberg, *The Life of Jean Jaurès* (Madison, 1962), 324–28.

74. Hilferding, "Parlamentarismus," 813, 816.

75. Bebel quoted in Schorske, *German Social Democracy*, 43.

76. Hilferding to Kautsky, November 14, 1905, KDXII, 597 (ISH). Quotations in the following two paragraphs are from ibid.

77. V. I. Lenin, "Was tun?" *Werke* (Berlin, 1978), 5:446–47, 468. Writing in 1902, Lenin stressed that his view of political organization and tactics applied specifically to Russia. Only later, after the events of 1917, did he universalize his conception.

78. Hilferding, "Der Funktionswechsel," 280.

79. Hilferding to Kautsky, October 27, 1905, KDXII, 596 (ISH).

80. Steenson, *Karl Kautsky*, 78.

81. Friedrich Stampfer, *Erfahrungen und Erkenntnisse* (Cologne, 1957), 77.

82. Blum, *The Austro-Marxists*, 13.

83. On Hilferding and Victor Adler see Adolf Sturmthal, *Democracy under Fire: Memoirs of a European Socialist* (Durham, 1989), 25, 27, and Otto Leichter, *Otto Bauer: Tragödie oder Triumph* (Vienna, 1970), 25–26.

84. For Hilferding's mediation between Kautsky and Adler see his letter to Kautsky, September 27, 1905, KDXII, 595 (ISH).

85. Kautsky to Adler, October 18, 1904, *Victor Adler: Briefwechsel mit August Bebel und Karl Kautsky*, ed. Friedrich Adler (Vienna, 1954), 434.

86. Kautsky to Adler, December 8, 1904, ibid., 439–40. Little is known about Margarethe Hönigsberg. She was born in Vienna on June 20, 1871, and like the Hilferdings, her parents registered the family at the Israelitische Kultusgemeinde. Her father, Paul, was a medical doctor. Margarethe and Rudolf married on May 9, 1904. In the marriage register they entered "Konfessionslos" (No denomination) in the space provided under "Religion." They had two children, Karl Emil (1904) and Peter Friedrich (1908). Margarethe and Rudolf divorced in the early

1920s. After the divorce she lived in Vienna and published a book, *Geburtenregulung* (Vienna, 1926). Karl Emil attended the University of Vienna and received a doctorate in philosophy in 1930. Margarethe and Karl were arrested by the Nazis. In June 1942 they were sent to the concentration camp at Theresienstadt. Later on they were murdered in Auschwitz. Peter Friedrich eluded the Nazis and emigrated to England. He changed his name to Dr. Peter Milford and returned to Vienna after the war. See Minoru Kurata, "Rudolf Hilferding, Wiener Zeit: Eine Biographie (3)," *Economic Review* 30.1 (1979): 54–56.

87. See Hilferding's letters to Kautsky, April 27, 1904, and April 3, 1905, KDXII, 586, 589 (ISH).

88. Hilferding to Kautsky, March 14, 1905, KDXII, 588 (ISH).

89. Bebel to Kautsky, August 2, 1906, *August Bebels Briefwechsel mit Karl Kautsky*, ed. Karl Kautsky Jr. (Assen, 1971), 178.

90. Bebel to Kautsky, July 7, 1906, ibid., 176.

91. Bebel to Kautsky, July 11, 1906, ibid., 177.

92. On the Zukunft see Julius Braunthal, "Otto Bauer: Ein Lebensbild," in *Otto Bauer: Eine Auswahl aus seinem Lebenswerk* (Vienna, 1961), 234. For Hilferding's pride in the school see his letter to Kautsky, March 14, 1905, KDXII, 588 (ISH).

93. For Hilferding's objections see Bebel to Kautsky, July 11, 1906, *August Bebels Briefwechsel mit Karl Kautsky*, 177, and Hilferding to Kautsky, February 7, 1906, KDXII, 599 (ISH).

94. Hilferding to Kautsky, September 6, 1906, KDXII, 602 (ISH).

CHAPTER 2. *FINANCE CAPITAL* AND THE STRUGGLE FOR UNITY

1. Epigraphs are taken from Hilferding, *Finance Capital,* 220, and Otto Bauer, "Das Finanzkapital," *Der Kampf* 3 (1909–1910): 391–97.

2. On the role of "Kautskyism" in prewar social democracy see Erich Matthias, "Kautsky und der Kautskyanismus: Die Funktion der Ideologie in der deutschen Sozialdemokratie vor dem ersten Weltkrieg," *Marxismusstudien* 2 (1957): 151–97.; Hans-Josef Steinberg, *Sozialismus und deutsche Sozialdemokratie: Zur Ideologie der Partei vor dem 1. Weltkrieg* (Bonn, 1979); Pierson, *Marxist Intellectuals,* 227–55.

3. Dieter Fricke, *Die deutsche Arbeiterbewegung, 1869–1914: Ein Handbuch über ihre Organisation und Tätigkeit im Klassenkampf* (East Berlin, 1976), 245 (hereafter cited as *Handbuch*); Susanne Miller and Heinrich Potthoff, *Kleine Geschichte der SPD: Darstellung und Dokumentation, 1848–1983* (Bonn, 1983), 55.

4. Miller and Potthoff, *Kleine Geschichte der SPD,* 59–62; Vernon Lidtke, *The Alternative Culture* (Oxford, 1985); Guttsman, *The German Social Democratic Party,* 78–112.

5. Helga Grebing, *History of the German Labor Movement: A Survey* (London, 1985), 79; Hans-Ulrich Wehler, *Das Deutsche Kaiserreich, 1871–1918* (Göttingen, 1983), 196–97.

6. Detlef Lehnert, "'Staatspartei der Republik' oder 'revolutionäre Reformisten'? Die Sozialdemokraten," in *Politische Identität und nationale Gedenktage,* ed. Detlef Lehnert and Klaus Magerle (Opladen, 1989), 89–93. Lehnert's essay focuses on the Weimar SPD, but the milieu he describes was long in the making. I

believe its general characteristics also applied under the empire.

7. On the development of the party structure and its political importance see Schorske, *German Social Democracy*, 116–45; Abendroth, *Aufstieg und Krise*, 39–40.

8. Rudolf Hilferding, *Arbeiterklasse und Konsumvereine: Ein Vortrag arrangiert von der Propagandakommission für das Genossenschaftswesen* (Berlin, 1908), 18–19; Pierson, *Marxist Intellectuals*, 246–47.

9. Hilferding to Kautsky, March 14, 1905, KDXII, 588 (ISH).

10. Fricke, *Handbuch*, 498–504.

11. Ibid.

12. Hilferding to Kautsky, March 14, April 3, 1905, and August 20, 1906, KDXII, 588, 589, 601 (ISH).

13. Fricke, *Handbuch*, 498–500.

14. Ibid., 502; Stein, *Rudolf Hilferding*, 6.

15. In 1900 the party's newspaper editors in large cities were demanding a yearly minimum salary of 3,000 RM, a sum considerably higher than that earned by industrial workers. SPD editor Wilhelm Schroeder claimed that such an income allowed a journalist with a growing family to rent a four-room apartment and to cover clothing and traveling expenses. When one considers that *Vorwärts* was the SPD's central organ and that in 1892 its editor, Wilhelm Liebknecht, earned as much as 7,200 RM, it seems likely that Hilferding's income must have allowed his family at least a middle-class standard of living. See Guttsman, *The German Social Democratic Party*, 257–58.

16. See Hilferding to Kautsky, May 27, October 30, 1905, KDXII, 590, 594 (ISH).

17. Fricke, *Handbuch*, 418–20.

18. Ibid., 420; Bebel to Kautsky, July 11, 1906, in *August Bebels Briefwechsel mit Karl Kautsky*, 177.

19. I have not been able to locate any reference to Hilferding's official appointment as chief editor, but by 1910 he was clearly working in that capacity. In July 1910, Bebel expressed his satisfaction with the paper and urged Kautsky to "Make sure that *Vorwärts* does not lose its balance when Hilferding goes on vacation." There is no question that by 1914 he was in charge of the paper. See Bebel to Kautsky, July 23, 1910, in ibid.; Stampfer, *Erfahrungen und Erkenntnisse*, 140–70. For statistics on the growth of *Vorwärts* see Fricke, *Handbuch*, 421.

20. Hilferding's most important articles on economic and political matters during these years were "Die Konjunktur," *Die Neue Zeit* 25.2 (1906–1907): 140–53; "Die Krise in den Vereinigten Staaten," *Die Neue Zeit* 26.1 (1907–1908): 526–33; "Die industrielle Depression," *Die Neue Zeit* 26.1 (1907–1908): 591–94; Karl Emil (a pseudonym sometimes used by Hilferding), "Antimilitarismus," *Die Neue Zeit* 25.2 (1906–1907); and Hilferding, "Die Kolonialpolitik und der Zusammenbruch," *Die Neue Zeit* 25.2 (1906–1907): 687–88.

21. Bauer, "Das Finanzkapital," 397; Karl Kautsky, "Finanzkapital und Krisen," *Die Neue Zeit* 29.1 (1910–1911): 883.

22. The book was initially reviewed by some of Europe's leading socialists. See, for example, Edward Bernstein, "Das Finanzkapital und die Handelspolitik," *Sozialistische Monatshefte* 15 (1911): 947–55, along with Bauer, "Das Finanzkapital," and Kautsky, "Finanzkapital und Krisen." The most important more recent

reviews are Thomas Hagelstange, "'Finanzkapital': Hilferdings Erklärung des modernen Kapitalismus," *Beiträge zum wissenschaftlichen Sozialismus* 8 (September 1976): 52–77; Jerry Coakley, "Finance Capital," *Capital and Class* 17 (summer 1982): 134–44; Giulio Pietranera, *Rudolf Hilferding und die ökonomische Theorie der Sozialdemokratie* (Berlin, 1974); and Cora Stephan, "Geld und Staatstheorie in Hilferdings Finanzkapital," in *Beiträge zur Marxschen Theorie,* ed. Günther Busch (Frankfurt am Main, 1974), 2:111–54.

23. John A. Kautsky, "J. A. Schumpeter and Karl Kautsky: Parallel Theories of Imperialism," *Midwest Journal of Political Science* 5.2 (May 1961): 114; Kurata, "Entstehung," 82–83.

24. J. A. Hobson, *Imperialism: A Study* (1902; reprint, Ann Arbor, 1983), 94–95.

25. Hilferding, *Finance Capital,* 21.

26. Kurata, "Entstehung," 79–98.

27. Hilferding, *Finance Capital,* 95. Pages for citations will be set parenthetically in the text.

28. For a concise discussion of Hilferding's reliance on Marx's and Engels's earlier views on the corporation see Reinhard Schimkowsky, "Zur Marx-Rezeption bei Hilferding," in *Monopol und Staat: Zur Marxrezeption in der Theorie des staatsmonopolistischen Kapitalismus,* ed. Rolf Ebbinghaus (Frankfurt am Main, 1975), 195–99.

29. Karl Marx, *Capital* (Moscow, 1966), 1:587.

30. Ibid., 3:436.

31. Hilferding, *Finance Capital,* 107–9, 118.

32. See also Bottomore's introduction, 5–6.

33. Manfred Pohl, *Entstehung und Entwicklung des Universalbanksystems* (Frankfurt am Main, 1986), 9–13, 54–56; Richard Tilly, *Vom Zollverein zum Industriestaat: Die wirtschaftlich-soziale Entwicklung Deutschlands, 1834–1914* (Munich, 1990): 90–93.

34. Pietranera, *Rudolf Hilferding,* 30–31.

35. Hilferding, *Finance Capital,* 307.

36. Pietranera, *Rudolf Hilferding,* 31.

37. Ibid., 50–55.

38. Ibid., 25; Coakley, "Finance Capital," 137–39; Hagelstange, "Hilferdings Erklärung des modernen Kapitalismus," 68; Schimkowsky, "Zur Marx-Rezeption bei Hilferding," 200–201, 208–9.

39. Sweezy, *Theory of Capitalist Development,* 258; Pietranera, *Rudolf Hilferding,* 23–24.

40. Compare Hilferding, *Finance Capital,* 241–43 (243), and Marx, *Capital,* 3:484.

41. Hilferding, *Finance Capital,* 257.

42. Ibid., 296–97.

43. Cora Stephan, "Geld und Staatstheorie," 114.

44. Marx, *Capital,* 1:97–106.

45. Hilferding, *Finance Capital,* 25–38. Pages will be set parenthetically in text.

46. Marx quoted in Schimkowsky, "Zur Marx-Rezeption bei Hilferding," 195.

47. For Marx's comments on the likelihood of revolutionary violence see Karl

Marx, "Rede über den Haager Kongress," in *Ausgewählte Werke in sechs Bänden* by Karl Marx and Friedrich Engels (East Berlin, 1981), 2:173–74.

48. Hilferding, *Finance Capital,* 310–17, 326. Pages will be set parenthetically in text.

49. See also Bernstein, *Voraussetzungen,* 211; Goldberg, *Jaurès,* 203.

50. Rosa Luxemburg, *Die Akkumulation des Kapitals* (Berlin, 1913; reprint, Frankfurt am Main, 1966), esp. chap. 26. For her specific criticisms of Hilferding see the appendix, "Akkumulation des Kapitals . . . Eine Antikritik," same volume, 46–49. On the importance of economic determinism in Rosa Luxemburg's work see Manon Tuckfeld and Jens Christian Müller, "'Madame Geschichte' und die Kämpfe: Zur Kritik der Rosa-Luxemburg-Nostalgie," *Bahamas* 13 (spring 1994): 40–44.

51. Nikolay Ivanovich Bukharin, *Imperialism and World Economy* (New York, 1929), 95, 103, 121, 133, 139, 142; V. I. Lenin, "Der Imperialismus als höchstes Stadium des Kapitalismus," *Werke* (East Berlin, 1960), 22:280–90.

52. David McLellan, *Marxism after Marx* (London, 1979), 27–28, 96; Steenson, *Karl Kautsky,* 174–79; Karl Kautsky, "Der Imperialismus," *Die Neue Zeit* 32.2 (1914): 921.

53. In 1912, for example, 214 SPD journalists also held an additional 147 party offices: 20 sat in the Reichstag, 22 sat in the Landtage, 58 served in local government, and 47 others were either party chairmen or members of local party executives. See Guttsman, *The German Social Democratic Party,* 246–49.

54. Hilferding's appointment as a representative to the council is recorded in the *Protokolle der Sitzungen des Parteiausschußes der Sozialdemokratischen Partei Deutschlands, 1912–1921,* ed. Dieter Dowe, with an introduction by Friedhelm Boll (Bonn, 1980), 1 (hereafter cited as *Protokolle des Parteiausschußes*). On the formation of the council, see Boll's introduction, xi–xxiii.

55. Braunthal, *In Search of the Millenium,* 101.

56. See Stampfer, *Erfahrungen und Erkenntnisse,* 142–43; Karl Kautsky to Victor Adler, June 26, 1913, *Victor Adler: Briefwechsel mit August Bebel und Karl Kautsky,* 573; Luise Kautsky to August Bebel, December 28, 1910, *August Bebels Briefwechsel mit Karl Kautsky,* 250; and Sturmthal, *Democracy under Fire,* 62–63. According to Sturmthal, the gregarious Hilferding was too undisciplined to sit and write books, so Victor Adler forbade his friends to converse with him in cafés until *Finance Capital* was finished. This story is not very credible, and neither is Sturmthal's claim that, after moving to Germany, Hilferding expected to be offered the leadership of the SPD. Hilferding finished *Finance Capital* in 1909, three years after leaving Vienna, and there is no evidence that he ever expected or even wanted to become head of the party.

57. Trotsky to Hilferding, dated end of 1911 or beginning of 1912, TH, 21 (ISH).

58. This and the following remarks are all from Leon Trotsky, *My Life* (New York, 1970), 212–13.

59. Hilferding to Kautsky, August 2, 1907, KDXII, 603 (ISH); Steenson, *Karl Kautsky,* 137–38.

60. On the elections of 1907 see Schorske, *German Social Democracy,* 59–66. For Hilferding's views see Karl Emil, "Die Auflösung des Reichstags und die Klassengegensätze in Deutschland," *Die Neue Zeit* 25.1 (1906–1907): 388–93 (392–93); "Die Konferenz der Parteiredakteure," *Die Neue Zeit* 25.1 (1906–1907):

652–55; "Die bürgerlichen Parteien und der Militarismus," *Die Neue Zeit* 25.2 (1906–1907): 132–34; and "Antimilitarismus."

61. For Hilferding's view of the struggle for the franchise see Karl Emil, "Die Wahlen in Österreich," *Die Neue Zeit* 25.2 (1906–1907): 209–11; "Der Freisinn und unser Wahlkampf," *Die Neue Zeit* 26.2 (1907–1908): 85; and Hilferding, "Der Wahlrechtskampf in Preußen," *Der Kampf* 3 (1909–1910): 313.

62. Hilferding quoted in Braunthal, *In Search of the Millenium,* 106–7.

63. Ibid.

64. Compare Karl Emil, "Alter und neuer Despotismus," *Die Neue Zeit* 25.2 (1906–1907): 409–11, and *Finance Capital,* 364–70, with Karl Kautsky, *Der Weg zur Macht* (Berlin, 1910). See also J. P. Nettl, "The German Social Democratic Party, 1890–1914, as a Political Model," *Past and Present* 30 (1965): 65–95, for a concise and penetrating analysis of the SPD's various intellectual and political currents.

65. Klara Zetkin, quoted in Schorske, *German Social Democracy,* 185.

66. Hilferding, "Der Parteitag von Magdeburg," *Die Neue Zeit* 28.2 (1909–1910): 896–97.

67. Social democracy's factional struggles during these years have been described in detail elsewhere. Compare Schorske, *German Social Democracy,* and Dieter Groh, *Negative Integration und revolutionärer Attentismus: Die Sozialdemokratie am Vorabend des ersten Weltkrieges* (Frankfurt am Main, 1973).

68. See, for example, Hilferding, "Sozialdemokratische Steuerpolitik," *Die Neue Zeit* 30.2 (1911–1912): 221–25, and "Zum Parteitag," *Die Neue Zeit* 31.2 (1912–1913): 873–80.

69. For Hilferding's views of the condition of the right and left see "Mit gesammelter Kraft," *Die Neue Zeit* 30.2 (1912–1913): 1001–4. On the center's loss of intellectual support, see Pierson, *Marxist Intellectuals,* 246–48; Steinberg, *Sozialismus,* 85.

70. On the SPD leadership's shifting views in the summer of 1914, see Schorske, *German Social Democracy,* 286–91; Groh, *Negative Integration,* 600–617; Arthur Rosenberg, *Imperial Germany* (Boston, 1964), 74–76; Hilferding, "Ein neutraler Sozialist über sozialistische Neutralität," *Der Kampf* 8 (1915): 270.

71. Kenneth R. Calkins, *Hugo Haase: Democrat and Revolutionary* (Durham, 1979), 50.

72. Erich Matthias and Susanne Miller, eds., *Das Kriegstagebuch des Reichstagsabgeordneten Eduard David, 1914–1918* (Düsseldorf, 1966), 13–14.

73. Ibid., 14; Groh, *Negative Integration,* 706. The declaration is reprinted in Eugen Prager, *Geschichte der USPD* (Glashütten im Taunus, 1970), 30–31.

74. Wolfgang Kruse, *Krieg und nationale Integration: Eine Neuinterpretation des sozialdemokratischen Burgfriedensschlußes, 1914–1915* (Essen, 1993). Even Rosa Luxemburg and the radical left felt paralyzed and isolated. For her initial response to the war see J. P. Nettl, *Rosa Luxemburg* (New York, abr. ed., 1969), 365–79.

75. Hilferding, "Der Revisionismus und die Internationale," *Die Neue Zeit* 27.2 (1908–1909): 161–74.

76. Karl Emil, "Der Internationale Kongress in Stuttgart," *Die Neue Zeit* 25.2 (1906–1907): 660–62, and "Alter und neuer Despotismus," 409–11.

77. Karl Emil, "Der Internationale Kongress in Stuttgart," 665–67; Hilferding, "Der Balkankrieg und die Großmächte," *Die Neue Zeit* 31.1 (1912–1913): 77–82.

78. Hilferding, "Totentanz," *Die Neue Zeit* 31.1 (1912–1913), 746.

79. Hilferding, "Taumel," *Die Neue Zeit* 31.1 (1912–1913), 849.

80. Hilferding, "Die Erneuerung des Dreibundes," *Die Neue Zeit* 31.1 (1912–1913): 458–66.

81. Victor Adler to Karl Kautsky, November 26, 1914, *Victor Adler: Briefwechsel mit August Bebel und Karl Kautsky*, 602–4.

82. Schorske, *German Social Democracy*, 300.

CHAPTER 3. THE REVOLUTIONARY

1. Lenin is quoted in Robert A. Goldberg, *Grassroots Resistance: Social Movements in Twentieth Century America* (Belmont, 1991), 91; Hilferding from "Taktische Probleme," *Die Freiheit*, December 11, 1919 (morning edition, henceforth noted [M]).

2. On the emergence of the various factions see Schorske, *German Social Democracy*, 294–308, and Susanne Miller, *Burgfrieden und Klassenkampf* (Bonn, 1974), 80–100.

3. Quoted in Schorske, *German Social Democracy*, 303.

4. Steenson, *Karl Kautsky*, 182–85. On Hilferding and Haase's views in the early months of the war see Calkins, *Hugo Haase*, chap. 5; *Protokolle des Parteiausschußes*, 100, 120–21.

5. Schorske, *German Social Democracy*, 303–6.

6. Ibid., 306–7.

7. Ibid., 295–97.

8. *Protokolle des Parteiausschußes*, 120–21 (120).

9. Ibid., 121.

10. The family lived at Favoritenstraße 67. Hilferding's first medical assignment was at the Rudolfspital III, Rudolfsgasse 1. See Hilferding to Luise Kautsky, April 29, 1915, and to Karl Kautsky, June 22, July 29, 1915, KDXII, 607, 608, 609 (ISH).

11. His address was Landsturmarzt Dr. Rudolf Hilferding, Steinach am Brenner, Notreservespital, Tirol. See Hilferding to Kautsky, August 1, 1916, KDXII, 612 (ISH).

12. Hilferding to Kautsky, December 20, 1916, KDXII, 627 (ISH).

13. Hilferding to Kautsky, October 6, 1916, KDXII, 619 (ISH).

14. "Das Gebot der Stunde" is reprinted in Prager, *Geschichte der USPD*, 72–74. See also Hilferding to Kautsky, June 22, July 29, 1915, KDXII, 608, 609 (ISH).

15. Hilferding, "Arbeitsgemeinschaft der Klassen?" *Der Kampf* 8 (1915): 321–29 (quotations in the next four paragraphs are from pp. 321–23).

16. Hilferding, "Ein neutraler Sozialist über die sozialistische Neutralität," 270–72 (270); Robert Michels, "Die deutsche Sozialdemokratie, Parteimitgliedschaft und soziale Zusammensetzung," *Archiv für Sozialwissenschaft und Sozialpolitik* 23 (1906), 527; Robert Michels, *Political Parties: A Sociological Study of the Oligarchical Tendencies of Modern Democracy* (1915; reprint, New York, 1962), 365–76.

17. V. I. Lenin, "Der Zusammenbruch der II. Internationale," *Werke* (East Berlin, 1968), 21:242–53; Lenin, "Der Imperialismus," 288, 306–7.

18. "Die Sozialdemokratie am Scheideweg," and "Kritisches Mißverständnis oder mißverständliche Kritik," *Die Neue Zeit* 33.2 (1914–1915): 489–99, 716–17 (497).

19. Hilferding, "Historische Notwendigkeit und notwendige Politik," *Der Kampf* 8 (1915): 206–15.

20. On Renner and Bauer see Blum, *The Austro-Marxists*, chaps. 10, 11.

21. Hilferding responded first to Neumann's book *Mitteleuropa*, and one year later to Renner's critique of his review. See his "Europäer nicht Mitteleuropäer!" *Der Kampf* 8 (1915): 357–65, and "Phantasie oder Gelehrsamkeit," *Der Kampf* 9 (1916): 54–63.

22. Hilferding, "Sozialistische Betrachtungen zum Weltkriege," *Die Neue Zeit* 33.2 (1914–1915): 843–44.

23. Hilferding, "Europäer nicht Mitteleuropäer," 357. Quotation is from Hilferding to Kautsky, August 8, 1916, KDXII, 613 (ISH). Hilferding, "Um die Zukunft der deutschen Arbeiterbewegung," *Die Neue Zeit* 34.2 (1915–1916): 171–73.

24. Hilferding, "Um die Zukunft der deutschen Arbeiterbewegung," 173–75; Hilferding, "Der Konflikt in der deutschen Sozialdemokratie," *Der Kampf* 9 (1916): 14; Hilferding to Kautsky, July 1, 1916, KDXII, 611 (ISH).

25. Schorske, *German Social Democracy*, 307.

26. Ibid., 308–10; Calkins, *Hugo Haase*, 110–11.

27. None of the participants actually advocated a break with the party. See Schorske, *German Social Democracy*, 311–12; Calkins, *Hugo Haase*, 104–24.

28. Hilferding to Kautsky, January 31, 1917, KDXII, 628 (ISH).

29. This article was the last in a seven-part critique of determinist theories of the collapse of capitalism. Hilferding's hope of publishing the series in booklet form was not realized. See "Handelspolitische Fragen," *Die Neue Zeit* 35.1 (1916–1917): 5–11, 40–47, 91–99, 118–26, 141–46, 205–16, 241–46.

30. Hilferding to Kautsky, October 13, 1917, KDXII, 630 (ISH).

31. Hilferding to Kautsky, December 3, 1917, KDXII, 631 (ISH).

32. Hilferding to Kautsky, September 8, 1918, KDXII, 632 (ISH).

33. Hilferding's request to Kautsky that fall to remind Alexander Stein (his past and future coeditor) to write to him indicates that the USPD had already selected him as editor and that he was thinking about his future tasks. See Hilferding to Kautsky, October 5, 28, 1918, KDXII, 633, 634 (ISH); and Stein, *Rudolf Hilferding*, 10. On Hilferding's close relationship with Haase, see Bebel to Kautsky, March 18, 1913, *August Bebels Briefwechsel mit Karl Kautsky*, 335.

34. See Hilferding, "Revolutionäres Vertrauen!" *Die Freiheit*, November 18, 1918 (M); and Hilferding, "Klarheit!" *Die Freiheit*, November 23, 1918 (M).

35. Walter Tormin, *Zwischen Rätediktatur und Sozialer Demokratie: Die Geschichte der Rätebewegung in der deutschen Revolution, 1918–1919* (Düsseldorf, 1954), 69–72; Sebastian Haffner, *Die deutsche Revolution, 1918–1919* (Munich, 1979), 68, 83–93.

36. David W. Morgan, *The Socialist Left and the German Revolution: A History of the German Independent Social Democratic Party, 1917–1922* (Ithaca, 1975), 127–38.

37. Ibid., 53–64; Hartfrid Krause, *USPD: Zur Geschichte der Unabhängigen Sozialdemokratischen Partei Deutschlands* (Frankfurt am Main, 1975), 116–21.

38. Hilferding, "Klarheit!"

39. "The Berlin USPD Debate on the National Assembly," in *The German Revolution and the Debate on Soviet Power, Documents, 1918–1919: Preparing the Founding Congress,* ed. John Riddell (New York, 1986), 127–34.

40. One East German history argues that on November 25, 1918, in an article in the *Leipziger Volkszeitung,* Hilferding also called for the Spartacists' departure because of their radical views. Although it is likely he would have written such a piece, I have not been able to locate the article cited. See Heinz Niemann et al., *Geschichte der deutschen Sozialdemokratie 1917–1945* (Frankfurt am Main, 1982), 54. For Haase's admonition to the Spartacists see ibid., 128–29.

41. Eberhard Kolb, *Die Arbeiterräte in der deutschen Innenpolitik, 1918–1919* (Düsseldorf, 1962), 208–9; and Calkins, *Hugo Haase,* 174.

42. Morgan, *The Socialist Left,* 191–98.

43. Hilferding, "Das Schuldbekenntnis," *Die Freiheit,* December 27, 1918 (Evening edition, henceforth cited [E]).

44. Krause, *USPD,* 122; Morgan, *The Socialist Left,* 251–53.

45. Hilferding, "Aufbau des Rätesystems!" *Die Freiheit,* February 5, 1919 (M).

46. Hilferding, "Die Einigung des Proletariats," *Die Freiheit,* February 9, 1919 (M).

47. As quoted in Morgan, *The Socialist Left,* 258, emphasis in the original.

48. For a similar view of Hilferding, see ibid., 60–61.

49. V. I. Lenin, "Die Dritte Internationale und ihr Platz in der Geschichte," *Werke* (East Berlin, 1961), 29:301–2, and V. I. Lenin, "Die Helden der Berner Internationale," *Werke,* 29:382–84.

50. V. I. Lenin, "I. Kongress der Kommunistischen Internationale," *Werke* (East Berlin, 1959), 28:484.

51. For Lenin's views on the methods and tactics necessary to achieve the victory of soviet power see "Was tun?" 357–79, and "Die proletarische Revolution und der Renegat Kautsky," *Werke* (East Berlin, 1959), 28:227–327, especially the section on the constituent assembly and the Soviet Republic.

52. Hilferding, "Revolutionäres Vertrauen."

53. Hilferding, "Die Einigung des Proletariats."

54. Hilferding cited in Braunthal, *In Search of the Millenium,* 242. Quotations in the next three paragraphs are from this work and pages will be set parenthetically in the text.

55. In addition to Hilferding and Kautsky, the commission included nine other economists drawn from USPD, SPD, and nonsocialist circles. For a complete list of the membership and background information see the *Verhandlungen der Sozialisierungskommission über den Kohlenbergbau im Winter 1918–1919* (Berlin, 1921), viii; Karl Kautsky to Reichsminister Rudolf Wissell, April 7, 1919, *Bildung und Auflösung der ersten Sozialisierungskommission,* vol. 1, Bundesarchiv Potsdam (henceforth cited as BAP); Winkler, *Von der Revolution zur Stabilisierung,* 75–82.

56. Hilferding, "Zur Sozialisierung des Wirtschaftslebens," in *Allgemeiner Kongress der Arbeiter- und Soldatenräte Deutschlands, vom 16. bis 21. Dezember 1918,* ed. Friedrich Helm and Peter Schmitt-Egner (Glasshütten im Taunus, 1972), 156–61, 171–72. Pages for citations will henceforth be set parenthetically in the text.

57. *Bericht der Sozialisierungskommission über die Frage der Sozialisierung des Kohlenbergbaus vom 31. Juli 1920. Anhang: Vorläufiger Bericht vom 15. Februar 1919* (Berlin, 1920), 34–40.

58. Ibid., 40–42; Heinrich August Winkler, *Weimar, 1918–1933: Die*

Geschichte der ersten deutschen Demokratie (Munich, 1993), 85–86.

59. Klaus Novy, *Strategien der Sozialisierung: Die Diskussion der Wirtschaftsreform in der Weimarer Republik* (Frankfurt am Main, 1978), 13–16.

60. Bauer to Hilferding, January 7, 1919, "Sozialisierungskommission, Privatbriefe von Kommissionsmitgliedern, vol. 1, Nr. 12" (BAP). On Bauer's concept of socialization see Otto Bauer, *Der Weg zum Sozialismus* (Vienna, 1919); Tom Bottomore, "Austro-Marxist Conceptions of the Transition from Capitalism to Socialism," in *Karl Kautsky and the Social Science of Classical Marxism*, ed. John A. Kautsky (New York, 1989), 109–13; and Walter Euchner, "Otto Bauer und die Sozialisierung in Österreich, 1918–1919," in *Otto Bauer: Theorie und Politik*, ed. Detlev Albers, Horst Heimann, and Richard Saage (Berlin, 1985), 32–34. On Hilferding's view of representative institutions see "Die politischen und ökonomischen Machtverhältnisse und die Sozialisierung," in *Zwischen den Stühlen, oder über die Unvereinbarkeit von Theorie und Praxis: Schriften Rudolf Hilferdings*, ed. Cora Stephan (Bonn, 1982), 121–22.

61. See, especially, Stephen F. Cohen, *Bukharin and the Bolshevik Revolution: A Political Biography, 1888–1938* (New York, 1973), 87–98.

62. Nikolay Ivanovich Bukharin, *Ökonomie der Transformationsperiode* (Hamburg, 1922), 67. Pages will be set parenthetically in the text.

63. Cohen, *Bukharin*, 90–91.

64. *Bericht der Sozialisierungskommission*, 8–27.

65. *Verhandlungen der Sozialisierungskommission über den Kohlenbergbau im Jahre 1920* (Berlin, 1920), 2:396, 399–400, 430–31. See also Wilfried Gottschalch, *Strukturveränderungen der Gesellschaft und politisches Handeln in der Lehre von Rudolf Hilferding* (Berlin, 1962), 173–84.

66. *Verhandlungen der Sozialisierungskommission im Jahre 1920*, 2:403.

67. Ibid., 398.

68. Hilferding, "Die politischen und ökonomischen Machtverhältnisse und die Sozialisierung," 116.

69. Winkler, *Von der Revolution zur Stabilisierung*, 338.

70. On the USPD's expansion see Morgan, *The Socialist Left*, 242–45, 350.

71. Ibid., 243. Stein claims that after six months *Die Freiheit*'s circulation reached 250,000, but in either case the figures are impressive. See Stein, *Rudolf Hilferding*, 10.

72. Stein, *Rudolf Hilferding*, 10. Stein admits that his personal friendship with Hilferding colored his appraisal of the latter's talents. He adds credibility to his description, however, by quoting Toni Sender's remarks on Hilferding. Sender was a member of the USPD's left wing and held Hilferding's editorial skills and work at *Die Freiheit* in high regard.

73. Morgan, *The Socialist Left*, 262–78.

74. See Hilferding, "Taktische Probleme," *Der Kampf* 12 (1919): 839–41; and *Protokoll über die Verhandlungen des ausserordentlichen Parteitages der USPD zu Leipzig vom 30. November bis 6. Dezember 1919* (Glashütten im Taunus, 1975), 2:265 (hereafter cited as *USPD Parteitag, Leipzig, Nov.–Dec. 1919*).

75. *USPD Parteitag, Leipzig, Nov.–Dec. 1919*, 266–68, 304.

76. See Robert F. Wheeler, *USPD und Internationale: Sozialistischer Internationalismus in der Zeit der Revolution* (Frankfurt am Main, 1975), 54–55.

77. Ibid., 53–54.

78. Quoted in Braunthal, *History of the International*, 2:44.

79. Jane Degras, ed., *Documents of the Communist International*, vol. 1, *1919–1922* (London, 1955), 170.

80. Hilferding, "Die Internationale," *Der Kampf* 12 (1919): 522.

81. Ibid., 522–24.

82. Hilferding, "Die Internationale," parts 1, 2, 3, appeared in *Die Freiheit*, July 19, 23, 24 (M). See also Wheeler, *USPD und Internationale*, 102.

83. Hilferding, "Die Krise der Internationale," *Der Sozialist* 5 (1919): 694–96; Wheeler, *USPD und Internationale*, 114–15.

84. Hartfrid Krause, ed., *Bericht über die Reichskonferenz der Unabhängigen Sozialdemokratischen Partei Deutschlands am 9. und 10. September 1919 im Abgeordnetenhaus zu Berlin* (Glashütten im Taunus, 1975), 18–20.

85. Compare Wheeler, *USPD und Internationale*, 124–25, and Morgan, *The Socialist Left*, 289–90.

86. *USPD Parteitag, Leipzig, Nov.–Dec. 1919*, 309–26. It should be noted that although Hilferding had essentially given up hope of rebuilding the old international, he still supported going to its Geneva congress the following summer in order to attack the SPD's policies. See his comments (324–25). Pages for citations will be set parenthetically in the text.

87. Wheeler, *USPD und Internationale*, 167–69; Morgan, *The Socialist Left*, (303).

88. Morgan, *The Socialist Left*, 303–4.

89. Hilferding, *Gegen das Moskauer Diktat* (Leipzig, 1920), 19–20.

90. For the text of Hilferding's speech see "Revolutionäre Politik oder Machtillusion?" in Stephan, *Zwischen den Stühlen*, 134–65. On the background to the congress and the proceedings see Braunthal, *History of the International*, 2:221–24; Wheeler, *USPD und Internationale*, chaps. 9, 10; Morgan, *The Socialist Left*, 364–80.

91. See Braunthal, *History of the International*, 2:230–36.

92. For the text of Hilferding's speech see "Die Wiedergutmachung und das internationale Proletariat," *Der Sozialist* 7 (1921): 200–207.

93. On the united front policy see Morgan, *The Socialist Left*, 389–94.

94. Hilferding, "Die Einigung der deutschen Arbeiterklasse," *Der Kampf* 14 (1921): 1–7.

95. *USPD Parteitag, Leipzig, January 1922*, 105–6.

96. See "Parteizentrale und 'Freiheit' Redaktion," and "Was wir wollen, Der 'Freiheit' Konflikt," *Die Freiheit*, March 23, 26, 1922 (M); Morgan, *The Socialist Left*, 415–16.

97. Morgan, *The Socialist Left*, 433–35; Krause, *USPD*, 243–54.

98. Hilferding, "Wandel in der Politik," *Die Frankfurter Zeitung*, December 31, 1922 (second morning edition).

CHAPTER 4. THE REPUBLICAN THEORIST

1. Epigraph is from *Protokoll des Kongresses der Sozialistischen Arbeiter-Internationale*, vol. 2, *Marseilles, August 1925* (Glashütten im Taunus, 1974), 266.

2. This is how SPD Reichstag delegate from Munich, Alwin Saenger, expressed it in 1926. Quoted in Lehnert, "'Staatspartei der Republik' oder 'revolutionäre Reformisten'?" 108.

3. Werner Abelshauser, ed., *Die Weimarer Republik als Wohlfahrtsstaat: Zum Verhältnis von Wirtschafts- und Sozialpolitik in der Industriegesellschaft* (Stuttgart, 1987); Peter Lösche and Franz Walter, "Auf dem Weg zur Volkspartei? Die Weimarer Sozialdemokratie," *Archiv für Sozialgeschichte* 29 (1989): 75–136.

4. Among the most useful general studies of Hilferding's theoretical and practical activities under Weimar are Gottschalch, *Strukturveränderungen,* chaps. 6, 7; Breitman, *German Socialism,* chap. 7; Harold James, "Rudolf Hilferding and the Application of the Political Economy of the Second International," *Historical Journal* 24 (1981): 847–69.

5. *Protokoll der Sozialdemokratischen Parteitage in Augsburg, Gera und Nürnberg, 1922* (Reprint, Bonn–Bad Godesberg, 1974), 192 (hereafter cited as *SPD Parteitag . . . .*).

6. Hans J. L. Adolph, *Otto Wels und die Politik der deutschen Sozialdemokratie, 1894–1939* (Berlin, 1971), 109–14; Breitman, *German Socialism,* 75, 120.

7. For Hilferding's most detailed theoretical explications in this period see "Probleme der Zeit," *Die Gesellschaft* 1.1 (1924): 1–17; *Für die soziale Republik* (Berlin, 1924); "Realistischer Pazifismus," *Die Gesellschaft* 1.2 (1924): 97–114; *SPD-Parteitag Heidelberg, 1925,* 272–83, and *SPD-Parteitag Kiel, 1927,* 165–84.

8. Hilferding, "Probleme der Zeit," 1. Pages will be cited parenthetically in text.

9. Hilferding, "Sozialismus und Eigentum," *Sozialistische Bildung* (February 1932): 32.

10. Hilferding, "Probleme der Zeit," 7.

11. *SPD-Parteitag Kiel, 1927,* 168. Pages will be cited parenthetically in the text.

12. Hilferding, "Probleme der Zeit," 13.

13. Ibid., 16–17; *SPD-Parteitag Kiel, 1927,* 219.

14. See, for example, Hilferding, *Für die soziale Republik,* 14; *SPD-Parteitag Kiel, 1927,* 173.

15. Hilferding, "Probleme der Zeit," 170.

16. On this aspect of Hilferding's thought, see the interesting discussion in Wolfgang Krumbein, "Vorläufer eines 'Dritten Weges zum Sozialismus?'" in *Solidargemeinschaft und Klassenkampf: Politische Konzeptionen der Sozialdemokratie zwischen den Weltkriegen,* ed. Richard Saage (Frankfurt am Main, 1986), 176–77.

17. Hilferding, "Introduction," in *Selbstverwaltung in der Industrie,* by G. D. H. Cole, translated by R. Thesing (Berlin, 1921); Otto Bauer, *Bolschewismus und Sozialdemokratie* (Vienna, 1921), 88–99.

18. Quoted in A. W. Wright, *G. D. H. Cole and Socialist Democracy* (Oxford, 1979), 74.

19. Hilferding, "Introduction," *Selbstverwaltung in der Industrie,* xvi–xvii.

20. *SPD-Parteitag Heidelberg, 1925,* 276–77.

21. Lösche and Walter, "Auf dem Weg zur Volkspartei?" 86–87, 132–33; Jürgen W. Falter with the assistance of Hartmut Bömermann, "Die Wählerpotentiale politischer Teilkulturen, 1920–1933," in *Politische Identität und nationale Gedenktage,* ed. Lehnert and Megerle, 302, 304.

22. For a detailed analysis of the SPD's relationship to various nonproletarian groups see Lösche and Walter, "Auf dem Weg zur Volkspartei?" 99–126.

23. Hilferding, "Theoretische Bemerkungen zur Agrarfrage," *Die Gesellschaft* 4.1 (1927): 421–32 (432).

24. For a concise description of the evolution of German agriculture through 1939, see David Schoenbaum, *Hitler's Social Revolution: Class Structure in Nazi Germany, 1933–1939* (London, 1967), 1–15, 159–86.

25. For the text of the program see *SPD-Parteitag Kiel, 1927,* 273–82.

26. Lösche and Walter, "Auf dem Weg zur Volkspartei?" 115–16; Winkler, *Weimar, 1918–1933,* 292; Hunt, *German Social Democracy,* 139–40.

27. Lösche and Walter, "Auf dem Weg zur Volkspartei?" 125–31; Hans Mommsen, *The Rise and Fall of Weimar Democracy,* translated by Elborg Forster and Larry Eugene Jones (Chapel Hill, 1996), 209–10.

28. Quoted in Loew, "Politics of Austro-Marxism," 25.

29. See ibid., 23–44, for a clearly argued, concise analysis of the SPÖ's policies between 1918 and 1934.

30. Otto Bauer, *Die österreichische Revolution* (Vienna, 1965), 259.

31. Otto Bauer, "Das Gleichgewicht der Klassenkräfte," in *Austromarxismus,* ed. Sandkühler and de la Vega, 91–96; Richard Saage, "Parlamentarische Demokratie, Staatsfunktionen und das 'Gleichgewicht der Klassenkräfte,'" in *Solidargemeinschaft und Klassenkampf,* 88–92.

32. Saage, "Parlamentarische Demokratie," 97–98.

33. Ibid., 92.

34. Loew, "Politics of Austro-Marxism," 40–46; Blum, *Austro-Marxists,* chap. 11.

35. Hilferding, "Realistischer Pazifismus," 111.

36. Ibid., 97–100.

37. Ibid., 101–10; Hilferding, "Die Weltpolitik, das Reparationsproblem und die Konferenz von Genoa," *Schmollers Jahrbuch* 45 (1923): 4, 7.

38. Quoted in Cohen, *Bukharin,* 147.

39. Ibid.

40. Ibid., 254–56; Nicholas N. Kozlov and Eric D. Weitz, "Reflections on the 'Third Period': Bukharin, the Comintern, and the Political Economy of Weimar Germany," *Journal of Contemporary History* 24 (1989): 389, 394–95.

41. Kozlov and Weitz, "Reflections on the 'Third Period,'" 396; Bukharin, *Imperialism and World Economy,* 127–28.

42. Compare Cohen, *Bukharin,* 256–57, and Kozlov and Weitz, "Reflections on the 'Third Period,'" 398–99.

43. See, for example, L. Leontjew, "Der 'organisierte Kapitalismus' und die 'Wirtschaftsdemokratie,'" *Unter dem Banner des Marxismus* 3 (1929): 660–87. The soviet Marxist point of view is concisely summarized in Heinrich August Winkler, "Einleitende Bemerkungen zu Hilferdings Theorie des organisierten Kapitalismus," in *Organisierter Kapitalismus: Voraussetzungen und Anfänge,* ed. Heinrich August Winkler (Göttingen, 1974), 12–13; and Günter Könke, *Organisierter Kapitalismus, Sozialdemokratie und Staat: Eine Studie zur Ideologie der sozialdemokratischen Arbeiterbewegungen in der Weimarer Republik* (Stuttgart, 1987), 85–86.

44. Max Adler, "Demokratie als Ziel und als Mittel: Über marxistische Staatsauffassung," *Der Klassenkampf* 2.10 (1928): 292. For Aufhäuser's view see *SPD-Parteitag Kiel, 1927,* 198. Hilferding's views on competition and economic crisis did meet with social democratic criticism, but most of his opponents were outside the party and trade union leadership. For a discussion of this criticism see Könke, *Organisierter Kapitalismus, Sozialdemokratie und Staat,* 77–84.

45. Novy, *Strategien der Sozialisierung,* 105.

46. Quoted in Könke, *Organisierter Kapitalismus, Sozialdemokratie und Staat*, 73.

47. Ibid., 77.

48. Ibid., 87–94, 224.

49. Leontjew, "Der 'organisierte Kapitalismus' und die 'Wirtschafts-demokratie,'" 669.

50. Hilferding, *Finance Capital*, 368.

51. Ibid., 296–97.

52. See Hilferding, "Die Eigengesetzlichkeit der kapitalistischen Entwicklung," in *Kapital und Kapitalismus*, ed. Bernhard Harms (Berlin, 1931), 1:20–37; and *Gesellschaftsmacht oder Privatmacht über die Wirtschaft* (Berlin, 1931), esp. 36–39.

53. See, for example, *SPD-Parteitag Heidelberg, 1925*, 294.

54. Krumbein, "Vorläufer eines 'Dritten Weges zum Sozialismus?,'" 181.

55. Ibid., 181–82.

56. On the usefulness of Hilferding's concept for understanding modern capitalist development in different countries see the debate in Winkler, *Organisierter Kapitalismus*.

CHAPTER 5. THE REPUBLICAN POLITICIAN

1. Epigraph is taken from *SPD-Parteitag Kiel, 1927*, 183.

2. On the WTB plan see W. S. Woytinsky, *Stormy Passage: A Personal History through Two Russian Revolutions to Democracy and Freedom, 1905–1960* (New York, 1961), 462–72; Winkler, *Der Weg in die Katastrophe*, 494–95; Rainer Schaefer, *Die SPD in der Ära Brüning: Tolerierung oder Mobilisierung? Handelspielräume und Strategien sozialdemokratischer Politik, 1930–1932* (Frankfurt am Main, 1990), 365–406.

3. For this quotation and the related ones that follow see Woytinsky, *Stormy Passage*, 471–72.

4. Winkler, *Der Weg in die Katastrophe*, 498.

5. The Reichswirtschaftsrat was intended as a type of economic parliament, in which employees and employers would be equally represented. Its role was strictly advisory. See Winkler, *Von der Revolution zur Stabilisierung*, 236–39; William Harvey Maehl, *The German Socialist Party: Champion of the First Republic, 1918–1933* (Philadelphia, 1986), 50–51; Dr. Hauschild, *Der vorläufige Reichswirtschaftsrat, 1920–1926: Denkschrift* (Berlin, 1926).

6. Harry Kessler, *Tagebücher, 1918–1937*, ed. Wolfgang Pfeiffer-Belli (Frankfurt am Main, 1961), 293–310.

7. For Hilferding's analysis of the Genoa Conference and the Treaty of Rapallo see "Die Weltpolitik, das Reparationsproblem und die Konferenz von Genoa"; *Deutsch-sowjetische Beziehungen von den Verhandlungen in Brest-Litovsk bis zum Abschluss des Rapallovertrages* (East Berlin, 1971), 593.

8. Hilferding, "Die Weltpolitik," 14–16; Kessler, *Tagebücher*, 293.

9. Some social democrats, including Ebert, had misgivings about the treaty because they feared alienating the Allies. Most, however, approved of the restoration of relations with Russia and thought that this development would weaken French

influence among the Western powers. See Maehl, *The German Socialist Party*, 74–75.

10. For a detailed discussion of Germany's situation in 1922 and the relationship between the exogenous and endogenous causes of the inflation see Gerald Feldman's *The Great Disorder: Politics, Economics, and Society in the German Inflation, 1914–1924* (New York, 1993), esp. chap. 10. The figures on the fall of the mark are given on page 5. See also F. W. Henning, *Das industrialisierte Deutschland, 1914 bis 1978* (Paderborn, 1979), 53–57, 63–65.

11. On the aftermath of Rapallo and the background to the Ruhr crisis see Maehl, *The German Socialist Party*, chap. 5; Ludwig Zimmerman, *Deutsche Außenpolitik in der Ära der Weimarer Republik* (Göttingen, 1958), 122–33; Winkler, *Weimar*, 186–88.

12. Erich Eyck, *A History of the Weimar Republic* (New York, 1962), vol. 1, chap. 8; Feldman, *The Great Disorder*, chap. 14; Henning, *Das industrialisierte Deutschland*, 65–66; Winkler, *Von der Revolution zur Stabilisierung*, 373–92; Gordon Craig, *Germany, 1866–1945* (New York, 1978), 448–56.

13. Winkler, *Von der Revolution zur Stabilisierung*, 388–91; Winkler, *Weimar*, 182, 204; Craig, *Germany, 1866–1945*, 451–52; Feldman, *The Great Disorder*, 272–305, 609–27, 840–47.

14. On the SPD's attitude toward Cuno see Maehl, *The German Socialist Party*, 81–83, and Breitman, *German Socialism*, 98–99 (Sinzheimer's letter, 98).

15. Feldman, *The Great Disorder*, 466, 473–90.

16. Breitman, *German Socialism*, 99.

17. Gustav Stresemann, *Vermächtnis*, vol. 1, *Vom Ruhrkrieg bis London* (Berlin, 1932), 144.

18. Ibid., 77; Winkler, *Von der Revolution zur Stabilisierung*, 601.

19. Hilferding, "Die Entwicklung der Valuta und die Ursachen der Wirtschaftskrise," a lecture series published in *Die Freiheit*, May 26, 28, 29, 1920 (M); Feldman, *The Great Disorder*, 473–74.

20. Hilferding, "Die Aufgaben der Reichsbank," *Vorwärts*, August 9, 1923 (E).

21. Ibid. For Hilferding's theoretical views on paper money's relation to gold see *Finance Capital*, 38–40.

22. On Hilferding's first period as finance minister the most important works are James, "Rudolf Hilferding"; Martin Vogt, "Rudolf Hilferding als Finanzminister im ersten Kabinett Stresemann," in *Historische Prozesse der deutschen Inflation, 1914–1924: Ein Tagungsbericht*, ed. Gerald Feldman and Otto Busch (Berlin, 1978), 127–58; Feldman, *The Great Disorder*, 698–753; Claus Dieter Krohn, "Helfferich contra Hilferding," *Vierteljahresschrift für Sozial- und Wirtschaftsgeschichte* 62.1 (1975): 62–92; Alex Möller, *Im Gedanken an Reichsfinanzminister Rudolf Hilferding* (Bonn, 1971), 9–19.

23. Vogt, "Rudolf Hilferding als Finanzminister," 128; Krohn, "Helfferich contra Hilferding," 84–86: John G. Williamson, *Karl Helfferich, 1872–1924: Economist, Financier, Politician* (Princeton, 1971): 383–94.

24. Vogt, "Rudolf Hilferding als Finanzminister," 129, 132–38, 153.

25. *Akten der Reichskanzlei, Weimarer Republik: Die Kabinett Stresemann I, 13. August 1923 bis 6. October 1923*, vol. 1, ed. Karl Dietrich Erdmann and Martin

Vogt (Boppard am Rhein, 1978), 10 (hereafter cited as *AdR: Stresemann I/1*); Vogt, "Rudolf Hilferding als Finanzminister," 129; Feldman, *The Great Disorder,* 710-11.

26. *AdR: Stresemann I/1,* 4-6, 30-31, 47; Vogt, "Rudolf Hilferding als Finanzminister," 129-30.

27. Feldman, *The Great Disorder,* 718.

28. Ibid., 711.

29. *AdR: Stresemann I/1,* 156-57; Vogt, "Rudolf Hilferding als Finanzminister," 133-34.

30. Vogt, "Rudolf Hilferding als Finanzminister," 138-39.

31. *AdR: Stresemann I/1,* 22-29.

32. Vogt, "Rudolf Hilferding als Finanzminister," 145-48 (145); Krohn, "Helfferich contra Hilferding," 86.

33. As quoted in Krohn, "Helfferich contra Hilferding," 88.

34. *AdR: Stresemann I/1,* 28-29.

35. On Hilferding's contacts with industry see Vogt, "Rudolf Hilferding als Finanzminister," 144-45. For detailed background on the various plans in circulation in August and September 1923 see Feldman, *The Great Disorder,* 720-27.

36. *AdR: Stresemann I/1,* 224-26.

37. James, "Rudolf Hilferding," 859; Vogt, "Rudolf Hilferding als Finanzminister," 147-49; Rosemarie Leuschen-Seppel, *Zwischen Staatsverantwortung und Klasseninteresse* (Bonn, 1981), 101-2.

38. *AdR: Stresemann I/1,* 256-62; Vogt, "Rudolf Hilferding als Finanzminister," 149-50.

39. Vogt, "Rudolf Hilferding als Finanzminister," 150-51.

40. Ibid., 151; Möller, *Im Gedanken an Reichsfinanzminister,* 14-15; Hans Luther, *Politiker ohne Partei* (Stuttgart, 1960), 117-18; Krohn, "Helfferich contra Hilferding," 89.

41. *AdR: Stresemann I/1,* 450; Vogt, "Rudolf Hilferding als Finanzminister," 152-53.

42. *AdR: Stresemann I/1,* 429-31; Breitman, *German Socialism,* 100; Winkler, *Weimar,* 217-19 (213).

43. *AdR: Stresemann I/1,* 450; Breitman, *German Socialism,* 100.

44. Stresemann, *Vermächtnis,* 1:141.

45. Otto Braun, *Von Weimar zu Hitler* (New York, 1940), 126-27.

46. Luther, *Politiker ohne Partei,* 115; Gustav Radbruch, *Der innere Weg: Abriß meines Lebens* (Stuttgart, 1951), 171.

47. Heinrich Brüning, *Memoiren, 1918-1934* (Stuttgart, 1970), 98, 110; Alex Möller, *Tatort Politik* (Munich, 1982), 89.

48. Möller, *Im Gedanken an Reichsfinanzminister,* 18; Vogt, "Rudolf Hilferding als Finanzminister," 153; Krohn, "Helfferich contra Hilferding," 90 n. 96. Despite the great detail with which Gerald Feldman describes the obstacles Hilferding faced in office, his judgment of his performance is harsher. See *The Great Disorder,* 727-29, 745.

49. *Verhandlungen des Reichstages: Stenographische Berichte der Sitzungen* (Berlin), vol. 423, July 5, 1928, 100-102 (hereafter cited as *VR*).

50. On Hilferding's orthodoxy see James, "Rudolf Hilferding," 858-60.

51. Breitman, *German Socialism,* 121.

52. Hilferding cited from *Sozialdemokratische Parteikorrespondenz, 1923–1928* (Berlin, 1930), 96–98.

53. Ibid., 97–98.

54. Breitman, *German Socialism*, 109–13. Hilferding's support for tolerating Marx rested largely on foreign policy grounds. He especially backed the Marx cabinet's negotiation of a new reparations agreement, which he regarded as essential for Germany's economic recovery. See Hilferding, *Für die soziale Republik*, 6–8.

55. Hilferding, *Für die soziale Republik*, 8–16 (15).

56. Detlef Lehnert, *Sozialdemokratie zwischen Protestbewegung und Regierungspartei, 1848 bis 1983* (Frankfurt am Main, 1983), 136–37.

57. Ibid., 137–38; Lösche and Walter, "Auf dem Weg zur Volkspartei?" 89.

58. Hilferding to Kautsky, December 29, 1924, KDXII, 640 (ISH).

59. Hilferding to Kautsky, January 8, 1926, KDXII, 642 (ISH).

60. On Hilferding's and the SPD's reaction to Koch-Weser's proposal see Breitman, *German Socialism*, 123–24, and Larry Eugene Jones, *German Liberalism and the Dissolution of the Weimar Party System, 1918–1933* (Chapel Hill, 1988), 247–48.

61. On Hilferding's appointment to the chairmanship of the program committee see Winkler, *Der Schein der Normalität*, 321. Heine is cited from an interview with the author, December 12, 1986, Bonn.

62. On Müller's and Wels's relationships with Hilferding I am drawing on Heine interview; Breitman, *German Socialism*, 116; Adolph, *Otto Wels*, 113–14.

63. Lösche and Walter, "Auf dem Weg zur Volkspartei?" 95–97; Winkler, *Von der Revolution zur Stabilisierung*, 446–47. For the text of the Görlitz Program see Miller and Potthoff, *Kleine Geschichte der SPD*, 334–38.

64. Maehl, *The German Socialist Party*, 78–79; Hunt, *German Social Democracy*, 229.

65. For Hilferding's explanation of the lack of a clear position on agriculture see *SPD-Parteitag Heidelberg, 1925*, 277. Pages will be set in text.

66. "Program der Sozialdemokratischen Arbeiterpartei Deutschösterreichs: Beschlossen vom Parteitag zu Linz am 3. November 1926," in *Austromarxismus*, ed. Sandkühler and de la Vega, 383–84.

67. On Bauer's views see Leser, *Zwischen Reformismus und Bolschewismus*, 402–12; Frank Heidenreich, "Das Linzer Programm und die Strategie des demokratischen Wegs zum Sozialismus," in *Otto Bauer*, ed. Albers, Heimann, and Saage, 43–55.

68. *SPD-Parteitag Heidelberg, 1925*, 285–87, 294–97.

69. Claus Inselmann, "'Die Gesellschaft': Ein Rückblick auf eine Zeitschrift der Weimarer Zeit," *Die Neue Gesellschaft* 11 (July–August 1964): 321–34.

70. Woytinsky, *Stormy Passage*, 457–58.

71. On the left's exclusion from the SPD's press see Gerhard Eisfeld and Kurt Koszyk, eds., *Die Presse der deutschen Sozialdemokratie* (Bonn, 1980), 43. On the issue of reviewing Riasanov's work see Hilferding to Karl Kautsky, October 6, 1927, and January 13, 1928, KDXII, 647, 649; Hilferding to Bendel Kautsky, January 4, 1928, KDXII, 648 (ISH).

72. Kautsky quoted in Steinberg, *Sozialismus und deutsche Sozialdemokratie*, 77.

73. *VR* 381, August 25, 1924, p. 815; *VR* 387, August 8, 1925, p. 4305. Strasser is quoted in Winkler, *Der Schein der Normalität*, 540.

74. Karl Korsch, *Marxism and Philosophy* (New York, 1970), 174–75.

75. Breitman, *German Socialism*, 120.

76. Kessler, *Tagebücher*, 451–52. Kessler's diaries are the richest source of information on Hilferding's daily social activities.

77. Gerhard Loewenberg, *Parliament in the German Political System* (Ithaca, 1966), 49. This is the figure given for 1927. In 1930, after the onset of the depression, it was reduced to 7,200 RM.

78. In conversations with the author, Susanne Hertz (a childhood friend of Rose Hilferding's daughter) and Fritz Heine both confirmed Rudolf's love of fine foods and cigars.

79. Lord d'Abernon quoted in Gottschalch, *Strukturveränderungen*, 15.

80. Kessler, *Tagebücher* (155) (122), 175. Kessler also refers to this club as a "Sozialwissenschaftlicher Verein" (social scientific association), 344.

81. Ibid., 125.

82. Leser, *Zwischen Reformismus und Bolschewismus*, 227–28.

83. Hunt, *German Social Democracy*, 63–78.

84. Kessler, *Tagebücher*, 84, 127, 345.

85. Author's interview with Fritz Heine, December 12, 1986; Adolph, *Otto Wels* (113–14).

86. In 1928 Müller told the other party leaders that he would not accept the chancellorship if they blocked Hilferding's appointment to the Finance Ministry. See Julius Leber, *Ein Mann geht seinen Weg: Schriften, Reden und Briefe von Julius Leber* (Berlin, 1952), 228. For Hilferding's obituary of Müller see "Hermann Müller," *Die Gesellschaft* 8.1 (1931): 289–92. On Hilferding's and Müller's political compatibility see Hilferding to Kautsky, April 15, 1931, KDXII, 652 (ISH).

87. Hilferding to Kautsky, November 19, 1924, KDXII, 638 (ISH).

88. Stein, *Rudolf Hilferding*, 3; Brüning, *Memoiren*, 115; Oscar Meyer, *Von Bismarck zu Hitler* (New York, 1944), 157.

89. On Braun's attitude toward Hilferding see Hagen Schulze, *Otto Braun oder Preußens demokratische Sendung: Eine Biographie* (Frankfurt am Main, 1977), 436–37 (437). For the remarks about Hilferding in the Parteiausschuß see *Protokolle des Parteiausschußes*, 120–21.

90. Hertz quoted in Adolph, *Otto Wels*, 114; Carl von Ossietzky, "Rudolf Hilferding, der Mann ohne Schatten," *Das Tagebuch* 5.2 (1924): 922–24 (922).

91. Von Ossietzky, "Rudolf Hilferding," 922.

92. Ibid., 923.

93. Ibid., 924.

94. Peter Lösche and Franz Walter, "Zur Organisationskultur der sozialdemokratischen Arbeiterbewegung in der Weimarer Republik," *Geschichte und Gesellschaft* 15 (1989): 524.

95. Werner Abelshauser, "Die Weimarer Republik—ein Wohlfahrtsstaat?" in *Die Weimarer Republik als Wohlfahrtsstaat: Zum Verhältnis von Wirtschafts- und Sozialpolitik in der Industriegesellschaft* (Stuttgart, 1987), 15–31; Dick Geary, "Employers, Workers, and the Collapse of the Weimar Republic," in *Weimar: Why Did German Democracy Fail?* ed. Ian Kershaw (New York, 1990): 100–101; David Abraham, *The Collapse of the Weimar Republic* (New York, 1986), 229–34.

96. Hilferding, "Politische Probleme, zum Aufruf Wirths und zur Rede Silverbergs," *Die Gesellschaft* 3.2 (1926): 289–302. On the willingness of other SPD

leaders to organize a new coalition see Ben Fowkes, "Defense of Democracy or Advance to Socialism? Arguments within German Social Democracy in the mid-1920s," in *Radical Perspectives on the Rise of Fascism in Germany, 1919–1945,* ed. Michael N. Dobkowski and Isidor Wallimann (New York, 1989), 252.

97. *SPD-Parteitag Kiel, 1927,* 169–72 (170).

98. Ibid., 173–74.

99. Ibid. (183); Hilferding, *Für die soziale Republik,* 15.

100. *SPD-Parteitag Kiel, 1927,* 184–89, 198–200, 217–23, 272.

101. Michael Schneider, *A Brief History of the German Trade Unions* (Bonn, 1989), 173–74; Fritz Naphtali, "Die Verwirklichung der Wirtschaftdemokratie," in *Protokoll der Verhandlungen des 13. Kongresses der Gewerkschaften Deutschlands (3. Bundestag des Allgemeinen Deutschen Gewerkschaftsbundes), abgehalten in Hamburg vom 3. bis 7. September 1928* (Berlin, 1928), 170–90.

102. Geary, "Employers, Workers, and the Collapse of the Weimar," 95–104; Harold James, *The German Slump: Politics and Economics, 1924–1936* (Oxford, 1986), 217–23; Heinrich Potthoff, *Freie Gewerkschaften, 1918–1933: Der Allgemeine Deutsche Gewerkschaftsbund in der Weimarer Republik* (Düsseldorf, 1987), 91–93; Jones, *German Liberalism,* 277.

103. Wels cited in Harsch, *German Social Democracy,* 28–32.

104. Lösche and Walter, "Auf dem Weg zur Volkspartei?" 133–34; Hans Mommsen, "Die Sozialdemokratie in der Defensive: Der Immobilismus der SPD und der Aufstieg des Nationalsozialismus," in *Sozialdemokratie zwischen Klassenbewegung und Volkspartei,* ed. Hans Mommsen (Frankfurt am Main, 1974), 117–33.

105. Richard Bessel, "Why Did the Weimar Republic Collapse?" in *Weimar: Why Did German Democracy Fail?* ed. Ian Kershaw (New York, 1990), 126–27.

106. The structural problems of the economy and their sociopolitical ramifications are succinctly described in ibid. and in Harold James, "Economic Reasons for the Collapse of Weimar," in *Weimar,* ed. Kershaw, 30–57.

107. Lehnert, *Sozialdemokratie,* 142.

108. James, *The German Slump,* 39–73; Ilse Maurer, *Reichsfinanzen und Große Koalition: Zur Geschichte der Reichskabinetts Müller, 1928–1930* (Frankfurt am Main, 1973), 13–18. The figures on the national debt are in Maehl, *The German Socialist Party,* 126.

109. On Hilferding's motivation for taking over the Finance Ministry see *VR* 423, July 5, 1928, p. 102; *SPD-Parteitag Magdeburg, 1929,* 198; Brüning, *Memoiren,* 127.

110. *VR* 395, March 28, 1928, pp. 13841–46.

111. Breitman, *German Socialism,* 148–51; Maehl, *The German Socialist Party,* 127–31; Winkler, *Der Schein der Normalität,* 541–55.

112. *Akten der Reichskanzlei, Weimarer Republik: Die Kabinett Müller II,* vol. 1, ed. Martin Vogt (Boppard am Rhein, 1970), 60–64 (hereafter cited as *AdR: Müller II/1*); Maehl, *The German Socialist Party,* 128.

113. Harsch, *German Social Democracy,* 48–49. Jensen is quoted in Schulze, *Otto Braun,* 548. For Hilferding's remarks see Gustav Noske, *Erlebtes aus Aufstieg und Niedergang einer Demokratie* (Offenbach am Main, 1947), 309.

114. *AdR: Müller II/1,* 229–30.

115. *VR* 424, March 14, 1929, pp. 1403–7; and Maehl, *The German Socialist Party,* 131–32; Breitman, *German Socialism,* 152; Maurer, *Reichsfinanzen,* 48–50.

116. *VR* 424, March 14, 1929, p. 1407.

117. Ibid., 1408–11.

118. Maurer, *Reichsfinanzen*, 57–60.

119. *AdR: Müller II/1*, 525–26.

120. Maurer, *Reichsfinanzen*, 61–63.

121. *VR* 424, March 14, 1929, p. 1405; *AdR: Müller II/1*, 498.

122. *AdR: Müller II/1*, 638–42; Maurer, *Reichsfinanzen*, 82.

123. Maurer, *Reichsfinanzen*, 83–84.

124. Maehl, *The German Socialist Party*, 153; Rudolf Wissell to Hermann Müller, August 29, 1929, Nachlaß Müller, II, doc. 177 (AdsD).

125. Friedrich Stampfer to Hermann Müller, September 4, 1929, Nachlaß Müller, II, doc. 178 (AdsD); Maehl, *The German Socialist Party*, 154; Maurer, *Reichsfinanzen*, 84.

126. James, *The German Slump*, 54.

127. Hilferding cited in *SPD-Parteitag Magdeburg, 1929*, 195.

128. James, *The German Slump*, 55–57; Maehl, *The German Socialist Party*, 146; Maurer, *Reichsfinanzen*, 78–79.

129. James, "Rudolf Hilferding," 863; Maurer, *Reichsfinanzen*, 96–98.

130. Maurer, *Reichsfinanzen* (98); *AdR: Müller II/2*, 1210–15.

131. The text of Schacht's memorandum is reprinted in ibid., 1220–29.

132. Ibid., 1238–44, 1263–64, 1270–72; *VR* 426, December 14, 1929, pp. 3572–77; Winkler, *Der Schein der Normalität*, 742–47.

133. *AdR: Müller II/2*, 1297–98 n. 1; Winkler, *Der Schein der Normalität*, 748–50.

134. *AdR: Müller II/2*, 1297.

135. Ibid., 1297–302.

136. Winkler, *Der Schein der Normalität*, 752–54; Leuschen-Seppel, *Zwischen Staatsverantwortung und Klasseninteresse*, 248–50; Wilhelm Keil, *Erlebnisse eines Sozialdemokraten* (Stuttgart, 1948), 2:363–64.

137. *AdR: Müller II/2*, 1299.

138. *SPD Parteitag, Magdeburg, 1929*, 88–90, 68–70; Winkler, *Der Schein der Normalität*, 764–65.

139. Knut Borchardt, *Wachstum, Krisen, Handlungsspielräume der Wirtschaftspolitik* (Göttingen, 1982), 166–73; Bernd Weisbrod, "Die Befreiung von den 'Tariffesseln': Deflationspolitik als Krisenstrategie der Unternehmer in der Ära Brüning," *Geschichte und Gesellschaft* 11.3 (1985): 321; Carl-Ludwig Holtfrerich, "Economic Policy Options and the End of the Weimar Republic," in *Weimar*, ed. Kershaw, 66.

140. *SPD Parteitag, Magdeburg, 1929*, 198–99; Hilferding, "Der Austritt aus der Regierung," *Die Gesellschaft* 7.1 (1930): 385–88.

141. Hilferding, "Der Austritt aus der Regierung," 389.

142. Schaefer, *Die SPD in der Ära Brüning*, 42–44; Eberhard Kolb, *The Weimar Republic*, translated by P. S. Falla (London, 1988), 107–8.

143. Harsch, *German Social Democracy*, 87–99; Schulze, *Otto Braun*, 637–39; Eberhard Kolb, *The Weimar Republic*, trans. P. S. Falla (London, 1988), 111–12; Lehnert, *Sozialdemokratie*, 148.

144. Hilferding, "In die Gefahrenzone," *Die Gesellschaft* 7.2 (1930): 290–93 (293).

145. Ibid., 294.

146. Ibid., 295–96.

147. *Vorwärts*, October 5, 1930, Nr. 467.

148. *Breslauer Volkswacht*, October 8, 1930.

149. Harsch, *German Social Democracy*, 97–99.

150. Brüning, *Memoiren*, 110, 115–16; Heinrich Brüning, "Ein Brief," *Deutsche Rundschau* 70 (July 1947): 8; Meyer, *Von Bismarck zu Hitler*, 155.

151. Harsch, *German Social Democracy*, 89; Erich Matthias, "Die Sozialdemokratische Partei," in *Das Ende der Parteien, 1933*, ed. Erich Matthias and Rudolf Morsey (Düsseldorf, 1960), 105–6; Schaefer, *Die SPD in der Ära Brüning*, 53.

152. Compare Kolb, *The Weimar Republic*, 114–15, and Mommsen, *The Rise and Fall of Weimar Democracy*, 360–64.

153. Matthias, "Die Sozialdemokratische Partei Deutschlands," docs. 2, 3, pp. 205–10.

154. Harsch, *German Social Democracy*, 135–36; Schaefer, *SPD in der Ära Brüning*, 127–31.

155. Sitzung des Bundesvorstandes, June 10, 1931, docs. 44, 47, in vol. 4, *Die Gewerkschaften in der Endphase der Republik, 1930–1933*, compiled, annotated, and introduced by Peter Jahn (Cologne, 1987), 312–20, 338–39, 342–43 (hereafter cited as *Gewerkschaften*).

156. Hilferding, "In Krisennot," *Die Gesellschaft* 8.1 (1931): 1–8.

157. Hilferding to Kautsky, October 2, 1931, KDXII, 653 (ISH). In 1927, Hilferding had refused to even read Max Adler's biting criticisms of his political views. On his growing impatience with left critics see his letters to Kautsky, January 13, 1928, and May 15, 1931, KDXII, 649, 652. For Max Adler's criticism's of Hilferding see "Zweck und Nutzen der Sublimierung der Parteien," *Der Klassenkampf* 2.2 (1928): 34, 39; "Eine Philosophie der Koalition," *Der Klassenkampf* 2.5 (1928): 134–39; and "Demokratie als Ziel und als Mittel über marxistische Staatsauffassung," *Der Klassenkampf* 2.10 (1928): 292–98.

158. Hilferding to Kautsky, October 2, 1931, KDXII, 653 (ISH).

159. Hilferding, *Gesellschaftsmacht oder Privatmacht über die Wirtschaft*, 32–36; Hilferding, "Ein Irrweg," *Vorwärts*, October 10, 1931; Woytinsky, *Stormy Passage*, 466–68, 471–72; James, "Rudolf Hilferding," 864–68; Cora Stephan, "Wirtschaftsdemokratie und Umbau der Wirtschaft," in *Sozialdemokratische Arbeiterbewegung und Weimarer Republik: Materialien zur gesellschaftlichen Entwicklung, 1927–1933*, ed. Wolfgang Luthardt (Frankfurt am Main, 1978), 1:281–91.

160. Sitzung des Bundesvorstandes, June 17, 1931, doc. 46, *Gewerkschaften*, 330–31; Holtfrerich, "Economic Policy Options," 66–67; Brüning, *Memoiren*, 221, 367, 503.

161. So argues Borchardt, *Wachstum, Krisen, Handlungsspielräume*, 169–70. For a convincing response see Holtfrerich, "Economic Policy Options," 65–84.

162. Hilferding, *Nationalsozialismus und Marxismus* (Berlin, 1932); Mommsen, *Rise and Fall*, 498–99.

163. Hilferding, *Für die soziale Republik*, 14; *SPD-Parteitag Kiel, 1927*, 173; Hilferding, "Zur Frage des Generalstreiks," 141.

164. On the formation and activities of the Iron Front see Harsch, *German Social Democracy*, 169–90.

165. Harsch, *German Social Democracy,* 189.
166. Hilferding, "Unter der Drohung des Faschismus," *Die Gesellschaft* 9.1 (1932), 3–6; Maehl, *The German Socialist Party,* 181–85; Fülberth and Harrer, *Die deutsche Sozialdemokratie,* 227–28; Gottschalch, *Strukturveränderungen,* 219–28.
167. Maehl, *The German Socialist Party,* 189.
168. Ibid., 190; Winkler, *Weimar,* 490–503.
169. Maehl, *The German Socialist Party,* 191–95; Breitman, *German Socialism,* 185–88; Winkler, *Der Weg in die Katastrophe,* 671–80.
170. Figures in Winkler, *Der Weg in die Katastrophe,* 774.
171. Ibid., 724–25.
172. "Sitzung des Parteiausschußes," November 10, 1932, doc. 2, *Anpassung oder Widerstand? Aus den Akten des Parteivorstands der deutschen Sozialdemokratie, 1932–1933,* ed. Hagen Schulze (Bonn–Bad Godesberg, 1975), 40–41.
173. Hilferding to Kautsky, December 1, 1932, KDXII, 658 (ISH).
174. Hilferding, "Zwischen den Entscheidungen," *Die Gesellschaft* 10.1 (1933): 1–9.
175. As quoted in Ben Fowkes, *Communism in Germany under the Weimar Republic* (London, 1984), 154.
176. Hilferding to Kautsky, April 15, 1931, KDXII, 652 (ISH).
177. SPD-Emigration, Mappe 2, Sitzung vom 30 Januar 1933 (AdsD).
178. Parteiausschuß, doc. 6, February 2, 1933, and doc. 7, February 5, 1933, in Schulze, *Anpassung oder Widerstand?* 159, 164.
179. Paul Baran quoted by Paul Sweezy in the introduction to Böhm Bawerk's *Karl Marx and the Close of His System,* and Hilferding's *Böhm-Bawerk's Criticism of Marx,* xviii. Sweezy did not identify Baran as the author of these remarks but later provided me with this information in a private communication.
180. On the norms that characterized the SPD leaders' thinking see especially Matthias, "Die Sozialdemokratische Partei Deutschlands," 196–99; and Harsch, *German Social Democracy,* 239–46.
181. Susanne Miller, "Politische Führung und Spontaneität in der österreichischen Sozialdemokratie," in *Otto Bauer,* ed. Albers, Heimann, and Saage, 71–73.
182. It remains unclear if he left Berlin alone or with other party members. See Stein, *Rudolf Hilferding,* 27; Brüning, *Memoiren,* 660.

CHAPTER 6. THE SWORD OF DAMOCLES

1. Epigraph is from Hilferding to Karl Kautsky, September 2, 1937, KDXII, 668 (ISH). Hilferding's travels to Saarbrücken and Paris are noted in letter from Friedrich Adler to Sigmund Crummenerl, May 20, 1933, SPD-Emigration, Mappe 15 (AdsD). On his meeting with exiles in Paris, see Kessler, *Tagebücher,* 719.
2. Hilferding to Kautsky, April 13, 1933, KDXII, 660 (ISH).
3. Ibid.
4. Ibid.; Hilferding to Kautsky, October 2, 1932, KDXII, 653 (ISH).
5. On this issue see Horst Lademacher, "Gewalt der Legalität oder die Legalität der Gewalt: Zur Theorie und Politik der SPD von Kiel (1927) bis Prag (1934)," in *Frieden, Gewalt, Sozialismus: Studien zur Geschichte der sozialistischen Arbeiterbe-*

wegung, ed. Wolfgang Huber and Johannes Schwerdtfeger (Stuttgart, 1976), 433–34.

6. Hilferding to Kautsky, September 23, 1933, KDXII, 661 (ISH).

7. Hilferding to Kautsky, April 13, 1933, KDXII, 660 (ISH).

8. Lewis J. Edinger, *German Exile Politics: The Social Democratic Executive Committee in the Nazi Era* (Berkeley and Los Angeles, 1956), 23–24.

9. Ibid., 29–33.

10. Hilferding to the Sopade, June 11, 1933, SPD-Emigration, Mappe 54 (AdsD).

11. Hilferding to Paul Hertz, June 14, 1933, Nachlaß Hertz (AdsD).

12. On the KPD's strategy in 1933–1934 see Edinger, *German Exile Politics,* 71–75.

13. Hilferding to "Lieber Freund," June 10, 1933, SPD-Emigration, Mappe 54 (AdsD).

14. Ibid.

15. Edinger, *German Exile Politics,* 48–55; Marlis Buchholz and Bernd Rother, eds., *Der Parteivorstand der SPD im Exil: Protokolle der Sopade, 1933–1940* (Bonn, 1995), xxxiv–xxxviii (hereafter cited as *Parteivorstand*).

16. Ibid., 57.

17. On Hilferding's appointment see Wilhelm Sollmann to Otto Wels, July 7, 1933, SPD-Emigration, Mappe 122 (AdsD); *Parteivorstand,* 7, 10–11.

18. Wels's ambivalence toward Hilferding was reflected in his decision in August 1933 to exclude him and Breitscheid from the party's official delegation to the Paris conference of the LSI. According to Breitscheid, Wels and Stampfer disapproved of their view that the LSI must immediately speak out against Germany's rearmament. See Peter Pistorius, *Rudolf Breitscheid, 1874–1944: Ein biographischer Beitrag zur deutschen Parteiengeschichte* (Cologne, 1970): 329–30; Hilferding to Stampfer, August 28, 1936, in *Mit dem Gesicht nach Deutschland: Eine Dokumentation über die sozialdemokratische Emigration, aus dem Nachlaß Friedrich Stampfer, ergänzt durch andere Überlieferungen,* ed. Erich Matthias (Düsseldorf, 1968), 283.

19. Edinger, *German Exile Politics,* 42–43.

20. Ibid., 45.

21. Ibid., 46–47.

22. On the origins and development of New Beginning see ibid., 83–90; Peter Grasmann, *Sozialdemokraten gegen Hitler, 1933–1945* (Munich, 1976), 115–23; and William David Jones, "Before the Cold War: On the Origins, Development, and Varieties of Leftwing Anti-Totalitarianism as shown in the Writings of Selected German Socialist Intellictuals, 1928–1944" (Ph.D. diss., Claremont Graduate School, 1992), to be published in 1998 by the University of Illinois Press.

23. The quotation is from Gottschalch, *Strukturveränderungen,* 230. For the Revolutionary Socialists' demands see Grasmann, *Sozialdemokraten gegen Hitler,* 22–23.

24. Hilferding hoped that the journal, at a cost of five Czech crowns, would have an initial circulation of about two thousand and eventually break even. Monthly circulation in 1935 was about one thousand, and debts mounted. On the founding of the journal, see the undated letters to Hilferding from the Sopade (probably July 1933) and Fritz Heine, August 16, 1933, in Nachlaß Hertz (AdsD). See also *Parteivorstand,* 7, 10–11, 101.

25. The following discussion is based on part 2 of Hilferding's essay, which remains unpublished. See SPD-Emigration, Mappe 54 (AdsD). Pages will be cited parenthetically in the text.

26. See, for example, Richard Kern (Hilferding's pseudonym in exile), "Totaler Staat, totaler Bankrott, verantwortungslose Wirtschaft im Dritten Reich," *Neuer Vorwärts*, June 18, 1933; "Finanzielle Reichszerstörung," *Neuer Vorwärts*, July 9, 1933; "Die Reichsbank als Geldmaschine," *Neuer Vorwärts*, October 20, 1933.

27. Richard Kern, "Sklaverei in den Betrieben, Despotie des Kapitals," *Neuer Vorwärts*, July 2, 1933; and "Korporationen, Stände und Monopole," *Neuer Vorwärts*, December 3, 1933.

28. Richard Kern, "Hitler ohne Maske, Verrat am Sozialismus," *Neuer Vorwärts*, July 16, 1933.

29. Hilferding was not the first to use the term "total state" to describe the fascist and communist countries; he himself ascribed its original use to the fascists. The antirepublican thinker Carl Schmitt used the term in the 1920s, as did Boris Sapir, a Menshevik critic of the USSR, in 1933. In the 1930s and 1940s, the German designation *totaler Staat* was generally translated into English as "totalitarian state." Usage of the term—compare, for example, Franz Neumann's *Behemoth* (1942) and Hannah Arendt's *The Origins of Totalitarianism* (1951)—varied, of course, depending on the context and the author's political perspective. By the mid-1930s some German and Russian socialists, including Hilferding, also began using the term "totalitarian" *(totalitär)* in their writings. On this development, compare Andre Liebich, "Marxism and Totalitarianism: Rudolf Hilferding and the Mensheviks," *Dissent* (spring 1987): 231–32; and Hans Buchheim, *Totalitarian Rule: Its Nature and Characteristics* (Middletown, Conn., 1986), 97–98.

30. Richard Kern, "Die Zeit und die Aufgabe," *Sozialistische Revolution* 1 (1933–1934): 1–3. Pages will be cited parenthetically in the text. *Sozialistische Revolution* was the original title given to the *ZfS*. Under Nazi pressure the Czech government demanded that the Sopade adopt a less militant title after the appearance of the first issue. See Edinger, *German Exile Politics*, 101.

31. See also Hilferding's letter to Paul Hertz, October 30, 1933, in which he requests that Hertz find authors from the party's left wing. Nachlaß Hertz (AdsD).

32. Hilferding, *Finance Capital*, 368.

33. On the manifesto's origins see *Parteivorstand*, 31–33; Edinger, *German Exile Politics*, 110–19; and Gerhard Gleißberg, *SPD und Gesellschaftssystem: Aktualität der Programmdiskussion 1934–1946, Dokumente und Kommentar* (Frankfurt am Main, 1973), 11–25. Quotations in the following discussion are drawn from the text of the manifesto, reprinted in Miller and Potthoff, *Kleine Geschichte der SPD*, 349–51.

34. Hilferding to Max Klinger (Curt Geyer), January 10, 1934, SPD-Emigration, Mappe 54 (AdsD). Compare also the manifesto's text with the much longer and more detailed text put forward by Friedrich Stampfer, Curt Geyer, and Erich Rinner, reprinted in Matthias, *Mit dem Gesicht nach Deutschland*, 197–212.

35. Hilferding's correspondence makes clear how difficult it was to synthesize the various competing drafts of the manifesto. In a letter to Paul Hertz, for example, he remarked that Aufhäuser, Böchel, and Crummenerl's draft was "especially poor with the exception of the part about socialization. . . . I have accepted most of this

despite some inner reservations that I have yet to clarify myself. . . . I have also adopted as much 'anticapitalism' as my conscience allows. As I've already explained in a letter to Klinger [Curt Geyer], I don't expect much from the mix of declamations about human rights, appeals to will, and calls on the most reactionary groups to march together." Letter to Paul Hertz, January 11, 1934, Nachlaß Hertz (AdsD). As the published version of the manifesto makes clear, the Sopade apparently elected to drop the section on socialization.

36. Richard Kern, "Revolutionärer Sozialismus," *ZfS* 1 (1933–1934): 148–51. Pages will be cited in the text.

37. For statements by Karl Marx and Friedrich Engels on the relationship between the "base" and the "superstructure" see Karl Marx, *A Contribution to the Critique of Political Economy,* ed. with introduction by Maurice Dobb (New York, 1970), 20–22; Karl Marx and Friedrich Engels, *Selected Correspondence,* ed. S. W. Ryazanskaya, trans. I. Lasker (Moscow, 1975), 227–28; Friedrich Engels, *The Origin of the Familiy, Private Property, and the State* (Moscow, 1977) (168).

38. For Hilferding's foreign policy views between 1933 and 1935 see Richard Kern, "Das Londoner Abkommen," *ZfS* 2 (1934–1935): 561–68; "Macht ohne Diplomatie—Diplomatie ohne Macht," *ZfS* 2 (1934–1935): 593–604; "Das Ende der Volkerbundpolitik," *ZfS* 2 (1934–1935): 621–37; and "Die Internationale vor der Entscheidung," *Der Kampf* 27 (1934): 41–47. Hilferding also wrote dozens of articles on foreign policy in *Neuer Vorwärts* after 1935. For a comprehensive listing see Minoru Kurata, "Rudolf Hilferding: Bibliographie seiner Schriften, Artikel und Briefe," *Internationale wissenschaftliche Korrespondenz zur Geschichte der Arbeiterbewegung* 10 (1974): 327–46. On the British Labour party's position during those years, see John F. Naylor, *Labour's International Policy: The Labour Party in the 1930s* (London, 1969), chap. 3. For an analysis of the European labor movement's foreign policy toward Nazi Germany see Braunthal, *History of the International,* 2:468–92.

39. Edinger, *German Exile Politics,* 187–89, 199.

40. For his role in this matter see Hilferding to Paul Hertz, January 29, September 30, 1935, Nachlaß Hertz (AdsD); Hilferding to Otto Wels, December 19, 1935, and January 3, 11, 1936, SPD-Emigration, Mappe 54 (AdsD); Matthias, *Mit dem Gesicht nach Deutschland,* 95. See also *Parteivorstand,* 130–33, 138–39, 149–51.

41. Paul Hertz to Hilferding, April 4, 30, 1935; Hilferding to Hertz, May 27, 1935, Nachlaß Hertz (AdsD); *Parteivorstand,* 159.

42. Report by Walter Ulbricht to Wilhelm Pieck, "Besprechung mit Hilferding," May 27, 1936, NL 182/198, Stiftung Archiv der Parteien und Massenorganisationen der DDR (SAPM/DDR) im Bundesarchiv, Berlin (former Zentrales Parteiarchiv der DDR); Hilferding to Paul Hertz, May 28, 1936, Nachlaß Hertz (AdsD).

43. Hilferding to Paul Hertz, January 29, 1935, Nachlaß Hertz (AdsD).

44. Ibid.

45. On Bauer's attitude toward the Soviet Union compare Norbert Leser, "Otto Bauers Haltung gegenüber dem Bolschewismus," in *Otto Bauer,* ed. Albers, Heimann, and Saage, 94–103; and Uli Schöler, "Otto Bauers Auseinandersetzung mit der Oktoberrevolution und dem sowjetischen Modell," in ibid., 104–17.

46. Hilferding to Kautsky, January 8, 1926, KDXII, 642 (ISH).

47. Hilferding to Kautsky, May 15, 1931, KDXII, 652 (ISH).

48. Hilferding to Paul Hertz, October 21, 1936, Nachlaß Hertz (AdsD).

49. Hilferding to Stampfer, August 28, 1936, in Matthias, *Mit dem Gesicht nach Deutschland,* 282–85.

50. Ibid.

51. Hilferding to Paul Hertz, May 27, 1935, Nachlaß Hertz (AdsD).

52. On Hilferding's relationship with Wels see ibid. On his standing in the executive see Matthias, *Mit dem Gesicht nach Deutschland,* 339, 341, 360; Hertz cited in *Parteivorstand,* 282.

53. Letter from the Sopade to Hilferding, June 14, 1935, SPD-Emigration, Mappe 54 (AdsD); Erich Rinner, ed., *Deutschlandberichte der Sozialdemokratischen Partei Deutschlands (Sopade): Februar 1938* (Frankfurt am Main, 1980), 195

54. Rose Hilferding to Paul Hertz, July 18, 1935, Nachlaß Hertz (AdsD).

55. I believe that, after 1935, the Hilferdings traveled on Czechoslovakian passports. Rose was born in Czechoslovakia and it appears from Rudolf's correspondence with Hertz that he depended on the latter's influence in Prague to secure his own papers. On Hilferding's visa problems see, for example, Hilferding to Hertz, October 31, 1936, and January 6, 1938, Nachlaß Hertz (AdsD). In 1931, Hilferding wrote an introduction to Blum's book *Ohne Abrüstung kein Friede: Die französische Sozialdemokratie im Kampf um die Organisation des Friedens* (Berlin, 1931). On Hilferding's new location in Paris see Stein, *Rudolf Hilferding,* 35.

56. Stein takes a similar view. See *Rudolf Hilferding,* 35–36.

57. Richard Kern, "Die Vorbereitung des totalen Krieges," *Neuer Vorwärts,* February 21, 1937.

58. Liebich, "Marxism and Totalitarianism," 223–40.

59. Liebich's analysis in ibid. focuses on Hilferding's writings in 1940. In my view, however, Hilferding had worked out the basic premises of his theory of the totalitarian state as early as 1935–1936. For this discussion, I am drawing on his article "Grundlagen der auswärtigen Politik," *Neuer Vorwärts,* November 15, 1936. Quotations in the next four paragraphs are from this article.

60. R. L. Worrall, "USSR: Proletarian or Capitalist State?" *Left* 39 (December 1939): 319–24; Hilferding, "State Capitalism or Totalitarian State Economy," reprinted in *The Marxists,* ed. C. Wright Mills (New York, 1962), 334–39. Pages will be cited in text.

61. See the "Grundsatzprogramm der Sozialdemokratischen Partei Deutschlands, Beschloßen vom Außerordentlichen Parteitag der SPD in Bad Godesberg vom 13.–15. November 1959," reprinted in Miller and Potthoff, *Kleine Geschichte der SPD,* 385–98. On the debate surrounding the program's principles, see 199–206.

62. Liebich, "Marxism and Totalitarianism," 240; Carl J. Friedrich et al., *Totalitarianism in Perspective: Three Views* (New York, 1969).

63. Franz Neumann, *Behemoth,* part 2, contains one of the earliest and most thorough criticisms of Hilferding's view of the Nazi economy. For more recent works dealing with the relationship between the economic and political spheres under fascism see Avraham Barkai, *Das Wirtschaftssystem des Nationalsozialismus* (Frankfurt am Main, 1988); and essays by Kurt Gossweiler, Brian Peterson, and John. D. Nagle in Dobkowski and Walliman, *Radical Perspectives,* 150–211.

64. Erich Matthias, "Bericht über das Schicksal Breitscheids und Hilferdings

(Mai 1940–Februar 1941)," in *Mit dem Gesicht nach Deutschland,* ed. Erich Matthias, 482 (hereafter cited as Matthias, "Bericht"). This report was prepared for the Sopade in the spring of 1941, probably by Fritz Heine. Kurt Kersten, "Das Ende Breitscheids und Hilferdings," *Deutsche Rundschau* 84 (September 1958): 843; Varian Fry, *Auslieferung auf Verlangen* (Vienna, 1986), 13–20, 75.

65. Kersten, "Das Ende Breitscheids und Hilferdings," 848.

66. Matthias, "Bericht," 482; Fry, *Auslieferung,* 34–35.

67. Fry, *Auslieferung,* 66–67.

68. Hilferding to Oscar and Margarethe Meyer, October 1940, Nachlaß Meyer, AR 7243, File 4, Leo Baeck Institute (LBI), New York; Matthias, "Bericht," 482–83.

69. Matthias, "Bericht," 483; Heinrich Brüning, *Brüning: Briefe und Gespräche, 1934–1945* (Stuttgart, 1974), 320, 326, 328–29; Hilferding to the Meyers, October (?), November 30, 1940, Nachlaß Meyer, AR 7243, File 4 (LBI).

70. Hilferding to the Meyers, October (?), 1940, Nachlaß Meyer, AR 7243, File 4 (LBI).

71. Hilferding to the Meyers, November 30, 1940, Nachlaß Meyer, AR 7243, File 4 (LBI).

72. Ibid.

73. Hilferding's essay was first published after 1945. Edited and introduced by Benedict Kautsky, it appeared under the title "Das historische Problem," in *Zeitschrift für Politik* (new series) 1 (1954): 293–324. See Gottschalch, *Strukturveränderungen,* chap. 8, for the best and most comprehensive discussion of this essay. Pages will be cited in the text.

74. Hilferding, *Finance Capital,* 23–24; Hilferding, "Das historische Problem," 296.

75. Here I agree with Gottschalch. For his detailed analysis, see *Strukturveränderungen,* 249–53. For Hilferding's discussion of Marx's famous comment on the relationship of the economic "base" and "superstructure" see "Das historische Problem," 301–3.

76. Hilferding, "Das historische Problem," 305.

77. Except where otherwise noted, the narrative below is based on Matthias, "Bericht," 482–87, and Fry, *Auslieferung,* 202–8.

78. According to Kersten, Geissler said, "Na, Ihr Sozialdemokröten!" Kersten did not provide his source for this statement. See "Das Ende Breitscheids und Hilferdings," 850.

79. On Hilferding's death see Masaaki Kurotaki, "Zur Todesursache Rudolf Hilferdings," *Beiträge der Miyagi-Gakuin Frauenhochschule* 61 (1984): 1–21. This article originally appeared in Japan. I used a copy located in the AdsD.

Hilferding died a prisoner but his wife, Rose, eventually escaped from France. After selling off most of her valuables, she left Paris in February and traveled southward to the border of the unoccupied zone. Upon her arrival she sold off the rest of her jewelry and hired a guide to smuggle her across the border. She succeeded and traveled to Arles, where she arrived at the Hotel Forum just after Hilferding's arrest. Unable to find out anything concrete about her husband's whereabouts, in March, she managed to go by ship to Portugal and—later on, via Trinidad—to the United States. The journey was extremely difficult and, after her arrival in New York, she was regarded as an enemy alien and had difficulty finding work. Eventually, she settled in

Massachusetts, where she died in 1959. On Rose Hilferding's flight, see Fritz Heine to the Sopade, March 27, 1941, and Rose Hilferding to Fritz Heine, June 24, 1941, SPD-Emigration, Mappe 54 (AdsD).

Rudolf Breitscheid was imprisoned first in Berlin and later on in Sachsenhausen and Buchenwald concentration camps. After the move to Sachsenhausen (1942), he was allowed to live with his wife in quarters allotted for special political prisoners. He was, in effect, a hostage. By 1943, the seventy-year-old was in terrible physical condition, but he remained alert and interested in politics. On September 14, 1944, Buchenwald was bombed. According to the Nazis, Breitscheid was killed in the attack, but it is also possible that he—like KPD leader Ernst Thälmann—was shot. Miraculously, Tony Breitscheid managed to survive the war. See Pistorius, *Rudolf Breitscheid*, 383–86.

AFTERWORD

1. For several years Hilferding's name has come up often in the politically charged discussions surrounding the renaming of streets in East Berlin. An early proposal by the "independent commission" responsible for renaming streets called for renaming part of the Rosa Luxemburg Straße after him (Luxemburg would retain "her" Platz). Then it was suggested that the Georgi Dimitrov Straße in Prenzlauer Berg become the Rudolf Hilferding Straße. Most recently his name—along with other deserving Weimar republicans—has been dropped from consideration. Monarchist heroes seem more acceptable to the commission. See "Straßen im Osten Berlins 'SED belastet,'" *Neues Deutschland*, January 20, 1994; Heinrich August Winkler, "Muß es unbedingt Otto Dibelius sein?" *Die Zeit* 27, June 30, 1995.

2. Beth Mintz and Michael Schwartz, *The Power Structure of American Business* (Chicago, 1985), 162–63.

3. Ibid., 220.

4. Rolf Behrens and Reiner Merkel, *Mergers and Acquisitions: Das Milliardengeschäft im gemeinsamen europäischen Markt* (Stuttgart, 1990), esp. chap. 2.

5. William Greider, *Secrets of the Temple: How the Federal Reserve Runs the Country* (New York, 1987). Greider's views have been largely confirmed by analysts across the political spectrum. See, for example, the works of Republican Kevin Phillips, *The Politics of Rich and Poor: Wealth and the American Electorate in the Reagan Aftermath* (New York, 1990), esp. chap. 6; and Communist Victor Perlo, *Super Profits and Crises: Modern U.S. Capitalism* (New York, 1988), chap. 9.

6. In the spring of 1994, the Deutsche Bank announced that its business volume for the preceding year had totaled 557 billion DM with a gross profit of 4.6 billion DM. As a point of comparison, the entire budget for the government of the Federal Republic was 480 billion DM. See "Deutsche Bank 'überrundet' Bundesetat," *Neues Deutschland*, April 5, 1994. For detailed information on the German banks see Rüdiger Liedtke, *Wem gehört die Republik?* (Frankfurt am Main, 1993), 113–16.

7. Hilferding, *Finance Capital*, 334.

8. John Cavanagh and Frederick Clairmonte, "The Transnational Economy: Transnational Corporations and Global Markets," reprint from *Trade and Development: An UNCTAD Review* 4 (winter 1982).

9. Cheryl Payer, *The World Bank: A Critical Analysis* (New York, 1982), 19.

10. Though, of course, capital remains dependent on the state to use force to secure its interests against any perceived threats. Thus, the capitalist powers, led by the United States, often intervene against societies that challenge the sanctity of private property and the "free" market system. Since 1945, although the threat of a war between the major imperial powers has been slight, imperialist military activity in the periphery—usually carried out in the name of "freedom" against "communism" or to protect "vital national interests"—has remained of central importance for the maintenance of the capitalist world order.

11. Among the flood of works recently devoted to this issue, a good starting point is William Greider, *One World, Ready or Not: The Manic Logic of Global Capitalism* (New York, 1997). See also the following two collections of articles: "Thema Weltmarkt," in *Die Neue Gesellschaft–Frankfurter Hefte* 8 (August 1995): 688–724; and "It's the Global Economy, Stupid: The Corporatization of the World," *The Nation*, July 15–22, 1996, pp. 9–32. The latter also contains an excellent resource guide for further exploration of the subject.

BIBLIOGRAPHY

THE PRINCIPAL WORK OF RUDOLF HILFERDING

BOOKS AND MONOGRAPHS

Arbeiterklasse und Konsumvereine: Ein Vortrag arrangiert von der Propagandakommission für das Genossenschaftswesen. Berlin, 1908.
Böhm-Bawerk's Criticism of Marx. Edited with introduction by Paul M. Sweezy. Translated by Eden and Cedar Paul. New York, 1949.
Böhm-Bawerks Marx Kritik. (Marx-Studien, vol. 1). Vienna, 1904.
Finance Capital: A Study of the Latest Phase of Capitalist Development. Edited and introduced by Tom Bottomore. Translated by Morris Watnick and Sam Gordon. London, 1981.
Das Finanzkapital: Eine Studie über die jüngste Entwicklung des Kapitalismus. Introduced by Eduard März. Frankfurt am Main, 1968.
Gegen das Moskauer Diktat. Leipzig, 1920.
"Das historische Problem." Unfinished manuscript. First edited and introduced by Benedikt Kautsky. *Zeitschrift für Politik* (New Series) 1.4 (December 1954): 293–324.
Nationalsozialismus und Marxismus. Berlin, 1932.
Preface (with Max Adler) to *Marx-Studien: Blätter zur Theorie und Politik des wissenschaftlichen Sozialismus, erster Band.* Vienna, 1904.

ARTICLES

Emil, Karl [pseudonym]. "Alter und neuer Despotismus." *Die Neue Zeit* 25.2 (1906–1907): 409–11.
———. "Antimilitarismus." *Die Neue Zeit* 25.2 (1906–1907): 241–45.
———. "Die Auflösung des Reichstags und die Klassengegensätze in Deutschland." *Die Neue Zeit* 25.1 (1906–1907): 388–93.
———. "Die bürgerlichen Parteien und der Militarismus." *Die Neue Zeit* 25.2 (1906–1907): 132–34.
———. "Der Freisinn und unser Wahlkampf." *Die Neue Zeit* 26.2 (1907–1908): 85.
———. "Der Internationale Kongress in Stuttgart." *Die Neue Zeit* 25.2 (1906–1907): 660–67.
———. "Die Konferenz der Parteiredakteure." *Die Neue Zeit* 25.1 (1906–1907): 652–55.
———. "Die Wahlen in Österreich." *Die Neue Zeit* 25.2 (1906–1907): 209–11.
Hilferding, Rudolf. "Arbeitsgemeinschaft der Klassen?" *Der Kampf* 8 (1915): 321–29.

———. "Aufbau des Rätesystems!" *Die Freiheit,* February 5, 1919 (M).

———. "Die Aufgaben der Reichsbank." *Vorwärts,* August 9, 1923 (E).

———. "Aus der Vorgeschichte der Marxschen Ökonomie." *Die Neue Zeit* 29.2 (1910–1911): 620–23.

———. "Der Austritt aus der Regierung." *Die Gesellschaft* 7.1 (1930): 385–88.

———. "Der Balkankrieg und die Großmächte." *Die Neue Zeit* 31.1 (1912–1913): 77–82.

———. "Die Einigung der deutschen Arbeiterklasse." *Der Kampf* 14 (1921): 1–7.

———. "Die Einigung des Proletariats." *Die Freiheit,* February 9, 1919 (M).

———. "Die Entwicklung der Valuta und die Ursachen der Wirtschaftskrise" *Die Freiheit,* May 26, 28, 29, 1920 (M). Lecture series.

——— "Die Erneuerung des Dreibundes." *Die Neue Zeit* 31.1 (1912–1913): 458–66.

———. "Europäer nicht Mitteleuropäer!" *Der Kampf* 8 (1915): 357–65.

———. "Der Funktionswechsel des Schutzzolles: Tendenz der modernen Handelspolitik." *Die Neue Zeit* 21.2 (1902–1903): 274–81.

———. "Grundlagen der auswärtigen Politik." *Neuer Vorwärts,* November 15, 1936.

———. "Hermann Müller." *Die Gesellschaft* 8.1 (1931): 289–92.

———. "Historische Notwendigkeit und notwendige Politik." *Der Kampf* 8 (1915): 206–15.

———. "Das historische Problem." *Zeitschrift für Politik* (New Series) 1 (1954), 293–324.

———. "In die Gefahrenzone." *Die Gesellschaft* 7.2 (1930): 289–97.

———. "Die industrielle Depression." *Die Neue Zeit* 26.1 (1907–1908): 591–94.

———. "In Krisennot." *Die Gesellschaft* 8.1 (1931): 1–8.

———. "Die Internationale." *Der Kampf* 12 (1919): 522.

———. "Die Internationale." Parts 1, 2, and 3. *Die Freiheit,* July 19, 23, 24 (M).

———. "Ein Irrweg." *Vorwärts,* October 10, 1931.

———. "Kampf und Ziel des revolutionären Sozialismus: Die Politik der Sozialdemokratischen Partei Deutschlands." *Neuer Vorwärts,* January 28, 1934.

———. "Klarheit!" *Die Freiheit,* November 23, 1918 (M).

———. "Die Kolonialpolitik und der Zusammenbruch." *Die Neue Zeit* 25.2 (1906–1907): 687–88.

———. "Der Konflikt in der deutschen Sozialdemokratie." *Der Kampf* 9 (1916): 14.

———. "Die Konjunktur." *Die Neue Zeit* 25.2 (1906–1907): 140–53.

———. "Die Krise der Internationale." *Der Sozialist* 5 (1919): 694–96.

———. "Die Krise in den Vereinigten Staaten." *Die Neue Zeit* 26.1 (1907–1908): 526–33.

———. "Kritisches Mißverständnis oder mißverständliche Kritik." *Die Neue Zeit* 33.2 (1914–1915): 716–17.

———. "Ein neutraler Sozialist über sozialistische Neutralität." *Der Kampf* 8 (1915): 270–72.

———. "Parlamentarismus und Massenstreik." *Die Neue Zeit* 23.2 (1904–1905): 804–16.

———. "Der Parteitag von Magdeburg." *Die Neue Zeit* 28.2 (1909–1910): 892–900.

———. "Phantasie oder Gelehrsamkeit." *Der Kampf* 9 (1916): 54–63.

———. "Die politischen und ökonomischen Machtverhältnisse und die Sozialisierung." In *Zwischen den Stühlen, oder über die Unvereinbarkeit von Theorie und Praxis: Schriften Rudolf Hilferdings,* edited by Cora Stephan. Bonn, 1982.

———. "Politische Probleme, zum Aufruf Wirths und zur Rede Silverbergs." *Die Gesellschaft* 3.2 (1926): 289–302.

———. "Probleme der Zeit." *Die Gesellschaft* 1.1 (1924): 1–17.

———. "Realistischer Pazifismus." *Die Gesellschaft* 1.2 (1924): 97–114.

———. "Der Revisionismus und die Internationale." *Die Neue Zeit* 27.2 (1908–1909): 161–74.

———. "Revolutionäres Vertrauen!" *Die Freiheit.* November 18, 1918 (M).

———. "Das Schuldbekenntnis." *Die Freiheit,* December 27, 1918 (E).

———. "Die Sozialdemokratie am Scheideweg." *Die Neue Zeit* 33.2 (1914–1915): 489–99.

———. "Sozialdemokratische Steuerpolitik." *Die Neue Zeit* 30.2 (1911–1912): 221–25.

———. "Sozialismus und Eigentum." *Sozialistische Bildung* (February 1932): 32.

———. "Sozialistische Betrachtungen zum Weltkriege." *Die Neue Zeit* 33.2 (1914–1915). 843–44.

———. "State Capitalism or Totalitarian State Economy." *Socialist Courier.* New York, 1940. Reprinted in *The Marxists,* ed. C. Wright Mills. New York, 1962.

———. "Taktische Probleme." *Der Kampf* 12 (1919): 839–41.

———. "Taktische Probleme." *Die Freiheit,* December 11, 1919 (M).

———. "Taumel." *Die Neue Zeit* 31.1 (1912–1913), 849.

———. "Theoretische Bemerkungen zur Agrarfrage." *Die Gesellschaft* 4.1 (1927): 421–32.

———. "Totentanz." *Die Neue Zeit* 31.1 (1912–1913), 746.

———. "Um die Zukunft der deutschen Arbeiterbewegung." *Die Neue Zeit* 34.2 (1915–1916): 167–75.

———. "Unter der Drohung des Faschismus." *Die Gesellschaft* 9.1 (1932), 3–6.

———. "Der Wahlrechtskampf in Preußen." *Der Kampf* 3 (1909–1910): 313.

———. "Wandel in der Politik." *Frankfurter Zeitung,* December 31, 1922 (second morning edition).

———. "Die Weltpolitik, das Reparationsproblem und die Konferenz von Genoa." *Schmollers Jahrbuch* 45 (1923): 1–28.

———. "Das Zuckerkontingent." *Die Deutsche Worte* 23 (1903): 278.

———. "Zum Parteitag." *Die Neue Zeit* 31.2 (1912–1913): 873–80.

———. "Zur Frage des Generalstreiks." *Die Neue Zeit* 22.1 (1903–1904): 134–42.

———. "Zur Geschichte der Werttheorie." *Die Neue Zeit* 21.2 (1902–1903): 213–17.

———. "Zwischen den Entscheidungen." *Die Gesellschaft* 10.1 (1933): 1–9.

Kern, Richard [pseudonym]. "Das Ende der Volkerbundpolitik." *Zeitschrift für Sozialismus* 2 (1934–1935): 621–37.

———. "Finanzielle Reichszerstörung." *Neuer Vorwärts,* July 9, 1933.

———. "Hitler ohne Maske, Verrat am Sozialismus." *Neuer Vorwärts,* July 16, 1933.

―――. "Die Internationale vor der Entscheidung." *Der Kampf* 27 (1934): 41–47.

―――. "Korporationen, Stände und Monopole." *Neuer Vorwärts*, December 3, 1933.

―――. "Das Londoner Abkommen." *Zeitschrift für Sozialismus* 2 (1934–1935): 561–68.

―――. "Macht ohne Diplomatie—Diplomatie ohne Macht." *Zeitschrift für Sozialismus* 2 (1934–1935): 593–604.

―――. "Die Reichsbank als Geldmaschine." *Neuer Vorwärts*, October 20, 1933.

―――. "Revolutionärer Sozialismus." *Zeitschrift für Sozialismus* 1 (1933–1934): 145–52.

―――. "Sklaverei in den Betrieben, Despotie des Kapitals." *Neuer Vorwärts*, July 2, 1933.

―――. "Totaler Staat, totaler Bankrott, verantwortungslose Wirtschaft im Dritten Reich." *Neuer Vorwärts*, June 18, 1933.

―――. "Die Vorbereitung des totalen Krieges." *Neuer Vorwärts*, February 21, 1937.

―――. "Die Zeit und die Aufgabe." *Sozialistische Revolution* 1 (1933–1934): 1–3. (*Sozialistische Revolution* was the original title given to the *ZfS*.)

PUBLISHED SPEECHES

Arbeiterklasse und Konsumvereine. Berlin, 1908.

Zur Sozialisierungsfrage: Referat auf dem 10. Deutschen Gewerkschaftskongress vom 30. Juni bis 5. Juli 1919 zu Nürnberg. Berlin, 1919.

Revolutionäre Politik oder Machtillusionen? Rede gegen Sinowjew auf dem Parteitag der USPD Halle. Berlin, 1920.

Die Sozialisierung und die Machtverhältnisse der Klassen: Referat auf dem 1. Betriebsrätekongress, gehalten am 5. Oktober 1920. Berlin, 1920.

Für die soziale Republik. Berlin, 1924.

Gesellschaftsmacht oder Privatmacht über die Wirtschaft: Referat gehalten auf dem 4. AfA-Gewerkschaftskongress Leipzig 1931. Berlin, 1931.

NEWSPAPERS AND PERIODICALS CONTRIBUTED TO OR EDITED BY HILFERDING

Breslauer Volkswacht (1930)
Deutsche Worte (1903)
Die Frankfurter Zeitung (1922)
Die Freiheit (1918–1922)
Die Gesellschaft (1924–1933)
Der Kampf (1907–1934)
Le mouvement socialiste (1899)
Die Neue Zeit (1902–1917)
Neuer Vorwärts (1933–1940)
Schmollers Jahrbuch (1923, 1928)
Der Sozialist (1919–1921)
Vorwärts (1907–1933)
Die Zeitschrift für Sozialismus (1933–1936)

PRIMARY WORKS

ARCHIVAL SOURCES

Archiv der sozialen Demokratie, Bonn.
Nachlaß Paul Hertz
Nachlaß Hermann Müller
Nachlaß Carl Giebel
SPD-Emigration
International Institute for Social History, Amsterdam.
Nachlaß Karl Kautsky
Nachlaß Leon Trotsky
Bundesarchiv, Koblenz.
Nachlaß Hermann Punder
Bundesarchiv, Potsdam.
Nachlaß Konrad Haenisch
Sozialisierungskommission, 1918–1923: 31.05
Bildung und Auflösung der ersten Sozialisierungskommission, vol. 1. Nov. 1918–April 1919.
Sozialisierungskommission und Sozialisierung: Überblick über die Arbeiten der Sozialisierungskommission und der österreichischen Staatskommission für Sozialisierung, vol. 1, Juli 1919–März 1922.
Privatbriefe von Kommissionsmitgliedern, vol. 1. Dez. 1918–April 1919.
Reichsarbeitsministerium 39.01, Nr. 10504, Film 37068
"Material über die Konferenz von Genua," 1, 23.
Vorläufiger Reichswirtschaftsrat: 04.01, Filme 53932, Nr. 129; Film 53949, Nr. 284; Film 53950, Nr. 287.
Leo Baeck Institute, New York.
Nachlaß Oscar Meyer
Stiftung Archiv der Parteien und Massenorganisationen der DDR im Bundesarchiv, Berlin.
Walter Ulbricht: Reden und Aufsätze. März–Mai, 1936. NL 182/198.

PUBLISHED DOCUMENTS AND RECORDS OF PARTY AND LEGISLATIVE PROCEEDINGS

Akten der Reichskanzlei, Weimarer Republik: Das Kabinett Stresemann I, 13. August 1923 bis 6. October 1923. Edited by Karl Dietrich Erdmann and Martin Vogt. Historische Kommission bei der Bayerischen Akademie der Wissenschaften und das Bundesarchiv. Boppard am Rhein, 1978.
Akten der Reichskanzlei, Weimarer Republik: Das Kabinett Muller II, 3. Juli 1928 bis 27. März 1930. 2 vols. Edited by Martin Vogt. Historische Kommission bei der Bayerischen Akademie der Wissenschaften und das Bundesarchiv. Boppard am Rhein, 1970.
Allgemeiner Kongress der Arbeiter- und Soldatenräte Deutschlands, vom 16. bis 21. Dezember 1918 im Abgeordnetenhaus zu Berlin: Stenographischer Bericht. Edited by Friedrich Helm and Peter Schmitt-Egner. Glashütten im Taunus, 1972.
Anpassung oder Widerstand? Aus den Akten des Parteivorstands der deutschen

Sozialdemokratie, 1932–1933. Edited by Hagen Schulze. Bonn–Bad Godesberg, 1975.

Bericht der Sozialisierungskommission über die Frage der Sozialisierung des Kohlen-berghaues vom 31. Juli 1920. Anhang: Vorläufiger Bericht vom 15. Februar 1919. Berlin, 1920.

Bericht über die Reichskonferenz der Unabhängigen Sozialdemokratischen Partei Deutschlands am 9. und 10. September 1919 im Abgeordnetenhaus zu Berlin. Edited by Hartfrid Krause. Glashütten im Taunus, 1975.

Buchholz, Marlis, and Bernd Rother, eds. *Der Parteivorstand der SPD im Exil: Protokolle der Sopade, 1933–1940.* Bonn, 1995.

Degras, Jane, ed. *Documents of the Communist International.* Vol. 1, *1919–1922.* London, 1955.

Deutsch-sowjetische Beziehungen von den Verhandlungen in Brest-Litovsk bis zum Abschluss des Rapallovertrages. East Berlin, 1971.

Die Gewerkschaften in der Endphase der Republik, 1930–1933. Compiled, annotated, and introduced by Peter Jahn. Vol. 4, *Quellen zur Geschichte der deutschen Arbeiterbewegung im 20. Jahrhundert.* Edited by Hermann Weber, Klaus Schönhoven, and Klaus Tenfelde. Cologne, 1987.

Protokoll der Verhandlungen des 10. Deutschen Gewerkschaftskongresses vom 30. Juni bis 5. Juli 1919 zu Nürnberg. Berlin, 1919.

Protokoll der Verhandlungen des 13. Kongresses der Gewerkschaften Deutschlands (3. Bundestag des Allgemeinen Deutschen Gewerkschaftsbundes), abgehalten in Hamburg vom 3. bis 7. September 1928. Berlin, 1928.

Protokoll des Kongresses der Sozialistischen Arbeiter-Internationale. Vol. 2, *Marseilles, August 1925.* Glasshütten im Taunus, 1974.

Protokolle der Sitzungen des Parteiausschußes der Sozialdemokratischen Partei Deutschlands, 1912–1921. Edited by Dieter Dowe, introduction by Friedhelm Boll. Bonn, 1980.

Protokolle der Parteitage der Unabhängigen Sozialdemokratischen Partei Deutschlands, 1917–1922. 5 vols. Glashütten im Taunus, 1975.

Riddell, John, ed. *The German Revolution and the Debate on Soviet Power, Documents, 1918–1919: Preparing the Founding Congress.* New York, 1986.

Rinner, Erich, ed. *Deutschlandberichte der Sozialdemokratischen Partie Deutschlands (Sopade): Februar 1938.* Frankfurt am Main, 1980.

Sozialdemokratische Parteikorrespondenz, 1923–1928. Berlin 1930.

Sozialdemokratische Partei Deutschlands. *Protokoll der Sozialdemokratischen Parteitage in Augsburg, Gera und Nürnberg, 1922.* Bonn–Bad Godesberg, 1922. Reprint, 1974.

———. *Sozialdemokratischer Parteitag 1925 in Heidelberg. Protokoll mit dem Bericht der Frauenfernz.* Bonn–Bad Godesberg, 1925. Reprint, 1974.

———. *Sozialdemokratischer Parteitag 1927 in Kiel. Protokoll . . . .* Bonn–Bad Godesberg, 1927. Reprint, 1974.

———. *Sozialdemokratischer Parteitag 1929 in Magdeburg. Protokoll . . . .* Bonn–Bad Godesberg, 1929. Reprint, 1974.

———. *Sozialdemokratischer Parteitag 1931 in Leipzig. Protokoll . . . .* Bonn–Bad Godesberg, 1931. Reprint, 1974.

Stephan, Cora, "Geld und Staatstheorie in Hilferdings Finanzkapital." In *Beiträge zur Marxschen Theorie,* edited by Günther Busch, 2:111–54. Frankfurt am Main, 1974.

————, ed. *Zwischen den Stühlen, oder über die Unvereinbarkeit von Theorie und Praxis: Schriften Rudolf Hilferdings*. Bonn, 1982.

Verhandlungen der Sozialisierungskommission über den Kohlenbergbau im Jahre 1920. Vol. 2. Berlin, 1920.

Verhandlungen der Sozialisierungskommission über den Kohlenbergbau im Winter 1918–1919. Berlin, 1921.

Verhandlungen des Reichstages: Stenographische Berichte der Sitzungen, 1920–1933. Berlin, 1920–1933.

Published Memoirs, Diaries, and Letters

Adler, Victor. *Victor Adler: Briefwechsel mit August Bebel und Karl Kautsky*. Edited by Friedrich Adler. Vienna, 1954.

Braun, Otto. *Von Weimar zu Hitler*. New York, 1940.

Braunthal, Julius. *In Search of the Millenium*. London, 1945.

Brüning, Heinrich. *Briefe und Gespräche, 1934–1945*. Edited by Claire Nix. Stuttgart, 1974.

————. *Memoiren, 1918–1934*. Stuttgart, 1970.

Emil, Karl [pseudonym]. See Articles by Rudolf Hilferding

Fry, Varian. *Auslieferung auf Verlangen: Die Rettung deutscher Emigranten in Marseille, 1940–1941*. Edited and with an appendix by Wolfgang E. Elfe and Jan Hans. Vienna, 1986.

Geyer, Curt. *Die revolutionäre Illusion: Zur Geschichte des linken Flügels der USPD. Erinnerungen von Curt Geyer*. Edited by Wolfgang Benz and Hermann Graml. Stuttgart, 1976.

Kautsky, Karl. *Erinnerungen und Erörterungen*. Edited by Benedict Kautsky. The Hague, 1960.

Kautsky, Karl Jr., ed. *August Bebels Briefwechsel mit Karl Kautsky*. Assen, 1971.

Kern, Richard [pseudonym]. See Articles by Rudolf Hilferding.

Kessler, Harry Graf. *Tagebücher, 1918–1937*. Edited by Wolfgang Pfeiffer-Belli. Frankfurt am Main, 1961.

Keil, Wilhelm. *Erlebnisse eines Sozialdemokraten*. Vol. 2. Stuttgart, 1948.

Krosigk, Lutz Graf Schwerin von. *Es geschah in Deutschland*. Tübingen, 1951.

————. *Memoiren*. Stuttgart, 1977.

Leber, Julius. *Ein Mann geht seinen Weg: Schriften, Reden und Briefe von Julius Leber*. Berlin, 1952.

Luther, Hans. *Politiker ohne Partei: Erinnerungen*. Stuttgart, 1960.

Marx, Karl, and Friedrich Engels. *Selected Correspondence*. Edited by S. W. Ryazanskaya. Translated by I. Lasker. Moscow, 1975.

Matthias, Erich, ed. *Mit dem Gesicht nach Deutschland: Eine Dokumentation über die sozialdemokratische Emigration, aus dem Nachlaß Friedrich Stampfer, ergänzt durch andere Überlieferungen*. Düsseldorf, 1968.

Matthias, Erich, and Susanne Miller, eds. *Das Kriegstagebuch des Reichstagsabgeordneten Eduard David, 1914–1918*. Düsseldorf, 1966.

Meyer, Oscar. *Von Bismarck zu Hitler*. New York, 1944.

Möller, Alex. *Tatort Politik*. Munich, 1982.

Radbruch, Gustav. *Der Innere Weg: Abriß meines Lebens*. Stuttgart, 1951.

Renner, Karl. *An der Wende zweier Zeiten: Lebenserinnerungen*. Vienna, 1946.

Schnitzler, Arthur. *Jugend in Wien*. Vienna, 1968.
Sender, Toni. *The Autobiography of a German Rebel*. New York, 1939.
Severing, Carl. *Mein Lebensweg*. Cologne, 1950.
Stampfer, Friedrich. *Erfahrungen und Erkenntnisse: Aufzeichnungen aus meinem Leben*. Cologne, 1957.
————. *Die vierzehn Jahre der ersten deutschen Republik*. Hamburg, 1947.
Stresemann, Gustav. *Vermächtnis: Der Nachlaß in drei Bänden*. Edited by H. Bernhard. Berlin, 1932–1933.
Sturmthal, Adolf. *Democracy under Fire: Memoirs of a European Socialist*. Durham, 1989.
Trotsky, Leon. *My Life*. New York, 1970.
Woytinsky, W. S. *Stormy Passage: A Personal History through Two Russian Revolutions to Democracy and Freedom, 1905–1960*. New York, 1961.
Zweig, Stephan. *Die Welt von Gestern*. Stockholm, 1944.

SECONDARY WORKS

Abelshauser, Werner, ed. *Die Weimarer Republik als Wohlfahrtsstaat: Zum Verhältnis von Wirtschafts- und Sozialpolitik in der Industriegesellschaft*. Stuttgart, 1987.
Abendroth, Wolfgang. *Aufstieg und Krise der deutschen Sozialdemokratie*. Frankfurt am Main, 1964.
Abraham, David. *The Collapse of the Weimar Republik*. 2d ed. New York, 1986.
Adler, Max. "Demokratie als Ziel und als Mittel: Über marxistische Staatsauffassung." *Der Klassenkampf* 2.10 (1928): 292–98.
Adolph, Hans J. L. *Otto Wels und die Politik der deutschen Sozialdemokratie, 1894–1939*. Berlin, 1971.
Albers, Detlev, Horst Heimann, and Richard Saage, eds. *Otto Bauer: Theorie und Politik*. Berlin, 1985.
Barkai, Avraham. *Das Wirtschaftssystem des Nationalsozialismus*. Frankfurt am Main, 1988.
Bauer, Otto. "Austromarxismus." In *Austromarxismus*, edited by Hans-Jörg Sandkühler and Rafael de la Vega, 49–51. Vienna, 1970.
————. *Bolschewismus und Sozialdemokratie*. Vienna, 1921.
————. "Das Finanzkapital." *Der Kampf* 3 (1909–1911): 391–97.
————. "Das Gleichgewicht der Klassenkräfte." In *Austromarxismus*, edited by Hans-Jörg Sandkühler and Rafael de la Vega, 91–96. Vienna, 1970.
————. *Die österreichische Revolution*. Vienna, 1965.
————. *Der Weg zum Sozialismus*. Vienna, 1919.
Behrens, Rolf, and Reiner Merkel. *Mergers and Acquisitions: Das Milliardengeschäft im gemeinsamen europäischen Markt*. Stuttgart, 1990.
Beller, Steven. *Vienna and the Jews, 1867–1938: A Cultural History*. Cambridge, 1989.
Bernstein, Eduard. "Das Finanzkapital und die Handelspolitik." *Sozialistische Monatshefte* 15 (1911): 947–55.
————. *Die Voraussetzungen des Sozialismus und die Aufgaben der Sozialdemokratie*. Berlin, 1921; reprint, Bonn, 1971.
Bessel, Richard. "Why Did the Weimar Republic Collapse?" In *Weimar: Why Did*

German Democracy Fail? edited by Ian Kershaw, 120–52. New York, 1990.

Blum, Mark E. *The Austro-Marxists, 1890–1918: A Psychobiographical Study.* Lexington, 1985.

Borchardt, Knut. *Wachstum, Krisen, Handlungsspielräume der Wirtschaftspolitik.* Göttingen, 1982.

Bottomore, Tom, and Patrick Goode, eds. *Austro-Marxism.* Oxford, 1978.

Boyer, John W. *Culture and Political Crisis in Vienna: Christian Socialism in Power, 1897–1918.* Chicago, 1995.

Braunthal, Julius. *History of the International.* 2 vols. New York, 1967.

———. "Otto Bauer: Ein Lebensbild." In *Otto Bauer: Eine Auswahl aus seinem Lebenswerk,* edited by Julius Braunthal. Vienna, 1961.

Breitman, Richard. *German Socialism and Weimar Democracy.* Chapel Hill, 1981.

Bronner, Stephen Eric. *A Revolutionary for Our Times: Rosa Luxemburg.* London, 1981.

Buchheim, Hans. *Totalitarian Rule: Its Nature and Characteristics.* Middletown, Conn., 1986.

Bukharin, Nikolay Ivanovich. *Imperialism and World Economy.* New York, 1929.

———. *Ökonomie der Transformationsperiode.* Hamburg, 1922.

Busch, Günther, ed. *Beiträge zur Marxschen Theorie.* Vol. 2. Frankfurt am Main, 1974.

Calkins, Kenneth R. *Hugo Haase: Democrat and Revolutionary.* Durham, 1979.

Cavanagh, John, and Frederick Clairmonte. "The Transnational Economy: Transnational Corporations and Global Markets." *Trade and Development: An UNCTAD Review* 4 (winter 1982).

Coakley, Jerry. "Finance Capital." *Capital and Class* 17 (summer 1982): 134–41.

Cohen, Steven F. *Bukharin and the Bolshevik Revolution: A Political Biography, 1888–1938.* New York, 1973.

Cole, G. D. H. *Selbstverwaltung in der Industrie.* Translated by R. Thesing. Introduction by Rudolf Hilferding. 5th ed. Berlin, 1921.

Craig, Gordon. *Germany, 1866–1945.* New York, 1978.

Deutscher, Isaac. *The Non-Jewish Jew and Other Essays.* Oxford, 1968.

Dieckmann, Hildemarie, and Johannes Popitz. *Entwicklung und Wirksamkeit in der zeit der Weimarer Republik.* Berlin-Dahlem, 1960.

Dobkowski, Michael N., and Isidor Walliman, eds. *Radical Perspectives on the Rise of Fascism in Germany, 1919–1945.* New York, 1989.

Ebbinghaus, Rolf, ed. *Monopol und Staat: Zur Marxrezeption in der Theorie des staatsmonopolistischen Kapitalismus.* Frankfurt am Main, 1975.

Edinger, Lewis J. *German Exile Politics: The Social Democratic Executive Committee in the Nazi Era.* Berkeley and Los Angeles, 1956.

Eisfeld, Gerhard, and Kurt Koszyk, eds. *Die Presse der deutschen Sozialdemokratie.* 2d. ed. Bonn, 1980

Engels, Friedrich. "Einleitung" [zu "Die Klassenkämpfe in Frankreich, 1848–1850," von Karl Marx (Ausgabe 1895)]. In *Werke,* by Karl Marx and Friedrich Engels, vol. 7. East Berlin, 1964.

———. *The Origin of the Family, Private Property, and the State.* Moscow, 1977.

Eyck, Eric. *A History of the Weimar Republic.* 2 vols. New York, 1962.

Feldman, Gerald D. *The Great Disorder: Politics, Economics, and Society in the German Inflation, 1914–1924.* New York, 1993.

Feldman, Gerald, and Otto Busch, eds. *Historische Prozesse der deutschen Inflation, 1914–1924: Ein Tagungsbericht.* Berlin, 1978.

Fowkes, Ben. *Communism in Germany under the Weimar Republic.* London, 1984.

Fricke, Dieter. *Die deutsche Arbeiterbewegung, 1869–1914: Ein Handbuch über ihre Organisation und Tätigkeit im Klassenkampf.* East Berlin, 1976.

Friedrich, Carl J., et al. *Totalitarianism in Perspective: Three Views.* New York, 1969.

Fülberth, Georg, and Jürgen Harrer. *Die deutsche Sozialdemokratie, 1890–1933.* Darmstadt, 1974.

Gay, Peter. *The Dilemma of Democratic Socialism.* New York, 1952.

Geary, Dick. "Employers, Workers, and the Collapse of the Weimar Republic." In *Weimar: Why Did German Democracy Fail?* edited by Ian Kershaw. New York, 1990.

Glaser, Ernst. *Im Umfeld des Austromarxismus: Ein Beitrag zur Geistesgeschichte des österreichischen Sozialismus.* Vienna, 1981.

Gleissberg, Gerhard. *SPD und Gesellschaftssystem: Aktualität der Programmdiskussion 1934 bis 1946, Dokumente und Kommentar.* Frankfurt am Main, 1973.

Goldberg, Harvey. *The Life of Jean Jaurès.* Madison, 1962.

Goldberg, Robert A. *Grassroots Resistance: Social Movements in Twentieth Century America.* Belmont, 1991.

Gottschalch, Wilfried. *Strukturveränderungen der Gesellschaft und politisches Handeln in der Lehre von Rudolf Hilferding.* Berlin, 1962.

Grasmann, Peter. *Sozialdemokraten gegen Hitler, 1933–1945.* Munich, 1976.

Grebing, Helga. *History of the German Labor Movement: A Survey.* 3d rev. ed. London, 1985.

———. *Der Revisionismus: Von Bernstein bis zum "Prager Frühling".* Munich, 1977.

Greider, William. *One World, Ready or Not: The Manic Logic of Global Capitalism.* New York, 1997.

———. *Secrets of the Temple: How the Federal Reserve Runs the Country.* New York, 1987.

Groh, Dieter. *Negative Integration und revolutionärer Attentismus: Die Sozialdemokratie am Vorabend des ersten Weltkrieges.* Frankfurt am Main, 1973.

Guttsman, W. L. *The German Social Democratic Party, 1875–1933.* London, 1981.

Haffner, Sebastian. *Die deutsche Revolution, 1918–1919.* Munich, 1979.

Hagelstange, Thomas. "'Finanzkapital': Hilferdings Erklärung des modernen Kapitalismus." *Beiträge zum wissenschaftlichen Sozialismus* 8 (September 1976): 52–77.

Harms, Bernhard, ed. *Kapital und Kapitalismus.* Vol. 1. Berlin, 1931.

Harsch, Donna. *German Social Democracy and the Rise of Nazism.* Chapel Hill, 1993.

Hauschild, Dr. *Der vorläufige Reichswirtschaftsrat, 1920–1926: Denkschrift.* Berlin, 1926.

Heller, K. D. *Ernst Mach: Wegbereiter der modernen Physik.* Vienna, 1964.

Henning, F. W. *Das industrialisierte Deutschland, 1914 bis 1978.* Paderborn, 1979.

Hobson, J. A. *Imperialism: A Study.* 1902. Reprint, Ann Arbor, 1983.

Holtfrerich, Carl-Ludwig. "Economic Policy Options and the End of the Weimar Republic." In *Weimar: Why Did German Democracy Fail?* edited by Ian Kershaw. New York, 1990.

Huber, Wolfgang, and Johannes Schwerdtfeger, eds. *Frieden, Gewalt, Sozialismus:*

Studien zur Geschichte der sozialistischen Arbeiterbewegung. Stuttgart, 1976.

Hunt, Richard N. *German Social Democracy, 1918–1933.* New Haven, 1964.

Inselmann, Claus. "'Die Gesellschaft': Ein Rückblick auf eine Zeitschrift der Weimarer Zeit." *Die Neue Gesellschaft* 11 (1964): 321–34.

James, Harold. "Economic Reasons for the Collapse of Weimar." In *Weimar: Why Did German Democracy Fail?* edited by Ian Kershaw, 30–57. New York, 1990.

———. *The German Slump: Politics and Economics, 1924–1936.* Oxford, 1986.

———. "Rudolf Hilferding and the Application of the Political Economy of the Second International." *Historical Journal* 24 (1981): 847–69.

Jones, Larry Eugene. *German Liberalism and the Dissolution of the Weimar Party System, 1918–1933.* Chapel Hill, 1988.

Jones, William David. "Before the Cold War: On the Origins, Development, and Varieties of Leftwing Anti-Totalitarianism as shown in the Writings of Selected German Socialist Intellictuals, 1928–1944" (Ph.D. diss., Claremont Graduate School, 1992). To be published in 1998 by the University of Illinois Press.

Kamenka, Eugene, and Krygier, Martin. *Bureaucracy: The Career of a Concept.* New York, 1979.

Kautsky, John A. "J. A. Schumpeter and Karl Kautsky: Parallel Theories of Imperialism." *Midwest Journal of Political Science* 5.2 (1961): 101–28.

———, ed. *Karl Kautsky and the Social Science of Classical Marxism.* New York, 1989.

Kautsky, Karl. "Finanzkapital und Krisen." *Die Neue Zeit* 29.1 (1910–1911): 74–83.

———. "Der Imperialismus." *Die Neue Zeit* 32.2 (1914): 908–22.

———. *Der Weg zur Macht.* Berlin, 1910.

Kershaw, Ian, ed. *Weimar: Why Did German Democracy Fail?* New York, 1990.

Kersten, Kurt. "Das Ende Breitscheids und Hilferdings." *Deutsche Rundschau* 84 (September 1958): 843–54.

Knapp, Vincent. *Austrian Social Democracy, 1889–1914.* Washington, 1980.

Kolb, Eberhard. *Die Arbeiterräte in der deutschen Innenpolitik, 1918–1919.* Düsseldorf, 1962.

———. *The Weimar Republic.* Translated by P. S. Falla. London, 1988.

Könke, Günter. *Organisierter Kapitalismus, Sozialdemokratie und Staat: Eine Studie zur Ideologie der sozialdemokratischen Arbeiterbewegungen in der Weimarer Republik.* Stuttgart, 1987.

Korsch, Karl. *Marxism and Philosophy.* New York, 1970.

Kozlov, Nicholas N., and Eric D. Weitz. "Reflections on the 'Third Period': Bukharin, the Comintern, and the Political Economy of Weimar Germany." *Journal of Contemporary History* 24.3 (1989): 387–410.

Krause, Hartfrid. *USPD: Zur Geschichte der Unabhängigen Sozialdemokratischen Partei Deutschlands.* Frankfurt am Main, 1975.

Krohn, Claus Dieter. "Helfferich contra Hilferding: Konservative Geldpolitik und die sozialen Folgen der deutschen Inflation, 1918–1923." *Vierteljahresschrift für Sozial- und Wirtschaftsgeschichte* 62.1 (1975): 62–92.

Krumbein, Wolfgang. "Vorläufer eines 'Dritten Weges zum Sozialismus?'" In *Solidargemeinschaft und Klassenkampf: Politische Konzeptionen der Sozialdemokratie zwischen den Weltkriegen,* edited by Richard Saage. Frankfurt am Main, 1986.

Kruse, Wolfgang. *Krieg und nationale Integration: Eine Neuinterpretation des sozialdemokratischen Burgfriedensschlußes, 1914–1915.* Essen, 1993.

Kurata, Minoru. "Die Entstehung von Hilferdings *Finanzkapital.*" *Review of the Liberal Arts* 62 (1981): 65–98. Published in Japan.

———. "Rudolf Hilferding: Bibliographie seiner Schriften, Artikel und Briefe." *Internationale wissenschaftliche Korrespondenz zur Geschichte der Arbeiterbewegung* 10 (1974): 327–46.

———. "Rudolf Hilferding, Wiener Zeit: Eine Biographie (1)." *Economic Review* 26.2 (1975): 17–25. Published in Japan.

———. "Rudolf Hilferding, Wiener Zeit: Eine Biographie (2)." *Economic Review* 29.2 (1978): 25–35.

———. "Rudolf Hilferding, Wiener Zeit: Eine Biographie (3)." *Economic Review* 30.1 (1979): 54–64.

Kurotaki, Masaaki. "Zur Todesursache Rudolf Hilferdings." *Beiträge der Miyagi-Gakuin Frauenhochschule* 61 (December 1984): 1–21. Published in Japan.

Lehnert, Detlef. *Sozialdemokratie zwischen Protestbewegung und Regierungspartei, 1848 bis 1983.* Frankfurt am Main, 1983.

———. "'Staatspartei der Republik' oder 'revolutionäre Reformisten'? Die Sozialdemokraten." In *Politische Identität und nationale Gedenktage,* edited by Detlef Lehnert and Klaus Megerle. Opladen, 1989.

Lehnert, Detlef, and Klaus Megerle, eds. *Politische Identität und nationale Gedenktage: Zur politischen Kultur in der Weimarer Republik.* Opladen, 1989.

———. *Sozialdemokratie zwischen Protestbewegung und Regierungspartei, 1848 bis 1993.* Frankfurt am Main, 1983.

Leichter, Otto. *Otto Bauer: Tragödie oder Triumph.* Vienna, 1970.

Lenin, V. I. "Die dritte Internationale und ihr Platz in der Geschichte." *Werke,* vol. 29. East Berlin, 1961.

———. "Die Helden der Berner Internationale." *Werke,* vol. 29. East Berlin, 1961.

———. "I. Kongress der Kommunistischen Internationale." *Werke,* vol. 28. East Berlin, 1959.

———. "Der Imperialismus als höchstes Stadium des Kapitalismus." *Werke,* vol. 22. East Berlin, 1960.

———. "Die proletarische Revolution und der Renegat Kautsky." *Werke,* vol. 28. East Berlin, 1959.

———. "Was tun?" *Werke.* Vol. 5. East Berlin, 1978.

———. "Der Zusammenbruch der II. Internationale." *Werke,* vol. 21. East Berlin, 1968.

Leontjew, L. "Der 'organisierte Kapitalismus' und die 'Wirtschaftsdemokratie'." *Unter dem Banner des Marxismus* 3 (1929): 660–87.

Leser, Norbert. *Zwischen Reformismus und Bolschewismus: Der Austromarxismus als Theorie und Praxis.* Vienna, 1968.

Leuschen-Seppel, Rosemarie. *Zwischen Staatsverantwortung und Klasseninteresse: Die Wirtschafts- und Finanzpolitik der SPD zur Zeit der Weimarer Republik unter besonderer Berücksichtigung der Mittelphase, 1924–1928/29.* Bonn, 1981.

Lidtke, Vernon. *The Alternative Culture.* Oxford, 1985.

Liebich, Andre. "Marxism and Totalitarianism: Rudolf Hilferding and the Mensheviks." *Dissent* (spring 1987): 223–40.

Liedtke, Rüdiger. *Wem gehört die Republik?* Frankfurt am Main, 1993.

Loew, Raimund. "The Politics of Austro-Marxism." *New Left Review* 118 (November–December 1979): 15–51.

Loewenberg, Gerhard. *Parliament in the German Political System*. Ithaca, 1966.

Lösche, Peter, and Walter, Franz. "Auf dem Weg zur Volkspartei? Die Weimarer Sozialdemokratie." *Archiv für Sozialgeschichte* 29 (1989): 75–136.

———. "Zur Organisationskultur der sozialdemokratischen Arbeiterbewegung in der Weimarer Republik." *Geschichte und Gesellschaft* 15 (1989): 511–36.

Luthardt, Wolfgang, ed. *Sozialdemokratische Arbeiterbewegung und Weimarer Republik: Materialien zur gesellschaftlichen Entwicklung, 1927–1933*. Vol. 1. Frankfurt am Main, 1978.

Luxemburg, Rosa. *Die Akkumulation des Kapitals*. Berlin, 1913. Reprint, Frankfurt am Main, 1966.

———. "Massenstreik, Partei und Gewerkschaften." *Ausgewählte politische Schriften in drei Bänden*. 3 vols. Frankfurt am Main, 1971.

Maehl, William Harvey. *The German Socialist Party: Champion of the First Republic, 1918–1933*. Philadelphia, 1986.

———. *Germany in Western Civilization*. University, 1979.

Marx, Karl. *Capital*. Vols. 1, 3. Moscow, 1966.

———. *A Contribution to the Critique of Political Economy*. Edited and introduced by Maurice Dobb. New York, 1970.

———. "Rede über den Haager Kongress." In *Ausgewählte Werke in sechs Bänden*, by Karl Marx and Friedrich Engels, vol. 2. East Berlin, 1970.

Marx, Karl, and Friedrich Engels. *Ausgewählte Werke in sechs Bänden*. 6 vols. East Berlin, 1981.

Matthias, Erich. "Kautsky und der Kautskyanismus: Die Funktion der Ideologie in der deutschen Sozialdemokratie vor dem ersten Weltkrieg." *Marxismusstudien* 2 (1957): 151–97.

———. "Die Sozialdemokratische Partei." In *Das Ende der Parteien, 1933*, edited by Erich Matthias and Rudolf Morsey. Düsseldorf, 1960.

Matthias, Erich. "Bericht über das Schicksal Breitscheids und Hilferdings (Mai 1940–Februar 1941)." In *Mit dem Gesicht nach Deutschland: Eine Dokumentation über die sozialdemokratische Emigration, aus dem Nachlaß Friedrich Stampfer, ergänzt durch andere Überlieferungen*, edited by Erich Matthias. Düsseldorf, 1968.

Matthias, Erich, and Rudolf Morsey, eds. *Das Ende der Parteien, 1933*. Düsseldorf, 1960.

Maurer, Ilse. *Reichsfinanzen und Große Koalition: Zur Geschichte des Reichskabinetts Müller, 1928–1930*. Frankfurt am Main, 1973.

May, Arthur J. *The Hapsburg Monarchy, 1867–1914*. Cambridge, Mass., 1951.

———. *Vienna in the Age of Franz Joseph*. Norman, 1966.

McLellan, David. *Marxism after Marx*. New York, 1979.

Meek, Ronald L. *Studies in the Labor Theory of Value*. New York, 1956.

Michels, Robert. "Die deutsche Sozialdemokratie, Parteimitgliedschaft und soziale Zusammensetzung." *Archiv für Sozialwissenschaft und Sozialpolitik* 23 (1906): 471–556.

———. *Political Parties: A Sociological Study of the Oligarchical Tendencies of Modern Democracy*. 1915. Reprint, New York, 1962.

Miller, Susanne. *Burgfrieden und Klassenkampf*. Bonn, 1974.

Miller, Susanne, and Heinrich Potthoff. *Kleine Geschichte der SPD: Darstellung und Dokumentation, 1848–1983*. 5th ed. Bonn, 1983.

Mills, C. Wright, ed. *The Marxists.* New York, 1962.

Mintz, Beth, and Michael Schwartz. *The Power Structure of American Business.* Chicago, 1985.

Möller, Alex. *Im Gedanken an Reichsfinanzminister Rudolf Hilferding.* Bonn, 1971.

Mommsen, Hans. *The Rise and Fall of Weimar Democracy.* Translated by Elborg Forster and Larry Eugene Jones. Chapel Hill, 1996.

———, ed. *Sozialdemokratie zwischen Klassenbewegung und Volkspartei.* Frankfurt am Main, 1974.

Morgan, David W. *The Socialist Left and the German Revolution: A History of the German Independent Social Democratic Party, 1917–1922.* Ithaca, 1975.

Naylor, John F. *Labour's International Policy: The Labour Party in the 1930s.* London, 1969.

Nenning, Günther. "Biographie Carl Grünbergs." *Indexband zum Archiv für die Geschichte des Sozialismus und der Arbeiterbewegung.* Graz, 1973.

Nettl, Peter. "The German Social Democratic Party, 1890–1914, as a Political Model." *Past and Present* 30 (1965): 69–95.

———. *Rosa Luxemburg.* Abr. ed. New York, 1969.

Niemann, Heinz, et al. *Geschichte der deutschen Sozialdemokratie, 1917–1945.* Frankfurt am Main, 1982.

Noske, Gustav. *Erlebtes aus Aufstieg und Niedergang einer Demokratie.* Offenbach am Main, 1947.

Novy, Klaus. *Strategien der Sozialisierung: Die Diskussion der Wirtschaftsreform in der Weimarer Republik.* Frankfurt am Main, 1978.

Ossietzky, Carl von. "Rudolf Hilferding, der Mann ohne Schatten." *Das Tagebuch* 5.2 (1924): 922–24.

Payer, Cheryl. *The World Bank: A Critical Analysis.* New York, 1982.

Perlo, Victor. *Super Profits and Crises: Modern U.S. Capitalism.* New York, 1988.

Phillips, Kevin. *The Politics of Rich and Poor: Wealth and the American Electorate in the Reagan Aftermath.* New York, 1990.

Pierson, Stanley. *Marxist Intellectuals and the Working-Class Mentality in Germany, 1887–1912.* Cambridge, Mass., 1993.

Pietranera, Giulio. *Rudolf Hilferding und die ökonomische Theorie der Sozialdemokratie.* Berlin, 1974.

Pistorius, Peter. *Rudolf Breitscheid, 1874–1944: Ein biographischer Beitrag zur deutschen Parteiengeschichte.* Cologne, 1970.

Pohl, Manfred. *Entstehung und Entwicklung des Universalbanksystems.* Frankfurt am Main, 1986.

Potthoff, Heinrich. *Freie Gewerkschaften, 1918–1933: Der Allgemeine Deutsche Gewerkschaftsbund in der Weimarer Republik.* Düsseldorf, 1987.

Prager, Eugen. *Geschichte der USPD.* Berlin, 1921; reprint, Glasshütten im Taunus, 1970.

Rosenberg, Arthur. *Imperial Germany.* Boston, 1964.

Rosenblitt, Marsha. *The Jews of Vienna, 1867–1914: Assimilation and Identity.* Albany, 1983.

Saage, Richard, ed. *Solidargemeinschaft und Klassenkampf: Politische Konzeptionen der Sozialdemokratie zwischen den Weltkriegen.* Frankfurt am Main, 1986.

Sandkühler, Hans-Jörg, and Rafael de la Vega, eds. *Austromarxismus: Texte zu "Ideologie und Klassenkampf" von Otto Bauer, Max Adler, Karl Renner, Sigmund*

Kunfi, Béla Fogarasi, und Julius Lengyel. Vienna, 1970.

Schaefer, Rainer. *Die SPD in der Ära Brüning: Tolerierung oder Mobilisierung? Handlungspielräume und Strategien sozialdemokratischer Politik, 1930–1932.* Frankfurt am Main, 1990.

Schimkowsky, Reinhard. "Zur Marx-Rezeption bei Hilferding." In *Monopol und Staat: Zur Marxrezeption in der Theorie des staatsmonopolistischen Kapitalismus,* edited by Rolf Ebbinghaus, 195–99. Frankfurt am Main, 1975.

Schneider, Michael. *A Brief History of the German Trade Unions.* Bonn, 1989.

Schoenbaum, David. *Hitler's Social Revolution: Class Structure in Nazi Germany, 1933–1939.* London, 1967.

Schorske, Carl. E. *Fin-de-Siècle Vienna: Politics and Culture.* New York, 1979.

———. *German Social Democracy, 1905–1917: The Development of the Great Schism.* Cambridge, Mass., 1955.

Schulze, Hagen. *Otto Braun oder Preußens demokratische Sendung: Eine Biographie.* Frankfurt am Main, 1977.

Schumpeter, Joseph A. *Ten Great Economists.* New York, 1951.

Spiegel, Henry W. *The Growth of Economic Thought.* Durham, 1983.

Steenson, Gary P. *Karl Kautsky, 1854–1938: Marxism in the Classical Years.* Pittsburgh, 1978.

Stein, Alexander. *Rudolf Hilferding und die deutsche Arbeiterbewegung, Gedenkblätter.* Hamburg, 1946.

Steinberg, Hans-Josef. *Sozialismus und deutsche Sozialdemokratie: Zur Ideologie der Partei vor dem 1. Weltkrieg.* Bonn, 1979.

Sweezy, Paul M. *The Theory of Capitalist Development.* New York, 1942.

———, ed. *Karl Marx and the Close of His System,* by Eugen Böhm-Bawerk, and *Böhm-Bawerk's Criticism of Marx,* by Rudolf Hilferding (New York, 1949).

Tilly, Richard. *Vom Zollverein zum Industriestaat: Die wirtschaftlich-soziale Entwicklung Deutschlands, 1834–1914.* Munich, 1990.

Tormin, Walter. *Zwischen Rätediktatur und Sozialer Demokratie: Die Geschichte der Rätebewegung in der Deutschen Revolution, 1918–1919.* Düsseldorf, 1954.

Tuckfeld, Manon, and Jens Christian Müller. "'Madame Geschichte' und die Kämpfe: Zur Kritik der Rosa-Luxemburg-Nostalgie." *Bahamas* 13 (spring 1994): 40–44.

Vogt, Martin. "Rudolf Hilferding als Finanzminister im ersten Kabinett Stresemann." In *Historische Prozesse der deutschen Inflation, 1914–1924: Ein Tagungsbericht,* edited by Gerald Feldman and Otto Busch, 127–58. Berlin, 1978.

Wehler, Hans-Ulrich. *Das Deutsche Kaiserreich, 1871–1918.* Göttingen, 1983.

———. *Imperialismus.* Düsseldorf, 1979.

Weisbrod, Bernd. "Die Befreiung von den 'Tariffesseln': Deflationspolitik als Krisenstrategie der Unternehmer in der Ära Brüning." *Geschichte und Gesellschaft* 11.3 (1985): 295–325.

Wheeler, Robert F. *USPD und Internationale: Sozialistischer Internationalismus in der Zeit der Revolution.* Frankfurt am Main, 1975.

Williamson, John G. *Karl Helfferich, 1872–1924: Economist, Financier, Politician.* Princeton, 1971.

Winkler, Heinrich August. *Der Schein der Normalität: Arbeiter und Arbeiterbewegung in Deutschland in der Weimarer Republik, 1924–1930.* Bonn, 1985.

———. *Von der Revolution zur Stabilisierung: Arbeiter und Arbeiterbewegung in der*

Weimarer Republik, 1918–1924. Bonn, 1985.

————. *Der Weg in die Katastrophe: Arbeiter und Arbeiterbewegung in Deutschland in der Weimarer Republik, 1930–1933.* Bonn, 1987.

————. *Weimar, 1918–1933: Die Geschichte der ersten deutschen Demokratie.* Munich, 1993.

————, ed. *Organisierter Kapitalismus: Voraussetzungen und Anfänge.* Göttingen, 1974.

Wistrich, Robert S. *Socialism and the Jews: The Dilemmas of Assimilation in Germany and Austria-Hungary.* London, 1982.

Worrall, R. L. "USSR: Proletarian or Capitalist State?" *Left* 39 (December 1939).

Wright, A. W. *G. D. H. Cole and Socialist Democracy.* Oxford, 1979.

Zimmerman, Ludwig. *Deutsche Außenpolitik in der Ära der Weimarer Republik.* Göttingen, 1958.

INDEX

Brauns, Heinrich, 133
Braunthal, Julius, 56, 58–59
Breitscheid, Rudolf, 145–46, 154, 165, 168, 200–202, 205–7, 239n, 243n
Breitscheid, Tony, 200–202, 205–7, 243n
Bremen, 26
Breslau, 164
Brest-Litovsk, Treaty of, 75
British Labour Party, 190
Brüning, Heinrich, 120, 122, 143, 147, 153, 164, 166–67, 169, 172, 202, 205; Hilferding's support for, 162–68; deflationary policy of, 165; fall of, 168
Brussels, 125, 183, 195
Bukharin, Nikolay Ivanovich, 5, 40, 53, 87–88, 191; theory of state capitalism, 114–16
Burgfrieden (civil peace), 68

Capital, 11, 40–41
cartels, 23–24; in the concentration and centralization of capital, 44–46; and competition, 49; and crises, 49, 69; and organized capitalism, 104, 119; and post-1918 foreign policy, 114; and inflation, 125
Casablanca, 201
Cassirer, Paul, 145
Catholic Center Party (Z), 89, 123, 125, 127, 132, 134, 137, 143, 151, 157, 162, 168, 171
Central Council, 79
Central Powers, 71, 86, 113
Chakhotin, Sergei, 168
Christian socialism, 12
Cold War, 210
Cole, G. D. H., 108
Colm, Gerhard, 120–21
colonialism, 23, 41, 53–55, 58
Commerzbank, 211
communism, 5, 17, 177, 210
Communist International, 81, 93, 179–80; and USPD, 91–96; twenty-one conditions of, 91, 96
Communist Party of Germany (KPD), 79, 96, 119, 120, 126, 135–38,

140, 151, 162, 164, 168–70, 177, 180; concept of social fascism, 170–71; Hilferding compares with NSDAP, 171; and proposed alliance with SPD, 192–93
corporations: development of, 42–45, 48, 104; emergence of transnational, 211–12
credit (*see also* banks): and corporations, 42; development of, 41–42; problems in Hilferding's theory of, 48–49
crises: causes of, 48–49, 69, 106
Crispien, Artur, 92, 98, 103
Crummenerl, Sigmund, 174, 176, 240n
Cuno, Wilhelm, 125–26
Curtius, Julius, 159
Czechoslovakia, 178, 191

Däubler, Theodor, 145
Däumig, Ernst, 90
Dawes Plan, 137–38, 150, 153, 158
Delbrück, Hans, 145
Denicke, Iurii, 196
Denmark, 172–73
Depression of 1929, 136, 163, 184, 210; and theory of organized capitalism, 117–19; onset of, 153; Hilferding's response to, 160–61, 166–68
Deutsche Bank, 46, 211
Deutsche Freiheit, 179
Deutscher, Isaac, 13
Deutschland Berichte, 178
dictatorship of the proletariat, 77, 81–82, 87, 111, 189, 198
Dietrich, Georg, 176
Dietrich, Hermann, 167
Disconto-Gesellschaft, 46
Dissmann, Robert, 140
Dittmann, Wilhelm, 79, 103, 166
Dresdner Bank, 211

East Germany, 209
Ebert, Friedrich, 36, 37, 77, 79, 82, 133
Eckstein, Gustav, 14
economic democracy, 104–5, 111, 150–51; and socialism, 105

Liebknecht, Karl, 57, 59, 66, 73, 180;
    death of, 80
Liebknecht, Wilhelm, 216n, 219n
Löbe, Paul, 176
Locarno Treaty, 150
Ludendorff, Erich, 73
Luther, Hans, 130, 132–34
Luxemburg, Rosa, 5–6, 13–14, 24, 27,
    35, 37, 39, 40, 53, 56, 57, 83,
    180; and mass strike, 58; and radi-
    cal left, 59; in World War I, 63, 66,
    73; and USPD, 78; death of, 80

Mach, Ernst, 14–16
Maltzan, Baron Ago von, 123
Marcuse, Herbert, 142
marginal utility, 12, 20
Marseilles, 200–201, 205
Martinique, 205
Marx, Karl, 3, 11, 13–14, 17, 19,
    20–22, 26, 29, 40–41, 48, 55, 82,
    103, 105, 110, 198, 203–5; and
    corporations, 42–43; and English
    capitalism, 46–47; transition to so-
    cialism, 51, 86; and workers' con-
    sciousness, 69; materialist concep-
    tion of history, 94, 189; and
    economic determinism, 189–90
Marx, Wilhelm, 137
Marx-Engels Archive, 191
Marxism, 8, 9, 12, 39, 81, 180, 185;
    Hilferding's contributions to, 3, 6,
    11, 17, 20–22, 40–41, 48–49, 55,
    69–70; as social science, 14–16, 21;
    and peasantry, 110; and WTB plan,
    121–22; and Hilferding's economic
    orthodoxy, 135–36, 142–43, 160,
    166–68; Hilferding's post-1933
    critique of, 189–90; Hilferding's
    break with, 197, 203–5; and totali-
    tarian state economy, 198–99; after
    1945, 208–9
Marxist center, 6, 19, 28, 35, 37, 55,
    58–60, 91, 100; and World War I,
    66–67, 71, 72
Marx-Studien, 16, 22
mass strike. See general strike
Mehring, Franz, 37, 39, 59, 66, 73

Meinecke, Friedrich, 142
Mensheviks, 80, 196, 199
Meyer, Margarethe, 202
Meyer, Oscar, 143, 147, 202
Michels, Robert, 70
militarism, 41, 58, 62
Mitteleuropa, 72
Mittelstand, 163, 184–85
Moldenauer, Paul, 159
Möller, Alex, 134
money: Hilferding's theory of, 49–51
Morgan, J. P., 47
Morgan Stanley, 211
Moscow, 4, 91
Müller, Hermann, 103, 127, 134, 139,
    146, 153–55, 157, 159–60,
    164–65, 167, 170, 200, 234n

Naphtali, Fritz, 142, 152
National Assembly, 77, 80–82, 85, 90
National Socialist German Workers
    Party (NSDAP), 3, 7, 110, 119–20,
    168, 172–73, 201, 206, 209; elec-
    toral breakthrough of, 162; social
    basis of, 163, 184–85; and SA and
    SS terror, 169; aggressive foreign
    policy aims of, 183; nature of state,
    199–200
nationalism, 41, 53, 70
Naumann, Friedrich, 71
neo-Kantianism, 15, 39
Neue Zeit, 11, 20, 22, 30, 31, 36, 39,
    56, 63, 69, 74, 142
Neuer Vorwärts, 177–79, 183, 191,
    193–95
New Beginning, 180, 191
New School for Social Research, 3
New York, 22, 201, 210
Nikolaevskii, Boris, 196
North American Free Trade Agreement,
    212

Ollenhauer, Otto, 176
Oran, 201
organized capitalism, theory of, 5, 7, 55,
    69–70, 103, 114; and class strug-
    gle, 104; and state, 105–6; Bolshe-
    vik critique of, 116; widespread